The HOUSEBUILDER'S Bible

Contents

Buy a timber frame kit from any UK manufacturer and this is essentially what you get – the superstructure.

Torus skirting, costs £1.30 - £2.50/lin.m, depending on quality

Dado rail, costs around £1.30/lin.m

Moulded architrave, costs around 75p/lin.m

Moulded picture rail, costs £1.60/lin.m

Mortar Mix Chart

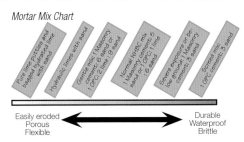

Easily eroded Porous Flexible ◄────────► Durable Waterproof Brittle

Tables

All Benchmark tables relate to the costings, labour and materials used in the Benchmark House which is featured in Chapter 2 and referred to throughout the book

Preface *by Mark Brinkley*

The Housebuilder's Bible first saw the light of day in 1994. It has always been my brainchild and over the past ten years it's success has transformed my life from being that of a working builder into that of a full-time writer. How did it come about?

From 1980 to 1994, I worked as a carpenter, small builder and developer in and around my home town of Cambridge, fifty miles north of London. That is what I would probably still be doing had it not been for the economic downturn in the early Nineties. This book is very much a by-product of that recession.

In 1986, I went into partnership with Robin Gomm, a designer-builder, and together we began buying up plots and development opportunities, borrowing money to finance the bulk of the deals. In common with tens of thousands of small builders and developers (and millions of homeowners), we were caught out when the property market turned sour at the end of 1988. During that fateful year, we were building a four-bedroomed house a few miles outside Cambridge and we had lots of interest. I remember turning down a cash offer of £180,000 on the house in the summer, deciding to hold off till we were completely finished in the hope of netting £200,000. But by the time we had finished, the market sentiment had turned and all deals were off. We ended up selling it for £154,000, virtually cost price, eight months later. At least we sold. Many developers refused to sell at these apparently knockdown prices and hung on far too long. They mostly went under.

Among the other bits of land we had accumulated was a building plot in Weston Colville, a small village east of Cambridge. We'd picked it up for £45,000 in 1986, seen its value double and then halve again. We decided that rather than try and build a house there for resale in this climate, we would just sell the plot. But in 1989 there were no takers, not even at £40,000. After a year on the market without an offer, it became obvious that it was time for a rethink. For during this period I had also married my wife, Charlotte, and together we were in the process of having three children in four years. A family house in the country suddenly seemed quite an appealing prospect. And whilst there was no market for rural building plots, even in 1990 it wouldn't take too long to sell a terraced house in central Cambridge. Thus we decided to go and build a house for ourselves on this unsaleable plot.

My business partner was meanwhile winning quite a bit of work from some farming contacts we had. A large new house, a series of barn conversions, some renovation work. It wasn't developing, it was design and build, but it kept us busy and paid the bills. My project took a back seat for a couple of years whilst we cracked on with the jobs in hand. It enabled us to spend a little time thinking about what we would build, how we would build it and how much we would hope to build it for. It was also during this time that the genesis of the Housebuilder's Bible occurred: initially just a little furtive note taking.

Work started on the house in Weston Colville in 1992, after the planners had had their say and re-worked many of our original thoughts. It was a sloping site, unusual for Cambridgeshire, and I was unprepared for just how much spoil we had to shift off site to get a level footprint. More note taking, plus a few calculations — the origins of Brinkley's Slope Law that features in Chapter 6. I took an active part in the groundworks and drainage, I serviced the brickies for a month and then worked as part of the carpentry team erecting the timber frame upper storey. After fourteen weeks we had the superstructure built and covered in. I then had to stop work whilst we negotiated a sale on the terraced house, whilst simultaneously helping my wife with the arrival of our third child in July. Finally we threw a whole mass of people at the house for eight weeks to enable us to move in before Christmas 1992.

Despite being the sixth house I had been directly involved in commissioning, I had found the process of housebuilding for myself and my family an amazingly rushed and frustrating experience. There simply wasn't anywhere to go to get a handle on the choices to be made, their costs and their pros and cons. There was at the time just one major book on selfbuild, Murray Armor's 'Building Your Own Home', which had sold in vast quantities since it first came out in the 1970s. It was, and indeed remains, an excellent book but it doesn't really deal with the technicalities of building. My idea was to put together a book which more or less started where Murray Armor's book left off — actually analysing the process of housebuilding from a builder's point of view.

The analogy of travel guides kept coming to mind. Imagine being dumped in a foreign city where you don't speak the language. You want to see the sights but you have no idea where they are or how to get to them. You have three days. You rush around like a whirling dervish, checking out likely looking buildings, catching buses all over the place and generally being pretty frantic. When the time comes to leave, you know you've "done" Rome or Barcelona or wherever it was you went, but you really don't have a clue whether you've seen the best bits or not. That was what it was like building a house in 1992. And so I figured there must be a market for guide book which would list the attractions, the admission prices, and the directions. That is more or less what the Housebuilder's Bible sets out to do.

I started the book-writing project by approaching a couple of publishers to see if there was any interest in such an idea. "Absolutely no way," said the first, "it's far too specialised." "Absolutely no way," said the second, "anything with prices in will date far too quickly." If anything, these responses just strengthened my resolve. I react well to being told I am crazy. I decided I would self-publish and concentrate on selling the book directly by mail order and at selfbuild exhibitions. First I had to write it.

All I had in 1993 was a series of notes on an Amstrad PCW plus masses and masses of price data in the office. It seemed a mammoth task to turn it into a readable book, especially with a young family to look after, a new house to finish off and an existing business to keep going. Looking back on it, I am not too sure how I got it all from an idea to a physical book in just 18 months with all that going on in the background. As I said, this book is a by-product of recession and recessions make you work that much harder. A key figure in all this was undoubtedly my mother who believed me when I said I was going to write a book and who kept us afloat during 1994 when I was taking three days a week off from the building business to get the first draft completed. I couldn't really work at home because of the distractions of three pre-school boys padding about the house. So I took a leaf out of the notebook of one of my heroes, singer songwriter Randy Newman, who, whenever he had to produce a new album, went and hired an office, put a piano in it and shut himself away in it for eight hours a day until the work was complete. Like Randy, I found a room in a village office complex and shut myself away. It worked. That is where I cracked it.

Come November 1994, I had something worth putting down on paper. I had bought an Apple Mac and taught myself how to use PageMaker and Photoshop, the tools of the desktop publisher. I had the costs all worked into one unwieldy Excel spreadsheet. It wasn't going to be glossy but I was sure it would be useful. My first print-run was tentative, a few hundred run out on a DocuTech machine, a sort of upmarket photocopier. Had they sat around for ages, I would have written off the whole project to experience and gone back to join Robin in the building business. But the first edition sold. They sold off the page in the selfbuild mags and

the sold by the hundred at a selfbuild exhibition at the NEC. Within a couple of months I had to do a reprint and the Housebuilder's Bible was on its way.

And ever since then there has been what I would describe as a very slow snowball effect going on. Each year has seen on average around 30% more Bibles sold than the year before. For the first couple of years I tried to get a presence in the major bookshops, making several appeals to WH Smith and Waterstones to stock my baby. But they were not in the least interested in such an amateurish product without a major publisher or a TV series behind it. Despite this, the sales kept climbing and the book sold very well through the selfbuild magazines and also through some professional titles as well. It surprises many who think of it primarily as a selfbuild title that around half the sales are made to 'professionals' - small builders and tradesmen, architects, surveyors, even estate agents. The fourth edition, the Millennium one, finally broke through into the retail market albeit via amazon.co.uk, the internet bookseller, whose sales depend to a large part on customer reviews. The Bible had some good ones — and no, I didn't write them myself! By 2002, the Millennium edition was regularly appearing in the top 100 of all Amazon's book sales and was frequently one of their top five Home and DIY titles. I believe that the Housebuilder's Bible has become their biggest selling independent (self-published) title, something that surprises them almost as much as me.

During this period, I have also turned my hand to a little journalism. Michael Holmes, the long time editor of the leading selfbuild magazine Homebuilding & Renovating, was an early fan. He asked me to write for his magazine in 1996 and I have been contributing pieces to it ever since. And David Birkbeck and Jo Smit, editors of Building Homes, were also very supportive. Thanks to them I have published over 200 articles, many of them deepening and expanding areas I had covered in the Bible. Journalism has also improved my skills as a writer — I don't waffle as much — and in 2001 I picked up my first ever gong, Residential Property Writer of the Year, at the Halifax Laing Homes Press awards.

In 2003, the book had become just a little bit too much for me to continue with on my own and I joined forces with a new business partner, Mark Neeter, to start a publishing venture called Ovolo which has taken on publishing this book in addition to commissioning new work in this field.

So much for me. What about this new edition, the 6th?
New editions seem to last between two and three years. The prices change, the regs change, the names change, the internet arrives, the range of products gets larger and the guide keeps gently expanding to reflect all this. I must admit that I am finding it an increasingly difficult subject to stay abreast of. Back in the early 90s, housebuilding seemed a much simpler task than it does now. In recession, value for money was king and all I needed to do really was point out how not to get ripped off and how to design in value. Today, there is a whole lot more money sloshing about and people are regularly specifying

stuff like Jacuzzis, granite worktops and gyms, things that really didn't feature ten years ago. There are stacks of products around that didn't exist back then — sunpipes, SIPS panels, photovoltaic cells, rainwater harvesters, CAT 5 cabling, I beams, self placing concrete, to name but seven. The first edition of the Housebuilder's Bible was very much a hands-on book. This edition is much more the work of a jobbing journalist and I recognise that as a weakness but also probably an inevitability. The market as a whole has expanded to such an extent that it would be almost impossible to have worked with everything that's now regularly used in housebuilding. The agenda has also moved on. Whilst material costs haven't really changed a great deal in ten years, labour rates have rocketed and, to make matters more difficult, they are now very variable across the country where once they were more nearly uniform. One of the key benchmark rates in housebuilding is how much bricklayers charge for laying a thousand bricks. Back in 94, it was more or less £180 per thousand across the country. Today it varies between £250 per thousand in some of our quieter backwaters to over £500 per thousand in and around London. In fact, as the chart in Chapter One indicates, there seems to be a close correlation between building trade labour rates and house prices and in mid-2004 neither show signs of levelling off.

Such is the pressure of these price rises that developers are beginning to abandon brickwork in favour of cheaper solutions. There is a huge and growing interest in housing solutions that remove as much as possible of the (expensive) sitework and replace it with semi-automated factory procedures, something the Japanese have been quietly doing for the past forty years. It's a very interesting time for housebuilders, large and small and it's been fascinating to watch it develop and change over these past few years. My hunch is that the technological changes will hasten if house prices continue to rise but will come juddering to a halt if the market takes another tumble.

In order to cover the innovation aspects more thoroughly, I plan to expand the editorial output of the Housebuilder's Bible. During the lifespan of this edition, expect to see occasional supplements appearing. I am not sure how often yet — plans are still formulating — but these digests will be able to keep abreast of the regulation changes — there are more happening today than at any previous time in our history— price movements, market trends and innovations. If you want to see one of these supplements, we will of course need to have your contact details — see the very last page of this book to find out more.

Housebuilding is a vast topic and no one can hope to know everything there is to know about it. I am no exception and I am aware that in some areas I am barely doing more than skating over the surface, handing out a few pointers. The value of a book like this derives in great part from pooling other peoples' expertise into one accessible source. Every edition of this book improves on the one before and many of these improvements are as a direct result of readers contacting me about little things which are unclear, misleading or just plain wrong. So I will finish with an offer of thanks to the many hundreds of people who have helped me with this project over the years and a plea to keep the feedback rolling in.

Thanks to the following who have helped with the Housebuilder's Bible over the years. Firstly, my family for putting up with it and me, especially my wife Charlotte. And to my mother, Diana, for helping get the project off the ground ten years ago. A whole cast of others who have helped in a variety of ways. Robin Gomm, Jeremy Pembrey, Steve Baldwin, Adrian Thurley, Andrew Allen, Anne Bragg, Mark and Dana Neeter, Norman Cox, Andrew Bailey, David Birkbeck, Jo Smit, Michael Holmes, Peter Harris, Jason Orme, David Snell, Bob Matthews, David Olivier, Phil Ayton, Tim Crump, Steve Mattick, Nick Jones, Brian Belton, Phil Goring, Nick Ellis, Rick Hughes and the many helpful members of the UK selfbuild list run by Yahoo. Also some very helpful institutions, notably the Building Research Establishment, The Centre for Alternative Technology, the NHBC, Zurich Insurance.

Dedication to:
David Thomas, my best friend from school days and university who met an untimely end, aged just 36, in a car crash in Kuwait in 1991, where he was reporting on the aftermath of the Gulf War for the Financial Times. He was an inspiration to me; it was partly his death which persuaded me to drop the hammer and learn to play the keyboard and start writing.

Mark Brinkley August 2004

Chapter 1
Background

The Builders' dilemma
Housebuilding in the UK
Selfbuild

▩ *The Builders' Dilemma*

The triangle on the right represents the age-old conundrum for all builders and would-be builders. It is said that you can have any two of these points in a building job but only at the expense of the third. Thus you can have a good, cheap job but it won't be quick, or a cheap, quick job that won't be any good.

So when you hear claims — as you may — of people having built (or more likely 'put up') a house in just eight weeks you can reply, confidently, "Ah, but how much did it cost you?" And, similarly, if you meet someone who claims to have built a house for £35 per sq ft, you can look them in the eye and exclaim "I bet it took you years" — and you'll be right. So before you set out to build a new house, first examine your motives and see where you fit into the triangle.

The Cheap House

The average new house is constructed entirely by builders; it takes about 6-8 months to complete and costs around £60 per sq ft (that's £645 per sq m). It is built to standards that meet — and do not exceed — the current building regulations.

[Triangle diagram with labels: Quick (top), Cheap (bottom left), Good (bottom right)]

If you want to maximise the financial return on your new house — in all but the most upmarket areas — it pays to keep it dead simple. Whether you plan to actually be a hands-on builder or not, for the cost-effective house the following advice should be carried out to the letter.

■ Dispense with any notions of individual design. Aim for a four-square box drawn up by a technician or a surveyor or better still from some already existing book of house plans — in fact anyone except an architect.

Avoid all of the following:
■ layouts with more than four external corners
■ anything round or curved
■ anything poking out through the roof (dormers, chimneys)
■ anything other than large format concrete tiles on the roof
■ anything other than face brickwork on external walls
■ anything other than straight stairs
■ complicated sites (unless at a bargain price)
■ fancy Continental plumbing systems
■ timber frame (except in Scotland where it's cheaper)
■ trying to build an 'Eco' house

- underfloor heating
- central vacuum cleaning systems
- kitchens that don't come from MFI
- bathrooms that don't come from B&Q
- anything but Magnet casement windows
- home cinema rooms
- handmade anything at all (bricks, tiles, etc)
- Agas
- garages – esp with remote-controlled doors
- porches and entrance canopies
- conservatories
- built-in cupboards
- hardwood floors
- data cabling
- any lighting that doesn't hang from a pendant in the middle of each room – especially if it's got the word halogen in it
- almost everything second-hand – it's only been salvaged because it's worth more than new.

Your sole remaining decision will be whether to paint or stain your woodwork. Received wisdom is divided on this topic; stain is quicker and easier but it's more expensive to buy and the joinery needs more careful preparation.

What you will end up with will have all the charm of a Fifties council house. But if space for bucks is your main motive in taking on a construction project, then you'll be very happy. Much of the book that follows is concerned with the options that might turn a cheap house into a good house and therefore much of the book will be of little relevance to you. I have, however, always tried to indicate what the cheapest option is in each element of the house.

The Quick House

The quick house will almost certainly be a kit house, which is largely prefabricated in a workshop or factory. It will also, very likely, be a timber framed house. They are rarely cheap; even the simplest box-type designs are likely to add a little to construction costs, though with most blocklayers now charging their labour out at over £1 per block this is no longer a universal truth. But neither are framed houses necessarily that much quicker to build. What really takes up a builder's time is the finishing tasks and these

are pretty much the same whatever your chosen building methods.

The Good House

Most would-be individual housebuilders are not hard up nor in a hurry – at least they're not when they're just planning it all; they might beg to differ when they're halfway through building. They can afford to browse and contemplate and research. They will look at many different options before embarking and will probably be keen that the finished product should somehow be an expression of their personality as well as a way of meeting their individual needs in a way that an off-the-peg house couldn't hope to.

Even if you are building for resale rather than personal occupation, you are more than likely to want to build an attractive house that passers-by will come to admire and occupants will love to call their home.

After all, the house is likely to be standing long after any transient profit is banked and spent, and may well still be there when they are burying your grandchildren. To build well, you have to know what's going on and not just rely on experts: the more you are involved in the design, the more you will appreciate the outcome, and the more you are involved in the building, the better that outcome will be.

Is this book for you?

What follows is housebuilding's first bodice ripper, a warts-n-all rough guide. It is not a DIY manual (there are enough of those) and it is not a disguised advertisement (I'm not selling anything apart from this book). Although primarily concerned with new housebuilding, there is also much information specifically tailored for people converting or restoring existing properties.

Many of the tricks and tips described I have learnt the hard way since I started as a selfbuilder in 1980. As the old saw goes: experience is the best education, but it is also the most expensive. My hope is that some of my 'experience' and research will help you avoid expensive pitfalls, many of which I've had the

Cambridge House Prices Plotted Against Local Brickie Rates

Source: House Prices, Cambridge Building Society
Bricklaying rates: Steve Baldwin

There is a remarkable correlation between house prices and building trade rates, as illustrated by this graph. The orange bars show average house prices in my local town, Cambridge: the thick black line indicates the brickies' rate per thousand bricks laid,

something of a benchmark for all the building trades and currently around £350/thousand. Whereas the prices of building materials are little changed during this period, it would seem the cost of labour followed house prices pretty closely.

doubtful pleasure of falling victim to myself.

In short, the aim of this book is to enable you to build a good house cheaply and quickly. Now hang on a minute, I thought that wasn't possible.

■Housebuilding in the UK

Housebuilding in Britain has always been a boom or bust activity, and this has never been more clearly illustrated than in recent decades.

The early Eighties saw a huge surge in private housebuilding, caused partly by post-war baby-boomers entering the housing market and partly by people choosing to live in smaller groups. This increased demand also led to a huge increase in house prices which, in turn, encouraged more people to jump onto the home ownership bandwagon, encouraged by the Thatcher government which made the supposed benefits of property-owning a key plank of its programme.

The Slump

This particular bandwagon came juddering to a halt on August 1, 1988 when Nigel Lawson, then our Chancellor of the Exchequer (but now better known as Nigella's dad) stopped a tax perk known as double mortgage tax relief.

I remember the day well. I was property developing at the time, owed the bank about a quarter of a million and had just learned that I was to become a father for the first time. It was also the day my business partner and I completed on purchasing a rather large barn for conversion in a village just outside Cambridge. The timing was about as bad as it can get.

Double mortgage tax relief sounds like rather an obscure tax perk, as indeed it was; these days we have no tax relief of any description on mortgages but back in 1988 both halves of an unmarried couple could claim tax relief on a mortgage, which was worth a few bob. It was an anomaly and Chancellor Lawson strove to eliminate anomalies.

The problem was that he announced his intention to do so in his budget speech in March, telling us all that the elimination of this particular anomaly would take place at midnight on the 31st of July. People who, in more normal times, would never have considered house purchase together were suddenly bounced into it by a fear that it was now or never for the housing ladder. The housing market, already toppy, duly went ballistic for four and a half months in the rush to get sales completed before the Chancellor's cut off point.

In Cambridge, average house prices jumped by 25 per cent overnight. Many of the 'Lawson couples' lived to regret the unwarranted emotional entanglement caused by this feverish speculation. All of them lived to regret the financial chaos brought on by the price bubble bursting on August 1st. For almost all of them, it would be ten years before the houses they bought at ridiculous prices in 1988 would be worth as much again.

For us property developers, it was more painful still. But then, as a group, we have never elicited much sympathy. What happened on August 1st was distinctly eerie. The housing market just came to a standstill. Viewing stopped. Offers to buy were withdrawn. People just lost interest in buying homes altogether.

Prices didn't fall immediately. But then, with hardly any house sales happening, it was hard to know what house prices were really doing. However, during 1989 it became apparent that all the estate agents' talk of the market 'just taking a breather' was bull and, as the number of sales continued to decline, the rout set in. Things weren't helped at all by another of Nigel Lawson's foibles, the decision to peg the pound to the Deutschmark (remember that currency?) which led to interest rates going up and up – the base rate was 15 per cent from October 1989 to October 1990. As you can imagine, housebuilders took a bath.

It wasn't until 1993 that house prices stopped falling. Even then, the recovery was painfully slow. Rather than being a return to the good old days before Lawson's bubble when house prices gently rose year-on-year (or so it seemed), everything remained resolutely frozen. Newspapers were full of stories of families stuck in 'negative equity' and of unhappy young homeowners just handing their keys back to the mortgage lenders and going back to live with mum and dad.

The climate all changed once again with the election of New Labour in 1997. Strange to think of a supposedly left-wing government riding to the rescue of the property-owning classes but then life was ever full of such ironies.

The fact is that average house prices were back to roughly the same level in May 1997 as they had been on that fateful day nine years previously when Nigel Lawson delivered his now infamous budget speech.

Since 1997, house prices have begun to behave exactly as they did from the Fifties through till 1988: in the prosperous parts of the country, they have been increasing by an average of nearly 15 per cent year-on-year. The Brits love this state of affairs. Never mind that the NHS is crumbling, the schools are appalling and that the trains keep crashing – just see how much our homes are worth. It contributes in no small way to the national feelgood factor. We could, as a nation, buy the whole of France and still have change for a couple of Spanish Costas and the heel of Italy.

For seven years this has been a major factor in keeping Labour in power. It's the Tories who have become embedded in the national psyche as the party which messed with house prices. New Labour has returned us to the status quo ante. Whether there will be a Gordon Brown bubble to rival Nigel Lawson's remains to be seen but if the past tells us anything, it's that the longer the good times roll in property, the bigger the hangover.

Mini-markets

It is a fact that, although commentators love to talk about 'the housing market', there really is no such thing. The painful bubble effect of 1988 was largely restricted to Southern England.

Generally speaking, the further away from London you travelled the less spectacular the effect. Away from the southeast price rises had been much more muted in the 1980s and sales activity far less frenetic; consequently, the market didn't fall off a cliff in 1989.

In Northern England and, in particular, Scotland, prices continued to rise gently for some time after that date: it is the idle boast of some Edinburgh estate agents that house prices have never fallen in that city. Ever.

Statistics published in the media about the national housing market are, therefore, usually next to useless because they tend to conceal the different trends going on in the various regional markets. To really get the feel for a market, it must be studied at a local level.

How we build houses

There are other interesting aspects to the British housebuilding scene besides the topsy-turvy nature of the housing market. Particularly pertinent to this book is the way we go about building homes – more particularly who builds them. Because it turns out that we are pretty unusual in this respect too. If you were to imagine a pie chart representing the total number of houses built each year in the UK – around 160,000 – there would be three slices in it marked:

■ speculative housebuilders (80 per cent);
■ social housing (12 per cent); and
■ others (eight per cent)

What do these descriptions mean? Let's start with the middle one, social housing. This is mostly homes built by housing associations for rent or shared ownership. Social housing has more or less taken over from the council housing schemes, which were such a feature of the middle years of the 20th century. It's an area alive with innovation and some fascinating schemes have been built in the past few years, notably by Peabody Trust, in and around London. But, by and large, these schemes are for multiple units, not really the essence of what this book is about.

Now let's move on to the first category.

Speculative housebuilders. First thing to note is just how big this section is, accounting for over 120,000 new homes every year. In most other countries, speculative housebuilding is an also-ran.

In Britain not only is speculative housebuilding by far the most common method of delivering new homes, but this huge market is dominated by comparatively few names.

In fact, the top twenty speculative housebuilders knock out around 70,000 homes between them. They are almost all national concerns, almost all quoted on the stockmarket which, incidentally, treats them as though they have all just been diagnosed with leprosy.

Beneath them are several dozen regional housebuilders accounting for around 30,000 homes in total, each of them building a few hundred homes each year.

And, beneath this, are the small housebuilders, doing anything from one site of maybe twenty at any one time, right down to the general builders who occasionally do a spec build.

And then there are the others. Sorry if I make it appear as though we are constantly sliding down the pyramid towards the bottom of the heap. Because this book is primarily intended for the builders down here at the bottom of the housebuilding heap. The small builders and the others. Particularly the others.

In many ways, this 'others' grouping is by far the most interesting. Although it may account for less than 10 per cent or so of new homes, that still amounts to between 15,000 and 20,000 each year. And the great bulk of these are built by individuals for their own occupation – what the media and everyone else has learned to call 'selfbuild'.

The crucial, defining distinction between selfbuild and 'spec' building is that selfbuilding is done for your own occupation and is, consequently, out of the tax net. It's not being carried out as a trade and therefore there is no profit being made and no income tax to pay. And additionally there is no capital gains tax to pay because principal residences are tax-exempt and always have been in this country.

Despite, or maybe because of, their simplicity, Walter Segal houses are instantly recognisable, even though the designs have undergone a few modifications over the years.

In the next section (and indeed throughout the book) I will be looking in greater detail at some of the pros and cons of selfbuild, but before getting stuck into that I think it's important to point out that there is a huge grey blanket of an area spread out between the sort of selfbuild featured in Channel 4's 'Grand Designs' and the output of a small spec builder who builds a house or two for sale every year and every so often builds a new one for himself – that way netting a nice little tax free earner. I have often heard builders referring to odd plots of land they own as 'their pension' and all good pensions should be tax free, shouldn't they?

Many good people, academics amongst them, have tried to assess the size of the UK selfbuild market and they get into all sorts of difficulties because selfbuild is not a clearly defined entity. The first 10,000 selfbuilds are easy to spot – they show up on the VAT returns – but the next 10,000 get murkier and murkier the higher the total gets. Hence I quite like the term 'others'. It covers a lot of nefarious undertakings.

■*Selfbuild*

Not that long ago, back in the Seventies and Eighties, selfbuild had a decidedly alternative flavour to it. Selfbuild was usually group selfbuild. This typically involved a number of individuals or families pooling their labour to build homes for themselves in a little estate.

Group selfbuild enjoyed a boom in the Eighties but came horribly unstuck when the Lawson bubble burst in 1988 (see previous section for more on this). Groups were left with homes worth less than they had paid for them and some of these schemes were abandoned half-built. Private group selfbuild all but disappeared off the radar screens after this.

But group selfbuild also existed in another guise where the schemes were done for rent rather than ownership – it's now known as Community Selfbuild – and this small sector continues to flourish though it rarely accounts for more than a dozen schemes each year.

In order to form a Community Selfbuild group, you need to have identified a number of people living in the same area who are in genuine housing need. Whereas the country is stuffed full of people in genuine housing need, not many of them have the time or inclination to go about meeting it by building a house which they then have to rent. So it remains a bit of a niche. The emphasis is often on building cheaply, simply and in an environmentally sound way, which often means building the Walter Segal way.

Walter Segal (1907-1985) was an innovative architect who designed and promoted a very simple method of building timber frame houses, which could be easily mastered by novices. The Segal Trust continues to promote his vision and should be a first port of call for anyone interested in pursuing these options. Another useful contact is the Community Self Build Agency who keep abreast of up-and-coming schemes all over the country and can act as a sort of dating service for would-be community self builders.

Whilst this specialised niche is alive and thriving, it is now dwarfed by the mainstream selfbuild market, which consists of people acting as what the Americans call paper contractors – do-it-yourself property developers.

This group tend to be fairly well-off and tend to build relatively high spec houses; some estimates reckon that over a third of all detached housing in the UK is now selfbuilt. For many of this new breed of selfbuilder there will be little or no physical involvement in the construction of their homes; they are instead providing the nous (and money) to get a plot of land purchased and to build a new home on it.

Throughout the postwar years, this group was typically buying and doing up old wrecks of houses, but as the wrecks with the most potential have mostly been snapped up now, their attention has moved on to building from scratch. Now it is recognised that there is such a thing as a selfbuild industry that supports many specialist businesses, three national magazines — 'Build It', 'Selfbuild & Design' and 'Homebuilding & Renovating' — and various exhibitions up and down the land.

Selfbuild has experienced something of a boomlet against a background of a housebuilding sector generally with no growth whatsoever. It would have experienced a full scale boom if only it wasn't so hard to buy land to build on: for every successful selfbuilder, there are four or five who give up the dream and go and do something else.

Much of the sales literature that is used to attract individuals to build their own homes is based on the fact that there is a large, tax-free profit to be had. Whilst the responsible end of the market likes to rein in such claims, you still come across examples of this hype. Here's one I dredged from my archives:

'Interested in a management activity for your spare time that should gain you more in a year than your regular salary? With the benefits completely tax-free? If so, you are looking at selfbuild. It is all based on the fact that the cost of a serviced building plot added to the cost of building a house on it using subcontractors is significantly less than the finished value of the property. Typically the savings will be around 25 per cent and on a £160,000 home this can be £40,000.'

Sounds too good to be true? You guessed it. I've already described the slump that followed the last housing boom. The current boom is now seven years old and keeps slowing down only to take-off again. Prices in most of the country have more than doubled in that time and painless paper profits are being made on house sales. London dinner parties are once again being burdened with tales of gazumping and thieving estate agents. Property development is back in fashion. In fact the above quote looks to be just about spot on. But (and it's a big but) the profits flowing towards today's selfbuilders and property developers are the result of the broad swell of a friendly economic tide, not of any brilliant ruse of making money out of the banks and the building trade. When the tide turns (as it did in 1988) you'd better watch out.

Land Costs are the key

The way in which prices for building plots are set is based on subtracting the building costs from the estimated value of the completed house. For example, if the estate agent or surveyor marketing a plot reckons that a nicely finished house there might fetch £300,000 and that it might cost around £120,000 to build, then he will probably recommend that the plot be sold for around £150,000, maybe more, leaving a small element of profit for the builder. There is obviously a return here but the problem is that there are many more costs involved than just the plot price and the building costs.

If house prices increase by 15 per cent during the time it takes you to build, all appears well and good and you do appear to get a fantastic return on your efforts; but if house prices don't go up you'll have to throw an almighty number of hours at your building project if you are to keep costs down to a level at which you appear to make a profit of more than a few per cent.

The bulk of the profit in a greenfield housing site tends to go to the landowner who succeeded in gaining planning permission to turn whatever was there into building land.

In most parts of the UK, agricultural land is worth around £3,000 per acre; in contrast, in SE England, half-acre building plots are currently fetching over £300,000.

Comparison of Costs for Developer and Selfbuilder		
	Developer	Selfbuilder
Plot	£100,000	£100,000
Stamp Duty	1,000	1,000
Purchasing Legals	400	400
Survey Fees	500	500
Design Work	3,000	0
Planning Fee	220	220
Building Control	300	325
Structural Warranties	500	1,400
Quantity Surveyor	500	0
Infrastructure Charge	480	480
Water Connection	600	600
Electricity Connection	350	350
Build Costs	130,000	130,000
Insurance	500	450
Marketing Costs	3,500	0
Legals/Agents Fees	6,100	0
Finance @5% for Plot (18months)	9,100	9,100
Finance @ 5% for Build Costs	5,200	5,200
Total Development Costs	£262,250	£250,000
Projected Sale Price	£300,000	£300,000
Profit before Tax	£87,750	£50,000
Proft after Tax at 40%	£23,430	no tax

Assumes that the design fees are included with a kit house option

One effect of this relationship between land costs and finished housing costs is that building plots tend to go up in value faster than house prices when house prices are rising; conversely, plot prices fall further than house prices when house prices slump.

As the money men would put it, land prices are geared to house prices so they experience faster rates of growth and decline. And recently, we have been seeing the phenomenon of land prices being bid up to unrealistic levels because the competition is so fierce.

Understanding the costs

The table on the next page compares the development costs for a professional developer and a selfbuilder using a timber frame kit house on an averagely profitable site. The costings reflect something akin to our standard house – see Chapter 2 'The Benchmark'.

If you just add plot costs and building costs together you'd see a 20-30 per cent profit (this is the margin that the press get so excited about), but a more thorough analysis reveals that the figure is nowhere near this amount. In particular, finance costs eat into the gross profit at an alarming rate and the effect of a) interest rates going up and b) failure to obtain a quick sale are disastrous.

Anyone who borrows to finance a project as large as a new house is extremely vulnerable to changes in interest rates.

When interest rates start to rise, professional developers get squeezed not just by the extra cost of this finance but also by the fact that the level of sales tend to decline, sometimes accompanied by the dreaded fall in house prices. Housebuilders are very vulnerable in these circumstances and what looks like a healthy profit on a house can evaporate within a matter of weeks.

A selfbuilder is in a subtly different situation to a speculative developer and this may mean exceptional, but their efficient execution is very dependent on a thorough working knowledge of the building trades and the local building practices and prices.

After three or four projects, you'll start to get halfway good; if it's your first time, you'll find it an almighty struggle and you'll be unlikely to do it well. Your subcontractors will very quickly realise they are working for a novice and the less scrupulous ones may be tempted to take advantage of this and to cut corners or to bodge, particularly if you've negotiated 'keen' labour prices.

Whilst your building inspector should ensure that the structure is adequate, very little professional checking takes place above foundation level and, in any event, most of the finishing trades are not covered by building regulations.

Furthermore, don't kid yourself that you're doing away with the overheads of employing a main contractor by managing the project yourself. Your phone bill will be up by £100-£200 a quarter; your mileage will increase two or three fold, even if you are living on site; you will need site insurance; you will suffer damage to materials which will have to be replaced at your own expense; you will end up with leftovers that you cannot easily get rid of; and at the end of the job, you'll have to chase yourself to get all those little snags finished.

More than half of a main contractor's mark-up goes on paying overheads that would be common to professionals and amateurs alike. And there is still the tricky little matter of finance. There are many other costs besides plot and building costs, and they all conspire to eat away your paper profit.

Still wanna selfbuild?

Having got all that off my chest, I will also readily point out that I have met many selfbuilders who have made a tidy packet out of their dealings. Nevertheless, I would argue that the rewards of selfbuilding are not chiefly financial. What it really allows is the freedom to design and build a new house to your

specifications, something that you will not be able to do by any other route.

For many people selfbuilding represents one of the great challenges in life. The more they are involved in the project, the more they get out of it and the whole attraction of selfbuild is the pure adventure of it all. If this is your motivation then more power to your elbow.

You may well end up just a little disappointed by the outcome and will perhaps be haunted by a whole host of 'what ifs' and 'if onlys.' Fear not, this is an experience common to all designers and builders. You'll just have to do it all again.

However, if your motivation is mainly financial then I warn you to look very carefully at the sums involved.

■ Yes, you can save money selfbuilding but it may not be as much as you might first expect.

■ Don't ignore the well-trodden route of hiring a designer (who in turn manages the job for you) just because you think it will be expensive.

■ Don't forget that property developing (for that's what you're doing) is a risky business.

Unlike many financial products that are now sold with warnings attached, building plots and the houses that go on them are sold on the understanding that the buyer knows the risks involved. You are assumed to be a sophisticated investor; make sure that you actually are.

Emotional investment

The selfbuilder has an emotional investment in their project and really wants to believe that all there work actually made sense financially; on the other side, the professional builder has good financial reasons for not wanting to exaggerate the profitability of any scheme they undertake. To do so would be to hand money over to the taxman. Thus the professional builder will account for every cost they possibly can whereas the selfbuilder will be inclined to overlook many of the legitimate overheads in order to make the final sum look more pleasing.

Nowhere is this discrepancy greater than in the area of finance. To a developer, finance is just another job cost, essentially no different than the cost of the land or the building costs. When the house is sold on, they will total up all the loan interest they have paid and add it in as a legitimate business cost.

The selfbuilder is in a rather different position. They may – probably will – already have a mortgage before they even think of taking on a major project like a new house or a major renovation. By transferring this mortgage from an existing house to a building plot they are not necessarily altering their cashflow at all and do not have to add this cost into their calculations.

What they are doing is exchanging a year or two's hardship (such as living with the in-laws or in a caravan on site) for the opportunity to live in a bigger or better house than they could otherwise afford. Whilst a cost accountant would probably say that the selfbuilders are deceiving themselves, it seems to me to be a perfectly legitimate approach to things.

If there is a danger for the selfbuilder in all this, it is that they will tend to get greedy and to overreach themselves. It is notoriously difficult to accurately predict building costs and the world is full of people with a vested interest in making building costs look cheaper than they actually are. Getting prices out of builders and subcontractors is often much easier said than done and the chances are that most selfbuilders will have to commit themselves to a building project before they have a clear idea of the actual costs. Often people realise at a comparatively late stage that they can't afford the scheme they have embarked on and desperately look for ways of reducing the costs.

Many will complain bitterly just how expensive builders are when the root of the problem is that they always had inflated expectations of what they could achieve with the money at their disposal.

Many people are bounced into becoming project managers because they think it is bound to be cheaper to build directly with subcontractors. This is not the way to become a selfbuilder; it's the way to become a headless chicken. Even hard-bitten professionals have problems reconciling their dreams with their budgets and it is essentially in response to this problem that I wrote this book – to help put you, the person paying all the bills, back in control of the situation.

Postscript

The bulk of this section appeared in the first edition of this book, published at the end of 1994. Several people have commented to me since that it's too gloomy in tone and that selfbuild isn't quite as bad, or as impoverishing, as I make out. Indeed since that time a number of selfbuilders have made a small tax-free fortune out of their dealings.

Perhaps the gloomy tone was affected by the times, when recession was still very present and the property market was mired in slump conditions. I did think of completely rewriting this section to reflect the more upbeat spirit of the age but then I figured that it served as a useful reminder to people that selfbuild is not a licence to print money.

If the property market turns sour in the next few years, I will be able to say, 'Told you so!' Not that it will do me much good. The chief reason I haven't changed the tone is because I have had feedback from others who are grateful for a counterblast, a view from the other side so to speak. A few have even said it encouraged them to take on some large building project because it enabled them to make a decent stab at evaluating the risks involved.

How Big is that House?			
	m²	ft²	Range of building costs
One-bedroom flat	40	430	£20,000-£30,000
Terraced two-bedroom house	60	650	£30,000-£50,000
Semi-detached, 3 bedrooms	90	970	£50,000-£75,000
Detached 3/4 bedrooms, integral single garage	130	1,400	£70,000-£120,000
Large detached 4/5 bedrooms, detached double garage	200	2,150	£100,000-£200,000

of foul drains laid out around the house. The foul drains connect to the village drains: the connection cost of £1,000 was shared between the four houses on the site, along with a water connection charge of £2,800 for all four homes plus an electricity connection fee of £1,100 just for Steve's house. There is no mains gas in Dullingham: the boiler is oil-fired, though they use LPG for their range cooker.

The brick chosen for the house is Hoskin's Westwick Mix, bought for £320 per thousand. They are laid in a white cement mortar, aping the look of old lime mortars but not using lime at all. 'I am not a great believer in lime,' commented Steve. 'It doesn't do much for me.

I just use Snowcrete cement and plasticiser.' Steve used Celcon aircrete blocks for the inner skin of the external walls because they give a better insulation value than ordinary blocks. Tarmac Hemelite – ordinary blocks – were used on the partition walls downstairs and on one or two walls upstairs. There are steel lintels – by Keystone – over all the openings and each is protected by a cavity tray. Steve commented: 'I am very careful to place cavity trays over the lintels even though I fail to see how they work when the cavity is stuffed with insulation. I have yet to see any moisture trickle out of the weep holes!'

The carpentry started with the first floor joists

Benchmark House Building Costs

	Mats	Labour	Plant	Total	Page no.
Groundworks	£ 5,130	£ 4,050	£ 1,680	£ 10,830	121
Drains & Services	£ 1,900	£ 1,170	£ 1,470	£ 4,540	137
Service Connection Charges	£ 1,800			£ 1,800	137
Inner Skin	£ 1,400	£ 2,600		£ 4,000	143
Internal Walls	£ 830	£ 1,370		£ 2,200	185
First Floor	£ 1,200	£ 2,100		£ 3,300	182
Cladding	£ 4,700	£ 4,700		£ 9,400	155
Internal Brickwork	£ 440	£ 440		£ 880	155
Chimney	£ 620	£ 350		£ 970	234
Joinery	£ 7,050	inc in blockwork		£ 7,050	169
Lintels	£ 870	inc in blockwork		£ 870	144
Steels	£ 350	£ 110		£ 460	186
Scaffolding			£ 1,200	£ 1,200	321
Roof Carpentry	£ 2,790	£ 2,900		£ 5,690	188
Roof Cover	£ 4,370	£ 2,950		£ 7,320	196
Insulation	£ 2,080	£ 740		£ 2,820	163
Rainwater Gear plus Fascia	£ 1,000	£ 1,350		£ 2,350	199
Plastering	£ 2,320	£ 7,790		£ 10,110	255
Painting	£ 750	£ 4,250		£ 5,000	271
Wall Tiling	£ 1,570	£ 1,010		£ 2,580	261
2nd Fix Joinery	£ 4,980	£ 2,920		£ 7,900	265
Electrics	£ 2,400	£ 2,400		£ 4,800	242
Heating	£ 2,550	£ 1,950		£ 4,500	236
Electric Underfloor Heating	£ 350	£ 240		£ 590	236
Sanitaryware & Plumbing	£ 1,960	£ 1,440		£ 3,400	299
Kitchen	£ 11,800	£ 1,690		£ 13,500	283
Floor Finishes	£ 7,040	£ 3,900		£ 10,940	261
Externals	£ 3,500	£ 2,600		£ 6,100	279
Rounded Total	**£ 76,000**	**£ 55,000**	**£ 4,000**	**£ 135,000**	
		Int FloorArea in m²		200	
		Cost/m²		£ 675	
		Cost/ft²		£ 63	

Rear view of the benchmark house. The extension is called the Sun Room on plan and it takes the place of a conservatory. The house was developed as one of four on a tight site.

that were built using conventional 47 x 200mm tanalised timber under 22 mm chipboard flooring. Some of the upstairs room partition walls are studwork. The roof carpentry was all bought in, in truss form, from Aspect Roofing in Norfolk for a total of £2,600. The roof took 18 man-days to erect. The roof cover is Forticrete Gemini tiles, a concrete tile designed to look like two plain tiles. They are a bit of a visual cheat: there are no cambers on them and if you look closely, you can see that every other tile divide is only for show. But the point is that people don't look closely. Only an expert would know they are not small format plain tiles. The three dormers were included with the other roofing supplies but they are covered with lead sheet — sounds expensive but it's actually quite a neat way to finish the dormer cheeks.

How is it all insulated? As you can guess, this is no eco-house and Steve has only chosen to insulate to the standards required by the building regs. But the 2002 building regs are surprisingly exacting: the cavity in the walls is filled with 75 mm of glass fibre insulation batts, the ground floor has 60 mm of Celotex (an efficient polyisocyanurate board) and the main roof has 200 mm of fibreglass quilt at ceiling level and 90 mm of Celotex within the sloping ceiling around the master bedroom plus an additional 25 mm underneath. Overall, over

£2,000 was spent on insulation materials. You can read up in much more detail on the thermal performance of this house in Chapter 13, Green Issues. The prediction is that this oil-heated house will spend £220 each year on space heating and £80 each year on hot water: Steve reckoned he was spending slightly more.

The external joinery is all white uPVC, except for the garage up and over door. Most of it is made by Speedframe, a supplier dedicated to new housebuilders. They use the traditional joinery sizes that house designers routinely work to. They also have a nifty clip-in fixing system that builds into the brickwork and enables you to just push the finished doors and windows into place - there is a photo of this in Chapter 7. The joinery in the sun lounge was sourced separately and Steve also used a separate supplier to fit the boxed eaves around the house and the guttering and downpipes – all done in white uPVC.

To erect all this, the house was scaffolded for a total of 16 weeks, which is about average for a detached house being built with brick and block.

Internally, the walls and ceilings received a wet plaster finish – render and skim onto the blockwork, plasterboard and skim onto the studwork and ceilings. The ground floor has a traditional screed, 65 mm deep. The internal

Floorplans of Benchmark House

Ground Floor

First Floor

10.150

Bedroom 4
Study
Bedroom 3
5.500
4.000

Family Bathroom
Stairs
Bedroom 2

A.C.

Joist/beam supports in grey

En-suite Showeroom

North

Master Bedroom
2.400
3.000

Sun Room
4.000
4.000

Kitchen
5.500
3.400
3.400

Lounge
4.000

Stairs

Shower Room

Entrance Hall

Footings marked up in solid grey

Utility
2.400

Office
3.000

Single Garage
3.000

Garage - no floor required

6.050
4.100

15.825
7550
3600
100
2200
100
1000
275
23000
100
5600
275
8275

275
2700
100
2700
100
4000
275

11.835

15.825
275
7.000
275
1.900
100
2.800
200
3.000
275

3.400

Bedroom 2 Window
1770x1200

Bedroom 3
1770x1050

Study Window
1200x1200

Bedroom 4 Window
1200x1200

Kitchen Window
1770x1050

50°

Garage Side Door
1018x2100

Garage Window
1200x1050

Lounge Window
1770x1350

West

Sun Lounge
Window
2750x1350

Kitchen French Doors
1200x2100

East

Bathroom window
1200x900

Velux
540x700

Dormer window
1200x1050

North

Sun Room Door/window assembly
2750x2100

Kitchen sink window
1200x1050

Kitchen door
918x2100

Shower-room
window
630x750

Utility window
630x900

Utility door
920x2100

Benchmark House Elevations

Note the joinery schedule. Normally this is written out like a shopping list but here I've indicated which opening is which. Read this in conjuction with the windows section in Chapter 7.

Dormer windows
1200x1050

Escape window
No Mullion

Garage Car
Door
2200x2100

South

Office Window
1200x1200

Entrance Door
1018x2100

Sidelight
300x2100

€ S.

The benchmark house is one of four very similar. The construction methods used on each were identical. This shot shows the neighbour's master bedroom taking shape, using a pair of dormer windows built off an attic truss roof

doors are timber – ledged and braced cottage style doors made by Jeld Wen, as was the staircase. The floors are finished with a variety of materials: 27mm (9 x 9 x 9) engineered oak planking from Creative Flooring in the lounge, the hallway and the office and 22 mm solid oak (from Barham & Sons, Mildenhall) upstairs. Interestingly the engineered flooring cost almost exactly twice as much as the solid oak planking used upstairs, £44 cu m and £22 per cu m respectively. The French door sets at either end of the lounge were made up as specials by local joinery firm, Soham Joinery.

The plumbing and heating took 12 days and

Benchmark house: the French doors to the Sun Room

is based around an oil-fired boiler, a Boulter Classic, and an unvented mains pressure hot water tank, a Megaflo. The space heating uses conventional radiators except in the bathrooms where there are, additionally, electric underfloor heating mats, manufactured by Devi.

There are three bathrooms: downstairs just has a shower, the upstairs family bathroom has just a bath and the en-suite bathroom in the master bedroom has a bath with a shower attachment. The kitchen has a simple ceramic Belfast sink unit and there is another sink in the utility room as well. All the pipework is run in copper, the waste in uPVC.

The electrics feature a large number of halogen downlighters: 24 upstairs (roughly four per room), 17 in the kitchen, another eight dotted around the ground floor. Also four outlets – in the entrance hall and stairwell – are energy efficient compact fluorescent lamps, as required by the building regs, as are the three smoke detectors. The lounge alone has a more traditional light fitting, a chandelier. There are also six external lights dotted around the house. Incidentally, that's a lot of lighting: I estimate that the electricity bill for lighting will be the same as the oil bill for space heating (both around £200 per annum). The sockets are arranged pretty conventionally, roughly three per room, more in the larger rooms. The house isn't 'wired for the future': the only concession to the internet is a regular BT outlet in every bedroom as well as three downstairs.

The kitchen, the largest room in the house, features a large number of distressed pine units, made by Pineland Kitchens, and granite worktops, produced on site by Affordable Granite. The appliances were all new – the most notable being a Rangemaster gas stove, fired by LPG bottles kept in the back alleyway. The Pineland kitchen units extend into the utility area but not the granite worktops: it's formica out here.

Finally the external pavings. On the back terrace and by the front door, Steve splashed out again using RMC's Chelsea Avenue Setts, three different sizes laid in a random pattern. Elsewhere the front access is laid under tarmac.

■ *Along the road*

Steve Baldwin's house is a pretty typical choice for a benchmark house for 'The Housebuilder's Bible'. It's designed very much with a view to selling on the new housing market, even though Steve built it for his family to live in. There are a few finishing details which wouldn't have been specified by a builder looking to make a sale, but in essence this is a straight developer-style house.

However, at the other end of the same village, Steve was involved in the construction of a much larger, more grandly specified house for Adrian and Beverly Thurley. The Thurleys' house makes an interesting contrast because it comes kitted out with a number of features which selfbuilders are very interested in and it makes a good case study for the more upmarket builds which have become commonplace during the past decade.

As a long haul pilot for Virgin Atlantic, Adrian Thurley spent a lot of time up in the sky with his thoughts close to the ground, dreaming of the house he would one day build. During the Nineties, the Thurleys were living in Bournemouth and were always on the lookout for building plots. However, Bournemouth is not an easy place to track down nice plots and they weren't meeting with any success. However, back in Dullingham, the village where Adrian had grown up, his parents were contemplating selling their bungalow and moving to something a little smaller.

Adrian realised that this was probably his selfbuild moment. The plot his parents' bungalow sat on was easily large enough for the house he wanted to build, the location was manageable for Heathrow and Gatwick

Rear elevation of the Thurley's house, which is over twice the floor area of Steve Baldwin's benchmark house.

and, of course, he still had ties in the village. He suggested to his parents that rather than moving, he should use the plot to create a house with a self-contained annexe for them to live in. It was an idea they were happy to go along with.

The bungalow had been largely untouched over the years and, in planning terms, it was clearly a candidate for replacement. However, it was only 100 sq m in size and the local council, East Cambs, had in place a policy stating that replacement dwellings could only be 25 per cent larger than the original and not significantly taller. Negotiations went on for eight months in 2001 with Adrian and his designer, Roger Peyton, edging forward their plans for a much larger house. Adrian recalled: 'The initial reaction of the planning officer to our plans was very negative: 'Far too big!' she exclaimed. So we moved the position of the house further back up the plot; this reduced the impact of the new house from the road. Then we agreed to step down the roofline a little and reduce the size of the front elevation by giving the house two rear additions, making it a U-shape. Finally, we went for a basement and a loft conversion. This way we got the space we wanted.'

However the size of the proposed house was

This was the bungalow that was replaced by the Thurley's new house. The footprint of the new house lies entirely behind the bungalow so this enabled them to leave the bungalow in place whilst they built the house. The driveway stayed in the same place and the newly-built garage block sits on the site of the old garage, pictured here top right.

still well beyond the council's guidelines for replacement dwellings and the planning officer had no choice but to refer the application to the committee. Adrian wrote a brief which he added to the application explaining that the new house would incorporate a number of sustainable features that should mean that it would use less energy and less water than the existing bungalow, even though it was apparently four times the size.

The planning committee actually paid a visit to the site in September 2001 and were impressed enough to grant planning permission later that day. It helped that Adrian and Roger had won over the planning officer and that she had recommended approval beforehand, even though the plans apparently drove a cart and horse through the planning guidelines. All that the council asked in return was that the external appearance of the house should be largely traditional; in particular, they required a slate roof and flint walling (adding approximately £15,000 and £10,000 to building costs respectively).

Having won an unlikely planning battle, the Thurleys had to arrange accommodation for themselves. Fortunately, the position of the new house was entirely behind the exisiting bungalow, which meant that they didn't have to demolish until after completion. But even so, the bungalow wasn't big enough for all of them so they started work by building the detached garage, which they then camped in for 18 months. They spent £30,000 on this structure; already you can see this was not going to be a cheap buiding process. It was then that Adrian also started his self build website, www.adethebuilder.co.uk, which he has kept faithfully updated ever since and which has subsequently logged over 75,000 hits, making it a valuable ongoing resource for many selfbuilders.

The building work was carried out by an assortment of specialists from around the country together with a core group of local tradesmen, marshalled by Steve Baldwin, and a huge input from the Thurleys. By early

From the front, the Thurleys' house looks like a large cottage, no more. This was a decision driven by the planning department which wished the house to be of a similar scale to the original bungalow

2004, some months after they had occupied the house, Adrian reckoned he had worked on average between three and four days a week for 120 weeks. In addition to this, his wife and his daughters had also contributed their time.

Basement

There are several aspects of the Thurleys' house that I want to highlight. Firstly, it includes a fully submerged 75 sq m basement, which itself incorporates a state-of-the-art heat pump and a rainwater harvesting system, all part of the negotiations undertaken with the planners. The basement was built using ThermoneX pre-cast panels, craned into place on a raft foundation. 'I think the basement has been tremendous value, even though I underestimated the amount of excavation. The total cost for the basement is around £33,000 which makes it quite a bit cheaper to build than the above ground parts of the house.'

Heat pump

The house is heated entirely by an Ice Energy

One of the things that the planners insisted on was the use of certain vernacular details, in this case flint walls. Adrian Thurley had a lot of trouble tracking down knapped flint and ended up buying it in from Somerset. The flint walling cost over £100 per sq m, adding considerably to the build costs.

Floor Plan for the Thurleys' 475 sq m House

Rooms in the Roof

bedroom 5

wc

landing

bedroom 6

bedroom 1

bedroom 4

en-suite

landing

First Floor

bathroom

bedroom 3

study

bedroom 2

Basement

kitchen

cloakroom

hall

dining

Ground Floor

livingroom

rainwater storage

utility

bedroom

bath

kitchen

Grannexe

lobby

lounge

The deal which Adrian struck with his parents was that he should provide them with a self-contained flat within the structure of the house. Theirs is the area shaded in orange.

Adrian was very much a hands-on selfbuilder. Here he is starting out on the kitchen floor tiling, something he had never done before.

the whole house ventilation system, the oak flooring, the guttering and the kitchen units as well as taking on all the tiling and decorating. He is particularly pleased with the fireplace and chimney details which were designed by the Fireplace Design Consultancy. 'They supplied some incredibly detailed drawings of how we should assemble the back-to-back chimneys together with a stainless steel flue. The fires work a treat and they look fantastic.'

The internal walls are lined with Fermacell board, a heavier alternative to plasterboard that doesn't require the same finishing skills. However, the ceilings use plasterboard: in retrospect, Adrian would have upped the spec on the ceilings because of the noise transmission between floors.

The joinery is all by Andersen, imported from the USA. These are timber windows covered with a PVC cladding externally.

Budget busters

As the accompanying table infers, Adrian had trouble keeping his building budget under control. No way was this ever going to be a cheap job but originally Adrian had planned on spending around £260,000 on the main house – £560 per sq m; his final bill was £327,000, a 25 per cent increase, working out at £700 per sq m, not including any of the sweat equity added by the Thurley's themselves.

To keep the project on budget, Adrian bought

HousebuilderXL, a project management and budgeting software package designed for the selfbuild market. 'You key in elements like walls and it works out everything you need for that wall including things like skirtings and ironmongery. It's exacting to learn but overall I thought it worked pretty well on all the standard features but not so well on the unusual parts of the build. For instance, the muck away costs for the basement spiralled out of control – I simply underestimated how much had to be taken out of the ground and I didn't get a quote beforehand.'

Because of cost overruns, there were some features which were abandoned. The home audio, budgeted at £6,200, and the HomeNet structured cabling, at £5,800, never saw the light of day.

The project has not been without its hitches. When I visited, Adrian was busy replacing many of the internal doors. 'I made a big mistake with those. I wanted a farmhouse, cottage look and went out and bought some pretty cheap external ledged and braced doors. But they have almost all warped and they look awful now. So we bit the bullet and had a local joinery company make up some hardwood specials. It's cost nearly £5,000 but I think in the long run it will be worth doing. I couldn't live with the other ones. The lesson to be learned is not to fit external doors internally — the moisture content is way too high and they almost always twist.'

In conclusion

Adrian and Beverley remain as enthusiastic about their project as ever, despite having been going hard at it for more than three years. Having moved into the house, they now find themselves with a highly serviceable self-contained flat above their garage which they plan to offer as a selfbuild bed and breakfast service. Anyone interested in meeting the Thurleys and spending some time finding out how they fared is welcome to book a night or a weekend and learn directly from them. Bookings can be made via the website.

Chapter 3
Pitfalls

Finding land
Renovate or rebuild
Legal pitfalls
Some planning traps
Problem plots
Bad design

■*Finding Land*

Every year in Britain around 15,000 selfbuilds, and probably as many major renovations and conversions, are completed. This number has held steady for many years, despite some people predicting that we would run out of plots and that every tumbledown old wreck had already been tarted up. The opportunities are out there, the business is being done. So, the question is, why do people find it so hard to get started?

I fear that the answer can be summarised in one uncompromising phrase — unrealistic expectations. Or, to put it another way, the opportunities are rather more expensive than people can afford.

The property market is pretty ruthless in valuing opportunity and the idea that you can pick up a really nice building plot for next to nothing is fallacious. The selfbuild exhibitions are full of people who are 'seriously looking at building a house' who basically can't afford to, or at least can't afford it in the expensive areas they already live in. They will make enquiries, log onto websites and register interest, and even buy books, without ever really realising that they haven't got the wherewithal to make

it happen. It doesn't help matters that TV is currently blitzed with programmes about doing up property and 'making it all happen': this just pulls even more people into the whirlpool. But without some serious financial assets and/or income, it's not really going to happen. After two or three frustrating years, would-be builders withdraw, saying they wanted to do it but they couldn't find a plot. But there are plots, and some people do make it happen.

So what are the essential ingredients for people who do get on and make it happen?

I think they tend to fall into three camps. Either they are rich and can afford to pay the prices needed to secure prime building plots. Or they are lucky and happen to already own a piece of land which is developable. Or they are not too fussy about where they live and will buy anything that comes up, within reason. This last group are the really keen selfbuilders who tend to do it over and over again because they love the whole process of building houses.

There are always dozens of opportunities on offer in every county during the course of a year: if people are deadly serious, they will find something. If they are just sticking a toe in the water, they will always find a reason to not go for a property or they will never bid enough to get it. Or they will complain that they can't afford the prices being asked.

Professional plot finding

Plot finding is actually becoming more organised and more professional. There are plot finding websites out there that will allow you to zoom-in in aerial photograph mode and get a pretty good idea of what the place is like before you visit.

You can subscribe to plot databases for individual counties and you can also check details of recent planning permissions granted in your district so you get advance warning of plots before they even come to market. Even so, tracking down opportunities is a time consuming process and it pays to be professional about it: always think like a developer, because that is what you are.

According to Buildstore, which runs the Plotsearch database, the average cost of a plot in Surrey is £350,000 whereas in Aberdeenshire it is just £40,000. Those are the two extremes: the rest of the UK is to be found somewhere between. It follows directly from this that selfbuild in Surrey is somewhat different to selfbuild as practised in Aberdeenshire. In Surrey, selfbuilders tend to either be replacing their own dilapidated houses or building in their back garden whilst selling off their original house; in Scotland, there is a more conventional selfbuild market with plots being bought by 'ordinary people.' It also means that selfbuild is far more common in the cheaper areas.

Of the 15,000 selfbuilds taking place each year in the UK, over half the total are in Wales, Scotland or Northern Ireland whose combined population is just ten million, compared to 50 million people living in England.

Single plots in SE England are so expensive that they attract professional developers whereas in the rest of the country they tend to be sold to amateurs wishing to build for themselves.

So it pays to be realistic. If you live somewhere expensive, you need a plot or a lot of money to make it happen; alternatively, you can move somewhere cheaper and upset the locals with all your flash big city money. The opportunities are out there.

Unconsented land

There are several companies selling 'land' for knock down prices, usually just a few thousand pounds. The adverts seem very enticing but, if you keep your wits about you, you will realise that this land has no planning permission and has very little chance of ever getting planning permission. It's on the wrong side of the planning boundaries and planning boundaries very rarely move, despite what the sales literature would have you believe. Usually the giveaway is that they advise you not to bother with a solicitor. Here's what Gladwish Land Sales suggests: 'No Solicitors necessary! Unlike buying a house, when buying land you do not need to ensure vacant possession (unless you want to scare birds away) nor do you have to ensure all the fixtures stay. Most land that we sell is cheaper than buying a car. Do you use a solicitor to buy a car? The car could be stolen

The market for small residential sites has been hot for several years now. When good sites come to market (and they do), they don't hang around long and they usually fetch rather more than can be strictly economically justified.

Development is controlled around every settlement in the country. The usual way of doing this is to draw dotted black lines on a map, known as framework boundaries. Outside the land is deemed to be agricultural and changes hands at £3,000/acre. Inside, within the development zones, land costs over £1 million an acre in southern England.

and the log book a forgery! With land, nobody can steal the land you buy and the transfer document you get, once signed, is irrevocable.'

All true. All true. But a solicitor might also advise you not to bother, which would be a shame for Gladwish, wouldn't it. Victor Gladwish isn't the worst offender. I have to hand a glossy brochure from an outfit calling itself UK Land Investments Group, head office in Berkeley Square in London, no less. They offer an "unparalleled level of expertise" and a "rare blend of knowledge and practical know-how which sets us apart" (who writes this guff?) and suggest that this is an opportunity for serious investors or, as they get called in Berkeley Square, private clients. Plots in East Sussex are being offered for £7,500. Better still, you can pay your 10 per cent deposit with a credit card. No need to bother with expensive solicitors. And you will become the proud owner of a slice of a field in Sussex with no realistic hope of becoming a building plot this side of the 22nd century.

There is nothing illegal about all this. They don't make any false claims. They make it clear

the plots don't have planning permission. They do, sort of, insinuate that they will get planning permission but are very careful with their choice of words here. 'We negotiate with local councils on your behalf so that you don't have to worry about getting planning permission.' That's good wording, isn't it. You 'don't have to worry about it' because nothing is ever going to happen on that front.

Don't buy land without planning permission from anybody unless you are certain what you are letting yourself in for. If you are tempted by any plot always talk to local planners who will be able to tell you about the history of any applications and the likelihood of getting planning consent.

Mechanics of Property Purchase

There are basically five methods by which property (including building plots) can changes hands in these islands.

■ Public auction: The best thing about this is that it's open. It gives the seller (or vendor in these circles) a legally binding agreement. On the other hand the expensive pre-sale work has to be undertaken with no guarantee of success. Sometimes, in the excitement of an auction, it doesn't get done at all. A ten per cent deposit usually taken at the auction so buyer has to have funds to hand.

■ Formal tender: as practised in Scotland. Once a bid is accepted, the deal becomes legally binding. Otherwise similar to the auction in pros and cons.

■ Informal tender: buyers are asked to send in sealed bids for the property by a fixed date, together with details of their own financial position. All the bids are opened at the same time and the sale is agreed, usually with the party considered to be in the best position to buy. Buyers are wary and object to the decision being made in private and with no opportunity to increase their bid. However it's probably less stressful than an auction and gives more flexibility to the vendor.

■ Informal telephone auction: the common method of property sales everywhere outside Scotland. It gives much more flexibility to both sides. This is both its strength and its weakness — you get flaky offers from purchasers and you get gazumping and other evils because the contracts are not binding until physically exchanged. And when there are more than three buyers competing for one property, it can get very difficult to organise proceedings because someone is often away or can't make up their mind. In these situations agents often decide to switch to informal tender (see previous point), to close the deal.

■ Private sales: often referred to as 'Sale by Private Treaty.' If a buyer and a seller can agree on a price, then there is no obligation for them to go through the more public channels indicated above. A lot of land changes hands this way. You'd be surprised. Or may be you wouldn't.

The actual process of buying land (or derelict buildings) is similar to that involved in buying houses. And indeed the principles are exactly the same, though the detail is very different. You don't buy a house if you think it's too expensive or if you think it's going to fall down; you normally employ solicitors and surveyors to ensure that you are not buying a pig in a poke. Likewise with plots, you want to ensure that you can build what you want on it at a price you can afford. Having said that, the whole process of buying plots (and, especially, renovation opportunities) is more complex because there are more things that can go wrong. When buying an existing property at least you know that it is there, even if it might just fall down next week! With a building plot you are buying nothing more than a field that comes with a promise, a hope for the future. And unlike the conventional house market, the chances are that you will have to purchase your chosen plot without knowing exactly what you can build.

The limits of professional help

You don't have to hire any help but it's usual to do so because the stakes are high and you don't want to make a silly mistake. If you hire the services of a solicitor or a licensed conveyancer, look for a property specialist. If you are buying in an area new to you, you'd be well advised to look for a local rather than sticking with someone you've used before who might be 200 miles away from the action. Now is the time you need as much information, official and unofficial, as you can get. A good solicitor will uncover more than just that which is revealed by undertaking searches and checking for legal complications and boundaries.

One common pitfall occurs when the planning permission only applies to one part of the building plot - a frequent occurrence when close to village framework boundaries and the like. Some solicitors spot this, others don't. But even the best solicitor is not going to be able to advise you as to whether the plot is an A1 purchase because there are a number of other areas that are outside the remit of even the most scrupulous legal beaver.

Purchase taxes

You pay exactly the same taxes on land purchase as you do on house purchase. It's called stamp

STAMP DUTY RATES as of 2004	
Plot or property price	Duty
Up to £60,000	0%
£60,000-£249,999	1%
£250,000-£499,999	3%
Over £500,000	4%

duty. The government likes stamp duty and they like increasing it: it's a stealth tax because, although people don't like it, it's not going to lose them the next election, and it's relatively easy to police. Only the buyer pays the stamp duty, which gives selfbuilders a small advantage because they are usually buying cheap (plots) and building expensive (houses).

Note that stamp duty is payable on the total value so a house or a plot bought for £249,000 would be charged stamp duty of £2,490 (one per cent of the total), whereas a house or plot bought for £250,000 would be charged £7,500 (three per cent of the total).

Stamp duty rates in the UK are still relatively low compared to other countries, so expect to see these rates continue to rise.

Any other charges? There are fees payable to bodies like the Land Registry (around £200) and for council searches, maybe another £200, but they are not significant in the scheme of things. And of course your legal fees.

■Renovate or rebuild

As virgin, greenfield building sites become more and more difficult to obtain, increasing numbers of people are looking to purchase dilapidated dwellings that they then seek to demolish and to build afresh. These are basically recycled building sites, sometimes referred to as brownfield sites.

Planning permission is usually much easier to obtain on a site with established residential usage and there are also usually considerable savings to be made because the service connections are already in place. A few sites will have problems with contaminated ground but mostly the requirements of today's foundations to go much deeper than was previously thought

necessary mean that any existing foundations will be excavated and disposed of. In addition to buying a serviced plot, you have an existing structure from which you may well be able to salvage some useful materials.

So far so good. The decision to demolish, however, is often not as clear-cut as this. For a start, few people care to sell their existing properties at building plot prices. To do so is to admit that your home is worthless which can be a bitter pill to swallow, even if it's true. In any event it's usually the case that the house is not worthless, it's just old and dilapidated and with a little bit of tender loving care and a whole lot of money it could continue to make a very serviceable home. So problem number one is the extra expense of buying such a site.

Then you are faced with a decision whether to knock down and start again or whether to work with what is already there. Now here things start to get complicated because the chances are that it is not a clear-cut issue, most renovation opportunities fall somewhere between the two extremes. Added to which it is a fiendishly difficult exercise to compare costs between the two approaches because this major decision has to be made at a pre-plan stage and you will have to work with ballpark figures. Whether the building is worth saving at all is an issue that only you (and the planners) can decide — each case has to be argued on its merits and there is little point making any broad generalisations here.

Comparison costs
Rebuilding from scratch is almost always cheaper than major renovations. It's hard to be too precise as to why this should be but that's the way it goes. For instance, the typical price for building a new home is currently around £600-£800 per sq m of internal floor area. For barn conversions, the ballpark costs tend to start at £800 per sq m and go up over £1,000 per sq m. At first this appears to be counter-intuitive: after all, with a major renovation or conversion, you already have much of the superstructure in place and so, logically, you

might think that the job would be that much less in scale. But logic and conversions don't sit that well together and experience tends to suggest that major conversions soak up money like a sponge.

Of course, it depends how major your major works are. But restoring a near-derelict superstructure is never quick and even minor repairs seem to cost. My business has been involved with many projects doing up Victorian houses where the superstructure has been essentially sound and still the costs have come out higher than with newbuild.

Is it a plot at all?

Don't assume that any building that has once been occupied by humans will automatically qualify for residential planning permission. Councils take widely differing attitudes to what constitutes abandonment and the most telling factor in whether or not an old building can be converted into a new home is usually the quality of the building, not its previous usage. Always check on the status of a derelict property in the local plan to see whether redevelopment is likely to be controversial. Often the planners will allow the conversion of a particularly fine old barn just to stop it from disintegrating and sometimes this permission is dependent on the structure being maintained, even when this is a costly and relatively dangerous course to take. There have been cases of planning permission being withdrawn from barn conversions after the builder has undertaken demolition of a few select walls.

▌*Legal pitfalls*

The prospect of buying a duff plot is a nightmare that haunts professional builders as much as amateurs, and the consequences of doing so are likely to be with you for many a year to come. There is no absolutely foolproof way of avoiding the lemons but a little bit of diligence (and a good lawyer) employed at the pre-contract stages of negotiations should uncover most of the problems.

Legal covenants

Building plots are often sold with legal constraints over what may and what may not be done to them. The most common form of constraint is the covenant whereby the vendor (i.e. the person selling the plot) requires that the purchaser should fulfil a number of conditions. Many of these might not cost a euro — i.e. no caravans to be stored in the back garden or no trees to be planted where they might block someone else's view — but others can involve substantial costs.

The commonest type of covenant deals with boundary fencing and would read something like this: 'The purchaser covenants to erect six foot high fencing to the southern and eastern boundaries of the plot before any building work takes place.'

Sometimes the covenant will be very much more specific and ask for a brick wall nine inches thick or something like that. A condition such as this is expensive to meet and should really be reflected in a lower plot price.

It is also common now to find covenants preventing any further development. The point behind such conditions is not to preserve the unique beauty of your setting but to hold on to any uplift in value you may be clever enough to negotiate with the planners. Covenants have beneficiaries and you can usually lift covenants if you are prepared to throw money at the beneficiaries. The going-rate for buying off a no-development covenant is around 50 per cent of the value created — an arm and a leg, in other words.

Sometimes there are some very old covenants lurking on the deeds and it's long since ceased to be clear who exactly the beneficiary is. Maybe they have died and their heirs are not very apparent: unfortunately, covenants don't disappear with the death of the beneficiary. In such cases, you can insure against anyone coming forward and laying claim to the uplift.

Boundary disputes

It is unfortunately very common to encounter problems with fuzzy boundaries. Just because someone offers a piece of land for sale, it doesn't follow that they own all of it — or even any of it sometimes. Plot boundaries are usually drawn in title deeds as relatively thick lines on OS maps and there is frequently lots of room for disagreement about where exactly these lines are on the ground.

Matters have been improving over the years as owners start to register their plots with the Land Registry but there are still over four million properties in the UK not registered and many of the large estates that routinely off-load land haven't bothered to register.

In 2003 an amended Land Registration Act was passed which establishes a framework for registering boundaries using satellite positioning technology. This should mean that having established site boundaries with sellers and neighbours on paper there should be no room for dispute when translating these to the site.

Ransom strips

Another potential problem occurs when part of the land needed to successfully develop a plot is owned by someone else. Typically, this is land needed to access the plot. This is sometimes referred to as a ransom strip. Ransom strips can usually be bought off although you may be staggered to find out that you will be required to pay over as much as half of the plot value – they are not called ransom strips for nothing.

Rights of Way and Wayleaves

There are any number of complications that should, repeat should, be uncovered by your solicitor's search: rights of way crossing the plot, existing wayleaves for services and cables to cross the plot, complex shared ownership of access roads, to name but three. Even if you can live with these arrangements, they may well affect resale values and make finance much harder to get and insurance more expensive. Many of these problems can be sorted out by throwing money at them — but the canny buyer should ensure it's the vendor's money not theirs.

Using Options

If it is any consolation, this is an area that causes big headaches to major professional developers as well as virgin housebuilders. If you are in any doubt about these issues, my advice is to use what muscle you have as a plot purchaser and, if possible, take out an option to buy your chosen plot rather than formally exchanging contracts.

What is an option to buy? The bare bones of a contract might look like this: you agree a price on a plot of land (though even this doesn't have to be fixed in stone). This remains in place for, say, two or three years; the length of the option is entirely up to you. During that time the vendor is prohibited from selling to anyone else. Some contracts involve interest payments to the vendor: this acts as a spur to the purchaser to get on with it and protects the vendor from time-wasters. The big plus from the purchaser's point of view is that an option protects you from gazumping and other forms of treachery.

How much would you be expected to pay for an option? Well, that depends. If the planning angle is difficult and you are taking on the costs of obtaining planning permission (which could be several thousand), then there may well be no payment made to the vendor at all. They would be very happy for someone else to do all this work for them. However if market conditions are buoyant, then you may have to part with up to five per cent of the plot price just to tempt the vendor into an option. Also the buyer may want to make the plot price conditional on what you manage to squeeze out of planning so that the price is £120,000 if you get one house but £200,000 if you get permission for two.

If there is a pitfall in all this, it is that you can spend a lot of money and get nowhere. But that's a pitfall that all property developers have to face.

■*Some planning traps*

Ever since they introduced the concept of planning permission in 1947, it's got progressively harder to obtain. Every government makes noises about reforming the planning system but that has invariably been code for introducing yet more controls. The planners, albeit accountable to elected local councillors, now have considerable and arbitrary powers over what you can and cannot do on a piece of land that you nominally own; in effect there is a level of 'state ownership' over each and every building plot which supersedes individual ownership and you must fulfil the conditions placed on you before you can begin to put your own ideas in place.

Time lapses

One potential problem for the unwary is the fact that planning permission has a time limit on it. Normally this lasts for five years from the date the permission is granted, but there is one kind of planning permission, known as outline permission, which basically expires after just three years. As many small or selfbuilders will be buying a plot which has only outline permission to build, please note that you have to get detailed permission before the end of the three-year period or you have a very expensive field on your hands.

Once the work has begun, you no longer have to apply for planning permission. Exactly what the definition is of 'work having been started' is a grey area, but it is usually accepted that if you have laid the footings then you have started. So if time is running short and you don't have the wherewithal to complete the building work, you can ensure your planning permission is permanent by undertaking just the foundations and footings.

Planning concerns

The planners are concerned with far more than whether a particular plot can be zoned for building. Some of the major areas they are likley to look at will be:

■ size of the house: is it 'too big for the plot?'
■ site of the house: don't assume you can build anywhere on the plot
■ neighbours' privacy and right to light
■ style of the house: design and materials 'must

be in keeping'
■ vehicular access and turning heads: a particular problem on narrow fronted plots, less than 12m wide. The highways department insists that not only will adequate visibility splays be provided, but that there must be adequate room on site for cars to turn around or, as they say in planning speak, 'enter and leave in a forward gear.'
■ trees and hedges: often have to be retained or replanted.

Visibility splays

Plots need access and this can of itself prove to be quite a planning nightmare. The Highways Department has a little routine know as the visibility splay – which prevents some plots ever being developed. The idea is that each new entrance onto the public highway should be safe and that to be safe it should have clear vision in both directions.

Visibility splays: the ground rules	
Speed limit	Clear of obstructions for:
20mph	45m each side
30mph	90m each side
40mph	120m each side
50mph	160m each side
60mph	215m each side
70mph	295m each side

In addition to this, the visibility splays have depth as well. At slow speed limits, you need clearance up to 2.4m back from the carriageway: this increases to 4.2m at the higher speed limits. In effect, you have to imagine two triangles of visibility on each side of your site access.

These are guidelines. You may well be able to develop a site where the visibility is marginal – i.e. it nearly meets the guidelines. But if you have, for instance, a large wall in your way then you have big problems.

It may be that you can negotiate with (bribe) a neighbour to reduce the height of a hedge or move a fence in order to meet the criteria. You may even have a ransom hedge on your hands!

Tree Preservation Orders

Tree Preservation Orders (casually referred

to in these circles as TPOs) can be slapped on inconvenient trees just to make life difficult for you. It doesn't have to be a big oak tree either: they can place TPOs on a tree with a girth of just 75mm or, failing that, little clusters of trees as well. Many people have been caught out over the years by inquiring if there were any TPOs in force at such and such a site, only to be told: 'There didn't use to be, but there will be within half an hour!' Well, it's never quite that brazen but it does happen – it's not an urban myth.

However, you can avoid this particular nightmare by asking to inspect the TPO register for your area; TPOs are a matter of public record and you aren't obliged to reveal your hand in order to take a look at it. If your site is TPO-free, you can then cut or mow down anything in your way that might cause TPO problems in future. In fact, if gaining planning permission is at all contentious, I would recommend that you do just that.

Frustrated selfbuilder Tim Cox proudly displays one of his tiny preserved trees. Huntingdon DC thoughtfully slapped TPOs across most of his road frontage which had the effect of disrupting his development plans.

Conservation Areas

These are areas defined by the planners as being especially sensitive and on which they maintain a whole raft of extra controls over what you can and can't do – for instance you need to fill out a three-page application in order to fell a tree.

Conservation areas are typically the older parts of a town or the core area of a village, perhaps surrounding the village green, and the fact that you are buying in such an area should be apparent when you purchase – after all it is usually used as an additional sales bullet in the blurb and passes as an excuse to hoick the price. It affects new builders less than renovators because new build is already subject to stringent planning controls. But be aware that you will be unlikely to get permission for anything unusual in a conservation area.

Logically the issue of conservation areas ought to be dealt with by regular planning controls but logic and local government make uneasy bedfellows and conservation area issues are not dealt with by regular planners. There is of course a trap in here waiting to catch the unwary: if, for instance, you apply to build an extension to an existing house in a conservation area which involves the removal of some existing structure, you could find that your permission to build the extension gets approved by planning but your permission to demolish what already exists is turned down by the conservation department. This is known, technically, as being kyboshed.

Listing

The other great wedge of planning control concerns the listing of buildings thought to be of merit and which, therefore, need extra protection from unscrupulous owners and developers. The lists of protected buildings are compiled by the Department of Culture, Media and Sport (DCMS), taking advice from English Heritage, Historic Scotland and Cadw in Wales. The following buildings tend to be listed:
■ all pre-1700 buildings in anything like their original condition
■ most buildings from 1700 to 1840

I am not alone in thinking that the listing of our nation's housing stock has gone too far. Here's a prime example from Cambridgeshire. Fake leaded lights? I don't mind. Aluminium patio doors? No problem, if you like them. But this house is listed. Who are we kidding?

■ buildings of quality and character from 1840-1914
■ post-1914, only the very highest quality.
  England & Wales have 500,000 listed buildings. Grade 1 accounts for just 2 per cent (i.e. 10,000), Grade II* is 4 per cent (20,000) and Grade II, the rest. Listing protects the interior and the exterior, as well as objects or structures fixed to the building, and objects and structures within the curtilage of the building, present since 1948. The curtilage is a fancy word for the outbuildings and garden walls: very often barn conversions are covered by listing arrangements because they are within the curtilage of a listed farmhouse.

  If you want to undertake any building work on a listed building you are required to apply for listed building consent, whether or not you need planning permission. There is dispute over just what constitutes 'building work.' Repainting the windows usually doesn't but something like re-pointing usually does. Obtaining listed building consent is often a slow business – anticipate at least a three month delay.

  Listed building officers are attached to each planning department and these are the people to head for in order to glean more information.

Expensive requirements

When considering the problem from a perspective of hidden costs, it is the planners' interest in the design and materials of the

house that is of most concern. Sometimes these concerns are easily predictable: if, for instance, you are building in one of the stone belts where there is a uniform vernacular style (as in the Cotswolds or the Yorkshire Dales), you will not be surprised to learn that you must build with similar materials. Expensive but not unexpected. However, most of Britain does not have a uniform building style and lowland England in particular is characterised by its great variety of building styles and materials. Despite this diversity, the planners can insist on any number of design details, examples of which now follow.

Slate roofs

Even in East Anglia, home of the (cheap) pantile, planners are frequently known to insist on slate roofs despite the fact that most roofing slate comes from North Wales and wouldn't have been known in England before the railway age. You may be able to argue that reconstituted slate will be adequate but it will still cost you an extra £6-£10 per sq m.

Dislike of rooflights

They sometimes insist on dormer roof windows. A small dormer will add at least £400-£500 to construction costs; in comparison, a flat opening rooflight (a Velux) would cost no more than £250. Paradoxically, on barn conversions the reverse is true: planners

When digging a trial hole, the convention is to go down somewhat deeper than the proposed (or existing) foundations. Normally, you dig two or three trial holes just outside the proposed footprint – not under it.

history or geology of the ground. The normal practice is for the pits to be dug to a depth of 3m (close to, but not under, the foundations) in the presence of a structural engineer who takes a long gander at the ground conditions before the digger fills the holes back in. The engineer then decides whether the house foundations can proceed as normal or whether a more complicated foundation solution is needed.

Expect to pay an engineer between £150 and £300 for this service, though their fees will be much higher if special foundation designs are needed; a JCB for an hour should cost an additional £50-£100 (depending on travel time). Augered boreholes are another alternative – likely to cost around £300 each (and you'll need two) but a good option where access to JCBs is not possible or you have other problems like high water tables.

But there is also a natural tendency for the experts, having been called in, to suggest very expensive, fee-swelling, solutions when they may not be necessary. Jeremy Bulbrook built three houses in the Cambridgeshire Fenland town of March during 2001 and he ended up feeling badly let down by his professional advice: 'I had a couple of boreholes drilled on my architect's suggestion. The soil report that came back from these recommended a piled foundation, on the basis that the first two metres or so could possibly be made ground, even though it was gravel/sand.

'My building inspector asked why I hadn't spoken to them first. He said that they would have been happy with strip footings, but as a recommendation for piles had been made, they had no choice but to force me down the piled route.

'Now whilst I don't want the houses to fall down,' he adds, 'I do wonder if some of the engineers that produce these reports are too scared to say that strip footings would be OK, because if it goes wrong in the future, then they have to bear some responsibility.

'After all, it doesn't cost an engineer a penny more to say he would recommend piled foundations. In fact he may earn more, if he gets to design the footings as well.

'If I was starting again, I would definitely talk to the building inspectors first. There's always the risk that when you dig you find something unexpected, but that could still happen even if you have boreholes drilled,' he said.

In some extreme situations the professional fees can end up costing more than the foundations. I have reports of people having spent around £5,000 on site investigations in areas where mining activity may or may not have occurred; boreholes down to 30 metres are very expensive. Selfbuilder Archie Hunter's case is a classic: he undertook a full geological survey which established that he didn't need a specialist raft foundation which he reckoned would have cost him an extra £2,000. 'Look we've saved over £2,000 on the cost of the foundations. OK, it cost over £4,500 to save this money but what the hell!'

Contaminated land

Where the problems with the site are caused by the natural characteristics of the land, the solutions are usually fairly straightforward, if expensive. However, there is now a trend towards recycling building land and an increasing number of new homes are being built on sites which have had buildings on before — these sites are sometimes known as brownfield sites. If the previous building was a house or a barn, then a pollution problem is unlikely but if the site has been used as a tip or as an industrial plant then it is quite likely that the ground may contain a whole cocktail of nasties such as heavy metals, toxic chemicals or methane gas. Now local authorities up and down the land are currently preparing registers of contaminated land and they will be empowered to issue Remediation Notices which will require the landowner to make the site safe, which usually means either excavating and burying the pollutants elsewhere (the Foot and Mouth option) or encasing them in concrete or clay (the Chernobyl option). Sometimes the solution may be relatively cheap – for instance specifying sulphur resistant cement – but it will be some time before housebuilders are able to accurately budget for contamination problems.

Access & services

When assessing a plot or a barn, you should take note of the distance you think you will have to take the services and the access you will have to build. Many backland developments come onto the market these days – typically the rear of someone's garden – and the prices asked for these sites are often little different to the prices asked for somewhere with a road frontage. Yet the budget cost of laying private driveways, drains, water and electricity combined with providing fencing is upwards of £100 per metre; that means that a plot set 50 metres back from a road is going to cost £5,000 more to develop than one with a road frontage. Whereas the layout of vehicle access arrangements are usually easy to work out, finding out about the services requires detective work.

Driveways

The basic cost of laying a drive can be budgeted at around £50 per linear metre, rather more if it is required to be fenced off as well. Often there is extra work involved in connecting to the public highway: typically you may have to construct a dropped kerb if you are crossing a raised pavement, at the very least you will have to provide a small apron of asphalt or tarmac so that there is no unsightly gap between your drive and the public highway. In some situations you may be required to create a visibility splay which may involve removing existing obstructions and rebuilding them further back from the road.

On the other hand, you may have to construct a bridge over a ditch or even make an opening through an existing building. There are, in fact, so many potential access problems that it is almost pointless trying to summarise them – you will, in all probability, discover them when you first visit the site. Just be aware that whilst a straightforward highway junction will cost a couple of hundred quid, complicated access arrangements may well set you back several thousand.

Drain connections

Many isolated plots are too far from mains drainage to make connection feasible. To find out what the position is on any given plot you must contact your local council and/or your local water or sewage company. The detail and accuracy of records varies from area to area but they will have some idea of the location of your nearest drain.

If the mains sewer is reasonably adjacent and it's not obviously uphill from your plot, then the omens are fairly good. Excavation and drain connections are, however, fiddly and expensive on even short runs, and if your drain is, say, 50m away from your house it is worth talking to a groundwork/drainage contractor about the other possibilities.

Sewage disposal via a non-standard route is going to add significantly to costs. A reasonable budget on a no-problem single site, draining straight into a main drain, would be £3,000. If you have to do something other than make a straightforward sewer connection, then you would be wise to budget these amounts in addition:

- septic tank – add £1,000
- mini-treatment works – add £3,000
- cesspool – add £2,500
- pumping station – add £2,000
- foul drain runs longer than 50m – add £20 per m
- rainwater drain runs longer than 50m – add £15 per m
- rainwater that won't soak away – add £300.

One frequently met problem is the development of a site that is located on backland or down a lane. Main drains are present under the main road but your site is maybe 150m or more away. How do you assess the situation? Probably the best solution is to get a groundwork contractor to have a look and give an estimate on how much a connection would be. If the figure goes up much over £2,500 then you would do well to think of using some of the alternative solutions. This is something else that is touched on in greater depth in Chapter 6: Groundworks.

Water Connections

Unlike drainage work, which is usually left to the housebuilder to organise, water connections have to be carried out by the powers that be. In England and Wales that means the private water companies and their fees are notoriously high, frequently higher than £500 for connections that need very little excavation, involving perhaps just three hours' work; if your connection needs a road to be dug up, then the connection fee will be in thousands.

All new houses in England and Wales are now fitted with water meters and these are conventionally placed at the boundary of the property so that at least you can control the costs of laying pipe from the boundary to your house; but all work carried out under or next to a public highway must be carried out by the water companies and it will cost.

Fortunately, the one ray of light in all this is that water companies will provide a free quotation for their work. They will need location and site plans, but there is no need for you to own the property, so it makes good sense to get this quotation before agreeing a plot price.

In Scotland and Northern Ireland the situation couldn't be more different. Here it is beholden on the local authorities to provide water and, providing the property is only a 'reasonable distance' from the mains supply, then work is carried out at the council's expense.

There is always the possibility of drawing water from under the ground via a borehole; this is almost invariably a costly option and can only be recommended if you have a very remote site (or you have a particular desire not to connect to your local water company's supply). Costs depend largely on depth of groundwater and can vary from as little as £1,500 to as much as £10,000; if you are interested, check out 'well borers' in your 'Yellow Pages'.

Electricity

Like water, installation to new sites is charged on a time and materials basis. Even a simple connection (say less than 25m from mains supply) is likely to cost in excess of £300 and charges rise in line with distance. However, the electricity companies offer a similar quotation service to the water companies and you should avail yourself of this.

Other services

It is unlikely that other service connections will result in budget busting costs. Gas supply to a new dwelling is either going to be reasonably cheap or it isn't going to happen at all. It all depends on how near the mains gas supply is. Very often supply is free if the gas main is nearby. Phone lines are costed on a flat rate: there is a one off connection charge, currently £74.99 (+VAT) per line for new BT residential lines, whatever the distance. Cable charges are set by local companies but, like mains gas, will tend to be either low or not available.

Overhead cables

Power cables running across your plot are bad news. They may intersect with your proposed building, in which case they will have to be moved; even if they don't they will detract from the resale value of the property. Burying them is the obvious solution but it can be horribly expensive; even a low voltage cable can cost over £20 per m to bury, which can easily make a short diversion cost £2,500 or more. Again, the trick is to get quotations for this before entering into any contract to buy.

Existing drains

This is one real nightmare for rookies and professionals alike: existing drains running across your proposed building. Do whatever you can to find out if drains are present, but sometimes there are no records and no surface evidence. Drains vary in their importance; small runs connecting one or two households to a sewer may very easily be diverted — depending on the lie of the land — but sewers and pumped drains cannot readily be moved and discovering one of these in your footings is a Grade A disaster, though thankfully this doesn't happen too often. Again the key is to find out as much as possible about the plot before you exchange contracts to purchase.

If there is any doubt in your mind, then try and place a retention in the sale contract which is only payable should nothing untoward be found under the ground.

■*Bad design*

There is a dangerous tendency for selfbuilders to cut right back on the design costs in order to cram more features into the house. I've been into new homes which are about as attractive as a cardboard box but are stuffed to the gunnels with home theatres, central vacuum systems, sprinklers, heat recovery systems, Agas, closed-circuit TV, saunas, gyms, you name it. Turns out the plans for the house were knocked out by some bloke in his spare time for about £300 because they thought that six grand for a proper architect was a rip-off. Well, maybe it is, maybe it isn't but, in terms of payback, good design really does seem to pay for itself and good design rarely (never) comes cheap. Skimping on design comes about from concentrating on the cost of everything rather than the value.

Borrowing money

I have already touched on the perils of property developing on borrowed money but it would be amiss not to touch on them once more because borrowing money, large dollops of the stuff, is perhaps the most dangerous peril of all.

If you already have a large mortgage and feel comfortable that you can meet the repayments, then the fact that you transfer this mortgage to an unbuilt or partially built property should not make very much difference to you. But never forget that there are many things that can come between you and the large paper profit that you start out with. Don't assume that this profit will flow effortlessly to you as you complete your building programme. Always be prepared for a situation where you cannot sell the finished house at the price you hoped for, or indeed at any price at all.

Over-specifying

It is said that the three most important factors

Pitfalls Checklist

Before buying a plot of land, you should check the following points. None of them is a reason for not buying, but all of them present potential extra costs which you need to be aware of and, perhaps, this knowledge may even enable you to negotiate a lower price.
■ are the described boundaries accurate?
■ are there any restrictive covenants on the plot?
■ are there rights of way crossing the plot?
■ would you own all the land necessary for access and services? If not, are wayleaves readily obtainable?
■ are there any tree preservation orders?
■ are there any other "legal encumbrances" which might hinder you in any way?
■ is access adequate for cars? What are the requirements for visibilty splays?
■ is the plot wide enough? Plots narrower than 12m can present problems for turning vehicles.
■ are there any planning conditions in effect?
■ does planning permission apply to the whole of the plot?
■ when does planning permission run out?
■ Is there a slope steeper than 1:25?
■ what are ground conditions like?
■ is there evidence of existing drains on site?
■ are there any large trees within 30m?
■ are there any overhead cables to be moved?
■ are there likely problems with services?
  Many of these potential administrative snags should be unearthed by your solicitor. The more technical ones are normally dealt with by building professionals — i.e. architects and structural engineers. If the plot looks dodgy in any way, don't hesitate to get help. Consider commissioning a feasibility study from your designer before contracts are exchanged – because this should unearth most of the bugs. At the end of the day though, it's caveat emptor – buyer beware – because you are where the buck stops and it'll be down to you to sort out any do-dos.

in property development are location, location and location. Like many other jokes, there is a pearl of wisdom here and one which rookie housebuilders would do well to heed. Building plots, just like existing houses, have to be assessed in relation to the neighbourhood they are located in and what goes on around them. If you are interested in maximising the return on your investment, then don't fall into the trap of specifying a luxury house on a plot that is surrounded by houses of a much lower quality. Rich people like to live in quiet secluded neighbourhoods, well away from the noise and grime of traffic and industry, and close by other rich people; poor people don't get the choice and have to make do.

If you have no intention of moving for many years to come and really don't give a hoot that your house is next to a council estate or a rubbish tip or a chicken farm, then go ahead and build your mansion on that nice cheap plot you found. However, if you are hoping to maximise your profit, it pays to take careful heed of the location you are building in and to specify a house in keeping with the neighbourhood. This is not hard to do, just look around and see who your would-be neighbours are and, more importantly, how much their houses are worth.

A well-built new house will tend to attract a premium price, perhaps as much as 15-20 per cent more than second-hand stock nearby but it is vital that you realise that however much money you pour into your house, you will not improve much on this premium.

This is a particular problem for selfbuilders in SE England who have to compete with each other and end up chasing up prices paid for quite humble plots of land. Naturally enough, they want to build the best house they can afford because they want to live in it but this often means ignoring the time honoured rules about the importance of location.

The general inexperience of selfbuild purchasers also means that the lessons contained in this chapter are frequently ignored or, more likely, just not known about so that there is often precious little difference in price between an A plus plot and a C minus.

Most estate agents have only the dimmest ideas about building costs and tend to value properties and plots far more by amenity and location than by assessing what the development costs might be. It is up to the buyers to assess these costs and the likely resale value. This is particularly so with barn conversions: these are usually considerably more expensive to build than equivalent new houses but the prices paid for derelict barns with planning permission don't reflect this at all.

Chapter 4
Design

Design
Planning permission
Building regs & the Party Wall Act
Choosing a designer
Two freelancers
Timber frame packages
Shape & size
Extra space

■ *Design*

House design is undoubtedly the trickiest issue faced by every potential builder. The central point that shouldn't be forgotten is that you want to build the best possible house for a price you can afford. Easily written, but how the hell do you do it? What is the 'best possible' house? And how do you go about designing it?

Questions abound. Is an architect necessarily an expensive option? What about using a designer who is not a qualified architect? Isn't it cheaper to use a package build design? Won't the planners force me to redesign the whole thing in any event?

Well steady on, I'll cover these issues in due course. But first let's take a look at the design process because...well, it's a good place to start. The design process can be subdivided into a number of parts, some fixed points with known costs and others elastic in the extreme. Below is a list of the stages that you need to go through. You don't have to do it in this order (you could for instance apply for building regulations approval before you have planning permission) but it would be frankly very strange not to do it this way.

■ site survey and feasibility study

■ design process, leading to sketches of options
■ commission drawings for planning permission
■ submit plans for planning permission (fee)
■ try and negotiate positive planning outcome
■ do this over and over again till outcome is positive
■ detailed designs and specifications
■ submit detailed designs for building regs approval (fee)
■ negotiate positive outcome.

Site survey

Unless you are very confident of your surveying and drafting abilities, you should have a professional carry out an accurate site survey to measure and plot all the existing buildings, boundaries, levels, access arrangements, trees, drains, neighbouring buildings and any other information thought to be relevant. On simple sites this might cost £100-£200. If by chance you've read the previous chapter then you'll realise that a smart plot buyer will have carried out much of this work before signing any contracts. Don't rely on professionals to sort these problems out for you after the event.

Feasibility study/sketches

Assuming you have a plot and a budget, the most important questions are: what can you build on it and how much will it cost? It may seem very early in the whole mysterious design process but you have already reached crunch point: this is the key moment when you start to commission the whole building process and your decisions at this point will have costly implications on down the line. I have distinguished between a stage called feasibility study and another called sketches of options; this is helpful in understanding how one grows out of the other but in reality there is no hard and fast dividing line between them, and how you and your designer get from an empty page to a full planning application is a very individual thing.

Nevertheless, there tends to be a clear path which leads from the site survey stage into a feasibility stage (which, if you like, is about eliminating impractical options) and then into outlining practical solutions and, from there, plumping for your best choice, at which point the designer changes gear and looks at the nitty-gritty decisions which spring from the choice you have made.

A professional at £30-£50 per hour may seem a luxury, but they will (or at least should) understand the issues and concentrate your thinking on the relevant areas. There may or may not be any consultation with local planners at this stage, depending on how confident you or your agent feels. If doing it yourself, then a visit to the planners would be advisable. Use books of house plans for inspiration (despite the fact that they're mostly anything but), but do not expect to fit an existing plan on to your plot; the chances of it working without amendment are small and amending existing plans can be almost as expensive as starting from scratch.

The cost of this stage is naturally very open-ended: some short-of-work designers will undertake the early parts of this process for free on the understanding that more work will follow. For many independent designers and architects, the early part of the process is the most challenging and the most interesting and they would anticipate spending around a third of their time on this stage. The biggest variable is you, the client. The more sussed out you are, the better your brief, and the shorter and cheaper this process will be.

Even if you are planning to build a kit house or use an off-the-shelf design, it is still worthwhile getting a professional designer to undertake some sort of study if only to sort out practicalities like drain runs (though note that many kit suppliers have their own designers who will undertake this work).

Planning Drawings

A good designer with a thorough working knowledge of local practices and trends will be able to help you marry your ideas with the views of the planners, hopefully pre-empting any potential areas of conflict. Planning departments are surprisingly diverse in their ideas, often reflecting the individual tastes of the chief planning officer, and knowing the whys and wherefores of local planning decisions is one way in which local knowledge scores heavily over nationwide services.

Whoever you choose, they will have to produce a set (in fact several sets) of planning permission drawings to present to the local planning department. Budget anything from £200 for pre-drawn plans through to £3,000 for architect one-offs.

For a detailed look at the mechanics of applying for planning permission, and the likely fees, see the following section. There are a number of plans and drawings that the planners require and your chosen designer/agent should know this rigmarole backwards – indeed if they don't I would tend to be rather suspicious.

Working details

If designing from scratch, it is conventional not to decide on all the construction details until planning constraints are established. This is simply to avoid having to do things twice. However, construction details on conventional houses are remarkably similar and often the details can be lifted from previous jobs. On simple projects, the plans, construction details and specification (known as the spec with a soft 'c') can all be contained on two sheets of A1 (840x592mm) plans which would detail:

■ floor plans
■ foundation plan
■ drainage plan
■ first floor joist layout
■ roof truss/rafter layout
■ n,e,s and w elevations (or views)
■ section or sections through the middle of the house, showing room heights, floor levels, wall constructions, joist depths, staircase dimensions
■ window and door schedule (list of joinery manufacturers codes)
■ text explaining construction standards (lots of bs numbers here).

On more complicated jobs, there may be extra plans perhaps running to many pages, showing various complicated details like eaves or dormer windows. Upmarket jobs tend to have the specification written separately from the drawings and a serious architectural practice may write a specification running to fifty pages or more. How much of this is necessary depends on a) the complexity of the work and b) the attitude of the client. Rookie builders would be well advised not to attempt anything too unusual first time around, in which case the standard two-sheet plans are probably adequate. Many experienced subcontractors never look at plans in any event – quite a few can't read – and complex plans could be wasted on many.

I know of a number of small builders who basically dispense with the working drawings stage. They work from little more than the planning drawings, littered with notes like 'To be confirmed on site' or 'To Building Inspector's Satisfaction'; they are on site every day and they prefer to work out these details as they go along. Once you've done it a few times, it works fine provided you stick to fairly standard solutions (they do). But if you are new to this game and/ or you can't be there on site a good deal, then you would do well not to skimp on working

drawings as these form, in effect, your detailed instructions to your builder.

Much of this detailed work and, in particular, the writing of the specification, forms the very heart of any forthcoming building contract. If you want an element of protection from the perils of badly executed building work, then a professionally written specification is worth far more than any off-the-peg contract that you might be tempted to sign.

In budget terms, these design details are the area with the most variance. If purchasing a set of predetermined house plans (typically for £300-£500), then all this detailed work will be included with the plans so the effective cost is zero. If using a package build, then again these details will come integrated with the package. But be wary of assuming that pre-drawn plans are necessarily the cheapest option, because 90 per cent of the time they require significant amendments and sometimes it proves to be just as expensive as starting with a blank sheet of paper. However, even a one-off design may cost no more than a few hundred pounds if it sticks to tried and tested solutions; on the other hand, this part of the design work can also very easily cost £2,000-£4,000 for unusual houses, as unusual features take time to design, not to mention build. Here you would expect workshop joinery, arched openings, fancy staircases, patterned brickwork – generally expensive features which are also expensive to design.

If you are building to a tight budget and are happy with conventional solutions, then make it clear that you do not want unusual detailing and, as a result, a) your working details should not cost too much, b) your house isn't likely to be expensive to build and c) it is much less likely to run over budget.

The danger in trying to put a price to all this is that you may lose sight of the fact that, as with so many things in life, you get what you pay for; if someone knocks up a set of plans for you over a couple of weekends for a few hundred quid, the chances are that your finished house will reflect the fact. On the other hand, if you are interested in creating a wonderful one-off home, you'd be daft to skimp on the design stages.

If you want to save money, you'd probably do better to build a smaller house. There is a real conundrum in here. People don't want to be ripped off by some fancy-dan architect charging the earth. Yet a good architect can often justify the fees because they actually add value to the finished product. If an architect or designer can do the business, then the thousands of pounds they want for employing them is money well spent.

Structural engineer

Having been called in during the digging of the trial hole, the structural engineer may have to make another appearance if the designs take on any non-standard features. All beams, lintels, roofs and foundations (the so-called structural elements) of a building require proof that they are sufficient to do the job asked of them. Standard solutions to standard problems are regarded as tried and tested, but anything out of the ordinary will require 'proving' to the satisfaction of the building inspector. A structural engineer will calculate the forces applied to beams or foundations and come up with adequate solutions. If the ground you plan to build on is at all dodgy, then an engineer will be required to prove your foundation design; also many very ordinary situations like using steel beams or opening up a loft space require structural proving. If you want to build in timber frame without going via a specialist supplier, you need to get the design proved by a specialist engineer qualified to issue an HB353 certificate — in Scotland it's called an HB210. This would normally cost between £300 and £500 per dwelling.

Detailed drawings and structural calculations (if needed) are presented to the local council's building control department for examination.

Sub-designs

Design and specification of finishes is often left to the client or builder to sort out and this is more often than not passed down the line to the tradesmen involved on the job. Therefore, the plumber designs the central heating system, the electrician designs the lighting, a kitchen specialist will take over design of the kitchen. This sort of arrangement obviously works, as it is what happens in 90 per cent of homes built, but arguably it could be much better co-ordinated by a single designer.

On large commercial contracts these areas are all dealt with separately by specialist professionals who draw up a specification and arrange quotes from it. One-off housing is really too small to justify the expense of all these extra professionals, and much of the work, designed and installed by the various tradesmen, is consequently very unimaginative. The degree of competence varies enormously: many act as much as salesmen as designers: most make no charge provided you buy their product, which is all very well but it makes you very vulnerable to uncompetitive practices.

It's really a very difficult area to negotiate, even for hard-bitten professionals. Many architects are not qualified to give advice on, say, lighting design or interior decorating. If you are happy with tried and tested solutions to problems then you will be well advised to keep it simple and deal directly with your chosen contractor; if, however, you want to explore the many and varied options open to you, then you could do worse than read the rest of this book which is peppered with contact names and numbers.

In conclusion

Design and professional expenses are the hardest areas to budget for because they are so variable. To a large extent, they are dependent on the brief that you, as a client, present to the designers. An off-the-peg house plan can be purchased for a few hundred pounds but will very probably require a great deal of alteration to fit both the site and your ideas. In contrast, an architect might charge over £5,000 for designing a detached four bedroomed house; however, it does not follow that the off-the-peg plans are necessarily better value. The resulting house might be £5,000 less expensive to build and might also be worth £10,000 more when finished! Here you must use your own judgement and intuition.

■ *Planning permission*

Planning permission and building regulations are two big hurdles that every would-be housebuilder will have to jump. They are complex and not easily mastered, and many building professionals have bald patches on their heads where they have torn their hair out from negotiating paths through or around the maze of regulations and precedents that govern our construction activities. For a rookie builder this can seem all rather daunting, especially when you're not even clear what's the difference between planning permission and building regulations – or regs as they are known in the trade, as in 'God, there's been another bloody change in the regs.' The regs are dealt with later in this chapter – first planning permission.

What exactly is it?

Various Acts of Parliament (notably the Town and Country Planning Acts) require that local authorities should control what can be built where, and how buildings (and land) should or should not be used. Planning permission is not concerned with how you build – that's the building regs – nor with who owns the land on which you wish to build. There are many small construction projects that do not require planning permission but something of the size of a new house invariably does.

The power-that-bees in this respect is your local council. Not your County or Metropolitan Council, but your District or City council. In Scotland and N.Ireland the system works slightly differently, as it does in National Parks, but then they wouldn't want to make it too straightforward, would they? It gets worse. Officially, the licence to build is granted by the elected councillors, but every council has

a full-time planning department staffed by planning officers, and these are the people who actually deal with planning applications. Indeed, the chief planning officer has powers to make certain decisions off his or her own bat. Even when they choose not to exercise these powers they make 'recommendations' to the committee of councillors as to whether an application should be accepted or refused. The planning committee rarely goes against the recommendations of its planning officers.

Foreplay

You don't have to have any contact at all with the planners before submitting your application, but it is commonplace to do so. Tactics are involved here and there is no such thing as a correct way of going about it — every case stands on its own. On the one hand, you don't want to be faced with the expense of drawing up plans only for the planners to fall about laughing at the very thought that anyone could build on that piece of land; on the other hand, if you wander into the planning department with questions like 'What sort of house could I build on this spot?' then you are inviting the planners to design the house for you. This they won't do, but what will happen is that they will get in their minds all kinds of constraints that will severely limit your options: 'You must do...' and 'You can't have...' Like our legal system and our parliament, our planning system is adversarial; you may not get exactly what you want out of it — most planning decisions are the result of compromise — but you stand a far better chance of getting more of what you want if you choose the battleground on which to fight; i.e. submit plans with minimal reference to the planners. Getting the planners too closely involved before submitting your application can be seen as ceding this battleground.

Now it may be that your planning application is not terribly controversial and that the planners will be delighted with your ideas. In which case you may think I am a paranoid old nutter. But don't forget that it's your money and that they have the right to make you shell out for things which you think are completely unnecessary. Adopting a 'lie down and think of England' pose may earn you brownie points at City Hall but may also fire off alarm bells around the corner at the bank or building society.

Submitting an application
The mechanics of submitting an application are straightforward, if time- and tree-consuming. There are, however, several different types of planning permission that can be granted and these are summarised in the adjacent box.

Application forms
The actual application consists of a number of forms that you have to fill out, together with your plans and your cheque. Exact requirements vary from council to council but are not likely to be less than six copies of each of the following:
- location plan (taken off OS map at a scale of 1:1250)
- existing site plan (boundaries outlined in red) at 1:500
- proposed site plan — showing position of house, garage, driveway, access
- layout plans and elevations of any existing structures on site
- layout plans and elevations of proposed dwelling at 1:100 or 1:50
- details of materials to be used
- details of trees to be felled – even though your application arrives in a wheelbarrow, they won't see the irony.

In addition to these, it often helps to have three-dimensional bird's-eye view drawings (isometric projections) which show how the house fits with its neighbours. Planning officers and committee members like a nice drawing, just like the rest of us, and apocryphal evidence suggests that they are likely to be better disposed towards a well presented application. Some people even go to the trouble of building scale models. This is probably over the top for routine applications but if there are close neighbours who will be affected by the new

buildings, it does help to have a contextual drawing or two so they can see just how the development sits in relation to what is already there.

Ownership Certificate
You also have to fill out a form stating ownership of the land in question. You don't actually have to own land in order to apply for planning permission over it but you are required to notify the owner of your intentions.

Fees
Outline fees in England & Wales are £220 for each 0.1 hectare (or 1000 sq m or a small plot) of site area applied for. Detailed permission for one dwelling is also £220 and if you apply for outline and then move on to a detailed application it will cost you twice £220; my calculator makes that £440 but it could be playing up. The only way to avoid this double fee is to go straight for detailed permission which involves more costly drawings: in some situations this is a risk worth taking but if the application is likely to be controversial, just go for the outline. There are no fees for consultation with planners or for making amendments to plans to satisfy planners' concerns.

Chances of success
After submitting your application, the planners then go to work on assessing it. These days they all seem to work in teams, and this makes it even harder to get any sense out of them as to how they think the application is progressing. They are meant to take eight weeks to reach a determination, but in practice it depends on how busy they are – it can all take much longer. Keep ringing them to find out what's happening to your application; sooner or later they will reach some sort of provisional verdict and this is the point at which negotiations start. If they are completely hostile, then you may do better to withdraw the application and start anew; if they express some reservations (they usually do), then you must be prepared

to compromise hard. Eventually, the planning officials will either grant planning permission (unlikely on a new house) or refer it to the planning committee of the local council who, typically, meet once a month. This referral will come with a recommendation either way which the committee habitually accepts. Planning permission is often granted with conditions attached; if you are Sainsburys wanting to build a supermarket, these conditions may be something big, but for a one-off housebuilder they are not likely to be terribly onerous though in some parts of England additional money is being asked for 'planning gain' – this can run to several thousand pounds.

Reasons for refusal

There can be any number of reasons why planners take a negative view of your proposals. In rural districts the land is zoned (via the 'local plans' which you can inspect at your library), and if you are applying to build in a non-building zone then you've got your work cut out trying to get anywhere. Assuming they accept that the site is suitable for development, here are several reasons why they may still not play ball:
■ lack of adequate parking
■ can't turn a car around on the hard standing
■ overlooking neighbours
■ roof too high
■ house too big for plot
■ not enough garden
■ development out of keeping with neighbourhood
■ wrong position on the plot
■ don't like your choice of materials or overall design.

I could go on. Suffice it to say that many of these reasons are perfectly justifiable and if you weren't so greedy and pig-headed you would be able to see the sense in them. But applicants are apt to feel aggrieved whenever the outcome goes against them.

Lobbying

You don't have to take the views of the planning officials lying down. Many people have taken to lobbying their councillors to overrule the recommendation for refusal. This is real grass roots politics and in many parts of the world sums of money would change hands in order to get planning permissions through on the nod, but in Britain, of course, we don't do that. I don't wish to sound too sarcastic because, by and large, this is true – people tend not to go into local politics for money, but they do have a tendency to self-importance and many are not averse to a little bit of flattery. This is the network at work: it all depends on personalities and who you do or do not know. Even if you don't get very far with councillors, you should at least consider lobbying your neighbours. A couple of letters from neighbours saying positive things about your plans is worth a lot at a planning committee meeting. However, there is every chance that your neighbours may not feel as enthusiastic about your plans as you do and this tactic can backfire.

Appeals v new applications

If you shoot your bolt and, despite all your lobbying, your application is refused you are faced with three choices:
■ give up
■ submit a new application
■ appeal.

The first is the cheapest but it doesn't get you very far. If you want to persist, then there is no reason why you can't go to appeal on your first application whilst simultaneously submitting a new one. Surprisingly, there is no charge for making an appeal but it does take time, around six months, and many people can't wait that long, especially if there's borrowed money riding on it. Appeals are presided over by an independent inspector, often a QC, sometimes an architect, and on small projects like individual housebuilding the usual way of going about it is to produce written evidence. Basically, you must write your side of the story and explain to the inspector why you think you should have been granted planning permission in the first place. On the due date the inspector

Planning Terms Explained

Outline
Often used by landowners who are trying to find out whether development would be acceptable in principle without going through the hassle of having detailed plans drawn up. Outline permission to build is what turns a garden or a field into a building plot; getting it makes you seriously rich but it doesn't, on its own, allow you to build. Outline permission lasts for five years, but a detailed application must be agreed within three years or else the permission lapses.

Full Application
As its name suggests, a full planning application seeks to approve both the principle and the details of development. It lasts for five years.

Approval of Reserved Matters
This is used to convert outline permission to detailed.

Renewal
Planning permission can be renewed, but only if consent has not expired so this route is used to get an extension to an existing permission. If the permission has lapsed, then a new application has to be made.

Relaxation
Sometimes planning permission comes with a load of irksome conditions. You can apply to have these lifted at a later date but don't hold out too much hope.

Amendments
If you purchase a plot with detailed permission for a house that you don't actually want to build, you may be able to amend the plans without submitting a whole new application. There is no charge for amendment but if your changes are substantial the planners may not accept them as amendments and you'll be back to square one.

Extensions/Conversions
If your building project involves work to an existing structure, you may not need planning permission. Phone your local council's planning department and ask their advice. They issue a free 22-page booklet called Planning – A Guide for Householders that makes a fair stab at explaining the rudiments.

will visit the site and shortly afterwards they will make their ruling known. That's it. There are alternative methods of appeal, notably using the informal hearing method which gathers all the interested parties together to discuss the issue at hand, but the written representation is the simplest and least time-consuming (and cheapest, if you are paying a professional to act for you).

Only one in three appeals succeed and from my limited experience it is difficult to predict the outcome in advance, so you are taking a big gamble in going to appeal. You can hire a professional to make the appeal for you, but this will be expensive and may not add to your chances. As there is no further drawing work to be undertaken – you can't amend your plans between first refusal and appeal – the appeal process can easily be undertaken by

any lay person capable of using pen and paper, although a thorough understanding of planning issues will obviously stand you in good stead.

For many people, it will be cheaper and much quicker to submit a new planning application. When an application is refused, the planners have to state grounds for refusal. In an ideal world these issues could have been sorted out before the application ever came before the committee, but sometimes it takes a refusal to actually bring the problems out into the open. Armed with refusal reasons, you can make suitable amendments in your next application and, provided you can genuinely sort out the issues, you should have a much better chance of gaining planning permission, although the outcome is likely to be some way from your original ideas.

Changes to the planning system are always

Take a hill-trekking holiday in the Himalayas as a comparison. Many people would want to go on such a holiday first time with a package deal, but having done it once, would realise that it was not so difficult to organise and that, if they ever went again, they would go on their own, have more independence and save money. Housebuilding is not so dissimilar; the comfort of having a professional organisation behind you in your first venture and a feeling that you know what the final bill will be is worth a lot more than the vague hope that you just might be saving money.

What buyers of package building services should realise is that they are not getting free design. Rather, the design work is being paid for within the package price. The package build companies all employ architects or designers and these people get paid just like their freelance cousins, and who do you think pays their salaries? Now the logic of using pre-drawn house plans is that the whole design process is reduced to a matter of a bit of photocopying which should be much cheaper for all concerned. However, British planning restrictions being what they are today, there are virtually no uncomplicated building plots on which you can plonk an off-the-peg house: the houses all require 'adaptation' which is tantamount to admitting that the brochure designs are just sales hooks to entice you, and that the actual house you have built will have had a fair amount of additional design work done to it in order to get it to fit both your ideas and the limitations of the plot. This extra work is invariably charged and you may well end up having a package build company designing your home from scratch.

Which begs the question 'Why start with an off-the-peg design at all?' In theory, a freelance architect or architectural designer should be able to provide a similar service to a package build designer and really shouldn't cost any more. But, for many people, the prospect of hiring a freelance is off-putting and not just because they think it will be expensive.

If you happen to know somebody in the trade, then there is every chance that you'll appoint them (however inappropriate) just because it takes away the difficult task of finding a compatible stranger. Many people without any contacts will, however, be lured into the package build option just because it's there. Eyeing up package build companies is like visiting Amsterdam's red light district: you can trawl up and down all night looking at the wares on offer but you don't have to consummate any deals if you don't like what's on offer. However, involving freelance architects and designers is much more personal: if you don't know them then it is akin to going on a blind date. You may or may not end up in bed together but you have to go through a courting stage just to find out where you want it to end up. It's a time-consuming and involved process and the outcome is just as likely to hinge on personal – not to say sexual – chemistry as it is on the designer's suitability and competence to carry off your briefs (shouldn't that read 'carry out your brief'? Ed).

Of course it doesn't have to be thus. If you're the professional, organised type, there is absolutely nothing to prevent you having a sort of beauty contest between three or four designers, in which you interview them and ask to see photographs of their previous work, ask for references and even ask them to prepare a quotation for design work, and possibly building work as well. The fact that architects hate this sort of thing is by-the-by: you'll be paying their bills and there is no reason at all why you shouldn't organise a parade of talents so that you can make an informed judgement.

Red light districts, blind dates, and beauty contests — it's all getting a bit far away from building houses. So who are all these people?

What's in a name?
Architect
Use of the very word architect is a touchy subject. The general public thinks an architect is someone who designs houses but the title architect is, in Britain at least, protected in law just like the titles doctor and lawyer. To

be qualified to call yourself an architect you must have completed seven years' training and passed all the relevant exams; an architect will regard him or herself as the natural choice for a commission such as designing an individual house and most architects love to take on such projects; trouble is, they may be rather high falutin' for your simple project and – worse fears – expensive. Just how expensive an architect is depends on how desperate they are for work but what can't be denied is that only a small fraction of new homes in this country are designed by architects.

Traditionally, architects worked on a percentage fee basis; three per cent of the contract value to prepare plans for planning permission, another three per cent for working details and doing the tendering work and yet another three per cent for administering the contract and (if you are lucky) certifying that the work has been done correctly – that's nine per cent in total for the full works. However this particular tradition is dying out and now architects work for what they can get.

Designers and architects have even been known to give quotations in advance for their work so they are showing every sign of rushing headlong into the 20th century.

A newly qualified rookie might cost less than a technician – say £200 per day – whereas a top-notch, in-demand architect could go out at that much per hour. One of our internationally renowned architects quotes £70,000 for designing and administering a one-off house – more than many more humble abodes cost to build. That's exceptional – though the house probably would be as well. But fees of £15,000 - £25,000 for upmarket projects costing a quarter of a million to build are now commonplace. But there are still loads of small architect's practices that work for much less.

Qualified architects are required to register with the Architects Registration Board. There is a body called the Architects' Registration Council, who you can call to check whether someone calling themselves an architect is fully qualified.

If they then choose to join the Royal Institute of British Architecture (RIBA) or its Celtic equivalents, they are able to call themselves Chartered Architects. The RIBA runs a nationwide Client's Advisory Service which will supply a list of suitable local practices who are actively looking for your sort of business.

There is a collection of architects (known as the Association of SelfBuild Architects or ASBA) who got together to cater specifically for selfbuilders and although as a collection of individuals it can't guarantee excellence, it has done some innovative marketing – including quoting for architectural services on a unit area cost basis. Incidentally, this rate was, until recently, around £30 per sq m, about the same as the cost of wall-to-wall carpeting.

Another useful lead is Design for Homes, a body set up to promote the use of architects in housing. The Design for Homes website has a searchable catalogue of architects where you can view their work.

Architectural technologists
There is a second body, the British Institute of Architectural Technologists, which issues a quite separate qualification (architects would say it is a lesser one) which is relevant in the field of house design. Traditionally this group was thought of as mere draughtsmen, beavering away in offices, turning architect's sketches into working drawings, but many of them work in practice independently. And some of them are very good. BIAT oversees and publishes a Directory of Practices and a regional list of self-employed members interested in taking on new work.

Building surveyors
Lots of good design work is carried out by chartered building surveyors. The problem is finding them. As a professional body, they are administered by the Royal Institute of Chartered Surveyors (known as the RICS) but this amorphous group includes every flavour of surveyor including estate agents and building inspectors. They key is to find the right

grouping – the Chartered Building Surveyors. If you ask for a list by post, you'll wait a long time but again you can search by region on the web at www.rics.org/resources

Many others

There is in fact no requirement for anyone to have any qualifications to design houses. The country is stuffed full of unqualified but nevertheless competent designers. Some may have undertaken some architectural studies but never qualified, some may have qualifications in other related fields, notably structural engineers, quantity surveyors and building inspectors. And there are whole rafts of individuals who are 'qualified by experience' – often designer builders – who do perfectly good work, some of it every bit as good as professional architects turn out. Obviously these designers are not regulated in the way that architects and surveyors are and you should be aware that if you hire an unqualified designer they are unlikely to carry professional indemnity insurance; on the other hand, unqualified designers are likely to steer you down a route where insurance is handled by third parties, such as the NHBC, so this is not actually as big a risk as you might imagine. You pays your money, you takes your choice.

Design and Build

This is a method of building that straddles the traditional distinction between designers and builders. In some ways it is similar to package build in that you are faced with an all-in-one solution but, unlike package build, there are usually no pre-drawn plans on the table, so in other respects, design and build is more akin to hiring a freelance designer.

In fact many design and build businesses are based around the skills of a designer who also happens to run a construction business. It is hard to generalise because individual businesses will go about things in markedly different ways and, indeed, may rarely have two similar contracts.

I worked in a design and build business for

ten years from 1986 to 1996 and if anything characterises this particular business it is the wide variety of projects taken on; some clients used us just as designers, some just as builders, most as both. Some clients subjected us to beauty contests, some to competitive tendering, some to both of these and some to neither, preferring to work in an atmosphere of trust all the way from initial contact to completion of building work.

Unqualified designers will tend to be a little cheaper and will also tend to be a little less imaginative, which can be a good thing if you want to build cheaply. Engineers and surveyors in particular have a reputation for designing to a cost, something which has been known to elude more upmarket architects.

CAD packages

Computer-aided design (CAD) has been around for decades but architects tend to look down their noses at it all: they continue to sketch stuff on paper in the time honoured fashion and then hire a 'CAD operator' to turn their works of art into engineered drawings.

Operating a full blown CAD package (the market leader is AutoCAD) is no mean feat but what has changed recently is that there are a number of really very cheap 3D software products around which anyone can pick up and play around with on their home PC. And some of it is very powerful indeed — a good example is Online Warehouse's ArCon which costs around £150. There is even passably good freeware that you can use — log onto www. povray.org if you want to check this out. If you like working with computers and you have plans for a home, you will probably love building virtual homes on screen and it may well help you work out some of your ideas.

DIY design

You can, of course, go the whole hog and design your own home. It's not as unusual as all that and it's not desperately difficult to undertake planning drawings – I have recently written an article for 'Homebuilding

& Renovating' magazine about a 77-year old grandmother who did just that, having sacked her architect because he kept trying to 'improve' her plans. She knew what she wanted and successfully undertook all the negotiations with the planners.

However, there is a large chasm of knowledge between doing outline sketches and filling in all the construction details, a chasm which can only realistically be filled by training and/or experience (preferably both). Most DIY designers get an experienced professional on board at some stage if only to satisfy all the building regulations – as indeed did my intrepid lady.

The problem with DIY design is that it's difficult to get pleasing results if it's your first time. Design sense and spatial awareness are not skills that can be quickly or easily mastered and you have to be supremely confident in your own abilities to be entirely happy with your own work. Fine if what you were producing was just a set of drawings but, of course, it's not, it's a recipe for a real, live house. People are naturally afraid that they will be building an ugly or impractical structure and so the vast majority are keen to get some professional opinion on board. Most architects expect to feed in ideas and improvements to your initial ideas and most people reckon that they are very good at this and welcome the added input. But not everyone.

There is in fact a groundswell of opinion that rates building professionals in general and architects in particular as nothing less than a cancer working to destroy an otherwise simple and healthy process called building. Colin Harding runs a medium-sized building business in Bournemouth called George & Harding and also contributes an occasional column in 'Building' magazine. In June 1999 he let rip on this topic:
'Very few architects have the construction management skills to justify their claims to be team leaders. Most of the contracts we work on suffer to a varying degree as a direct result of the designer's failure to do their job properly

and professionally. Typical lapses are
- specifying inappropriate materials and systems, then being incapable of devising professional solutions to overcome the technical problems created
- lack of knowledge of basic construction techniques
- no understanding of buildability
- unwillingness to accept budget constraints
- inability to manage the design process so that information is often late or inaccurate.

'What is so disappointing is that, in my opinion, the standard of professionalism among architects is still falling,' he wrote.

Harding's is not a lone voice. Here's selfbuilder Rick Hughes's assessment of the service he received on his project in Swansea: 'I would never use an architect again, this practice has proved difficult, frustrating, incredibly slow, and, although very good on conceptual items, struggle greatly once things leave the drawing board and enter the real world.'

Hmm. Doesn't look good, does it? But in defence of architects I hear of rather more successful relationships than failures. Indeed I have heard many selfbuilders go as far to say that their project would have been hell without an architect on board and that using one had got them a far nicer house for much less money.

Try this one for a counter blast from home extender Marc Arnall: 'I decided to build an extension and, in order to save money, I wanted to use a person to draw the plans as opposed to using an architect. Meanwhile I talked to an architect that I knew, after explaining to him that, unfortunately, I couldn't afford to make use of his services. He was most understanding and offered to check over my ideas and costings, with no charge to me.

'The end result? Richard (the architect) has designed a far better extension, organised and put in my planning application, organised a good discount with suppliers and has reduced my costings by some £8,000. He is going to supervise the work, thereby ensuring that I comply with all regulations and that any labour I hire fulfils his/her part of the deal. Thank goodness for architects!'

Well this game of architectural ping-pong could go on all night. It seems you either love 'em or hate 'em. What would be fair to say though is that there is a significant minority of architect/client relationships that are bedevilled with problems and that if you choose to work with an architect, choose very carefully. By and large, the design professionals who are not qualified architects don't arouse nearly so many hackles. It must be something they do to them in architecture school during those long seven years.

Selecting a designer

For many people there is no selection procedure, they just happen upon someone. Perhaps the chap plays golf with you or you went out with his sister when you were students or maybe she's an old friend of your mother-in-law – the network. Logically, this a daft way to pick on a designer, but it doesn't half take away the difficult decisions of how to choose, and it does provide some limited protection from hiring a real bozo.

Building is one of the ultimate network businesses, there being very little formal long-term work around so it is not surprising that your designer should arrive on your (yet to be) doorstep by word of mouth. But bear in mind that all designers have tastes and quirks that are individual to them and even the simplest house commission is likely to receive radically different treatments. Make sure that you can at least live with your chosen designer's ideas by taking a look at their previous stuff. If you have very particular ideas yourself, then you would be well advised to seek out a like-minded soul.

The key to hiring an architect or designer and not paying through the nose is to be very upfront about money from the first meeting. Conventionally, architects like to work on a percentage fee basis: typically this would be three per cent of the overall job cost for initial designs and planning, followed by another three per cent for detailing and handling the tendering process and a final three per cent

for contract administration and certification. But there is no reason why you should pay on a percentage basis – some argue it encourages architects to make you spend more than you want – and you can arrange to pay by the hour or in other ways too.

Ask for an estimate to undertake design of your house and don't be afraid to specify that your project should cost no more than £XX,000 and that it has to be designed to a budget. Most architects/designers would actually appreciate such specific requests from their clients – a lot get very tired of the polite to-ing and fro-ing that goes on around issues like this. The more specific your brief, the better pleased you will be with the results.

If it's a safe, packaged product that you are looking for then the package build route may well be your best choice. Package build also wins out if speed of construction is paramount. There is much going for the package build route but it won't get you a unique home nor will it get you a cheap home. Whilst you would expect to turn to a freelance designer for a one-off house, surprising as it may seem, I think they are also the route to use if you want to build very cheaply, though I doubt very much if it would be the same designer.

◼ Two freelancers

Whilst it is relatively straightforward to analyse the ins and outs of using package build systems, it is very much harder to pin down what you get from using a freelance designer. The service varies, as you would expect, from the excellent to the incompetent. As with the rest of the building trade, freelancers usually find work by word of mouth – the old network again – but there are more formal routes through which you can contact designers which I've looked at in the last but one section.

Rather than list a load of old tripe about how much money an architect will save you or how you'd be crazy not to use one, I thought it would be more interesting to look at the work of a couple of designers who work in this area and to examine just what it is that you get for your money. Neither of these guys is cheap and you'd be most likely to end up with a building cost of £800 per sq m or even more these days. But then Mercedes cost more than Fords and this doesn't make Mercedes poor value. Both men are exceptional designers and provide a very specialised service some way removed from the average jobbing architect.

A traditionalist

Steve Mattick is a designer – not a qualified architect – who works from an office in the Essex village of Newport and who has a nationwide reputation for building houses in the old styles. And I'm talking old styles, not the Olde Worlde styles of the showhouses at the 'Ideal Home Exhibition' with their timbered beams and leaded double-glazed sealed units.

A new Mattick house will look almost indistinguishable from a 200-year-old one; the walls may not be perfectly perpendicular, the windows may not be exactly level and the roof will almost certainly sag (or 'have movement'). The materials he uses are almost always natural and are often salvaged, and windows and doors are always made locally in a joiner's shop.

Much attention is given to getting details right and many of these are worked out on site by Mattick and his crew for, above all, he is a designer builder. Or he used to be. In recent years he has eschewed building and concentrated on design.

Now, going to the trouble of building roofs that gently undulate along the ridge is expensive. Carpenters are taught to erect roof trusses by hauling them up off the back of a lorry and arranging them all like a pack of cards, stringing lines along the ridge to ensure perfect alignment. In contrast, Steve Mattick's roofs will all be hand cut on site and will actually be packed out in certain spots to ensure that they do not align along a string line.

Builders working for him tend to have to re-learn the old craft skills, long since abandoned in the rush towards mass production and streamlined products that are more and more made off-site. Coupled with his insistence on detailing workshop joinery, handmade tiles and cast iron guttering, Mattick's building costs are 50-80 per cent higher than the standard fare of the big developers.

Mattick tends to have few problems from planners (who by and large drool over his work) and yet is often in conflict with building inspectors. Many of the techniques he employs

Traditionalist Steve Mattick works in the Arts & Crafts style, using handmade or local materials wherever possible. Although all the details are period, every house is designed as a one-off.

are no longer considered adequate though, as he points out, they have stood the test of time. He particularly dislikes the current mania for double-glazing, which makes it that much harder to build good-looking, traditional windows.

One of his trademarks is the sideways sliding sash window, once common in eastern England but now all but abandoned. You can't really draught proof such a window; you can't even stop water penetration when it is lashed by gales and so it has been relegated to the status of a vernacular has-been. Mattick is quite aware of the problems but reckons it's a price worth paying to achieve an authentic reproduction. As well as being well-heeled, Mattick's clients need to be enthusiasts capable of living with such minor inconveniences.

Somehow, we assume that because a house is a new product it must perform to the same standards as a new camcorder or a new car; but if we bought an old wreck to do up we would expect to have a few wonky things going wrong with it from time to time, even after we'd shovelled a fortune into it. To some extent, an authentic new/old house is bound to perform in the same way.

The current trick of aping old styles with modern materials and techniques comes

at a price; it reduces art to artlessness, style becomes pastiche. As a nation we know this intuitively because we flock to National Trust properties and to villages like Castle Coombe and Lavenham to see beautiful buildings, but as a nation of house buyers we seem to be happy with imitations that are usually executed rather poorly.

A modernist

Which all rather begs the question why – if we want to live in smoothly functioning machines which never break down – don't we design houses that look like cars or computers? Well, why not? There are many architects working in the machine tradition but most of their work goes into commercial developments. Jonathan Ellis-Miller is one of the few who are interested in housing.

He designs in the modern style, has been much written up in the architectural press but was until recently ignored by all the selfbuild magazines (unlike Mattick). This is a shame because his approach has much to offer the selfbuilder who wants something out of the ordinary.

Ellis-Miller's most widely seen house is a timber frame built by Stewart Log Homes at the FutureWorld exhibition held in Milton

Modernist designer Ellis-Miller's first house looks more like an office but it won him a big reputation, not to mention a neighbour who used a very similar design!

Keynes in 1994, which attracted rave reviews from most visitors, but here I will describe the glass and steel home he selfbuilt on a plot at Prickwillow in the Fens near Ely.

The plot was bought for £20,000 in 1987, the price being that low because the ground was poor and the foundation work was complex. He chose to build using a raft foundation rather than the more conventional pile. Either way it proves expensive and for a floor area of 110 sq m (not all of which is built on) he had to pour 60 cu m of concrete. In all, substructural works came to £10,000. In areas like the Cambridgeshire Fens where ground conditions are difficult, most plot buyers are aware of the problems involved and the plot prices tend to be cheaper to reflect the excess works needed.

The total building costs were £45,000 for a building which measures 70 sq m. Apart from the £10,000 substructural works, another £6,000 went on made-to-order patio doors, £1,000 on blinds by Hunter Douglas. Parquet flooring from the local salvage yard was cheap, granite worktops in the kitchen were not. The kitchen doors came from IKEA (cheap) though the handles and door furniture throughout is by Modric (expensive).

Internally, the house is thus fitted with a mixture of cheap, off-the-shelf items intermingled with some pricey architectural fittings. The style is unashamedly modern (in the old-fashioned sense of the word) and Ellis-Miller is striving for that simple, uncluttered look which characterises the style. The quiet, slightly monastic feel to the house would suit anyone with a lifestyle to fit; children, I suspect, would not fit in so easily.

His building cost is around £645 per sq m, though had he been building on good ground this figure would have fallen to £540 per sq m. Had he not used expensive patio doors and spent money on fancy fittings, then he might have got the price down to near £430 per sq m, but then he would have lost a lot of the style he was striving for. Other expensive detailing includes galvanised steel box guttering that drains to a soakaway via the centre of the house,

bespoke aluminium windows at the back of the house, floor lighting and underfloor heating.

This style would be unlikely to appeal to more than a few aficionados of modern architecture, but it is by no means as avant-garde as you might think. If you have a site with a good view where single-storey development is preferable, this solution could provide a stunning house. In the case of his own house, the view out through the west-facing glazed wall looking over Ely Cathedral is a Fenman's delight, and despite the cool, semi-industrial look of the building it sits remarkably well in a side road in a fen village.

Some people's immediate response to the thought of living in a glass-walled home is 'What! No privacy?' but this problem is reasonably overcome with the use of external louvre blinds which are adjusted to suit conditions. Ellis-Miller's glass wall faces on to the road in order to get the view he wanted and there would probably be few people who would be happy with such a degree of overlooking. However, if the orientation had been more conventional (so that privacy could be maintained) then I think there would be few people who would not be bowled over by the effectiveness of the idea.

If you want to build in an unconventional style, you will likely have problems obtaining planning permission.

Only estate agents are more conservative than planning officers and Ellis-Miller had a planning officer who was implacably opposed to such a dwelling. No way is Prickwillow a sensitive, conservation type area (quite the reverse) and no way does his plot impact on the casual visitor. Yet when he approached his local council planning department, he met with stares of disbelief and what can only be described as prejudice against his submitted plans. However, despite a recommendation of refusal from the planning officers (which 80 per cent of the time wins the day), councillors on the planning committee saw otherwise and let him build.

Without some support from more enlightened planning officers, plans to build in any but the tamest vernacular styles will be stillborn.

If you're interested in building in an unusual style, then first check with your local authority to get their views about your favoured site. Obviously, if the area is a conservation area or next to a listed building or the church, then you will expect to have to stick to a prescribed style. On the other hand, most building plots are not in such sensitive positions and arguably it's really none of the planner's business what style of building goes up. Needless to say, planning officers do not see it thus. To them, everywhere is sensitive, which unfortunately translates as: 'If you want planning permission you'd better conform.' Ellis-Miller's tale indicates that there is still room for innovation.

■Timber frame package build

When arranging the running order for the 'Housebuilder's Bible', I initially thought that I should bung this section into the superstructure chapter, up there with walls and roofs. 'Because, if you buy a timber frame kit, then it's basically the superstructure you are buying. Logic would seem to dictate that that's where it should go, and indeed there is a piece on timber frame as an inner skin up there in Chapter 7. But the main piece is here in the chapter on Design. In truth, it was a close call. But I believe that the main reason for choosing a timber frame package build is not to do with the merits or otherwise of selecting timber as your walling material, but rather to do with selecting a specialist custom home builder as your supplier; the fact that they choose to build with timber is secondary. And, as if to prove my point, there are one or two package home suppliers who don't build in timber frame. So it's the fact that it's package build which makes it end up here in the Design chapter.

In England, Wales and Ireland (though not Scotland), the building trade traditionally builds houses using masonry blockwork for the structural walls. In Scotland, they have taken to timber frame in a big way and it accounts for the majority of new houses there. In the rest of Britain, builders are of course happy to use timber in the roof and usually for the floors above ground level so, in a sense, even these houses have some timber framing in them but masonry walls have been the preferred way of building homes since we ran out of forests around three hundred years ago.

Timber frame is an upstart. Although in some parts of the world, notably North America, building houses out of timber is the standard way of doing things, in Britain it's always been a bit of a novelty and most builders don't know that much about it. Nor do architects.

Timber frame housing in Europe has developed down a very different path to North America; we tend to make them in factories, far away from the building site, and consequently timber frame housebuilding seems to be set apart from other methods of housebuilding.

It's harder for builders to 'add value' by using timber frame. By taking much of the labour input off-site and putting it into a factory, builders are in effect doing themselves out of a job and there is little incentive for them to change their ways. Architects are similarly disadvantaged in that timber frame construction requires an extra stage of panel drawing and extra structural calculation, both of which are technical in nature and best dealt with by specialists. There is thus an unwritten understanding between design professionals and builders to leave things as they are.

Advantages

Selfbuilders, of course, don't have to run along with the crowd and selfbuilders throughout the UK have taken to timber frame in a big way for much the same reasons as Scotland as a whole has. Not only is a timber frame house potentially much quicker to build than a masonry one, but — because the frame itself is largely hollow — it is easy to insulate to a high standard and yet still maintain a clear cavity between the frame and the outside walling material. Timber frame houses are therefore inherently energy efficient and they are warm and comfortable to live in, even in the depths of the coldest winters.

Timber Frame comes in many different guises. Top: Border Oak, our first and best-known green oak builder, specialise in recreating Tudor manor houses. Below: It looks like a kit from up-market German manufacturer Huf Haus – but in fact it's not: it's built by a German business called DaVinci which uses many of the same design ideas.

At least as important as any technical differences between the building systems is the question of procurement. I've touched on the fact that most architects and most builders like to use traditional masonry construction because it suits their own purposes. Because of this, there has grown up a quite distinct timber frame industry in the UK which has had to specialise in meeting all or most of the would-be housebuilder's needs. A timber frame company can't just build a factory, set up its jigs and wait for the orders to come rolling in — they won't. Instead they have to go out and grow the business by attracting the end users. As there are few independent architects prompting clients down the timber frame route, the companies themselves need to attract selfbuilders at the initial design stage and, by and large, they do this with attractive brochures of houses they have already built or a set of off-the-peg house types which you can choose or adapt to your own requirements. In effect, most timber frame companies design your house as well as provide and erect the superstructure.

It follows therefore that the timber frame is only one part of the service provided by these businesses. What they are really about is what is known as design and build or what the Americans call custom home building where you can pitch up with a few ideas, maybe a few sketches, and they will transform these into a workable home, delivered and erected on your site.

The fact that your superstructure is made of timber is almost incidental to the procurement process – in order to sell you a timber frame kit, it is first necessary for them to capture your imagination and your confidence. Often they have a range of standard house types from which you can choose or adapt but most of them admit to rarely, if ever, building these standard houses.

These days, selfbuild clients are choosing to have a much greater say in how their houses should look and function and consequently most timber frame houses start life as a sketch done by the selfbuilder or a more detailed drawing carried out by their architect.

Even companies with an established reputation for standard house ranges such as Potton find they are doing more and more 'one-offs'. Potton's Mick Jewell commented to me: 'Planning permissions are getting increasingly difficult to obtain and we find ourselves getting more and more involved with bespoke designs so, although we are best known for our standard ranges, we now undertake to work with almost any designs.

The businesses

There are a surprising number of timber frame businesses throughout the country catering for the selfbuilder. By and large they tend to offer a similar range of services. Almost all the businesses offer a design service to turn your

preliminary drawings into a fully engineered structure. In this respect a timber frame house is quite different to a masonry brick and block house: the design for a timber frame structure needs to be proved so that the building inspector is satisfied that it won't collapse in a heap or that it won't take off in the wind. This work is normally carried out in-house, though you can commission a structural engineer to undertake it for you if you want. To do it on a one-off basis is a complex and time-consuming process and you also need to draw up technical drawings for the timber frame wall panels which, by hand, can take almost as long as it does to actually assemble them. This is all work which can be carried out easily on computer and this is another contributory factor helping to develop the timber frame industry into a unique entity, quite distinct from the mainstream building industry.

Beyond the design and assembly of the timber frame, the businesses offer various levels of service from frame erection right through to a complete build, often known as a turnkey service. Many of the businesses tend to offer different levels of service depending on distance – for instance, they will be happy to quote for an entire build or a waterproof shell within, say, a forty mile radius but beyond that feel that they are bound to be uncompetitive. Others have developed contacts all over the country and feel comfortable taking on entire builds far away from home – indeed some of the timber frame builders think nothing of going overseas. If anything characterises the industry it is the word flexibility. Having said that, it often pays dividends to work with a local business – the level of service is usually better.

Some of the businesses are known for specific styles or designs. Market leader Potton are best known for their Heritage range, half-timbered Tudor cottages. They have spawned several imitators. There are a clutch of Scandinavian or Scandinavian-inspired companies, a couple of American ones and one well-known German one, the much admired Huf Haus. The selfbuild magazines are the best place to get information and contact details and the selfbuild exhibitions, particularly the annual jamboree at Birmingham's NEC each March, are where you can most easily make face-to-face contact.

The majority of timber frame companies offer to work with any and every style. In all there are around sixty businesses active in the field, although around half are based in Scotland, reflecting the popularity of timber frame there. Many of the larger firms have joined together to form an umbrella group known as the UK Timber Frame Association. There are one or two offering to do very similar things with steel frames and Design & Materials is unique in working in a similar method to timber frame companies but actually supplying masonry materials to build houses in the traditional way.

Generally, the concept homes are expensive; for instance, a Potton Heritage home of equivalent size to our benchmark house is going to cost about 12 per cent more to build. A 200 sq m Gamlingay house kit from Potton costs £40,000 – the kit really just covers the superstructure of the house. Foundations and finishes are additional costs. In contrast, Steve Baldwin spent just £25,000 on providing the equivalent work on our benchmark house. However, if you strip out the vernacular elements of the Potton Heritage style – notably the posts and beams – the cost differential between the timber frame kit and our developer house all but vanishes. Typically the price of the kit is between a third and a quarter of the overall build costs though the amount of goods supplied with the kit varies quite considerably.

When making comparisons you have to become adept at looking at the small print to see what's provided and what isn't. The Scandinavian kit home suppliers tend to provide the bulk of what you need but at a considerable price; they also have a nasty habit of listing their floor areas gross – that is including the external walls – which makes the homes appear to be 15 per cent larger than the competition which works with net floor areas. Watch out for this. In Scotland, the timber frame market is more mature than elsewhere and there tends to be a standard Scottish package (which includes the plasterboard), which makes cost comparisons more straightforward.

Prepayment issues

Because a large amount of work is being carried out off-site, most timber frame companies want some form of prepayment. The timing and amounts of deposit required vary enormously from some businesses who want 100 per cent of the frame costs before delivery to others who expect payment after work has been carried out.

From a client's point of view, the nightmare lurking over the horizon is that the company they are dealing with may be about to go bust and that their cheque will be cashed before anything has arrived on site. Timber frame companies are no more secure than any other type of business and one piece of advice frequently given to selfbuilders is 'Never pay for anything upfront'. On the other hand, the suppliers have legitimate fears that the customer can't or won't pay and many have learned the hard way that a contract as large as a timber frame house, usually measured in tens of thousands of pounds, should not be undertaken without some form of deposit and some form of guarantee that the client is able to pay. Unlike other expensive items such as cars, timber frame kits are bespoke and can't just be sold on to another customer.

One way around this problem is to use a solicitor's stakeholder account where the majority of your payment is lodged, usually about a week before delivery of the main frame. This way the supplier can see that you have cleared funds in place, but they are not drawn down until the frame is on site. Another often acceptable solution, used widely for car purchases, is to get a bankers draft or a building society cheque – i.e. the sort of cheque that won't bounce – made out to the supplier a week or so before delivery. This is then shown but not handed over until goods are on site.

However, this raises another problem for selfbuilders borrowing to fund their build. Many lenders will not release funds against goods still being fabricated in a factory and consequently many selfbuilders get caught in a Catch 22 situation where they are unable to proceed.

However, there are now mortgage products on the market, like Buildstore's Accelerator Mortgage, which are designed to unlock funds before a critical stage is reached. Alternatively, many timber frame suppliers will accept undertakings from lenders to pay them directly on delivery.

The important thing to bear in mind is that you must plan ahead and discuss the matter with your chosen supplier and your lender.

Timber frame: fact and fiction
Green oak post and beam houses
The oldest and most traditional form of timber frame building is to use hardwood post and beam systems. This is typical of how the Tudor's built all those manor houses. Large trunks, usually of oak or elm, were cut down, roughly shaped and then used to build the superstructure of walls, floors and roof. Oak post and beam building died out in Britain partly because we ran out of forest but in recent times it's been making something of a comeback.

There are several businesses using oak posts and beams and re-creating the Tudor techniques: the oak is said to be 'green' because it has to be worked in a two-year period after felling before it gets too hard. The best known 'traditional oak' business is Border Oak.

Other companies, such as Potton with their post and beam Heritage range, are using similar designs but employing cheaper softwoods and simpler jointing techniques. Green oak building is not quick and it's not cheap but it produced superb houses in the past and it continues to do so today: the green oak revivalists are much in demand today not only in Britain but all over the world.

Modern timber frame
Volume timber framing is a very different animal. It is reputed to have been invented

in Chicago in the 1830s: it was at the time a revolutionary method of construction. Instead of walls being built in situ as the house went up, they were hammered together in frames on the ground and then hoisted into place. It was called balloon framing because the houses went up so quickly. There was some scepticism at the time that they would come down just as fast, but the technique was used to transform Chicago within twenty years from a 100 inhabitant cattle station into one of the largest cities in America and many of the original homes are still standing. It became – and remains to this day – the standard way of building homes throughout North America.

Speed of erection was of the essence and this is still one of timber frame's main attractions. There is a huge pool of North American construction workers who have grown up with this method of timber framing and the frames are still conventionally built on site, a technique which is also sometimes called stickbuilding. In Europe, the framing tends to be done in factories and then gets transported to site for erection.

Either way, the actual construction techniques are similar. Step One: relatively lightweight softwood timber studs are first cut to length and then nailed together in a rectangular frame. Step Two: a thin (usually around 8-10mm thick) board is then nailed to the outside of the frame – this both strengthens the frame and locks it into a rectangular shape. It's essentially that simple. Most designs call for the addition of extra layers, a breather paper on the outside, a vapour check barrier on the inside and, of course, insulation within the voids of the frame, but these are often added at a later stage on site.

The skeleton of the house can be erected in a matter of days and then one can turn one's attention to finishing off the internal and external details; even here there is a speed saving because on a masonry built house you have to complete the external elements of the house before you can roof it and you have to cover the roof before you can start work on the internal finishes. With timber frame, the roof is conventionally left watertight by the erection crew which allows work to start on the inside immediately their work is done.

If it's that quick and simple why doesn't everyone use timber frame? Well, as already discussed, in many parts of the world they do, though admittedly these are usually the cold northerly latitudes, from which Scotland should not be excluded – current estimates suggest that between 60 per cent and 70 per cent of newly built homes in Scotland are timber frame, a figure on a steady upward trend. In the rest of Britain, timber frame housing accounts for less than 10 per cent of housing starts, though this figure is also rising. There are three discernible reasons for low uptake of timber frame overall.

Comparison costs

Timber frame is perceived to be more expensive than masonry construction. Straight cost analysis suggests this is true but the difference is marginal, of the order of one per cent or two per cent on overall construction costs. And in areas where the blocklayers can charge more than £10 per sq m for their handiwork – now most of southern England, timber frame kits manufactured in cheaper parts of the country start to work out cheaper. Timber frame advocates claim that the added speed of timber frame construction produces cost savings in itself. In Scotland, timber tends to be cheaper – though curiously only the external boarding, Stirlingboard OSB, is sourced from Scotland – and this will tend to make timber frame a cheaper option overall.

Prejudice

There is, or at least was, a prejudice against timber frame, much of it dating from an infamous 'World in Action' TV documentary screened in 1983 which exposed some sloppy housebuilding practices of the time and, erroneously, pointed the finger of suspicion at timber frame. You still hear all manner of things against timber frame houses such as 'They are harder to sell', 'They are difficult to insure', 'They don't last as long.' All complete rubbish.

Timber frame homes actually enjoy a better claims record with Zurich and the NHBC than do masonry ones. Factory production produces fewer errors.

If there is one area where timber frame is inferior, it's in its sound proofing qualities between floors and rooms. But using timber joists and studs for internal elements is common with all forms of housebuilding, not just timber frame; for one thing, it is much cheaper than using concrete or masonry.

If you want better soundproofing you can get it if you are prepared to spend a little bit of money on it. You don't have to switch away from timber frame because of noise issues. More information on sound topics can be found elsewhere in the book; details of improving sound insulation in internal walls and floors can be found in the Superstructure section and right at the end, in the Apocrypha, at the back of this book, there is a section 'All about sound'.

Stickbuilding

The American school of timber frame housebuilding is known over here as stickbuilding. Here the timber and boards are delivered to site and the frame is constructed and erected by carpenters working directly for you. It has its advocates: many claim it to be substantially cheaper than factory prefabrication, but you need to have people around who know what they are doing and there is a shortage of them in Britain. You also need to allow for panel drawings and structural calculations, both of which are time consuming and expensive.

Closed-panel systems

Usually timber frame houses are delivered to site with only one side of the walls boarded. The insulation and the inner linings are put in after the frame as a whole is erected. However, it's a common practice in Scandinavia and Germany to deliver walls and floors to site with both sides boarded out, with the pre-glazed joinery and the services already in place. You get a much faster pace of construction and you tend to get very good quality control as well. There has been some experimentation with such closed-panel systems in the UK but they haven't met with universal approval.

Whilst we marvel at the speed and efficiency of the likes of Huf Haus, who have it all down to a fine art, when we try and do it in the UK, we are beset by customers who keep changing their minds and deciding that they actually don't want a socket on that wall but they do want two on the other wall instead.

Such is our indecision that one of two timber frame businesses that have stuck their toes into the world of closed panels have beat a hasty retreat back to what we know well, the relative flexibility of the open panel systems. Closed-panel type systems need organised clients who know what they want: if you are the dithering type (and most of us are), then avoid.

SIPS

Structural Insulated Panels or SIPS appear to be an alternative to standard timber framed walls and roofs. With SIPS, much of the timber element in the timber frame wall or roof

Murus polyurethane SIPS panels on site in Sevenoaks, July 2000. This was one of the first homes to be built in the UK incorporating SIPs. Where SIPs have run into problems, it's always because the joints between the panels haven't been executed properly, causing air leakage and condensation.

panel is eliminated and instead the panels get their strength from bonding insulation (either expanded polystyrene or one of the polyurethane types) to OSB boards, making a sort of sandwich panel. It's both very strong and very quick to erect though not as quick as the closed panel systems beloved by the Germans. SIPS have been around in North America for some time but recently a number of British businesses have got interested and we are starting to see a lot of interest from selfbuilders and the selfbuild press.

Energy efficiency

Good insulation has always been a feature of timber frame houses because they're essentially hollow skeletons. But as of 2002, the thermal regulations require U-values better than those which standard timber frame walls used to provide. The standard wall thickness of timber frame houses is 90mm which has a U-value of around 0.4 when stuffed with fibreglass or Rockwool. The requirement is now for a U-value of just 0.35 (even lower in Scotland, 0.3) which means that the walls have to either be thickened or a better insulation has to be specified instead. It's not difficult to meet these new standards in either timber frame or masonry builds – but the standard designs will be changing a little. In 2005, U-values are set to be tightened again so expect more changes to how basic timber frames are constructed.

Breathing Walls

There is a very different school of ecological house building, usually in timber frame, that is based on a branch of pseudo-science called building biology. It's very much the organic school of building and it postulates that the fabric of the house is a sort of semi-living entity which absorbs and releases moisture in order to balance out the indoor humidity levels. It's dead set against the use of vapour barriers and it's very much in favour of hygroscopic insulation materials, principally cellulose fibre or recycled newspapers. Advocates claim that a breathing wall design will give you a healthier home with reduced condensation levels: by implication, if you choose to build using conventional materials you will have an unhealthy home with lots of condensation. However, there is scant evidence for this. Condensation is extremely rare in warm, well insulated homes, however they are built. Indeed, if you manage to keep temperatures above 12°C (which isn't hard in a well insulated house) and relatively humidity levels under 70 per cent (which is also not hard, unless you have no ventilation at all), then you will not get any internal condensation, full stop. It's not that breathing walls don't work, but they do seem to me to be the answer to a non-existent problem.

Interstitial condensation

A related but subtly different problem associated with timber frame is interstitial condensation. This is condensation occurring within the wall or roof fabric and thus causing all manner of rot and damp. There is some substance to the fears because on a cold winter's day the temperature difference between inside and out is such that there is almost always going to be a dew point occurring within the fabric of the house. A dew point occurs when the temperature drops to a point at which the relative humidity reaches 100 per cent and at which condensation occurs. However, significant amounts of research carried out in North America (Canada in particular) over the past few decades have concluded that the only significant risk to timber walls and roofs comes when there is a passage of air from inside to out. Moisture doesn't migrate through walls in significant quantities without being driven by air pressure. Cases of interstitial condensation and the related mould growth are thankfully pretty rare and are almost always due to gaps or holes around the walls or roof — i.e. its a workmanship issue. Build it right, build it tight and there is never a problem.

◾ *Shape and size*

Before you even approach a designer or a package company, you would do well to take on board a few home truths about the cost implications of your design decisions. If you are after cheap space, then you need to build your house in a simple shape, preferably a simple box with a simple roof. This doesn't have to look cheap – indeed it doesn't have to be cheap – but the point is that it is almost always going to be the simplest (and therefore cheapest) form of construction available to you. Many traditional houses take this form and they are not all peasants' cottages.

So why should a rectangular box shape be cheaper than say two rectangular box shapes stuck together? In a word, junctions. You are introducing junctions at every stage of the building process and junctions always involve head scratching and usually expensive detailing. Your brickwork will take just that little bit longer to build, your carpentry will become just that little bit more complicated, your roofing will become much more complicated.

However, it is important not to exaggerate the cost implications of building complex shapes: I estimate that the cost effect of these junctions is probably of the order of between 0.5 and one per cent on your total building budget per junction. Therefore if you were to build in an L shape, for instance, you would scarcely notice the extra cost.

But wherever you interrupt the basic shell shape of a house you are adding junction costs and if you choose a complex form with extensions, dormers, porches and the like then you can take it that the overall cost will increase by much more than the unit cost per square metre at which you build the main shell.

Circulation space

There is another hidden cost brought about by using non-standard shapes in house design and this is to do with having adequate circulation space – i.e. hallways, stairwells and landings. This is virtually impossible to quantify because no two situations are the same, but the basic tenet holds that the more complex your form, the more difficult it becomes to provide and frequently do take on the role (and risk) of a general builder and do the hiring and firing of tradesmen together with all the other activities. However what should not be underestimated is the amount of time and energy this all takes up. Realistically, you need some sort of professional management help if you can't be on site every day (although not necessarily all day). For many people, hiring a general builder makes a lot of sense.

Why aren't builders any good?

However much sense it makes in theory, in practice many people end up feeling let down by their main contractor. More often than not, this is because contractors tend to be incredibly busy people and they are forever juggling timetables and deadlines. Whilst the typical general contractor would make a good project manager on one particular job, the wheels start to fall off when the number of sites being supervised gets above three. Yet in order to make a decent living and to keep a run of work going for various tradesmen, most general contractors simply have to keep going at several jobs simultaneously. I know from experience that it's incredibly demanding and stressful trying to co-ordinate building work going on across a wide area. As a builder you may start out with the best intentions in the world but you rapidly end up employing the same knee-jerk excuses used by everyone else in the trade (and despised by its clientele). Appointments start to get missed, calls start to go unanswered, promises start getting broken.

Why can't builders deliver?

I'm not sure there is an easy answer to this. The glib answer is 'You try doing it and see if you are any better.' But that's not terribly helpful. In truth, most general contractors do deliver eventually but often at a standard well below their customers' expectations. So perhaps the advice should be by all means use a main contractor but don't set your standards too high. Or perhaps we are not prepared to pay enough for the level of service we want.

What scares the builders?

Money for a start. It is an axiom often repeated that you should avoid paying a builder upfront for anything, wherever possible. However there is another side of this coin – it is the builder who is consequently extending you credit, which immediately puts him at a disadvantage. And despite the so-called power of the consumer these days, the levels of unsecured credit you are likely to get from a builder are way beyond anything else you are going to be offered on the high street.

Try buying a new car by offering to pay in 30 days only if you are completely satisfied and then withholding five per cent of the price for six months. Little wonder that so many builders experience cashflow problems. Sure, they are buying their materials on credit but this only lasts 30 to 60 days and the subcontract labour they employ will down tools if not paid much more quickly than that.

So one way you can smooth your relationship with your builder is to agree how payments will be met before the contract starts and then stick rigidly to those terms. If you are having to borrow large dollops of money to finance your building work and this money is only released in stages, then be open with your builder about this and make it clear just what he has to do to trigger the stage payments – at least he'll know that you are being realistic about money.

One of the bugbears of today's builder is to be told at the end of the job that although the client is perfectly happy with the finished result, the final £20,000 is going to have to wait a bit because they've overspent and run out of money: yet it happens all the time, builders getting used as sources of interest-free finance.

Another frequent scam foisted on builders is the excuse that the money is locked into a 30 or 60 day savings account and that payment is being withheld until the full withdrawal period is up. The builder is quite likely to be struggling with an overdraft as big as a mortgage. Yet such behaviour by clients is all too common and is verging on being really abusive but, when the builder is the creditor, he can basically do very little about it.

As you can see, the builder is actually in a very vulnerable position. But clients play still worse tricks; some will withhold payment of many thousands of pounds on the flimsiest of excuses, such as resolving a few snags that might be worth just a few hundred pounds. Sometimes these machinations are born of frustration with the performance of the builder but sometimes the client uses these excuses to cover up for the fact that they never had enough money in the first place. Yes, these are the real cowboy clients.

My business was 'locked out' on a couple of occasions on the excuse that the standard of workmanship was not good enough when subsequently it emerged the real reason was that the client was in financial difficulties and simply had no way to settle the bill. Rather than admit to the humiliation of being unable to settle a debt, it is altogether easier and more convenient to tell everyone that the builder is an incompetent rogue from whom you have had to withhold money – or even more likely, an extortionate bill for extras.

Whilst the client is telling everyone who will listen just how awful the builders are and receiving a sympathetic ear, able to point to work which is half finished in evidence, the builder is often forced to bear such indignities in silence. Often the amounts at dispute are too large for the small claims court but not large enough to warrant risking a full-blown legal challenge and many thousands of pounds get written off this way. Clients withholding money for whatever reason is easily the commonest reason for builders going bust and it can happen to even the best builders.

Does the builder choose the client?

Small wonder then that builders are just as wary of potential customers as the customers are of them. The vetting process that goes on between contractors and clients is very much a two-way thing and part of the skill of being a good builder is knowing which clients to work with and which to avoid. You are chosen by your

builder as much as you choose your builder. It's back to that marriage thing again. More often than not, a builder who suspects that a job is a potential lemon will not even bother to quote for it or, if they do, they will add a very high percentage to the overall profit figure to cover their back should they win the contract.

What's wrong with competitive tendering?

One practice which is now becoming prevalent is for busy builders to get together and divide up the work in a way (and for a price) that suits them – it's called covering. It works like this. A job is put out to tender – typically by an architect – to four or five local builders. Some of them are so busy that they simply don't want to take on any more work. Architects tend to regard refusals to quote rather badly and the builders feel that, rather than risking losing the possibility of quoting for future work, they would like to put in some price, any price. So the next step is to chat with the competition – it's not hard, it happens naturally anyway – and soon an informal cartel is in place.

Reg: 'Have you been asked to quote for the old Rectory Job at Chipping Butty?'

Charlie: 'Yes. I like the look of it.'

Reg: 'I really can't see any way we could do that one – could you do us a favour and cover us.'

Charlie: 'Sure – I've no doubt you'll be able to return the favour soon.'

So Charlie puts in his price and tells Reg to put in a price maybe £20,000 higher. Reg knows he won't get the job but he hasn't spent any time or money quoting for it and he hasn't upset the architect so he'll stand a chance next time around when he does want the work.

Occasionally the builders know all the other tenderers on any given job – in matters like this the grapevine works extremely efficiently – so that there are cases where every builder on the tendering list has been in on the scam. They all know who is providing the lowest quote and, consequently, the lowest quote is in reality quite a high one. Such a complete stitch-up is perhaps rare but frequently two or three of the quotes are to be deducted from the overall contract value if the work is not completed to an agreed schedule. For some reason I've not been able to fathom, these are conventionally referred to as liquidated damages. Again, it's one to sort out right at the outset and it's a very adversarial condition to place on a builder.

Time penalties make sense when you will suffer financial hardship (such as paying extra rent). However, when a job overruns it is more often than not very hard to decide who is to blame. You have to be prepared to keep your side of the bargain, which means no delays in agreed payments along the route and no changes to the specification of works. This still leaves the messy grey area of unavoidable delays (weather, strikes, illness, disputes with architects), which could keep an impartial referee busy for weeks. You need a very tight specification to be able to argue your side effectively.

These added conditions are really nothing more than specialised forms of insurance and, if you load a contract with retention clauses and time penalties, you can expect to pay more overall for the works described.

Extras

The biggest single contractual nightmare any builder faces is how to adequately negotiate what the trade calls variations but what everyone else refers to as extras. People call them extras because, like Topsy, they seem to grow and grow. Some do shrink (hence variations being a more accurate term) but for every one that shrinks or even disappears there must be a dozen that expand. It's a particularly critical problem with renovations and smaller works (where often 40 per cent of the final bill is made up of items not originally quoted for), but the new housebuilder is not immune from catching these particular bugs. If you've got plenty of time and money and like a nice loose specification where you can make up your mind as you go along then you'll be wondering what all the fuss is about, but if you belong to the 95 per cent of builders who break out into a sweat every time a bank statement arrives you will

want to know how to avoid these nightmares.

The good news is that you can inoculate yourself against most of them. The bad news is that immunisation is itself expensive and time-consuming. Many extras can be avoided by having a professionally written specification, but people wanting to save money will probably have avoided paying for one in the first place and are usually the same people who can least afford extras.

As if the fact that extras occur at all isn't bad enough, when they do occur, you, the client, are negotiating with a gun to your head; you can hardly hire another builder just to do the extras. If you've gone in a bit hard at the beginning, including onerous time penalties and retentions, you can be sure that the builders will have their revenge here. Not only can they potentially stitch you up pricewise, but they have a cast-iron excuse for blowing your time penalty clauses out of the water. Even if things haven't descended to this sabre rattling, adversarial level there is still ample scope to misunderstand and to misconstrue – 'Oh I didn't realise that meant the glass had to be toughened as well.' 'Well that's an extra £200.' If you are the kind of client who expects your builder to give you fully costed options for free throughout the job, as in 'How much extra would it be if we had a bidet in the kitchen?' you probably deserve to pay over the odds in any event.

Each little decision forms a mini-contract in itself and accounting for them can take up over half the total admin time spent on a job. The golden rules are:
■ make it clear that extras need to be authorised by you before work starts on them
■ always negotiate extras direct with the main contractor – that is the person with whom you placed the initial contract, not with anyone working for them
■ write down what you've agreed – even if it's just in a site diary.

The reasons for extras are many and various. Sometimes it is down to unquantifiable works discovered after the building work has begun

– in new building this type of problem usually occurs underground. Most often it is down to the client adding to the original specification of works as the job progresses or, as it's known in the trade, 'changing their bloody minds again'. There are two specialised forms of extras, or variables, which deserve closer attention.

PC sums

PC Sums are not a new form of anti-sexist arithmetic but a good old builder's routine for dealing with loose specifications. Prime cost sums are put into contracts to allow you, the client, the freedom to select a particular product at a later date. For instance, you might put a PC sum of £300 for a bathroom suite into a specification. The contractor will have included this amount in the quotation but the actual figure you pay will be down to which bathroom suite you choose.

There is a nasty little problem here because things like bathroom suites have list prices and they have trade prices – indeed the trade price is a matter for negotiation. Don't bulldoze in and buy the kit yourself, because the builder (or perhaps plumber in this case) is expecting to make a profit on this deal and they would have every right to expect you to reimburse them for their lost profit.

The normal arrangement is that the builder buys what you specify and that you get to pay list price and the builder pockets the difference between list price and his trade price, but this can work out very expensive, particularly if you up the spec. There is no reason why you shouldn't negotiate a radically different deal whereby you pay trade prices, but make damn sure that you negotiate it beforehand – preferably right at the beginning. Again, the sure way to avoid these sorts of problems is to have a tight specification and that mean ones without PC sums. This means deciding on things like kitchen and bathroom finishes before the job starts.

Provisional sums

Like their cousins, the PC sums, the provisional sums are placed in contracts where there is an element of doubt about the amount of work to be carried out. They are much more common in renovations than in new building but there are nevertheless areas – notably underground works – which most builders will only estimate rather than enter into a fixed price quotation. Understandably so. It's a buck-passing device, a way of saying that if there's more work to do than can reasonably be anticipated, then you, dear client, will be the one who has to pay. Well, you knew it was a risky game. Provisional sums are just one of the things that makes building work such a gamble. You can try to force contractors to take on the risk themselves but their understandable response is to hoick prices through the roof; more realistically you can establish guidelines for how provisional works will be charged: a labour rate, a mark-up applied to materials, that sort of thing.

Running a site

Plan your site as if you were Wellington planning the downfall of Napoleon, or Montgomery about to attack Rommel. Think of it as a military campaign. Montgomery defeated Rommel because he realised that a battlefield was like a building site and that the best building sites were well organised with things happening when and where you wanted them to happen.

Don't just order 14,000 bricks and think how clever you are to have got them so cheaply. Think about how much space 14,000 bricks will take up, where that space is to be found, who or what will put them there, whether they will stay there when you dig a trench in front of them and whether your hod carriers will be able to get to them if there are 200 sq m of concrete blocks stacked in front. Build the house in your head before you pick up a shovel in anger and you will be some way towards having a strategy for negotiating the obstacles that you will encounter along the way.

Always assume the worst. Plan for rain, lots of it; plan for sub-zero temperatures in which your tap freezes and your bricklaying sand sets hard like rock; plan for delays as your subbies slip off to finish another job. Don't be gobsmacked if materials turn up damaged or if the wrong materials get delivered or if nothing gets delivered at all. Keep calm when your mortgage advance fails to come through on time and four large roofers move threateningly towards you demanding payment.

It'll be alright. It won't be that bad.

Who? When? With what?

I cannot stress how much it is worth sitting down with a blank sheet of paper before you start building. In my experience, builders actually find this incredibly hard; they are, by nature it would seem, always wanting to 'push on' or 'get ahead' and they think admin is for accountants and blank sheets of paper are for poets.

It's almost as if the child in us can't resist the lure of the sandcastle whereby you start digging and piling and gradually the structure appears as if by magic, because everyone is digging and piling. Perhaps it is the natural way to build – after all how many children do you see designing sandcastles before going onto the beach. Natural or not, building this way is a luxury which only the rich and frivolous can afford.

Your preparation doesn't have to look incredibly professional – it may indeed look like nothing so much as a glorified shopping list – but it does need to identify who is going to do what, when and with what. As a rule of thumb, every hour spent planning the job beforehand saves between three and four hours tying up the loose ends at the end of the job.

Some of these whos? and with whats? will be blank at the beginning of the job – for instance, you may not know your plumber or your plasterers at that stage – but the key point to take on here is that you need to identify a time by which you should make a decision, otherwise you will lose the so-called critical path and the whole building programme will slide gently off the rails.

How to finish

Following on from this thread, there is another identifiable problem which you need to address from the word go and that is to do with the finishing details, the key ones listed below:

- kitchen
- bathroom furniture
- light fittings
- socket placement
- decorating schemes
- wall tiles
- floor finishes
- shelving, cupboards
- pavings, driveway finishes.

Very often, and quite understandably, people don't want to make decisions about these features until the structure is finished and they can walk around it and visualise everything. Architects' drawings (and 3D computer walk-throughs) are no substitute for being there any more than watching 'The Travel Show' is a substitute for going on holiday. The ability to successfully visualise completed building projects when they are still on plan is something that is generally only picked up after years of experience. If you feel unhappy about making these crucial buying decisions before you have a building you can walk around, then be realistic about the scheduling of these delayed purchases.

Refer back to the eight-month building schedule that appears at the beginning of this chapter Notice that your first fix wiring and plumbing are taking place whilst the roofing is being completed, in Month 4. Well first fix wiring and plumbing can't actually take place until there has been some decision making about what is being wired and plumbed in and this effectively means that you will have had to plan both the kitchen and the bathroom layouts, even if you have yet to decide on what the fittings are to be. Usually these layout options will have been drawn in on the initial plans but note also that the socket outlet and lighting positions will also have to be inked in at this stage and this will affect your positioning of beds and desks and TVs, which is normally left off the plans.

Plan for a pause

If you refer back to the timeline diagram at the beginning of this chapter, you will note that the finishes are booked in to Month 6. Note also that the plastering stage isn't booked to be completed before the middle of Month 5 and realistically this is the point at which the visually challenged can at last see what their schemings have produced.

Most people are surprised to find that some rooms seem larger than they had imagined, some seem smaller, some lighter, some darker. If you are of the sandcastle persuasion of builder, you've reached the natural point at which decision making about finishes should take place. Well you know, a dark oak kitchen would look just so, or perhaps you feel like stretching to those sensational Provençal tiles you saw in the Fired Earth catalogue which would look a wow behind the bath. Now phone up your chosen supplier, be they MFI or Smallbone kitchens.

'Yes, madam, we'd be pleased to supply you with these items. They will be shipped to you in six weeks time.'

'Six weeks! But I've only got ten days!'

'Well perhaps madam would like to choose from our Salmon Slash range which can be delivered to you in three working days.'

'But I don't like any of those.'

I could go on but my point is made. If you want the time to step back and think and then seek out obscure items, and you don't want to do it before your house is plastered out, then plan a quiet period in the building programme so that you can engage on a second stage of the planning. If you are working to stage payments, then try and arrange for a stage payment to coincide with the completion of the plastering stage so that the financial pressure is taken off.

Site tidy

A clean site is a happy site. It is also a more productive site and a safer site. However, keeping a site tidy takes time and some people regard this as wasted time. It's not. Take time out each day to clear away the crap and to return tools to the spot where they should be kept and it will repay dividends in time saved later on.

Subcontractors tend to be very messy; if someone is working for you on a price then they will tend to think that clearing up after them is your business. Typically, the issue doesn't even get discussed when the subbies are being hired but as a general rule if the subbies are supplying materials then they should be responsible for seeing that they clear their waste away after they've finished – after all, in this instance they own the waste materials.

On the other hand if you are supplying materials then they are yours and it's down to you to decide what to do with them. If you demand that your subbies spend half an hour at the end of each day clearing up their own mess they may well turn around and demand extra money for work which would normally be done by an apprentice (whatever happened to them?). Clean subbies are a blessing, but if yours aren't don't just stand there and moan, get on with it yourself.

Rubbish disposal

Often the reason a site degenerates into something resembling the aftermath of a small bomb is that there is no coherent way of disposing of all the rubbish. Indeed, many builders are a) loath to spend money on keeping a site clean and b) loath to throw anything away because it might come in handy later on the job, or on another job. There is a balance to be struck here between a sensible amount of recycling of waste materials and a stubborn refusal to admit that 98 per cent of what is not used the first time will never get used anywhere else. What this invariably hides is the refusal to admit to an earlier buying mistake.

The easiest option for most small sites is to have a skip on site all the time. It costs around £5 per week to keep a skip in an off-the-road location which I reckon is very good value. The expense comes when skips are exchanged – expect an exchange to cost £100 or more, depending on your location, but don't forget that you can have sand and aggregates delivered economically in the new skip, which can make a considerable saving. Many builders are tempted to economise on the rubbish and let the pile grow bigger and bigger, thinking that they'll sort it out later on.

Just piling rubbish up in one corner can cause more problems than it solves – a windy day may send it all out over the site again, and into your neighbours' gardens as well. Another solution is to dig a pit on site which you will cover on completion – this sounds attractive but it is usually rather a dodgy way of going about things because you'll find that covering it over is easier said than done and you'll be unlikely to use the resulting land for anything useful because it will keep subsiding. Bonfires are OK for disposing of timber offcuts but most building waste is either inert (which won't burn) or is plastic (which shouldn't be burnt).

Whatever you do, do plan to do something. Building work produces copious quantities of all kinds of waste and it won't just go away.

Security

Theft is a problem on building sites the world over. It's usually on a small scale and it's typically tools that get nicked, often by casual ne'er-do-wells rather than organised gangs. Fortunately, the way most sites work, the early stages of the work involve a large amount of largely low value commodities like concrete and blocks, which are not easily stolen. Only after the shell is watertight (and hopefully lockable) do the expensive fittings arrive on site. If you want to beat the threat of any potential theft, then don't provide any tempting morsels for light fingers:

■ Have valuable materials (joinery, sanitaryware, kitchen goods) on site for as short a time as possible before fixing.
■ If you have nowhere to lock up kit like cement mixers, barrows and handtools then at least hide them so that the casual visitor does not see them from the road.
■ Take small tools (especially power tools) home with you.

■ Get the windows glazed and the external doors hung as soon as is practicably possible.
■ If your site is particularly vulnerable, consider building the detached garage first (if you have one) to use as a strong room. Alternatively, do what many of the professionals do and hire a container for the duration.
■ Temporary fencing-off is expensive and usually unjustified on small sites. However it may be worth considering if you are in a particularly high crime area or if your site is particularly hazardous and it is likely that people may be wandering around after hours. You can hire 2m high steel fencing such as SGB's Heras Readifence for around 50p per metre per week – less for longer periods. If you need security fencing for more than five months it will probably repay you to buy it and re-sell when you have finished.

Safety

Building sites are by their very nature dangerous places. We demand finished buildings that are themselves structurally sound, weatherproof and safe to live-in but in order to create them we have to go through a series of steps which are inherently unsafe. Anyone managing small building sites is legally required to be aware of these risks and to take measures to minimise their impact. New housebuilding is actually one of the safer sectors of the construction industry – a fact borne out by lower insurance premiums – but there are still a large number of potential hazards to be negotiated.

Excavations

Trench work is usually fairly safe at levels down to about 1m (waist height), but thereafter the dangers of trench collapse become very much greater. There are well proven techniques for shoring up trenches and if you are not sure what you are doing then for God's sake get hold of someone who is.

Deep foundations are potentially very dangerous and you need to guard against not just trench collapse but also materials and people falling down into them. If you are working close to or underpinning an existing structure there is the additional problem that you could undermine it and cause a potentially catastrophic collapse.

Another problem to always be aware of is encountering buried cables and pipes, something that is common when you are opening roads to make service connections. You can reduce this risk by doing your homework and trying to establish just where cables are likely to be buried.

Plant
Control machinery. Heavy plant can kill or maim if not properly controlled. If you get behind the wheel of a dumper truck don't play silly buggers, be very wary. They are not difficult to drive but they can be difficult to control, particularly if it's wet and muddy. They can easily end up crushing someone. Dumpers are often used to pour concrete into foundations and this frequently leads to accidents. Also, ensure cement mixers are properly seated before you start loading.

Ladders
Don't be tempted to be macho – anchor the top end on to something secure. Don't make do with funky old ladders with broken rungs. And wonky step ladders are a nightmare you can live without.

Scaffolding
Don't be afraid to spend money on extra scaffolding. If you are uneasy about doing some task off a ladder (or a scaffold tower) then get proper scaffolding erected. It's surprisingly cheap and you'll get the job done in half the time. Also be very wary about 'rearranging' scaffolding. Usually, this means nicking boards off the scaffolding to use elsewhere. Think who might be going to use the scaffolding in the near future and make sure they know what's been going on.

Power tools
If you don't already have a kit of power tools but are planning to buy some, then buy 110v ones rather than 240v. You'll need a transformer to get them to work but they are far safer. When you hire power tools you should be offered a choice of 110 or 240v. If you are committed to using 240v power tools then ensure that your temporary electricity supply is protected with RCDs (Residual Current Devices).

Electric cables
Long extension leads are a menace (though sometimes unavoidable). Try and avoid trailing them across site where vehicles may drive over them. Get a cordless screwdriver – they are brilliant and you won't need all those extension leads. Cables on building sites tend to get gashed and generally bashed about and it's not unusual for bare wires to get exposed. Keep your eyes open for this sort of thing and if you come across badly frayed cable then replace it, don't bodge it with insulating tape.

Isolated barns provide rich pickings for ne'er-do-wells. With reclaimed slates fetching over £1 each, it's a bit like leaving your car unlocked with the keys in the ignition.

– for instance no one is going to insure you against your finished house being worth less than it cost to build. But there are various catastrophes that you can, to a certain extent, guard yourself from. The basic level of insurance here is covered by the Contract Works or All Risks policy, used to cover theft of plant and materials from site (usually with a hefty excess) together with fire or structural damage to any structures that you may be working on. Your lender will probably insist that you have all risks cover just as a conventional mortgage lender will insist that buildings insurance is in place on any property they mortgage.

If you are employing a builder to erect your house, again you shouldn't need to take out your own policy as well but again you must check to see that they have current all risks insurance in place and that it's large enough to cover the value of your completed house – very often the policies stipulate a maximum contract value above which they won't pay out.

One important point to note is that contract works insurance does not cover any existing structure you may be altering, converting or extending. You would be expected to have this covered by a regular buildings insurance policy.

There is another particular problem which occurs with unconverted barns with valuable planning permission riding on the back of them. The nominal value of the structure may be very low indeed – in fact it may well be a liability rather than an asset – but the planning permission depends on the building continuing to exist. Were it to burn down before conversion work is started, you could theoretically have the planning permission revoked which would be far more expensive than replacing the original fabric. So the risk you are insuring in these cases is not the value of the building but the value of the planning permission.

Make sure that your insurance company understands the difference.

Contracts Works or All Risks policies are not mandatory and they usually come with dozens of options for you to pick and choose just which risks you want to cover. These go from the catastrophic (such as the building being destroyed) down to the inconvenient (such as some kid nicking your power tools). Just where you draw the line and just what excess you choose to bear yourself has an enormous impact on the cost of the policy.

There are only a handful of insurance companies active in the construction market and most of them are open to the needs of selfbuilders as well as the professionals. The names with the track records currently are DMS Insurance, Holbrook (Buildcare), Project Builder and Belmont (Self-builder.com).

Expect to pay around 0.5 per cent of the total project value to get most of the cover you really need to build with a safety net. That translates at around £600 for a house such as our 200 cu m benchmark, four-bedroom detached house. Small builders pay much the same rate on their overall turnover. This would cover you for all the main areas that professional builders are supposed to cover, being employer's liability, public liability and all risks insurance, all summarised above.

If you are selfbuilding, then these policies cease to have any validity once you have completed and so then you need to transfer to regular building and contents policies.

Warranties

Most people have heard of the NHBC (the National Housebuilding Council) – usually because it's being attacked in yet another TV programme about bad housebuilding practices. But most people are only dimly aware that the NHBC is actually an insurance company and that the so-called NHBC guarantee is really nothing more than a latent defects policy. A what?

If you buy a car or a computer, it is usual for it to come with a one-year or two-year guarantee, provided free of charge by the manufacturer. The new homes market once operated in exactly the same way – i.e. the builder supplied their own guarantee – but back in the Thirties depression, there was such a huge number of housebuilders going bust that the housebuying public lost all confidence in the guarantees being offered by individual builders. Those housebuilders who remained in business decided to pool together the risk and that's how the NHBC was born. It's really rather a peculiar organisation because it's part policeman, part arbitrator, part insurer and partly a club for housebuilders. The builders themselves pay the premiums (based on their turnover and their claims record) and sell it to the purchasers as a ten-year guarantee. But it's not the same thing as buildings or contents insurance and many housebuyers have had cause to feel very poorly done by the NHBC policies when they finally get around to reading the small print and find out just how little is covered.

But over the past fifteen years there have been a lot of changes in this area. For a start there is some competition, principally from Zurich Municipal and latterly Premier Guarantee. Partly driven by this competition and partly by wave after wave of bad publicity, the NHBC has substantially improved its terms of cover to include things like roof tiles and double glazing. In 1998, the NHBC introduced a policy called Solo aimed specifically at selfbuilders. Zurich CustomBuild had been around for a lot longer and was market leader but on recent form Zurich quotes have been coming out considerably more expensive. Premier Guarantee is the new kid on the block; they only do warranties and they work with a team of independent inspectors across the UK and Ireland. Many of the selfbuild insurance brokers have links with them.

How do warranties work? Well, any substantial piece of building work has to be inspected to insure it's been carried out correctly. This work is traditionally undertaken by your local authority's building inspectors.

Initially, you submit your plans, which they scrutinise and often call for one or two amendments. Then they carry out onsite inspections to see if you are building what your plans suggest you should be building. Having satisfied themselves that you have carried out the building work correctly, you then get a

completion certificate. If you are just building an extension, that is basically the end of the story.

The NHBC warranty worked under a rather different system that used building inspectors to carry out random checks before issuing a completion certificate. But now the two systems have overlapped and the distinction is becoming confused. The crucial difference between ordinary building control and a warranty scheme is that the latter is turned into an insurance policy, which allows you to make a claim against the builder (or its insurance company) in the event of defects arising in the future. But, of course, you have to pay for this policy and, for selfbuilders, it's an expensive exercise – invariably costing over £1,200 per dwelling and up to £2,000 for larger ones.

You don't have to have it in place but you may well find your mortgage lenders insist on some form of warranty. It's worth mentioning that the cover offered by NHBC's Solo policy is remarkably limited: subsidence, structural damage and defective drains seem to be about the limit of it. If you choose to use an NHBC builder to erect the watertight shell, then you should be able to piggyback on their insurance at rather more competitive rates.

Local authority building control doesn't come with any guarantee. The local authority building inspectors have the power to act as construction policemen, making you redo bits of your work so as to satisfy the building regs. And they are able to issue (or withhold) a completion certificate for your works, which is a mighty handy thing to have when you come to sell your house. But you have no redress against them if their inspections should prove to be negligent.

Architect's certificates

There is an alternative to buying warranties. If your job is being supervised by an architect (or in some cases a surveyor or a chartered builder), you can elect to have them issue progress (and completion) certificates throughout the job, which say, in effect, that the work has been done to their satisfaction.

Most lenders are more than happy to take the word of a suitably qualified (and insured) professional instead of a latent defects warranty such as NHBC or Zurich. However, your professional is unlikely to provide such a service for free and the overall cost may well end up being very similar to third party insurance.

There is a pitfall here too for the unwary. Your architect is not an insurance company and making a claim against an architect is no easy matter. If your double glazing (say) was to fail after five years you would have difficulty establishing whether this failure was down to poor design or to manufacturing defect. If you think the blame lies with your architect's design or supervision, you would then have to pursue the architect for compensation.

Now it is part of a properly qualified architect's job to have Professional Indemnity (PI) insurance in place for just such eventualities so they can't just roll over and play dead the moment you get heavy, but what isn't often understood is that their insurance policy will cover their costs but not yours. And unless you have all costs awarded to you (which is extremely rare) then you are likely to end up with huge legal bills.

Another financial risk looming and, lo and behold, there is yet another policy available to cover this particular risk, although I only know of one such policy, the Selfbuild Legal Protection scheme. It will pay reasonable legal expenses for actions you might wish to take against a whole raft of characters over and beyond your architect: your main contractor, your subbies, your materials suppliers, even your solicitor. It costs about £125 and is valid for up to two years after you move in.

What if you are using a designer who doesn't carry PI insurance? Many very good house designers are not formally qualified and would find it very difficult to get PI cover. In these instances, your protection would lie in using one of the third party warranty providers instead. Once your plans are accepted by the

likes of the NHBC or Zurich, then they are taking on responsibility for their outcome.

■Book-keeping

Site diary

Even if you loathe the thought of record keeping, do try and keep a site diary and write down a summary of every day's action:

- Weather
- What work was done
- Who was on site and how many hours they worked
- Quotations, orders, deliveries, shopping trips
- Payments made
- Contacts made, phone numbers
- Site visits by building inspectors, surveyors, etc
- Comments, feedback from casual visitors, neighbours
- Accidents (however small), breakages, theft.

Not only does this provide a fascinating historical record, but a site diary has a more immediate benefit if a dispute arises; you have a written record of transactions as they occur. Whether you choose to work with or without a formal contract, a site diary will provide you with loads of unexpected ammunition should things ever turn nasty.

Basic accounts

What level of accounts you keep on a project like a selfbuilt house is very much up to you. Because you are able to reclaim VAT on most purchases going into a newly built house, it is a must to keep every VAT receipt that comes your way (I recommend a lever-arch file and a hole puncher for filing). When the time comes to make your claim, you will have to total all the figures, but whether it's worth keeping a running total of costs going whilst the job is in progress is doubtful.

Running trading accounts with builder's merchants and plant hire shops can be a big help; not only is buying more convenient (and often cheaper) but just the fact that tax invoices get sent by post to your home address makes it much easier to keep tabs on paperwork. Trading accounts is a subject dealt with in greater length in Chapter 12 'Shopping'.

Management accounts

If money is tight then you should consider putting a lot more effort into job accounting. You need an early warning system in place to warn you when costs start to overshoot. The key to doing this is to split your whole project down into a number of little joblets such as groundworks, external masonry, roofing, etc. Prepare a detailed budget for your house showing how much you expect to spend on each joblet and prepare a job schedule sheet showing how long each stage of the job should take. Analyse costs as they occur and use your site diary to estimate how much of each stage is completed each week.

You don't go into a project like building a new home without some sort of a budget. Sticking to the budget is obviously crucial to the success of the project, but in my experience you are more likely to come adrift through making an unrealistic budget in the first place rather than overspending on budgeted items. The other great budget breaker is the unavoidable extras (often to do with extra foundations or drains). There is only one safe way around this and that is to make a largish – say five per cent – contingency sum available for such eventualities. If your budget doesn't stretch to this, then how about building a smaller house? The more loosely organised your management of the job is, the higher the chance there is of encountering unavoidable extras. No amount of clever management accounting will make up for an incomplete specification.

Correspondence

Keep handy copies of all correspondence to do with your house from plot purchase to suppliers' terms. A lever-arch file with about ten subdividers should be sufficient. Don't forget that correspondence means keeping copies of your letters as well as ones received, so work out some system of making and keeping copies of your side.

Literature

When you express any kind of an interest in building, you soon find yourself getting snowed under with mailshots for this, that or the other. Some of this is junk, some of it is incredibly useful, but you will need to be on the ball about organising it or you'll never be able to retrieve the useful bits when you need them. Again, a subdivided lever-arch file is a real winner here, though you may need to invest in a heavy-duty hole puncher (round about £25) to pierce the thicker tomes. In addition, get a pack of cardboard magazine files which you can use to hold really thick literature like you get from kit home suppliers and certain kitchen manufacturers.

◼ VAT

Important notice: VAT rates can change. Indeed they may well do during the lifespan of this edition. It only takes a single announcement in the House of Commons. This edition is based on the situation that applied in 2004: all prices mentioned in this book are VAT-free (unless otherwise stated). If there are major changes, they are likely to receive wide publicity but if you are not sure what has happened, you are advised to contact the VAT query line – 0845 0109000. Also note that Customs & Excise now have a national centre in Birmingham for dealing with selfbuild claims: you can contact it directly on 0121 697 4000.

New housebuilding (and conversions of non-domestic property into homes) enjoy a privileged position in the UK VAT world. They are zero-rated. This means, in layman's terms, that you can reclaim almost all the VAT charged to you in the course of creating your new house. This is something of an anomaly. Since the introduction of VAT in 1983, almost all other building work has been standard-rated, which means that you cannot reclaim the VAT.

The reason new housebuilding survives VAT-free is that VAT cannot be levied on second-hand house sales since such sales are private, and so it would be regarded as inequitable for new housebuilders to have to charge VAT on their product when 85 per cent of all house sales escape it. Nevertheless, the imposition of VAT on new housebuilding is a possibility that all new housebuilders must face and it's recently come to the fore in the political debate about the future of housing.

Change may well be on the way during the lifetime of this edition so that VAT reclaims may become a thing of the past. Having warned you of that, the changes in VAT rules for homebuilders recently have actually been pretty helpful. The definition of a non-domestic property was widened in 2001 to include anything that hadn't been lived in for ten years so conversions of all kinds of buildings into homes was brought into the zero-VAT net – prior to that they had to have been unoccupied since 1973.

Chancellor Gordon Brown also introduced a new five per cent VAT band which applies to work on properties empty for more than three years and also to changing the number of living units in a building. This latter was presumably brought in to encourage builders to convert large houses into flats but it seems to equally well apply to people who want to turn a block of flats into a large house.

Reclaiming VAT

So much for politics. Here follows an explanation of the VAT position in Great Britain as of 2004. The position varies depending on how you organise your construction. If you are a professional builder undertaking a spec build for the first time, it could hardly be simpler; you just reclaim the VAT inputs each quarter when you do your VAT returns. The only complexities come with certain costs where VAT is not reclaimable. More on these in a minute. For selfbuilders, Customs & Excise runs a special scheme called VAT refunds for DIY builders and converters. Really, this claim pack is a must-have item unless, of course, you think the government deserves the money more than you do. You can use the DIY reclaim scheme even if you have very little input into a new house: if a builder undertakes a turnkey project for you,

you can still reclaim VAT on items like fencing and paint that you might put in yourself.

How you run a job has a bearing on the VAT situation. Design fees and professional services are not normally eligible for VAT refunds but if you start by appointing a builder who then subs out design and other fees, then it's all considered one design and build contract and you can reclaim all fees (provided the invoicing doesn't separate out the fees from the construction). It's called creative invoicing.

If you are taking on the project management yourself, there are quite a few ground rules you need to be aware of.

■ You can't reclaim VAT from subcontractors for their labour. Make sure they don't charge VAT in the first place. Just to make things complicated, if the project you are undertaking is classed as a conversion not a new build, then you are able to reclaim VAT on labour, even though VAT on the labour is probably being charged at the reduced rate of five per cent.

■ You can only make one claim and this must be within three months of completion. Completion is not the same thing as occupation: they expect you may well occupy before technical completion but if the delay between the two is longer than six months then they become suspicious and will demand explanation. Tread cautiously here.

■ All purchases you wish to reclaim the VAT on must be supported by valid VAT receipts, made out to you. A VAT receipt is one that includes the supplier's VAT No. (but doesn't necessarily separate out the VAT). Credit card slips, cheque stubs, delivery notes are not VAT receipts. Also Customs & Excise want to see the originals; they don't accept photocopies. Note also that if some of your material supplies are purchased through a subcontractor who is not VAT registered, you will not be able to reclaim VAT – the original invoice must be made out to you.

What is zero-rated?

As discussed already, recent changes in VAT rules have somewhat simplified the rules and made definitions of what can and cannot be zero-rated much easier to grasp. There are two areas to consider. Firstly, how does the job as a whole stack up in the VAT reclaim stakes? And secondly, which costs incurred can you reclaim? The first area has always been looked on as a minefield. If you are in doubt, you can get hold of the rules on the web at www.hmce.gov.uk where you want to get hold of two documents, VAT notice 708 (Buildings and Construction) and VAT information sheet 0501 (which explains the 2001 changes in a mere 11 pages). There are of course still grey areas — for instance what happens when you convert a pub that has a self-contained flat — but it's still simpler than it was. A bit.

Provided you can establish that your project is a new build, almost all the construction costs are eligible for zero-rating of VAT. That is to say, that suppliers who are knowingly supplying a zero-rated project should not add VAT to their invoices and if VAT is applied (currently at 17.5 per cent) you should be able to reclaim it. The situation with conversions is subtly different. Here you are expected to pay VAT on all supplies, including labour albeit at the new reduced rate of five per cent. You can still reclaim using the DIY builders VAT refund system (snappily referred to in these circles as VAT notice 719)

As your house nears completion, you will find a number of items that Customs & Excise, in their wisdom, regard as fittings that lie outside the zero-rating net. If there is any ground rule at all it is that if the items are fixed into the building then they are zero-rated but if they are removable then you must pay the VAT.

However, there are many exceptions to this rule and the rules are often subject to review. I present the following list for general guidance only; the VAT office may view things differently and please don't jump down my throat if you find you are unable to reclaim VAT on something I've said you can. It's the VAT office you should be arguing with and, if you're canny, you will do this before you start construction. VAT Notice 719 includes a similar list, which you should refer to for the latest

views from the VAT office.

Having tried to get myself off this particular hook, let's look at the current state of play. Personally, I find this catalogue of what's in and what's out ridiculous, and I'd be tempted to laugh at it if there wasn't so much damn money riding on it. Don't keep telling your VAT official that 'This is crazy!'; they know it and they've heard it a thousand times before.

■ Kitchens: Fitted kitchens are zero-rated but white goods (cookers, washing machines, dishwashers, etc.) are not. There is no distinction made between integrated and freestanding equipment — you must pay VAT on them — so things like waste disposal units and water softeners are standard-rated. However there are some zero-rated appliances, most notably cooker hoods and built-in vacuum cleaners.

■ Agas: standard-rated except when they have an integral boiler; then they are regarded as part of the heating system and VAT can be reclaimed.

■ Fitted cupboards: At present the ruling seems to be this — if you build the cupboards (i.e. fitting doors across alcoves formed in the walls) then it seems that you can reclaim the VAT on all the materials, but if you buy in fitted cupboards then you can't. If that's not clear then ask your VAT office.

■ Flooring: All forms of carpeting are standard-rated. Everything else is zero-rated.

■ Heating/plumbing/sanitaryware: All zero-rated except water treatment units. Fireplaces are also zero-rated. Solar panels, heat recovery systems and air conditioning also qualify for zero-rating.

■ Electrics: All zero-rated. Light fittings should be OK provided they are fitted, but a zealous inspector may disagree.

■ Alarms: Both smoke alarms and burglar alarms are zero-rated. Also fire safety equipment is now zero-rated.

■ Furnishings: Movable furniture is invariably standard-rated. The status of fitted shelves is unclear. Curtains and blinds are standard-rated but you can reclaim VAT on curtain rails.

■ Decorating: Paint is zero-rated and you

shouldn't have any problem with wallpaper. Also, if you want to have decorative finishes (like pine matchboarding) you should be able to reclaim the VAT.

■ Garages and driveways: Zero-rated.

■ Landscaping: They will generally accept a limited amount of turfing and paving as zero-rated. However, trees, shrubs and plants will all be VATable.

■ Swimming pools: Standard-rated unless it's inside a building which is at least attached to the main house.

■ Outbuildings/conservatories: Detached outbuildings (except garages) are standard-rated. However, attached extensions like conservatories are zero-rated.

■ Plant hire, scaffolding: These are standard-rated items which you cannot reclaim, although note that scaffolding erection and dismantling is technically zero-rated whilst the hire is not. Therefore you can save money by getting your scaffolder to invoice separately for the two services.

■ Professional fees: standard-rated.

End of the party

A selfbuilder can only make one reclaim from the VAT office and so when it's done, it's done. This presents a major cashflow problem to many as there is usually several thousand pounds waiting to be reclaimed, several thousand pounds which most selfbuilders could well use to finish off their project; many end up forgoing further VAT reclaims in order to get their hands on this money before the house is complete. If you employ a VAT registered builder to construct your house this reclaim problem does not occur as the builder's invoices are zero-rated for all but the exempt items though note that you can still use the DIY reclaim scheme if you buy just the odd can of paint and a few curtain rails on your own account.

Listed buildings

If you think the list of what you can and can't reclaim VAT on has just a touch of the Alice in Wonderland about it, then Lewis Carroll must have gone into overdrive when dreaming up just how the tax should be applied to listed building work. The purpose of listing buildings is to preserve them so you might think that the Treasury might just help out a bit with repairs. But no, what actually happens is that alterations to listed buildings are zero-rated whilst repairs to them have VAT charged on them at the standard-rate. So there is a tax incentive to alter a listed building but none to keep one in good repair. Yes, I agree, it's an extraordinary state of affairs. Enter the creative specifier who can save 17.5 per cent of the building costs with a nice turn of phrase!

Most major works on listed buildings involve a mix of repairs and alterations and the usual route taken is to agree a proportion of the two with Customs & Excise before work commences. If it's 60:40 alteration:repair, then they should allow you to charge (or be charged) VAT at 40 per cent of the standard-rate. So if the total bill was, say, £100,000 net of VAT then you would be expected to pay just 40 per cent of the standard VAT amount of £17,500.

VAT in the EU

The VAT regimes for new housebuilding vary substantially around the EU. There is no such thing as zero-rating anywhere else (as far as I can establish). In the Republic of Ireland, VAT is collected at over 20 per cent on all building materials though there is a tax break if you employ a registered builder on a new house – you pay VAT at 12.5 per cent instead.

But one piece of good news is that if you are undertaking zero-rated building in the UK you can reclaim VAT on materials purchased anywhere in the EC. This is particularly useful for selfbuilders in Northern Ireland who want to buy stuff from the Republic. Also note that there is an increasing cross-Channel trade in light goods, which currently seem to be significantly cheaper in France and Belgium than in the UK.

French DIY sheds Castorama and Leroy Merlin are now getting almost as many UK visitors as the wine warehouses (I'm exaggerating) and there is an IKEA in Lille, which seems to be much cheaper than its UK counterparts. This arbitraging of building materials is something which may grind to a halt if (or is it when?) the UK joins the euro. But of course by that time we may no longer have zero-rated building supplies.

■*Other taxes*

Whereas professionals and selfbuilders are on a level playing field when it comes to VAT, selfbuild really comes into its own when you start to look at other taxes. If you are building your one and only house, then you really don't have to pay any taxes at all on the profits you make. The two taxes which you might expect to get clobbered by are income tax and capital gains tax (CGT). If you are a professional, you will get caught by one of these two. Typically, income tax is levied on you if your livelihood involves building homes for sale, and CGT cuts in if you buy and sell second homes or houses to let out. Here you would be expected to pay income tax on any rental income, and CGT on any gains you make when you come to sell the house. However neither income tax nor CGT have ever been levied on 'your principal private residence' so any profits you make on your private homebuilding are consequently tax-free. Even if you sell off part of your garden for someone else to build a house, you don't pay any tax on the proceeds, although you can trip into the tax net if the garden area exceeds 0.5 hectares.

Now the selfbuilders' tax exempt status raises a few interesting possibilities. What if you move into a house you have built, make it your 'principal private residence' and then sell it shortly afterwards? What if you step from one selfbuild house to another to another? Welcome to the world of the serial selfbuilder. It's actually a long established practice in the UK. I remember a builder doing exactly this in the Cambridgeshire village I grew up in. My parents bought a house from him in 1950. By the time we left the village when I was 13, he'd

moved house about five times and was at work on another, all in the same village.

Many small builders live a semi-nomadic, selfbuild lifestyle like this, interspersing regular work with the odd homebuilding or renovating project. As long as you establish each house as your 'principal private residence' you should be in the clear tax-wise, although there are signs that the Revenue is beginning to take an interest in this area. There is no published guidance on how long you have to stay in a house before it is accepted as your 'principal private residence' which would distinguish you from a commercial developer but 12 months is often quoted as a broadly acceptable period. The key point to establish isn't how long you live in a house but that the project wasn't undertaken with profit in mind. 'Private residence relief is not intended to relieve speculative gains,' reads the Inland Revenue Help Sheet 283. 'Relief is not therefore available where you acquire or spend money on your dwelling-house wholly or partly to realise a gain on its disposal.' Ominous wording, especially as it could be applied to just about anyone who ever bought a house in Britain. It's worth bearing in mind. Although the number of people pursued for tax on their 'speculative' profits on selfbuild is tiny, it would be as well not to make too much of a song and dance about how much money you may have made.

In reality, not that many people will keep on moving house and building and moving and building indefinitely. Whilst it's a great way to build up equity and reduce mortgages, it doesn't actually bring in any extra cash (unless you start trading down) and it's also pretty exhausting and doesn't fit easily into the requirements of family life. But it probably beats babysitting as a way of eking out a little bit extra. Until such time as the property market decides to take another tumble…

Chapter 6
Groundworks

Excavations
Foundations
Ground floors
Slopes, bad ground & trees
Services
Drains

Groundworks is the term most often used to describe all the things that builders do beneath ground level. It's actually a hotch potch of different activities – excavation, drainage, service connections, concreting, some brickwork. It also conventionally includes the laying of the ground floor but I deal with that in the next chapter where ground floors can be more easily compared with upper floors.

The advent of JCBs, readymix concrete and plastic drainware has taken a lot of the graft out of this part of building, but it still remains an exacting and potentially hazardous task. It is also incredibly messy, especially when there's rain about. Whilst neighbours will look on in horror as you recreate the battlefield of the Somme, you must shrug your shoulders and utter asinine comments like 'You can't make an omelette without breaking eggs.'

Groundworks is really a question of getting from A to B as cheaply and easily as possible. There are many reasons for using something other than the standard solutions for your underground work, but all of them involve sorting out or avoiding problems, not increasing amenity value. This is not to say that the housebuilder does not face choices of how best to get the groundworks completed, but

these choices are for the most part to do with ease, speed and cost of installation. This chapter concentrates on these issues as well as taking a closer look at how some of the problems, outlined in Chapter 3 'Pitfalls', are solved.

Given a straightforward site and a straightforward house design, the groundworks can progress with remarkable speed at a comparatively low cost. However, a problem site can easily double or even treble the base costs, so I cannot emphasise enough how important it is to thoroughly analyse the costs involved in just getting your house out of the ground.

Groundworks is also one of the areas of housebuilding most prone to mistakes being made. The setting out of foundations and levels and the correct siting of drain terminals is not a job to be undertaken lightly; add a slope into the equation and you have a job to tax the most skilled surveyor. Yet the supervision of groundworking is often left to harassed digger drivers who 'want to get on with it' and often barely refer to any plans that may have been drawn up. The horror stories that you occasionally hear of completed houses having to be taken down because they were put up in the wrong place are a testament to the consequences of rushed excavations.

Benchmark House Groundworks Costs Summary

	Quantity	Going Rate	Total	Mats	Lab	Plant
Clearing Oversite	36 m³	£ 15 per m³	£ 540			£ 540
Setting Out Foundations	146 m²	£ 2 per m²	£ 220		£ 220	
Excavating Foundations	60 m³	£ 15 per m³	£ 900			£ 900
Dumper Hire	3 days	£ 80 per day	£ 240			£ 240
Foundation labour	39 m³	£ 11 per m³	£ 410		£ 410	
Readymix in Trenches	39 m³	£ 50 per m³	£ 1,950	£ 1,950		
Footings Blockwork (area doubled for 2 skins)	112 m²	£ 16 per m²	£ 1,800	£ 630	£ 1,180	
Footings Brickwork below DPC	14 m²	£ 45 per m²	£ 640	£ 340	£ 320	
House Floor	110 m²					
Beam and Block Floor		£ 29 per m²	£ 3,190	£ 1,870	£ 1,320	
Ventilation & Airbricks		£ 3 per m²	£ 310	£ 140	£ 170	
DPM		£ 2 per m²	£ 210	£ 40	£ 170	
Garage Floor	17 m²					
Hardcore & Blinding		£ 12 per m²	£ 200	£ 70	£ 130	
100mm Concrete Slab		£ 13 per m²	£ 220	£ 90	£ 130	
		Totals	£ 10,830	£ 5,130	£ 4,050	£ 1,680
Overall Footprint 127 m²			£ 85 m²			

This table covers the excavations, foundations and ground floor work up to DPC level, the traditional point at which groundworks is said to end. However there are some new systems on the market – such as Hanson Jetfloor, Abbey Pynford's Housedeck – which give you an insulated finished floor as part of the package, elements missing from the above table. To compare like with like, you would need to add another £15 or £20/m² to the above total of £85/m² to get to a comparable stage of the work

If you've never been involved in setting out foundations, you can sit back and laugh at the incompetence; not until it's just you and a stroppy JCB driver do you begin to realise just how difficult it is and how easy it is to go badly wrong. Of all the areas of housebuilding, groundworks is the one that needs the most management and the best management. If you are a DIY project manager, this is the big one. Crack this and you will have no problems on down the line.

Most builders choose to subcontract all the groundworks but, whilst this makes it very much easier to navigate this stage, it is still vital to check that you are getting exactly what you asked for. You must check that the foundations are in the right place, are square, and are at the right height (this last can be difficult to measure). You must check that the access arrangements have been properly constructed, with falls going the right way and that the drains and the services have been installed correctly. Your building inspector will provide some guidance and should be able to pinpoint errors and bad practice but is not paid to be a surveyor and will have no idea if your trenches are off-square or in the wrong position. It is much harder to ferret out mistakes on

groundworking than on later parts of the build and usually much more expensive to rectify at a later date.

■ Excavations

A flat site is a cheap site; clearing debris off the oversite will not take long and digging normal depth foundations for a four-bedroom house will take a JCB no more than a day. Note, however, that the crucial task of setting out the foundations on the ground has to be carried out after the undergrowth is stripped away. It's not a job to rush, especially if you are new to the game, and so you ideally want to leave a couple of days between site clearance and the start of excavation. The consequences of setting out in completely the wrong place are often disastrous.

Unless you are working in a confined area where mechanical plant cannot reach, then you will want to get hold of a JCB or some similar digger. Some builders have diggers and digger drivers in their armoury, but most just have contacts with guys who are self-employed and own their own machine. They tend to charge for travelling time so it's worth getting someone local and – depending on how busy they are – they often charge for a minimum of half a day even when they're only around for a couple of hours. But at around £150-£200 per day for driver plus JCB, they can do the work of around ten to twenty men and therefore represent a bargain not to be sniffed at. They can also do a lot of damage. The one-man-band digger drivers tend to be the most helpful, but they do like to get on with it. If you're not 100 per cent on top of what's to be done then chances are that you'll get rushed into mistakes. Trench excavations happen remarkably quickly: expect around 50m per day, enough for a small house. Inexperienced groundwork managers will have their work cut out to keep up.

Demolition man?

If you've an existing structure to demolish, then you'll have a choice of taking it down slowly and salvaging materials, or getting a machine to demolish it which is not very green but it's far more exciting – one for the camcorder. I'd suggest that it is almost entirely dependent on the value of the salvaged materials. There are also health considerations, whichever method you employ: watch out for asbestos, which was very common in much of the 20th century housing now being demolished.

Muck away

Charming expression for getting rid of the spoil. The topsoil is stripped off and stored on site for later use, but the subsoil is usually dumped somewhere else. Many digger drivers operate in tandem with a 15- or 20-tonne lorry and will have local dumping contacts. Alternatively, it is worth chasing up local landowners to see if they have any holes to fill. Subsoil taken out of the ground 'bulks-up' at least 30 per cent when piled in a heap (or on a lorry). This means that just under 12 cu m dug out of the ground will fill the 15 cu m space on a 20-tonne lorry: those sorts of calculations are typical when doing muck away sums – a cubic metre in the ground tends to weigh between 1.5 and two tonnes. Some ground conditions, notably clay, bulk-up at much more than 30 per cent: a 50 per cent or even 60 per cent bulk-up rate can be expected. Make sure if you get a quote per cubic metre whether you are dealing with muck in the ground or bulked-up on the lorry.

Landfill Tax

Since 1996, a tax has been applied to muck away at a rate of £2 per tonne if the spoil is

Foundation/Excavation Key Element Prices

Groundworker	£ 18 per hr
JCB Hire with driver	£ 30 per hr
JCB digs in easy ground	5 m³ per hr
JCB Digs in hard ground	2 m³ per hr
20 tonne lorry	£ 80 per trip
20 tonne lorry holds	15 m³ spoil
Landfill tax (inert)	£ 2 per tonne
Spoil bulk up rate	1.3 m³ per m³ in ground
Readymix Concrete	£ 50 per m³
Concrete Pump Hire	£ 200 per day
Dumper Hire	£ 80 per day

Composite Rates for Excavation

Easy Dig Excavation rates	
Excavation with JCB	£ 6 m³
Muck away in lorry rate	£ 5.30 m³
Plus Landfill tax	£ 3.20 m³
Total	£ 15 m³

Hard Ground Excavation Rates	
Excavation with JCB	£ 15 m³
Muck away in lorry rate	£ 5.30 m³
Plus Landfill tax	£ 3.20 m³
Total	£ 24 m³

I have made a distinction between easy and difficult excavation to reflect the fact that it's a job that can vary enormously in time and cost. This sort of thing can make it difficult to estimate groundworks – especially if you are digging out a basement, which may be as much as 400m³ for a benchmark-sized house.

classed as inert and up to a whopping £15 per tonne if it has man-made detritus in it. The tax is paid when spoil is tipped at a licensed pit and it has had the effect of increasing the cost of a 20-tonne muck-away lorry from around £70 per load to £100 per load. Our benchmark house had around 100 cu m of muck taken away during the excavation stage and this will have resulted in a Landfill Tax bill of about £300 (for 150 tonnes), adding 25 per cent to excavation costs.

Ouch. A stealth tax if ever there was.

All the more reason to find a friendly farmer with a hole to fill. Many builders are choosing to put all excavated spoil in the back garden, then compacting it with heavy machinery and placing topsoil back on top. It's an option to consider but it's just not possible on all sites.

On many sites you will be unable to get heavy plant like JCBs to the back of the house once you have completed the trench excavations. If you have plans for landscaping or drainage or even plan to build a swimming pool or a summer house at a later date, this may be your only opportunity to get the groundwork done quickly and cheaply and a change of plan or an oversight can have costly ramifications later. Another area to sort out on day one is the site access; it pays to get your drive levelled and hardcored as early as possible.

Summary

To work out your likely excavation and muck away costs, first work out the volume you need to remove. If it's fairly easy digging, it's likely to cost around £5 per cu m to dig out of the ground and an additional £8 to £10 per cu m to remove it to a licensed tip (of which £3 will be tax). If the digging is hard (rock, for instance) the excavations costs can double or even treble but the muck away costs should be unaffected.

■*Foundations*

If you ever get involved in working around the foundations of some pre-20th century buildings, as you might if you were building

The reality of foundations for many people. You dig 'em – they fill up with water before you can order the readymix

an extension on to a Victorian house, you will be amazed at how shallow and how basic the existing foundations appear to be compared with what we have to build off now. 'How come this house is still standing?' will be your first thought. Followed by 'If these foundations have supported this house for so long, what am I doing messing around two feet deeper underground?' Both good questions. Neither has a simple answer.

The history of foundations is vaguely interesting and a little instructive. The current idea of building up off slabs of concrete at depths of a metre or more below ground level is relatively new, very much a 20th century innovation. The Victorians used to step the walls out at the base, pyramid style, over a depth of just three or four brick courses, that way spreading the load of the house across a wider area. These below-ground courses were known as footings and the footings were effectively the foundations. Today we still refer to footings but we put concrete foundations under them. 21st century footings are simply the brick or blockwork sandwiched between the concrete foundations and the damp proof course which is usually installed at 150mm above ground level.

When concrete foundations were first adopted widely, in the Twenties, they were sold to builders as being a cheaper and quicker method of building-in adequate load bearing. In fact, the load imposed by a typical house (which maybe weighs around 100 tonnes in total) really isn't that great – it's similar (on a weight per area basis) to that imposed on the ground by your feet when you stand up. The problems arise from the fact that the ground has a nasty habit of shifting about which itself has a nasty habit of causing all manner of disruption on the very rigid structures placed on it. Building foundations out of concrete may sound very hard and solid but when the ground starts moving then they look as feeble and spindly as you could want.

The Building Research Establishment, our premier research science group, investigated the phenomenon of ground movement in the early Nineties and found a site which regularly heaved up and down by 50mm over the course of a year, not to mention a 60mm sideways movement as well. Mostly it's sites with large trees and clay soils but it's also rather unpredictable so consequently the momentum is towards deeper and deeper foundations, which means more and more concrete. This usually works but we still have a large number (approx 1,000 a year) new houses that subsequently suffer from foundation failure.

The best advice is to follow the advice you are given as closely as you can – don't cut corners. Readymix concrete and excavations are moderately expensive but nothing like as expensive as having to fix later failures.

As foundation requirements have grown deeper over the years, there have evolved two options about how to construct them – at least, on largely problem-free sites. One is to pour the minimum amount of concrete possible into the foundation trenches and then build upwards in brick or blockwork – known as strip footings. The other system reverses this logic altogether and pours as much concrete as possible into the trench before starting on the bricklaying – this is usually called trenchfill. Both methods have pros and cons.

The traditional method, laying footings below ground level, is cheap on materials but heavy on labour; it is also slower. In contrast, trenchfill is much quicker but, of course, uses more concrete. When pouring concrete into clay soils, you will probably have to use the trenchfill method.

An important consideration when designing foundations is to set the level of the concrete so that it 'works blocks.' Blocks are laid either flat in courses of 110mm or in the vertical in courses of 225mm (ish). If you have surveyed the site accurately, you will know exactly where

Traditional Strip Footings

brick and block cavity wall
blockwork footings
trench dug 600mm wide
concrete min 250mm thick
external ground level

Trenchfill

ground floor
concrete fills trench

the damp proof course will be so you can ensure that you stop the concrete at 225, 450 or 675mm below that point. That ensures that you keep the fiddling about and cutting to a minimum. – provided, of course, that you pour your foundations level!

The benchmark house went for the 675mm mark which meant that Steve Baldwin poured no more than 450mm of concrete into his trenches which technically makes this house a strip footing one, but only just. Most builders these days pour right up to the 225mm below DPC mark. They value the speed and comparative ease with which trenchfilling is done: much of the graft of foundation pouring has been taken away by the increasing use of concrete pumps which do away with the need for barrowing, at a cost of around £200 a go.

A new development is the arrival of self-placing concrete that finds its own level around a set of foundation trenches. This reduces the labour input still further and may partly do away with the use of pumps. The most widely available self-placing concrete is RMC's Foundation Flow.

The depth and length of the trenches are not in your control, but the trench width is largely down to which bucket the JCB uses to dig with (the general choices being 450 and 600mm wide). Using a 450mm wide bucket is going to reduce the amount of readymix used by a quarter (as well as reducing excavation costs) but it is not to be recommended to rookie builders. Cavity walls – generally now 300mm wide – sit uncomfortably on such a narrow trench; internal load bearing wall foundations are obviously less of a problem, but the key factor in all this is accurate setting out of trenches.

Unless you are an experienced surveyor, you really want to play safe and set trenches at 600mm wide, because not to do so is to risk not having square footings. This will end up costing you far more money than the few hundred quid (maximum) you may save through having narrow foundation trenches.

You can – and some people do – design a

house so that it sits on a series of concrete pads rather than a continuous trench. It helps to have a relatively lightweight structure – timber frame is ideal – and you need an external skin that doesn't have to sit on the ground. It's much more of a fiddle setting it all up but it is possible to reduce the amount of foundation concrete used by around 70 per cent when using pad foundations, though any cost saving here is likely to be clawed back in structure above.

Many people ask if timber frame homes require less in the way of foundations. In theory, being much lighter than masonry ones, they should but in practice it doesn't make much difference. As already discussed, the weight of the house is often not the principal issue with foundation design: it's more important to be confident that the load bears on ground that won't move. One area where timber frame can win out is that the walls tend to be a little thinner which can mean that trenches can be a little bit narrower but again this is not always to be recommended.

One issue that does require close scrutiny if you are building a timber-framed house is that the overall accuracy of the foundations has to be spot on. Whereas brick and blocklayers are well used to making up the odd 30mm discrepancy in height and squareness, frames require accuracies of plus or minus 5mm. Ensure that your groundworkers know this.

■ Ground floors

The 'industry standard' is to build a concrete or masonry ground floor and a timber first floor. This is how the benchmark house was built, and it's how 90 per cent of single homes are built in the UK. Only in Scotland does the practice change – there they still love timber ground floors. Intermediate floors are in a section all their own in the next chapter. Here, I just look at ground floors.

Comparing floor costs is a bit of a nightmare. It gives me nightmares, at any rate. The problem is to know where to begin and end. I was struck

Ground Floors — Key Element Rates

	Materials		Labour	Combined
	Unit Cost	m² rates	m² rates	m² rates
Beam and Block Floor		£17.00	£ 12.00	£ 29.00
Hanson Jet Floor		£19.00	£ 12.00	£ 31.00
Hollowcore Floor		£30.00	£ 12.00	£ 42.00
Telescopic Vents	£ 3.50 ea	£ 0.90	£ 1.50	£ 2.40
Airbricks	£ 1.40 ea	£ 0.40		£ 0.40
100m² DPM	£ 29.00 roll	£ 0.40	£ 1.50	£ 1.90
60mm Celotex Insulation		£ 6.00	£ 1.50	£ 7.50
100mm Jablite Insulation		£ 4.00	£ 1.50	£ 5.50
65mm Screed		£ 4.30	£ 7.50	£ 11.80
100mm Concrete	£ 50.00 m³	£ 5.00	£ 7.50	£ 12.50
Reinforcing Mesh		£ 1.00	£ 3.00	£ 4.00
150mm Hardcore	£ 18.00 m³	£ 3.00	£ 6.00	£ 9.00
Sand Blinding over Hardcore	£ 20.00 m³	£ 1.00	£ 1.50	£ 2.50
50x200mm Timber Joists	£ 2.20 m	£ 7.70	£ 13.50	£ 21.20
50x200mm I-beams	£ 5.00 m	£ 12.50	£ 9.00	£ 21.50
22mm Chipboard	£ 5.00 sheet	£ 1.67	£ 4.50	£ 6.17

Ground Floor — All-in Rates per Square Metre

Concrete Slab (Un-reinforced)	£ 45 inc insulation and screed*
Concrete Slab (reinforced)	£ 49 inc insulation and screed*
Beam and Block floor	£ 51 inc insulation and screed*
Hollowcore floor	£ 62 inc insulation and screed*
Hansons Jet Floor	£ 48 inc screed (NB insulation built-in)
Timber Ground floor	£ 50 inc base concrete and chip board floor cover
I- beam Ground floor	£ 50 inc base concrete and chipboard floor cover

AN IMPORTANT DISTINCTION Groundworks are conventionally costed 'up to DPC level' which means that floor finishes are ignored. But because underfloor insulation is now mandatory, there are solutions around that provide insulation and consequently the All-in Rates per Sqaure Meter include costs for a semi-finished floor — i.e. a screed or at least some chipboard on top of the structure. Underfloor heating is ignored but it tends to add about another £20/m² to the costs.

* Jablite 100mm and 65mm screed finish

by this looking around Buildstore's permanent exhibition space in Livingston, near Edinburgh. They have a small display showing how the structure works on the main floor types, being timber, solid slab and pre-cast concrete suspended floors.

On the solid slab exhibit I counted seven different layers in the sandwich: from the bottom, hardcore, sand, DPM, concrete, insulation, screed, floor cover. In total, nearly 500mm in depth. That's just phenomenal. If it were all, miraculously, to turn to jelly, you would be wading about up to your knees in floor. Add in a little re-inforcement in the concrete (not uncommon), maybe some underfloor heating pipes laid on some sort of backing board in the screed, and another plastic DPM layer above the concrete (sometimes specified) and you have a very complex as well as a very thick construction.

The problem from a costing point of view is that the floor finishes are usually considered separately. On top of that, it's also common practice to consider the intermediate layers such as the underfloor heating and the screed in yet another compartment. Yet they are also all related. Ideally, you need to start with your floor finish and work downwards to get your most cost effective floor. But most builders work the other way.

What I am saying is that it's tricky to compare floor costs because you actually want them to do different things. Anyway, I digress. Let's look at the options in a little more detail.

Solid slabs

A solid concrete slab is usually laid 100mm thick over a layer of compacted hardcore. This is the most labour intensive system and, conversely, the cheapest on materials, which

The concept behind the beam and block floor is dead simple. The concrete beams form an upturned 'T' section, enabling the blocks to sit loosely between the beams. This technique was introduced in the 1970s and has been widely taken up across the country. Builders like them because they are quick, dry and relatively easy to use, but they are expensive on smaller footprints, below 100m².

makes it suitable for DIY builders with access to cheap or free labour.

You have a choice of placing the insulation layer – you have to have an insulation layer – either above or below the concrete.

It's sort of conventional to finish a concrete slab floor off with a cement screed on top, laid at a later stage of the build. But there is no requirement to do so and some builders dispense with the screed layer, choosing to get a smooth finish on the concrete using a power floater. There is no reason why you couldn't place your insulation beneath your slab, and sink your underfloor heating pipes (if you want them) into the concrete: it's just that not many people think this far ahead.

Pre-cast flooring

Pre-cast concrete floors are not economic below areas of 50 sq m but become increasingly cost-effective on larger areas. Beam and block has been gaining in popularity with developers since it first appeared in the Seventies, largely because it's fast and largely dry. It's also preferred by the NHBC and building inspectors where you have a large amount of space to fill under the ground floor: if the gap is more than

600mm, they would rather you bridged it than filled it in.

Beam and block floors are provided by specialists who work from drawings supplied. A number of businesses cater for this market and many have links with builder's merchants who act as middlemen; if you want to go direct, try Tarmac Topfloor or Rackhams or Hanson. Note that the infill blocks that are laid between the concrete beams are the same in size and specification as the standard 100 x 225 x 440mm blocks used in wall construction, and you may be able to effect savings if you supply the blocks.

These floors, in common with all suspended ground floors, require venting, which is usually done by providing airbricks in the external walls; indeed the presence or absence of airbricks around the damp-proof course is very often the only clue as to what sort of ground floor a new house has.

Understand also that pre-cast flooring is an engineered solution for each situation. There is very often more than one way to run the beams and you may be able to take advantage of a system like Rackhams 225 beams which can span up to 8 m and can sometimes enable you to do away with sleeper walls within the main floor area.

Another thing to watch out for is the 1:300 camber on these pre-stressed beams. It's surprisingly large: as much as 13mm on a 4 m long beam. If you lay a screed over the floor you can of course get a nice level finish but if you want a dry finish or a floating floor, consider the fact that the floor won't be level.

Also consider lead times. Pre-cast floors need to be manufactured to order and you may well find that you have to wait six to eight weeks for them to be delivered. Not something to decide about on the spur of the moment.

Jet Floor

This is a unique variation on the standard beam and block floor that uses polystyrene infill blocks to fill the voids between the beams. It was developed by a company called Trent in the late Eighties and was for many years a bit of a green curio. But changes to the insulation requirements in 2002 meant that all ground floors have to be heavily insulated and suddenly Jet Floor became a very efficient, cheap and thin way of doing floors. It's a little bit (10 per cent-ish) more expensive to buy than a block infill floor but it does away with an added layer – you can just place a structural screed on top of it. Jet Floor is now part of the Hanson stable.

Jet Floor works fine but it has to have a structural concrete screed placed over it immediately – the polystyrene blocks are not a working platform. The longer spans (over 4.2 m) also require some element of interplay between the concrete and the beams in order to get sufficient strength. This can make it difficult to work with underfloor heating.

Hollow core

Hollow core planks are another form of craned-in precast floor. Instead of concrete beams being laid and infilled with blocks, the whole floor is laid in a series of wide concrete planks – hollowed out to reduce the weight, hence the name. Hollow core is the most expensive of the options but leaves you maximum flexibility:

you don't have to align your bedroom walls above load-bearing walls or supporting beams, you can build anything anywhere. However, the internal walls where the planks meet end to end have to be double thickness in order to bear the weight. It's used more for intermediate floors than ground floors. They are particularly good if you want to cantilever a balcony out from the main support walls.

Timber

Timber ground floors are discriminated against by the NHBC, which insists on there being a concrete capping and damp proof membrane laid over the oversite underneath the suspended floor, which effectively adds around £5 per sq m to the costs. Upstairs, of course, no such extra work applies and here timber joisting is easily the cheapest option.

On the ground floor, timber makes a lot of sense if you want a timber floor cover: you can have an entirely dry construction. Around £10 per sq m– 50 per cent of the cost of a timber ground floor – goes into the sheeting (usually chipboard or plywood) that is laid over the joists and where a plank floor finish is desired this sheeting can be dispensed with. The problem with doing this is that either the planking will be exposed for the duration of construction, which will almost certainly lead to damage, or some form of temporary sheeting will have to be installed, which will cancel out most of the perceived cost advantages. However, the technique works well with reclaimed boards which need to be sanded and sealed and can serve as both temporary and finished floor covering.

Insulation

Underfloor insulation on the ground floor is not quite mandatory but the 2002 changes to the building regs make it expensive to avoid. There are several methods of insulation available, the cheapest and most readily understood being to lay flooring grade expanded polystyrene at 75 or 100mm thickness over the sub-floor and under the

Brinkley's Slope Law

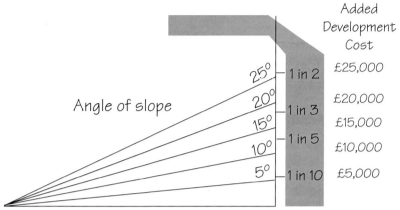

Angle of slope

Added Development Cost

25°	1 in 2	£25,000
20°	1 in 3	£20,000
15°	1 in 5	£15,000
10°	1 in 5	£10,000
5°	1 in 10	£5,000

screed or chipboard. Alternatively, you could opt for the nu-Trenchfloor system being championed by the Readymixed Concrete Bureau – this places the insulation under the concrete slab itself. Or you can use a thinner layer of one of the more efficient insulation boards such as Polyfoam, Kingspan or Celotex.

These techniques of underfloor insulation are relatively new and there are possibly problems building up in the future should the insulation not prove to be as rigid as expected: more cautious builders will continue to use some form of reinforcement in their screeds to counteract any such failures. The really cautious can specify Celcon's Jamera flooring planks which are 250mm deep and don't require any additional insulation to meet the U-value standard of 0.25.

Aficionados of underfloor heating will wonder what all the fuss is about. Such systems only work well with very high levels of underfloor insulation – otherwise much of the heat would be lost – and, whatever problems there may have been with underfloor heating systems, laying insulation under heavy cement screeds does not appear to be one of them.

■*Slopes, bad ground & trees*

If you have worked through the book to this

point from 'Pitfalls' you will have twigged that, though groundworks can work out to be relatively cheap, they can also turn into a budget-crippling nightmare. Whether you have or haven't, the crucial groundworky bits went as follows:

There are three basic causes of alarming cost expansion:
■ slopes
■ bad ground
■ trees.

Slopes

Obviously, it all depends on how much it slopes, but even quite gentle slopes can create havoc with a tight budget. Brinkley's Slope Law states that, no matter how you deal with it, each one degree of slope will add £1,000 to your development costs. Obviously this represents an enormous over-simplification of different situations but you will be disappointed to discover that it rarely works out less than this and sometimes it can be a whole lot more, especially if you are constructing a mansion larger than 200 cu m.

You just can't get away with building a sloping house and so adjustments have to be made between the lie of the land and the lie of your house and these adjustments are expensive. It's not just excavating out the ground so you can build on the level; if the slope is greater than five degrees, there are complications with access roads and pavings, drains, and landscaping. Steeper still and you are likely to require retaining walls and possibly even safety railing. Faced with a sloping site, there are basically three options for the new housebuilder.

Excavate and cart away

Here you dig large, house-sized hole out of your slope, dispose of all the excavations and fit the house into the hole. This is perhaps the simplest and the one that the planners are likely to prefer, as it will keep your roofline low. There will be the cost of excavation and carting away which, depending on the lie of the ground, could easily cost £1,000-£4,000. Add to this the cost of any retaining walls that might have to be built: budget £100 per lin m for a 1 m high retaining wall.

Build out from high point

Here you substitute the cost of excavating with the cost of building supporting walls. There may not be much to choose between the two in cost terms, but this method is likely to leave you with expensive steps to build up to the back/front of the house. The overall structure is also likely to be far more imposing and, consequently, much less likely to pass muster with the planners.

Fit house to slope

Arrange the house as a series of steps, running up the slope. Building basements and/or mezzanine split-levels may well be architecturally the most pleasing but it is also the most expensive. Split-levels have cost implications at almost every stage of the building works: stepped foundations, shuttering for floor slabs, special stair joinery, complex service routes, and complex roof details. Split-level building adds between 10 and 20 per cent to your overall building costs.

Whichever method you choose to overcome the problems set by a sloping site, you will be faced with extra landscaping expenses – steps,

turfed banks, rockeries. Although these costs can generally be deferred over a number of years, they will add significantly (£1,000 plus) to the overall development. The extra thousands might be better spent on building a semi-submerged basement.

Bad ground

A variety of problems are dealt with under the category of bad ground. The commonest are clay soils and the presence of tree roots, but also you must be prepared for bog conditions, mining subsidence, wells, water courses, old factory workings, disused refuse tips, even problems when ancient remains are discovered. It's worth carrying out any amount of detective work to ascertain exactly what has happened on your site because the ramifications can be expensive.

A site appraisal is likely (but not definitely) going to uncover the problems you will meet below ground and your foundation design is almost definitely going to be in the hands of an engineer.

The key to understanding the cost implications of these alternative foundation solutions is to hang on to the ballpark figure that applies to normal foundations. This is currently around £80 per sq m of footprint. By way of example, the footprint on the benchmark house is 146 sq m: this includes the ground covered by the single attached garage and all the ground built over by the house. Its foundations, which are deeper in one corner only, footings and ground floor cost just over £12,000, that's £83 per sq m.

There are three likely solutions to bad ground:
■ deeper foundations (sometimes reinforced with steel)
■ raft foundations
■ piling

Deeper foundations

You will have to excavate to good bearing ground (if it's there). If it's just a question of going down to 2.5 m, you may get away with the regular trenchfill foundation. But this will be expensive; on a four-bedroom house it will add around £3 to the ballpark footprint figure (remember base equals £80 per sq m) for every 100mm deeper you have to dig.

So if, for instance, you were asked to dig foundations 2 m deep all round instead of the standard 1 m deep, it would ratchet your overall footprint costs up from around £80 per sq m footprint to £110 per sq m footprint. Deeper than 2 m, it starts to look like other, engineered systems will save you money – see next items. Trouble is, if you are discovering how bad it all is as you dig, then it's realistically too late to switch to one of the alternative foundations systems.

Clayboards

One technique commonly used in clay areas is to fit a collapsible board against the side of the trench, rather like lining paper on the side of a cake tin. The idea is that clayboard is flexible enough to allow the clay to heave without moving the enclosed concrete foundations. There are a number of dedicated products available for this application; the two best known are Claymaster which is made of polystyrene and Clayboard which uses a honeycomb filler very similar to that used in moulded doors.

Rafts

On a problem-free site, the floor slab is laid a couple of stages further on than the foundations. However, with rafts, you pour the foundation concrete together with the floor slab concrete in one operation. With various cambered design profiles and a whole mass of steel reinforcement, you create a concrete raft, which will move as one. If subsidence occurs, the raft will absorb the changes without imposing extra strains on the superstructure above.

A raft foundation uses vast amounts of concrete and steel and, if one had been specified for the benchmark house and garage, it would have cost as much as £20,000 giving an unit cost of around £135 per sq m footprint.

Piling

Reckoned to be cost effective in situations where foundations would otherwise have to

concrete piles are sunk into the ground, often several metres deep

be deeper than 2 m. The number of piles and the depth of each pile can only be determined by a test pile being dug (budget £300), but a typical installation would place piles 2.5m apart under every load-bearing wall (including detached garages) and each pile would go down till solid ground was reached. All the piles are then filled with concrete and tied together with a concrete ground beam, which would be all that you would eventually see of the operation, and would look much like a regular trenchfill concrete foundation. Budget prices are £30 per metre depth for individual piles (depth anywhere from 3-10 m) and £60 per lin m for ground beams. A 5 m depth piled foundation for the benchmark house and garage would cost around £20,000, around £8,000 more than standard footings or trenchfill on a non-problem site.

There are various other techniques which can be used as an alternative to concrete piling or reinforced rafts but these are really the province of the specialist engineer. One interesting

concrete raft extends under the entire building, acting as both a wall foundation and a floor slab

option is Abbey Pynford's Housedeck, which is designed to be cost effective for single house developments; it's actually a floating or suspended raft, which gives you a well-insulated slab. Housedeck will typically cost between £15,000 and £25,000 for a 150 sq m footprint. Abbey Pynford's Phil Jones commented to me: 'Our unit area rate gets to site whilst construction is underway but you have to do a bit of construction work first to create a suitable housing for it.

Gas

If you have a mains gas supply to lay, then you are usually best advised to install ducting (available free from British Gas) at the groundworks stage. You are conventionally aiming to get from the gas main to an external meter box, which you can place pretty much where you please. British Gas supply a semi-concealed meter box that is mostly buried in the ground and is much less obtrusive than the wall boxes. The incoming gas service pipe, which connects the gas main with your meter, should be buried at least 375mm below ground level.

Telecoms, cable

Both BT and the cable companies will supply plastic ducting for free. The BT supply may be overhead, in which case, you needn't trouble yourself with underground routes. My local cable company will supply ducting for their service even in areas that may not receive a supply for many years to come. The routes and the depths of these runs are up to you though note that they prefer their lines to come out of the ground on the outside wall of the house, rather than inside.

Mains water, electricity, gas and telecoms are often laid in ducting, which is laid across the site during the drain-laying excavations. The water company will want to inspect the ducting but the other services will let you fend for yourself, so you need to know exactly where you want them to run. Industry standards are to set electricity and gas mains at least 450mm below ground level.

Infrastructure charge

First introduced in England and Wales in 1990 to help pay for environmental improvements, these charges are raised by the local water companies and are additional to their already high connection fees. The infrastructure charge

is nothing more or less than a tax on new building. It's applied to every new dwelling created – including flats converted from existing houses – and it is applied at exactly the same level regardless of the size of the dwelling.

Until 1994, water companies were free to set their own charges and – surprise, surprise – they tended to charge the earth (often over £1,500) but then OFWAT, the water regulator, stepped in and set a ceiling for the infrastructure charges (£245 for water and an additional £245 for mains drainage connections in 2003). In Scotland and N Ireland the situation is very different; there the water industry is still publicly owned and infrastructure charges are unheard of.

Despite OFWAT's success in limiting the scale of these charges, this sort of backdoor tax (which loses few votes) is probably the coming thing and expect other similar charges to appear over the coming few years. In America they are called impact fees and they get levied not just by utility companies but also by the local councils as well to pay for such things as roads, schools, etc. which the new development is deemed to need.

Drains

First things first: it is important to understand the difference between foulwater and rainwater.
■ Foulwater is the waste generated by normal household usage – flushing loos, emptying baths and sinks, washing machines, dishwashers, etc. Foulwater is sometimes subdivided as black water (toilets) and grey water (most other outlets).
■ Rainwater, as its name suggests, is what falls out of the sky and flows down the gutters and downpipes from off the roof.

Generally our sewage systems are working at near capacity levels and therefore it is a standard requirement that rainwater is not added to the load. Hence it is normal to lay two separate drain systems to dispose of their respective wastes in different ways. In certain locations it may be possible to run rainwater into the main

Ballpark costs for drains - costs per metre run							
	Pipe & Fittings	Excavation	Accessories	Mats	Time in mins	Lab @ £18/hr	Combined
Foul Drain Runs	£ 12	£ 4	£ 2	£ 18	80	£ 24	£ 42
Rainwater Drain Runs	£ 12	£ 4	£ 2	£ 18	60	£ 18	£ 36
Service Trenching		£ 4		£ 4	40	£ 12	£ 16

sewerage system (refer to your water company) but it would be unwise to assume that this is the case. You will need to prove that there is no alternative.

Our benchmark house has its foul drains running into the village main drains; its rainwater drains collect in a soakaway at the back of the house. This is the usual arrangement for UK housing.

Rainwater drains typically cost more to install than foulwater drains. Bear in mind that there are downpipes at every corner of the house and this contributes to some very long drain runs.

When planning rainwater drains it is sometimes possible to replace a relatively expensive underground drain run with a relatively cheap gutter run overhead. Alternatively, you can sometimes use a larger size of guttering, which will enable you to cut down on the number of downpipes and therefore the length of rainwater drains. But I digress; this stuff really belongs in the section on rainwater – see Chapter 7 'Superstructure.'

Where to?

In assessing the likely costs of any individual scheme there is one overriding question that must be answered at the outset. That is, 'Where the hell am I going to dump all this crap?' There are other questions as well, notably: 'How do I get it there?' but 'Where to?' is the 'big one'. So, though it may seem illogical to start at the end, we'll look at the drainage options this way around.

All these dumping options are extremely variable from case to case. The tables indicate ballpark figures for many options but – I can't emphasise enough – you would be wise not to set too much store by these figures as they can often prove to be higher.

Key Element Costs for Drainage	
Road Openings	£ 300- £4,000
Septic Tanks	£ 500
Mini Treatment Works	£ 3,500
Cesspools	£ 2,500
Soakaways	£ 50
Storm Drain Connections	£ 200
Main Drain Interceptors	£ 200

Running into the main drains

Even a relatively simple mains drainage connection can be an expensive business. In England and Wales, you'll have to pay a sewage infrastructure charge – currently £245 – from which off-mains disposal is exempt. Locating main drains can be a problem; what records exist are held by the water companies and, whilst access is open to all, accuracy is not guaranteed.

The amount of work in excavating and connecting to the main drain (usually referred to as 'doing a road opening') can vary enormously depending on the depth of the drain, whether there are vacant junctions (known as laterals) already present to connect on to, the presence/absence of other utilities, and the attitudes and charges of local authorities and water companies.

To open a public highway, you must contact the council highways department in order to purchase a road-opening permit (prices start from £300). Inspections of the opening and connection need to be carried out by a) your water company, b) your own building inspector and c) the council highways department, who inspect no less than five times to ensure the surface reinstatement is in order. A busy road may require traffic lights and if your main drain runs under the other side of the road, the whole process becomes very much more complicated.

The water company is going to insist that you employ a competent groundworker to make the connection and therefore it is a sensible idea to get some quotes for this work before proceeding.

Backdrop manholes

It is much cheaper, easier and safer to lay house drains at depths of between 600 and 1200mm below ground level. Normally, drains are best laid at gentle falls (around 1:80) and sharp inclines are discouraged. If your main drain level is way beneath your optimum house drain level, you will probably find it easiest to construct a backdrop manhole near your boundary line (cost £200-£400). A backdrop manhole works a bit like a waterfall: it's a sudden drop from one level to another and it requires special construction methods and access arrangements.

Pumps

If your main road drain is higher than your house drains you have the option of pumping the waste up hill. This is often done by building in a tank of some description, similar to a small septic tank (say, 2m deep and 1m in diameter) into which the house drains run, and fitting either a solid handling pump or a macerator or grinder pump. The macerator pump is the more expensive but allows the waste to be expelled in a 32 or 50mm pipe, which makes it a better bet for long distances. A control panel is placed somewhere indoors or in a weatherproof casing.

Expensive though a pump is, it can be cost effective to install one when the main drain connection is further than 300m away, even if it is downhill. This is because it can pump out into a small bore pipe that can be laid in a flat trench, much reducing excavation costs. On the other hand, any system that works by gravity alone is ultimately preferable because it isn't going to break down.

Budget between £2,000 and £4,000 for making a road opening and maybe a further £3,000 if you need a pumping station.

Occasionally road openings can be done for less but don't count on it. However if your costs look like being any higher than this you should start to look at an off-mains drainage solution.

Off-mains drainage

The simplest and the cheapest off-mains solution is usually to install a septic tank. It's a tried and tested method and there are millions of them in operation, dotted around the countryside. A septic tank is one of the simpler concepts to understand in the field of sewage treatment: it is an underground chamber (traditionally constructed of brick, more recently from concrete or GRP), into which your foul waste system empties. The septic tank first separates the solids from the liquids before carrying out a limited amount of bacterial treatment on the liquids that form by far the greater part of the waste. The solids collect at the bottom of the tank and need to be pumped out, usually annually, but the liquid (or liquor as it gets called in these circles) passes out of the septic tank to end up, conventionally, in a series of linear soakaways – called a leaching field – located downstream from the tank, probably underneath your lawn. Here the liquor soaks away into the subsoil. As waste water enters on one side of the tank, the semi-treated liquor overflows on the other side. There is no power needed, there are no moving parts and, as long as the solids at the bottom of the tank are regularly pumped out (or desludged), then the septic tank should give decades of trouble-free service.

The cost of the tanks varies depending on the volumes they are designed to deal with but single household units are often priced between £400 and £600. Added to this is the cost of the groundworkers installing the tanks (often around £1,500) and the cost of excavating and installing a herringbone soakaway system – again depending on the volumes to be dealt with and also ground porosity. It would be wise to budget £3,000 to £5,000 for a new septic tank system.

However, in order to be able to install a septic

Benchmark House - Drainage and Services Costs

		Rate	Cost	Mats	Lab	Plant
Foul Drains	40 m	£ 42	£ 1,680	£ 720	£ 480	£ 480
Rainwater Drains	60 m	£ 36	£ 2,160	£ 1,080	£ 540	£ 540
Service Trenching	25 m	£ 16	£ 400	£ 100	£ 150	£ 150
Road Opening	Shared and simple		£ 300			£ 300
		Total	**£ 4,540**	**£ 1,900**	**£ 1,170**	**£ 1,470**

Service Connection Costs	
Electrics	£ 1,100
Water (inc infrastructure charge)	£ 700
Total	**£ 1,800**

tank, you need to convince your building inspector that the ground on which you are building is capable of actually absorbing the liquor and this you attempt to do by undertaking a porosity test, sometimes known as a percolation test. Carrying out such a test couldn't be simpler. You dig a hole in the ground, you fill it with water once and let it soak away: you fill it with water again and this second time you stand there with a stopwatch and note how long the water takes to drain away. The quicker it drains away, the more porous your subsoil. The length and complexity of your leaching field is determined by the time the water in the hole takes to soak away. If the water level takes longer than 15 minutes to fall 25 , then you have a problem: your building inspector will tell you your subsoil is officially non-porous and you have to find some other method of disposing of the liquor.

This is where the Environment Agencies step in. For in most circumstances, especially if the ground is non-porous, there will be a ditch, a stream or a burn within striking distance of your property and if you clean your liquor to a higher standard than that achieved by a septic tank – which means using one of the systems described below – then you will be allowed to discharge it into this water course. But in order to do this, you need to apply for a Consent to Discharge.

Consent to Discharge

In England and Wales, sewage disposal comes under the aegis of the Environment Agency:

national number 08459 333111 – should be the only contact number you need but paperwork is done via local offices, listed in phone books under Environment Agency. A Consent to Discharge currently costs £103 (no VAT) if the plant is outputting less than 5 cu m per day – a typical single household discharges between 0.5 and 1 cu m per day so virtually all single households will discharge less than this amount. It can take up to four months to get an approval. You can start to install the plant but you can't discharge from it until you have the consent.

In Scotland, you need to contact the Scottish Environmental Protection Agency (SEPA) and in N Ireland it's the Environment Heritage Service. If you can't get away with a septic tank or don't have a water course to discharge into then your options are limited to having a cesspool.

Cesspools

Sometimes confused with septic tanks, a cesspool is different because there is no outflow at all. Everything that empties into your cesspool has to be pumped out and removed from site. Whereas a septic tank or a treatment plant need be desludged perhaps once a year, a cesspool is likely to fill up every few weeks: tank desludging usually costs between £50 and £80 a time, so you can see that a cesspool is very expensive to keep on top of. They are also traditionally rather larger than septic tanks or treatment plants so that their installation cost is also pretty high. A cesspool is the option of last resort, only to be specified if every other avenue is closed. And the cesspool is not acceptable at all in Scotland.

Package treatment plants

If you can obtain consent, then the normal

The advent of plastic pipes has made laying drains easier. Pre-formed inspection pits have a number of outlets: use the ones you want and block off the others. Laying in pea gravel helps protect the pipes. Building inspectors will usually want to have sight at this stage

can be run off into a nearby watercourse – in contrast, the outflow from a simple septic tank is unlikely to meet the required standards. In effect, a package treatment plant works rather like a super-charged septic tank and the outflow is measurably cleaner.

The simpler plants use little more than an air pump whilst the unique Klargester Biodisc is designed around a series of rotating metal discs. And there is one, the Bio Bubble, which acts like a super-super-charged septic tank and eats the solids as well as the liquor and therefore doesn't need any desludging.

What they all have in common is that they consume a certain amount of electrical power in order to work. This means that they also need looking after, to a much greater extent than a simple septic tank. Consequently, all the package treatment plant suppliers offer annual service contracts – indeed in order to obtain a Consent to Discharge into a watercourse, you have to sign a declaration confirming that you will pay annual charges. The cost of these service contracts vary between suppliers and also vary by region so it is important to be aware of these charges when comparing systems.

Typical service contracts are currently costing between £80 and £150 per annum – though note that these do not include desludging costs, which are paid to the local council to remove solid wastes.

Not everyone will be installing an entirely new drainage system. Repairing or upgrading an existing septic tank is a commonly met problem. Many of the existing septic tank systems have been around for a long time and have been either poorly maintained or just become saturated – often the ground soakaway drains become blocked and the effluent going into the tank just backs up as if it was a cesspool. In situations like this it may be possible to reuse part of the old system – typically the original tank – and to bolt-on a smaller treatment plant downstream. If you have an existing septic tank that's not functioning as well as it should, then don't automatically assume that the whole system has to be replaced.

course of action is to install a small sewage treatment plant. There are around twenty businesses in the UK producing such plants suitable for single dwellings and they employ a wide variety of different technologies to achieve their aims. What they all have in common is that they are all designed to treat your foul waste to such an extent that you will be able to obtain a Consent to Discharge, so that the outflow

Alternative options

There is a growing interest in alternative forms of sewage disposal. Some of these are seen as being greener than the conventional methods but it's a tag that many of the alternative practitioners themselves are reluctant to emphasise: most readily admit that there is a time and place for almost all the sewage systems on the market and it is often stretching things a bit far to make out a case that any one system is greener than another.

The best known of the alternative disposal systems is the use of reed beds (aka Constructed Wetland Sewage Systems). A reed bed system can be used to upgrade the effluent coming out of a tank so that it meets the same discharge standards as a package treatment plant and can, therefore, be discharged into a watercourse. Although it sounds very organic and natural, successful reed bed drainage involves a surprising amount of construction and no way is this a cheap option – installation costs are similar to a package treatment plant and you require an area the size of half a tennis court. And like a septic tank or package treatment plant, you still have to pump out the solids, which are collected in a primary settlement tank. Reed beds also require some weekly maintenance so they tend to attract enthusiasts rather than the fit-and-forget brigade.

Reed bed treatment is well accepted as a sewage treatment method and is now being specified on a large scale by some of our water companies. There are however other options, including the use of dry composting toilets. Increasingly, selfbuilders are turning their attention to the whole picture of water and waste management and seeking to combine aspects such as rainwater harvesting and grey water recycling with efficient treatment of sewage waste.

Normally it is a principle of all foulwater drainage systems that rainwater should be disposed of separately: the problem being that whereas most sewage digestion systems need a steady supply of blackwater to keep working smoothly, rainfall has a habit of arriving in large quantities which can disrupt the workings of the sewage systems. However, if rainwater is being collected separately, it is usually used to flush toilets and this way the two systems can be effectively combined at one stage removed.

Siting of tanks

Any off-mains drainage system that uses a tank which needs desludging (and that includes most of the options) has to consider tanker access – 30m is reckoned to be the limit that a tanker's hose can extend to. In Scotland, tanks must be a minimum of 15m from the house. No minimum exists in England and Wales but if you have a sensitive nose you would do well to stick to the Scottish standards.

Rainwater disposal
Soakaways

The normal destination of rainwater is a simple soakaway that is nothing more than a 1m deep hole in the ground, usually filled with free draining hardcore or brick rubble. Soakaways are conventionally sited 5m away from buildings, but the building inspector must be convinced that the water will percolate away. In heavy clay soils, for instance, a soakaway may not be appropriate and you may have to look at other ways of disposing of rainwater. Budget £50 if machine dug, £75 if hand dug.

Storm drains

Common in urban areas, rare in the country, they are actually designed to stop the roads flooding, but can sometimes be used for house rainwater. Budget £300 to make a connection to a storm drain. Storm drains are often over 100 years old and in a poor state of repair, and locating them can be a hit and miss affair. Typically, they are managed by the highways department of the local council (rather than the local water company) and they often flatly refuse to accept any additional rainwater discharge, even when it is obviously the best option. If you have well-honed negotiating skills, here's a good place to use them.

Eight drain tips

The plans need...

Drawings and specifications should include drain layout, invert levels (depths), junctions, inspection chambers and access (rodding) points.

Plastic or clay?

Although the trade is still split between using clay and plastic (uPVC) drainage, someone new to the game would do well to use plastic. There is little to choose between the systems on price but the plastic systems are more user-friendly. There are six major players in this field and, underground at least, there is little to choose between them on quality or price. Osma are the market leaders and their installation guide tells you much of what you need to know about laying drains. They do a free (but slow) design service but you must know your main drain invert (drain depth) levels for it to be worthwhile.

Buying plastic pipe

Plastic pipe is sold with heavy discounts off list price. A new house project should be able to get discounts of 30-40 per cent. All the manufacturers produce guttering and internal waste fittings as well and, if you combine your order, you will have more muscle to negotiate better discounts.

Excavation of trenches

Drain trenches are normally 450 mm wide (the width of a digger's narrow bucket). If drains are to run parallel and close to wall foundation trenches, then you will be doing yourself a favour if you can set the drains higher than the concrete in the adjacent trench – NB this won't work with trenchfilled foundations. Where this is not possible, drains will have to be concreted-in, whereas they are normally just bedded in pea shingle.

Drain sizes and depths

100 mm drain (the standard) is going to be adequate for all situations where there are less than five loos. There is no set depth, but less than 600 mm and you may have to cover the pipe with paving slabs, deeper than 1200 mm and you will have problems working. The optimum fall is 1:80 which is equivalent to 250 mm on a 20 m run. If you have to cope with gradients much steeper than this then take specialist advice, don't assume that drains will work just because they are going downhill.

Pea shingle

Plastic pipe should be bedded on pea shingle, which is a particularly fine grade of gravel. Allow one ton of pea shingle (cost £6-£15 per ton) for every 8 lin m of drain. When calculating excavation quantities, allow for 80 per cent of excavated material to go back into the trenches once the pipes are laid.

Rodding access

It is good practice not to have to rod from inside the house, so try to give every waste point a direct run to a manhole rather than joining drain runs together under the house in the assumption that they can be rodded from above.

Drains under driveways

Plastic drains are prone to deformation if loads are placed upon them. They therefore require more protection than clay drains. This becomes an issue if you are laying drains under roads or drives: anything less than 900 mm deep will require some form of concrete capping over the drain. Allow £5 per lin m extra for this, but note that it is a very useful place for excess Readymix to be dumped, which can effectively reduce price to near zero.

Rainwater into main drains

Attitudes to this vary from area to area, but nowhere is it encouraged. But when soakaways and storm drains are impracticable, this course will often be accepted as a last resort. There must be an interceptor between the two drain systems to prevent unpleasant pongs coming back up the rainwater gullies.

Rainwater harvesting

The sensible Germans have practised the art of saving rainwater for household use (rather than just spraying on the garden via a water butt). There are now a handful of businesses in the UK selling (mostly German) gear with which you can filter, collect and pump rainwater around the house for flushing loos. More information can be found on this in Chapter 10 'Green issues'.

Routes

This is the other major decision to be made when looking at drain runs. The idea is to get from the house to the final dumping point with as few bends as possible. Drains have a tendency to get blocked, so access is important at all but the gentlest bends, and access is expensive.

Ballpark drain run costs

Straight 110mm plastic drain runs can be machine excavated (to average depths), laid and buried for around £15 per lin m. The building inspector may allow you to have a few gentle radius bends on your drain runs, provided they don't prevent rodding — that is clearing future blockages with drain rods — but generally the accepted practice is to have access to the drains every time there is a bend. The addition of inspection chambers, gullies, rodding access, etc. ('fittings') more than doubles the basic metre rate for drain laying to between £25 and £40 per lin m — the cost of one manhole is equivalent to 10 lin m of straight drains. So the general idea is to plan your drain runs with as few bends as possible.

Chapter 7
Superstructure

▉Introduction

Superstructure is a long and pretentious word and I would like to use some funky Anglo-Saxon alternative, altogether more down-to-earth. Trouble is, I don't know one. Some use the term shell – as in 'Putting up the Shell' – and perhaps this isn't bad, especially if you think of it in terms of sea shells, not egg shells. But, to confuse matters, the outer walls that make up the shell get referred to as skins or, sometimes, leaves; one suggests bodies, the other trees, neither eggs nor sea creatures. It all seems a bit of a mess; hence I'll stick with the term Superstructure.

Definition? Well you have hopefully figured it out by now – it's all the above ground bits of a house up to but excluding the finishes and the wiring and piping. Literally, the super (i.e. above) structure as opposed to the sub (i.e. below or under) structure. So in Superstructure we'll look at walls (as in inner and outer skins),

external doors and windows, roofs and all the fiddly bits that hold them together. Floors? The ground floor details are in the previous chapter, the first floor and above – known as intermediate floors – are buried in this chapter. If you buy a timber frame house kit, it's the superstructure that you are getting. Or at least part of the superstructure. The roof covers and the external wall finishes are left to you to sort out, along with the substructural works and the finishes.

▉The Inner Skin

The inner skin refers to the structural, load-bearing part of the external walls. For many years that was just about all there was to it, but these days the requirements for insulation have made the decision of just how best to build the inner skin a complex and involved

Inner Skin: Key sq m Costs

Masonry Materials	Basic Mats	Accessories (inc mortar)	Time taken in mins	Labour at £18.00/hr	Combined
Celcon 100mm blocks	£ 6.70	£ 0.70	35	£ 10.50	£ 17.90
Hemelite blocks	£ 5.00	£ 0.70	35	£ 10.50	£ 16.20
Thin-Joint Blocks	£ 6.70	£ 2.30	25	£ 7.50	£ 16.50
Timber Frame					
47x90mm Frame	£ 3.00	£ 4.20	50	£ 15.00	£ 22.20
47x140mm Frame	£ 4.50	£ 4.20	50	£ 15.00	£ 23.70

Timber frame is costed as if it was being built on site, which it rarely is in the UK. Normally it's created in a factory and erected on site, a much quicker process. Also note that though timber frame external walls are more expensive than masonry ones, the reverse is true on internal walls. Overall, there is very little difference in cost between the two main walling systems.

Inner Skin: Benchmark House Example

Inner Skin Area - minus joinery openings	191m²	
Celcon Blocks laid in mortar	£ 7.40m²	£ 1,400
Inner Skin Area - measured straight through openings	243m²	
Blocklaying price based on above	£ 10.50m²	£ 2,600
Total		**£ 4,000**
Switch to 90mm Timber Frame		£ 4,250
Switch to 140mm Timber Frame		£ 4,600

The other thing to pick up here is the brickies' cute habit of measuring their work straight through joinery openings. The logic is that they spend time fixing joinery, not charged elsewhere. But the overall effect is to make blockwork more expensive than its headline rate suggests.

subject. Our benchmark house is built in brick and blockwork, the traditional and commonest form of house construction in England, Wales and Ireland; it is well understood and relatively cheap to construct and its only serious challenge, at least on single house sites, comes from timber frame.

Cavities

The practice of building two separate walls separated by a cavity became widespread in the Thirties. It came about because it enabled builders to incorporate large format concrete blocks – only then becoming widely available – into house walls whilst retaining a brick skin on the outside. Prior to this, brick walls had been built nine inches thick (i.e. a double skin of bricks), which was both slower and more expensive.

The cavity was advertised as being an 'improvement' in house construction because it introduced a barrier across which rain supposedly couldn't jump. But rain often does find a route across cavities: they are very difficult to build well, easy to get wrong. For along with cavity walls came brick ties (to knit the inner and outer walls together), returns

(for joinery to sit in) and cavity trays (to divert water trickling down the inner skin across to the outer skin). Cavities had a nasty habit of filling up with bits of crud, or snots as they are lovingly referred to, which would cling to the ties and form tracks for the water to cross the cavity. As regards protecting the house from water damage, cavity walls are only marginally better than solid walls.

In the Eighties, we started to become concerned about heat loss through walls and builders began to put insulation into the cavities. Now you might think that these two alternative uses for a cavity – i.e. to stop water going one way and heat the other – are completely at odds with one another and, essentially, you'd be dead right. Yet, bit by bit, builders are learning that insulation and cavities are not an impossible marriage and many builders are now enthusiastically stuffing their cavities with all manner of insulants without suffering horrendous damp penetration problems. But an even greater number of housebuilders continued to build homes with empty cavities; up till 2002, over half of all new homes in Britain were built this way – i.e. with no insulation in the cavity.

Steel Lintels – Key Rates

- Convention is that they need 150mm bearing at each end
- Thus 1200mm wide window requires 1500mm lintel
- These costs are averages per metre run

Regular Type	£ 14 per metre run
Heavy Duty	£ 18 per metre run
Regular with Wide Inner Leaf	£ 20 per metre run
Heavy Duty With Wide Inner Leaf	£ 32 per metre run
Box Type (internal)	£ 10 per metre run
Timber Frame Type	£ 6 per metre run

Lintel Costs on Benchmark House

	No	Total length	Cost
External - Heavy Duty	15	27.6m	£ 500
External - Regular	5	7.65m	£ 150
Internal	6	6.8m	£ 220
		Total	**£ 870**

No labour cost - inc. in blockwork

Lintels and Wall Ties

Cavity walls need to be knitted together. And the openings in them need to be bridged. And the bases of them need protection against rising damp. All told there are a number of things you have to think about when you build a cavity wall. The knitting is done with wall ties. Conventionally galvanised steel, in a figure of eight shape, these need to be placed in regular patterns, dictated by the building regs. Lintels are now conventionally steel and need to bear at least 150mm at either end of the openings they bridge. You also have to consider how water will behave inside a cavity: it has a tendency to funnel across to the inner skin so you have to take great care to ensure that any water trickling down the inner face of the cavity has to be directed outwards at openings. There are a number of companies producing cavity tray products designed to keep cavities dry, a very specialised niche within the building trade.

Blocks

In many countries blocks are manufactured with feature finishes and are used extensively, instead of bricks or stone, as external wall finishes in their own right. But in Britain this hasn't proved to be a popular technique, except where cheaper substitutes for stone are sought.

So when we look at building blocks we are analysing how well they perform structurally, not how good they look.

Block Strength

Block strength is calculated in Newton per sq mm, known in the trade as 'Newtons' or just plain 'N'. Roughly speaking the more cement in the block, the higher the strength (or the more Newtons it is said to have). Most blocks qualify for the basic 3.5N strength, though some applications require 7N blocks (i.e. below ground and, some say, floor blocks). You will find a number of utility blocks on the market, often at a price less than £5.00 per sq m, but their strength is not guaranteed. Having said that, there aren't many applications in housebuilding that call for extra-strength blocks.

Block Types

There are many shapes and sizes of block made but there is an industry standard, which is 440mm by 215mm. This is the equivalent of six standard bricks and you need 10 of these blocks to build a square metre of wall: they are conventionally bought by the square metre – a ten-pack. They are usually 100mm thick, though some of the super-lightweight varieties are thicker in order to get their insulation values up to par.

The Dense Block

Uncomfortably heavy to lift, they are usually used below ground, often at 7N strength. Cheap – full loads cost just around £5.00 per sq m. Have done for years, in fact.

Lightweight Clinker Blocks

Almost half the weight of a dense block, these are often used on the inner leaf of insulated cavities and in partition walls. They provide an excellent keying surface for plasters. They are also widely used in beam-and-block flooring; they are very similarly priced to dense blocks.

Aerated Blocks

Introduced from Scandinavia in the Sixties,

The Empty Cavity struggles to get a U value below 0.6. Since U values were tightened in 2002 it's history

Cavity Fill Insulation: U values are low but there is effectively no cavity to prevent damp penetration

Partial Cavity Fill: insulation is pinned against the outer face of the inner skin

Insulated Dry Lining: used on conversions and renovations but rare on new builds

Timber Frame: the insulation fills the void between the timber studs, which is easy, plus you still get an empty cavity

these blocks have become a huge hit in the UK market and more than 70 per cent of new homes use them somewhere. This includes our benchmark house, which uses these blocks on its inner skin only. There are three manufacturers, Celcon, Thermalite and Tarmac, who bought the fourth, Durox which is still obtainable as a separate brand. Their big plus was that they packed enough insulating properties into them to allow builders to carry on with empty cavities.

Aerated blocks met all the thermal requirements thrown at them until 2002, when the newly revised Part L of the Building Regulations began calling for U-values of 0.35. At this level, aerated blocks struggle without

some additional insulation. However, the superior insulating value of aircrete still allows you to build with less insulation in the cavity: maybe just 10mm less but that still leaves you with a narrower cavity and hence a bigger house.

Brickies love aircrete blocks because they are light and easy to cut. Plasterers are not quite so fond of them: they have a reputation for causing cracking. This is one of the reasons for the rapid uptake of plasterboard stuck onto walls (dot and dab), taking over from the old wet plastering routines.

Trade Rates
An all-in rate of between £10 and £12 per sq m for laying blocks is OK, depending on area. All-in rate means that your brickies would fix wall ties, cavity wall insulation, joinery, lintels, airbricks, DPCs, etc. as they go, but excludes the cost of laying an outer skin, which likely as not will be in a different material.

Using an all-in rate saves the hassle of measuring non-standard runs like chimneys. A two-and-one gang should be able to lay between 30 and 40 sq m of blocks in a day. Combined with the cost of blocks and mortar, it creates an inner skin walling cost of around £20 per sq m, against which all other options have to be compared. Note that when working on measured rates, brickies conventionally treat joinery openings as if they were part of their work (which arguably they are, as they fit the joinery as they go). This makes a considerable difference to overall costs, as highlighted in the Inner Skin table.

Insulation
The preferred way for the majority of English builders to knock-out the inner skin/cavity detail up till 2002 was to use an aircrete block and an empty cavity. That all changed with the introduction of the new thermal standards in 2002. Just how builders choose to achieve the new U-value standards will appear in due course but if they stick to blockwork as the preferred material for inner skins, they are

confronted with four basic options: fill the cavity with insulation, put insulation in the cavity but leave a gap (known as partial fill), insulate on the inside of the wall or on the outside of the outer wall.

Cavity fill insulation

This is both cheap and easy to do – but you do lose your empty cavity. Cavity batts designed to completely fill the void between the walls – known as Full Fill – are invariably made out of one of the woolly insulators such as glass fibre or mineral wool; these are 'wicked' (rhymes with licked) to stay rigid and are cut to fit in around cavity ties. An alternative would be to blow the insulation (either polystyrene beads or glass fibre) into the cavity after construction. Cavity fill is only acceptable in the more sheltered parts of the country: in the rainswept west, you have to maintain a 50mm air gap in the cavity. In other words, you look for a partially filled cavity solution…

Partial fill

Most of the regular insulation materials are available in formats designed to partially fill the cavity. Despite making special 'retaining' wall ties being available (which, at 25p each, actually cost more than the insulation), the wet Tuesday in February syndrome means that it is often extremely difficult for brickies to maintain a partially clear cavity. If you want a decent amount of insulation plus a 50mm cavity, your overall wall thickness is starting to blow up to 300mm plus, and this starts to eat a significant chunk out of your internal floor area.

Insulated dry lining

This method involves using either plasterboard laminated to insulation and sticking the whole thing on the room side (i.e. inside) of the inner skin wall. Or, more frequently, insulation fixed to the wall with battens onto which the plasterboard is fixed. The insulation value depends on the choice and depth of insulation. Although it gets around the problem of having to partially fill the cavity wall, it leaves

a number of cold bridges between floors and where internal walls meet external walls and this makes it hard to meet the 0.35 U-value rating required for walls (let alone the 0.3 in Scotland). It's often used in renovations where you don't want to disturb the outer wall but it's not common in newbuild.

External insulation

Also rarely used in new build, but there is nothing to stop you placing insulation on the outside of your walls and finishing off with a waterproof render. It's really only a common practice when renovating or upgrading existing structures which either don't have a cavity or have reason not to insulate the inside. It actually works pretty well in that you make the whole structure inherently warm.

Timber Frame

Tinkering around with where you put the insulation in relation to the blockwork is all very well but there is a mainstream alternative that enables you to place the insulation inside

Key elements of a timber frame wall

polythene vapour barrier

90mm timber stud

plywood sheathing

breather paper

Buy a timber frame kit from any UK manufacturer and this is essentially what you are getting – the superstructure. This lot will have taken around four days to erect

the wall which is, in many ways, the most elegant solution. We are of course talking timber frame here. Timber frame housebuilding is very common in other parts of the world, notably North America and Scandinavia, and is currently in a period of sustained growth in Britain and Ireland. More than 60 per cent of houses built in Scotland are timber frame and over the UK as a whole it has breached the ten per cent mark, many of these being selfbuilds. However, switching to timber frame requires a much greater leap of the imagination than just juggling figures. It doesn't have to be built off-site – but it usually is – and it involves different skills and expertise which tend to mark timber framers out as a race apart. Even the follow-on trades (plumbers, electricians, kitchen fitters, second-fix carpenters) have to rethink the way they go about things when the walls are made of studwork and the first floor is a structural element holding the whole building together. Lintel and wall ties change, and allowances for differential movement between brickwork outer skins and timber frames have to be built-in.

Whilst timber frame internal walls are cheaper to build than blockwork ones (£12 per sq m as against £15 per sq m), when these walls become external and structural, as required for timber framing, they become slightly more expensive because they usually have structural

sheathing, breather paper and vapour barriers added; these combined nearly double the cost of the basic studwork. The benchmark house has an external wall area of 190 sq m and an internal wall area of around 144 sq m. On current trade rates, the total cost of building the walls would have been around £7,000 by either route.

Such sums are almost entirely hypothetical because what would actually happen is that the basic structure of a timber frame house would be made off-site and delivered as one. There are a number of companies that perform this service, converting plans for brick and block houses into plans for timber frame houses and then quoting for manufacture and erection. Factory prefabrication is, however, relatively expensive and you would expect to pay between £2,000 and £5,000 more for such a service. So on a straight labour and materials basis timber frame looks more expensive than blockwork built on site but, timber framers would argue, you get a number of advantages for taking the process off site. Not only is the erection process much quicker, but you get a structure that is more likely to be square, plumb and level and this in turn means you will spend less time on finishing details such as flooring, roofing and fitting doors, kitchen units and cupboards.

Many timber frame firms will convert

drawings as part of their quotation. The best known name in England and Wales doing this service is Taylor Lane, based in Hereford but operating across the country. In Scotland, there are dozens of companies who supply whole house packages either working to their own designs or adapting others. In fact almost any timber frame company (there are currently around 70) will offer to convert a masonry designed house into a timber one. Check the selfbuild press for more contacts.

Other Differences

■ Wall ties: brickwork built against a timber frame background requires a different shape of wall tie and slightly more of them. They are more expensive to buy than blockwork wall ties (£25 for 100 instead of £10 for 100) but overall the difference in cost is negligible. Our benchmark house required around 750 wall ties: the difference in cost would be around £150.

■ Brickwork built against a timber background also requires a different shape of lintel over windows and doors. Here the timber framers win out because the special timber frame lintels are half the price. The benchmark house used £900 of steel lintels. Had it been built using timber frame, this figure would have fallen to under £400.

■ Where timber frame really wins out is when you choose to abandon brickwork or any other form of heavy, foundation-bearing, outer skin. If you opt for a lightweight cladding, such as timber boarding, tile hanging or render on a metal mesh backing, then you save a considerable amount of money in not having to construct an outer skin to hang them off.

■ Timber frame also gives you a narrow wall profile. This is because the insulation is mostly placed inside the timber wall panels, whereas with blockwork construction, the insulation is usually placed within the cavity, which adds to the cavity width. Timber frame houses require just a 50mm cavity if wrapped in brickwork, less if a lightweight cladding is hung off the frame.

■ Perhaps the most significant extra cost of timber frame comes from having to have the design proved by a structural engineer. Your building regs officer will require an HB353 certificate (HB210 in Scotland) which may cost you £500 per house, unless you are buying an off-the-peg design.

■Alternative skins

The previous section 'Inner skin' covers the two main building systems for UK housing. Needless to say, there are dozens of others and each year there is a steady trickle of pioneers doing something rather different. Some of these are definitely minority interests, others are gunning very much at the mainstream of housebuilding. I can't possibly hope to do any of them justice in such a short space so let's hope I manage to avoid any injustice.

Green oak/post and beam

The traditional way, that is to say Tudor way, of building large timber houses was to erect a large post and beam skeleton (usually using oak) and then to hang the house off it. Whereas modern, industrial timber frame is a fast, lightweight, cheap way of erecting walls, here we are working in an altogether different idiom. Post and beam housing has undergone a revival in recent years and it's used for both retro designs (Border Oak, Potton Heritage) and modern (Carpenter Woodland Oak, Huf Haus). It's also essentially the form you get when you take on a timber barn conversion. It's very good for creating large open plan spaces as you don't require structural walls. However, you do require an external weatherproof cladding. Here you have basically two options, infill between the posts or clad the entire structure. The infill technique used to be carried out with wattle and daub but today's insulation requirements rely on rather more hi-tech solutions. Attention has to be paid to the fact that green oak shrinks so that what starts out as a nice tightly fitting infill panel can work itself loose by year three. This is addressed by using flexible foam gaskets which expand to take up the slack.

Post and beam frames are invariably load-bearing but they are rarely essential: you can usually opt to spread the load onto the walls instead. Consequently, the cost of the posts and beams is almost always an extra to the cost of building the house in a simplified, modern format.

A typical large detached house (they are rarely small) will use between 20 and 30 cu m of green oak to make up the frame. The cost of the oak alone will be at least £12,000 (it's around £450 per cu m for French oak, £500 per cu m for English) and the cost of making up and erecting the frame will be around three times as much as this on top – it's a slow, painstaking business.

The point I am labouring to get to is that green oak frames are expensive and completely unnecessary – a complete luxury, in other words. You won't build a green oak home for under £1,000 per sq m. You may save a bit by switching to a softwood – Douglas Fir gets used on occasion – but saving money isn't what this is all about, is it? What's interesting, to my mind, is that there are a number of small developers out there who willingly pay all

that extra money to get an oak framed house because they can make it back and more on the asking price.

If you are an aficionado of Channel 4's 'Grand Designs' you will be familiar with the sight of its presenter, Kevin McCloud, salivating over green oak. Bizarre as he may seem, he's not alone. Alone of all the major building materials, oak seems to posses some magical properties, an instant wow factor which plays some primaeval chord within the British psyche. Interestingly, other countries build post and beam too but they only ever use softwoods. They think we are mad to use oak: what do they know?

SIPS

SIPS stands for Structural Insulated Panels and they are an American way of homebuilding that can best be described as timber frame without the timber. By laminating sheets of plywood or OSB around a core of insulation board, you get an incredibly strong building board which combines many of the qualities of plywood with great insulation values. Ideal for our new exacting U-values? Many people think so, hence the excitement. SIPS are very flexible. You can

Kingspan Tekhaus SIPS panels being craned into position on a TJ Crump Oakwright house in Lincolnshire. SIPs panels can be used for walling, roofing and even flooring

turn up on site with a load of blank panels and simply cut window holes and door holes into them wherever you choose – only the widest openings require stiffening. You can also build roofs with them. Where they are not so clever is that they are heavy, requiring a crane on site, and when it comes to jointing the panels together they use lots of foam sprayed out of cans to get a good airtight fit.

Like many overnight sensations, SIPS have actually been around a while, in this case since the Fifties, but never really developed beyond the prototype level because they were too expensive to build compared to traditional methods. But in the early Nineties, American post and beamers (known confusingly over there as timber framers) started to use SIPS to clad their newly built homes and this seems to have kick started the market.

In North America there are a hundred or more producers and some developers have started using SIPS to build estates. In all, around 12,000 SIPS homes are being built each year across the Atlantic. To date developments in Britain are in their infancy but several small manufacturers have started to produce SIPS and, in 2001, Kingspan, one of our big insulation producers,

acquired a small German system (Tek Haus). SIPs have begun to be used on projects with a lot of repetition, such as the chalets at Center Parcs holiday camps, but there remain doubts as to whether they will ever be big players in the individual homes market.

I beams

Timber I beams have become a common sight on British housebuilding sites. Being an engineered product (basically like a steel RSJ, only made of wood products), I beams are lightweight and stable and they don't shrink. Like SIPS, they are also comparatively strong. Where they have been getting used mostly is to replace conventional timber floor joists. But some people have been building whole houses out of them. It's not really as flexible as SIPS (you can't cut it up on site very easily) and it shares the same jointing problems but because of the strength of the I beams it can span huge distances which makes it suitable for applications like floors.

Steel

In some parts of the world – notably Australia – steel-framed housing is big bananas. In

Steel frame housing has been around since the 1940s but has never really caught on. But recently one or two developers have grown interested. Redrow and Barratt have both started to use steel frame and, in Ireland, Fusion Homes are producing insulated steel panels for housing (pictured here), available in the UK as well as the Republic

Britain, its heyday came and went in the Forties in the post war prefab boomlet. Since then, it's remained something of a curio. There are two approaches, mirroring timber frame. You can have a post and beam structure (which is what most office buildings are) or you can build lightweight wall panels (which is where most of the housebuilder's interest is). Advocates reckon it's superior to timber frame in many ways – it's lightweight, it's fast, it's accurate – but it's mostly been aimed at the mass housing end of the spectrum.

For several years, British Steel's (now known as Corus) Surebuild was the only game in town and they regularly produced about 1,000 homes a year from an antiquated plant in South Wales. For a couple of years, their supply simply couldn't keep up with demand as one or two of the plc housebuilders began to get interested. The situation is changing thanks to some new kit developed in Australia and New Zealand that allows you to cold press steel without having a huge plant – indeed one of the systems works from the back of a lorry with just three people needed to press the steel into channels and assemble it into frames. And Irish housebuilder, Fusion Homes, is planning to offer a bespoke steel housebuilding and erection service across the UK. Their design fuses insulation around a steel frame so that you end up with something not a hundred miles from a SIPS panel. Steel has traditionally only made much sense when you have an order for many identical units but the new CAD CAM techniques potentially change all that. Another space to watch.

Pods and prefabs

The past few years have seen renewed interest in prefabrication as a solution to our housing needs. Bathroom pods in particular are migrating from commercial office space into housing. They are assembled and finished in a factory and then craned into place on site, bolted into place and the plumbing is connected from the outside. Completely prefabricated dwellings are also back – steel-framed containers have been used to build

hotels and MacDonalds for years and now innovative housing groups such as the Peabody Trust have started using them as well. However, neither pods nor prefabs are likely to be of the remotest interest to self builders or small developers because, to make economic sense, you have to replicate the work many times – opinions vary as to how much many consists of but it's not less than 30 and it may be as much as 100.

Timber and steel frame homes are conventionally supplied in what kitchen suppliers would call a flat pack state, wall and floor units ready to be assembled on site. In contrast, pods and prefab units are supplied as ready assembled units – indeed they tend to have as much work done in the factory as possible. Transportation thus becomes the limiting factor – you can't realistically transport anything which won't fit onto the back of a lorry.

Close panel timber frame

A sort of halfway house between regular timber frame, as practised in the UK, and prefabs is the closed panel systems, as used by the Germans and the Swedes. Here the wall, floor and roof sections are finished in the factory, right down to the services and decorations, and then craned into place on site. It's quicker than regular or open panel methods, which require internal finishing on site, but it only suits builders who are very organised and know exactly what they want. It has been tried once or twice in the UK but has never really caught on because the average British client wants the flexibility to change their mind every two days or so.

ICFs

Another technique. Another three letter acronym. Just to prove not all innovation is happening in the lightweight framing, this one uses polystyrene moulds and lots of concrete. ICF stands for Insulated Concrete Forms. Rather like SIPS, ICFs have taken off in North America where again they are reckoned to be building more than 10,000 homes each year using this

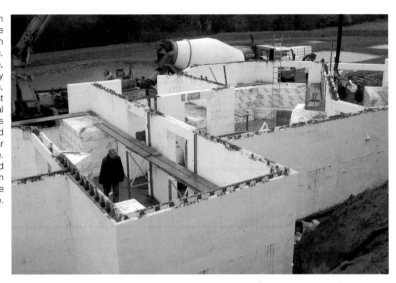

A Beco Wallform pour taking place on a selfbuild in Banbury, Oxon. For a long time, Beco were the only ICF show in town, But in the past four years, several alternative suppliers have appeared — Styrostone, Polar Wall, Eurozone. They have formed an ICF Association to help raise the profile.

technique. Unlike SIPS, it's originally a German idea – it's still widely used there as well though not in equivalent numbers to the USA and Canada.

In the UK, by far the best known name is Beco Wallform, started in the early Nineties by Robin Millar, who has built around 250 homes using this technique. In 2004 there were no less than five ICF suppliers at the 'Homebuilding & Renovating' show at the NEC and Beco seem no longer to be ploughing a lone furrow.

The idea behind ICFs is that you start with a delivery of hollow polystyrene blocks that you then stack up into a house shape. You stop at each floor and get lorry loads of readymix which you pour into the hollows in the polystyrene walls. It's a clever variation on how concrete building work is usually carried out, where you take down the formwork after the concrete has set. With ICFs, the polystyrene acts initially as formwork (or mould) for the concrete and stays in place to become the insulation for the finished house.

The polystyrene can be covered on the outside with polymer (flexible) renders; inside, however, there are many unusual techniques for fixing internal walls, frames and floor joists which would probably completely flummox the average British builder. And whilst the idea is

engagingly simple, it's not without its problems as I've seen on site when the wet concrete sometimes bursts through the side of the polystyrene blocks.

ICFs have an undoubted appeal to people wanting to take a hands-on approach to building their own walls. They don't need bricklayers and blocklayers, anybody can do it. However, there are some cost implications that have to be addressed. Even using your own sweat labour, ICFs are more expensive than blockwork or timber frame, both of which have an external walling cost of under £25 per sq m including insulation and labour.

ICFs give very good insulation levels, for sure, but adding extra insulation is cheap, whichever system you use. When you see an ICF walling system costing less than £15 per sq m, let me know because then they will be serious players. But mostly they come in around twice as much.

Thin-layer blockwork

Thin-joint or glue mortars are widely used in Germany and were introduced into Britain by Durox in 1991 but their uptake hasn't been as fast as the manufacturers would like and their use has been limited in the housebuilding arena.

There are two key elements that make it

different to conventional blockwork. Firstly, it uses a very sticky mortar, more akin to tile adhesive than a traditional sand and cement mix. This thin-layer mortar starts to set within ten minutes and this makes it possible to work with much bigger block sizes – this is the second key element and the one from which the speed advantages derive. The limit on block size is set by what a man can easily handle: in fact, in response to feedback from site, Celcon's currently preferred size – 610 x 270mm – is slightly smaller than the format they launched with. Blocklayers who have moved over to thin-layer reckon that it's around 30 per cent quicker. Any increase in material costs is more than offset by a decrease in labour rates.

The techniques used are quite different to mortared blockwork. In many ways, it's closer to carpentry than masonry: tooling up for thin-joint blockwork also requires a bandsaw, a mortar spreader, a block rasp, a mortar whisk and a wall tie puncher – you can't use traditional wall ties. Thin-layer work also requires a very level base to work off; with just a 2mm bed between the blocks you can't make good any initial errors as you go. As with many of these new techniques, the problem for would-be adopters is that there simply

aren't any (or at least many) blocklayers around who know anything about thin-joint. When faced with the thin-joint option, the knee-jerk reaction is to hoick the labour rates up through the roof when, going on the evidence, they ought to be actually lowering them.

Celcon's Jämerä

Thin-joint blockwork is a relatively minor innovation in the grand scheme of things. It still leaves a big problem in insulation terms because, though aircrete blocks are moderately good insulators, on their own they are way short of meeting the current U-value requirements. Or, at least, they are at conventional block widths of 100 or 140mm. But peek into the 'Green issues' chapter and take a look at the section on how to calculate U-values and R-values and you will understand that, given enough thickness, any material can provide adequate insulation. Aircrete blocks get there at about 350mm thickness which just happens to be the width of a convention brick and block cavity wall. Well, the width plus maybe another 50mm.

Why not build houses out of solid aircrete blocks 350mm thick? Well, it turns out that they have been doing just this in Scandinavia and

The advantages of thin-bed masonry are many. But, as with all new techniques, there are disadvantages as well. Here builder Steve Hicks returns to a thin-joint site after a 200 mile round trip to collect the steel bed reinforcement mesh. If you want to try something different, don't expect the local building suppliers to have everything you need on tap.

Germany for some time and H+H Celcon, one of our main aircrete manufacturers, happens to be part of a group that owns a Finnish company that builds this way. The system is called Jämerä and it is capable of providing floors and roofs as well as walls. Celcon see a big future for Jämerä and have tooled up their plant in Pollington in Yorkshire to produce everything you need to build a Jämerä house. Thus far the uptake has been slow. Several major housebuilders have trialled Jämerä but none has placed a really big order yet. The problems as they see it are that British housebuyers like to see brick facings and to add a conventional brick facing onto the outside of an already very thick wall is impossible. The alternative is to switch to a brick cladding system but these are themselves still expensive. In Finland, they simply render the outside and paint the inside and the houses look stunning but they also look very Scandinavian...

One part of the system that is achieving significant sales is the flooring panels, which are proving to be an attractive and cost effective alternative to beam and block flooring.

Others

Having been very traditional in our approach to homebuilding for decades, suddenly there has been an explosion of interest in how differently we might do it in future. All I've tried to do here is summarise some of the methods which are putting themselves across as mainstream alternatives. There are several more ethnic methods about which I know very little and can't really do much more than point you in the right direction.

Here are some useful contacts:

■ Earth-sheltered or underground homes: these take the concept of a basement to its logical conclusion and build the entire house underground. Actually, more typically, earth is banked up on three sides so that you still end up with one wall of glass. However don't assume this is a natty way of avoiding the planners. Current contact via website www.besa-uk.org

■ Centre for Earthen Architecture, University of Plymouth, Nottle Street, Plymouth (01752 233630). All things to do with building in cob and earth, increasingly of interest in restorations. Linda Watson runs courses and acts as an informal contact for other regional groups.
■ Straw bale homes: a small phenomenon in North America, they have started to sprout in Britain and Ireland as well. Our best known straw bale builder is Barbara Jones who runs straw bales futures (aka Amazon nails). 01706 814696.
■ Hemp: architect Ralph Carpenter of Modece Architects is the man - 01284 761141.
■ Centre for Alternative Technology, Machynlleth, Powys (01654 702400). Mine of information, especially on timber and also straw bales. Wide number of residential courses on offer and good bookshop with details of all these and more.
■ Construction Resources: a green builder's merchant specialising in unprocessed building materials (as well as many other things). 16 Great Guildford Street, London SE1 0HS (Tel. 0207 450 2211).

The one thing you will have noticed about this section is that I haven't mentioned any prices – not once. Most unlike Brinkley. There is a reason for this. Most of these non-traditional techniques are expensive. Several of them are still in their infancy and haven't really sold enough for meaningful prices to develop. Where prices have emerged, they tend to look high. For instance, the standard Beco wall costs around £30 per sq m just for the insulation blocks. And SIPS panels are certainly no cheaper than conventional timber frame.

■Outer skins

If you've arrived here from the previous section, 'Inner skins', you will have noticed that it started with a short (very short) history lesson about the introduction of cavity walls into British housebuilding. Round about 1930, if you weren't paying attention. This split the external walls into an inner and outer skin. Whilst there have been numerous developments and changes in the techniques used to build the structural inner skin, the outer skin has remained largely unchanged over the years. Other than some very modern houses which tend to swap glass for cavity walls, most of the materials used to clad homes haven't changed that much.

The basic choices are fairly limited. Brick – still easily No 1 in England; stone – expensive, tending to be used where local styles dictate; cement renders – top choice in the wetter parts; or lightweight claddings such as timber board or tiles – commonly used for odd decorative panels but rarely for whole houses.

There is surprisingly little difference between the prices you pay for external claddings. It's hard to build an outer skin for less than £35 per sq m though it's not difficult to vastly increase this figure if you specify expensive materials and finishes. Before embarking on a look at what the regular options are, a word about mixing up walling materials, something that's become very popular with developers (though not with our benchmark house builders, who stick with brick). Mixing materials invariably creates an extra layer of complexity and therefore adds to costs. Not only are different

materials and trades being brought in for relatively small amounts of work, but junction details need to be built in as well. It's difficult to be too precise about this because every situation is different but bear in mind that simplicity helps if your primary aim is to hold down costs.

Brick

Bricks remain the preferred material for external walls throughout England and Wales. They are reasonably cheap, they are well understood by the building trade, they can look attractive and, above all, they are durable. Not only should a brick wall not need any further care after construction, it should actually improve with age.

There are dozens of brick manufacturers and thousands of bricks to choose from. There is also a substantial business in reclaiming bricks from old buildings – though it only amounts to one per cent of total brick sales, that's still 40 million bricks reclaimed each year. If you are limited by budget you will probably find your choice is rather narrow, but if you are prepared to pay more than £250 per 1,000 (that's 25p per brick) then a whole world of choice opens up. Choosing a brick is quite an involved process and it is notoriously difficult to visualise what a brick wall will look like from

External Cladding Costs – Square Meter Rates

Heavyweight Claddings	Basic Mats	Accessories	Mats	Time in Mins	Labour at £18/hr	Combined
Brickwork @ £350/k	£ 21	£ 2	£ 23	75	£ 23	£ 46
Natural Stone	£ 35	£ 2	£ 37	240	£ 72	£ 109
Artificial Stone	£ 15	£ 2	£ 17	120	£ 36	£ 53
Stone Sladding	£ 40	£ 2	£ 42	120	£ 36	£ 78
Painted Render on Outer skin blockwork	£ 11	£ 1	£ 12	110	£ 33	£ 45
Lightweight claddings						
Painted Render on Mesh	£ 14	£ 1	£ 15	90	£ 27	£ 42
Tile Hanging	£ 17	£ 7	£ 24	70	£ 21	£ 45
Sawn + Stained Weatherboard	£ 9	£ 4	£ 13	90	£ 27	£ 40
Unpainted Cedar	£ 28	£ 4	£ 32	50	£ 15	£ 47

The Benchmark House only uses one external wall cladding, a Hoskins Westwick mix cream brick

Brickwork Costs on Benchmark House

All brickwork @£320/k	Area in m²	Rate	Mats	Lab	Total
External wall cladding	205	£ 46	£ 4,700	£ 4,700	£ 9,400
Internal feature brickwork	19	£ 46	£ 440	£ 440	£ 880

rigmarole is more or less restricted to bricks, although it is rumoured to occur with up-market roof tiles and pavings.

Mortar

You can't lay bricks without mortar and mortar actually makes up around 20 per cent of the area of a brick wall. So what the mortar looks like is arguably as important as what the bricks look like. The current fashion is for very pale mortars, aping the lime mortars that the Victorians used. One way to get this is to use pure lime mortars instead of cement, but lime mortars are expensive and not as easy to use as cement. If you want the look but not the hassle, you can use Steve Baldwin's (our benchmark house builder) mix which is white cement (Snowcrete) and sand mixed with plasticiser. There is a section on mortars in Chapter 12.

Render

Rendering is the expression most commonly used for an external plastered finish, a treatment which has been enjoying something of a return to fashion in contemporary house designs. In Scotland it's known as harling, and in Ireland it's never gone out of fashion.

Two alternative techniques are used to get a rendered finish – rendering directly on to blockwork or rendering on to metal lathing which is nailed on to battens. The first would normally be used on masonry-built houses, the second on timber frame. Render, if done properly, does give a very good waterproof surface, something bricks don't do. This is why it's usually seen in exposed coastline areas.

Decorative render

A nearly lost art which is undergoing a small revival. The finish is rather like an upmarket artex applied to the face to enliven the outlook. In East Anglia it is known as pargetting and there are so few exponents that ballpark figures are meaningless.

Pebble dash

Uncommon on new build nowadays, pebble dashing involves throwing (or sometimes spraying) small stones into wet render to make a rough cast finish. Now perceived as downmarket, it costs little more than conventional smooth finished render. Rough casting and Tyrolean finishes are two other variations on this theme.

Timber and boards

Plain timber boarding (sometimes known as clapboarding) is coming back into fashion with the increasing popularity of barn conversions. There are several different styles which you can use. Roughsawn timber (featheredge) looks more rustic; planed timber (shiplap) can look a shade more sophisticated. In their raw states, they make remarkably cheap claddings, costing between £5 and £8 per sq m (materials only). But they drink wood stains by the gallon and, of course, they require extensive maintenance to keep looking the business. Supply and fix rates for featheredge are around £20 per sq m and three coats of woodstain adds another £10 per sq m on top. This still looks like a cheap cladding method but you need to factor in a re-application every seven or eight years, costing maybe £5 per sq m each time. If you pay for the labour, then weatherboard is actually one of the most expensive of claddings after thirty years has elapsed.

Step forward a number of timber or near-timber solutions that don't require staining in the first place, let alone frequent re-applications. Cedar – usually western red cedar – is the best known timber promising to be fit and forget. It's five times the price of basic sawn featheredge but it lasts for sixty years. Roughly, anyway. It's being sold on the proposition that it lasts 60 years and there are many acres of cedar claddings going up all over the place in locations that are often hard to reach so it had better last sixty years! It goes a mellow silvery-grey after a couple of years.

There are a number of mid-priced alternatives between cedar and the basic whitewood boards. Native larch is sometimes specified — it's £22 per sq m instead of cedar's £28 per sq m, but of course it doesn't last as long. There are some interesting heat-treated timbers coming onto the market: one is Thermowood, from Finland, which is a treated redwood with a 30 year lifespan, costing £16 per sq m. And Eternit, the tile manufacturers, produce a convincing fibre cement board, pre painted, for slightly less than this. It's known as Weatherboard 50 – for a fifty year lifespan. Right at the bottom end of the spectrum is uPVC: sure, it doesn't rot but it doesn't really have much going for it as a cladding.

There are also a number of semi-industrial boards which can be used to clad buildings. These live really in the commercial sectors of the building trade but one or two adventurous architects sometimes specify them on housing.

Incidentally, with all external timber that requires painting or staining, it is good practice to put at least one coat of paint or stain on the boards on the ground before fixing. Timber shrinks, and if the whole board is not covered with a uniform colour you will end up with 1-2mm flesh-coloured strips wherever boards overlap.

Half-timbered tudor look

This is usually achieved by planting 50x100mm or 50x125mm timber on to either a blockwork or timber frame backing. A typical gable would have between six and twelve verticals and two or three horizontals, plus framing around any windows. A simple arrangement such as this with planed timber would add around £8 per sq m (Mats £3 Lab £5). Complex patterns with distressed timber or oak could easily treble this figure.

Further expense could be added by doing the infill panels in brick rather than cement render. This is a beautiful old technique (called brick noggins) and it can be carried out in several different ways. It is very time-consuming and it would only look good with interesting bricks and timber, so allow £60 per sq m.

Vertical tiling

Using vertical tiling is another Victorian building feature that is coming back into fashion, particularly in SE England. Costs are very similar to plain tiles laid on roofs, although vertical hanging tends to be a little more expensive because there is more work involved in cutting corners, angles and around openings. Generally it looks best with small format plain tiles or slate and it is more important to select a good looking (i.e. expensive) tile for a wall than it is for a roof. Cedar, in the form of small tiles called shingles, also features as wall cladding.

Rubble walls

If you know the right quarries this kind of walling material can be extremely cheap to buy, but it tends to be very time-consuming to lay. Traditionally rubble walling was independent of any backing materials, but now it is much cheaper to lay if it is set against a background of blockwork – which makes it a bit like very rough pebble dash. Each area of the country has its own local 'rubble' stones and seaside locations often tend to find theirs on the nearby beaches.

In East Anglia, flint is the usual material and prices vary enormously depending on how it is finished. Flint can be laid as wholestones – which gives a rough 'agricultural' look – or it can be knapped, which involves breaking the stones open to reveal a shiny black inside which is then set as the facework. Wholestone is available for under £20 per tonne, but knapped flint is up to ten times this amount. Expect to pay around £6-10 per sq m for rough walling materials (inc sand and cement) and around £100 per sq m for laying. As you can see from these prices, laying is slow. It is, however, not particularly difficult and it could well suit a DIY builder who has more time than money. You can now buy pre-finished flint blocks which take all the hard work out of it – you just lay them like a conventional block.

Stone

If you live in one of the so-called stone belts you may well have to build in stone to satisfy the local planners. You may actually want to build in stone – it's usually very attractive – but it's likely to be very much more expensive than the developer's standbys: brick and render.

There are basically three approaches: you can use real stone quarried out of some hillside, you can use reconstituted stone which is stone dust glued together with cement, or you can use stone cladding which usually gets stuck on the outside of cheaply erected blockwork.

Natural stone

Building stone tends to be a very local affair. It was, after all, hewn from quarries and, in the days before cheap transportation, could only be carried the shortest of distances. Many of these old stone quarries survive and supply the demands of the local construction trade. In some areas there are thriving second-hand markets in stone walling materials, yet nowhere is natural stone a cheap material. You may be given brownie points for using natural stone in your house – more likely the local planners will insist on it – but you'll probably be adding £10,000 to the overall cost.

Reconstituted Stone

A cheaper alternative is to use a reconstituted stone. Marshalls and RMC Peakstone are two of the largest producers. Although, to the practised eye, reconstituted stone will never look as good as the real thing, it will cost about half as much and, if done well, looks as good as many of the cheaper bricks.

Cladding

Stone cladding has got a reputation for being naff as hell, but this is because it's often associated with people who fix it to their brick terrace houses to 'make a statement' (such as 'I'm naff as hell'). Out of context like that it does look more than a touch ridiculous, but on a new house in a stone village chances are most casual passers-by would not even know it was stone cladding. However, artificial stone claddings are now virtually unobtainable and natural stone cladding is very expensive – it is unlikely to cost less than £50 per sq m – so if

Stone facades are occasionally used – and much photographed – by professional developers. This one by Prowting Homes, now part of Westbury Homes

you are starting from scratch you might just as well use real stone.

One interesting option is to use reconstituted stone cladding. It sounds awful but Fernhill produce a very convincing product which is set in moulds and is so realistic that it's virtually impossible to tell from the real thing. But realism comes at a price: it costs around £35-£45 per sq m to buy the tiles and laying is as expensive as brickwork. It can be placed on a polystyrene backing (useful for people building with ICFs) but it's usually stuck onto an outer blockwork wall.

Glass

Certain designs call for lots of glass, so much that you have to start thinking in terms of glazed walls rather than large windows. In the accompanying table, I've costed up for a screen wall of sliding patio doors and fanlights, the sort of thing you might use around a swimming pool or a conservatory. The glass has to be suitably energy efficient to meet the new building regs and on the surface it appears to be an amazingly expensive walling option even when you take into account the low fixing costs and the reduction in costs from not having to build an inner skin. There is a basic costing law at work here. Windows cost twice as much as the walls they sit in.

Porches and bays

Thus far I've been looking at exterior finishes but there is, of course, much more to the external design of a house than just the materials used. Features like bay windows and porches have been coming right back into fashion despite the fact that they are expensive to build. It's quite hard to separate out how much extra these features cost because they tend to get lost in the whole job costings.

A bay window, for instance, involves minor additions to almost every aspect of the construction – excavations, foundations, flooring, brickwork, joinery, roofing, guttering, carpentry and decorating (to name just nine). Individually these changes are not great but added together I estimate that a two-storey bay may add as much as three per cent to the costs of erecting the house superstructure. For an area less than 3 sq m that's expensive – getting on for double the amount spent on ordinary living space.

Porches are easier to quantify, although bear in mind that the standard of construction varies enormously from something little more than a rain shelter to what amounts to a mini-extension. Being (usually) rectangular in shape, porches are not appreciably more expensive to construct than the main structure, but bear in mind that any complications that might ensue will end up taking a disproportionate amount of supervision time. One recent development is companies producing GRP bolt-on porches and bay window canopies; it's proved to be a big hit with developers. One company, Storm King, produces a whole range of architectural conceits such as pseudo-lead infill panels and clock towers. Their bolt-on porches start at just over £100.

Cills, arches

One of the classiest effects you can get on external facades is to use feature lintels above and cills below your openings. There are a number of options for doing this. The cills and lintels can be formed from special bricks or made on site with a granite and cement mixture, which is fine if they get painted afterwards. Another variation is to have reconstituted stone ones made up in a workshop: this is the most expensive option but also probably the most attractive.

Insetting joinery into the facade is not a merely decorative process. By its very nature it helps to protect windows and doors from the worst of the weather, and the building regulations acknowledge this by making recessed joinery compulsory in Scotland and in many exposed parts of the rest of the country.

Don't ruin it

Having gone to all that trouble to get good-looking materials correctly proportioned, it is worth taking on board a cautionary word about the effect of those little elements which can ruin the overall effect – like a wart on the face of a much loved friend (shouldn't that have been a carbuncle? Ed). Whether you go for period charm or ultra-modernism really makes no difference, just think about the details – remember the devil is in the details. Here are a few style tips:
■ rainwater downpipes – the fewer the better
■ plastic meter boxes – hide them round the side
■ security floodlighting – don't point it straight at people walking towards it
■ alarm bells – potential burglars will still see them on a side wall
■ satellite dishes – they can sometimes go out in the garden.

■ Insulation

All materials insulate to a greater or lesser extent – see section on U-values in Chapter 13 – but only since the Seventies have we seen the widespread adoption of materials that do very little else except insulate. By and large, these materials are not prohibitively expensive and most will pay for themselves within a few years. So whilst you could design your home to avoid using insulation wherever possible, there would be very little point in doing so.

Material choices

There are several materials available to insulate housing. All have pros and cons and not all are suitable in every application; mostly they are available in a number of different formats – often in combination with other materials like chipboard and plasterboard – which makes describing them all extremely complicated. The basics are as follows. First the woolly ones.

Fibreglass

Cheap, reasonably good insulator. Excellent when laid flat in lofts but when placed in walls it will sag. But help is at hand: it can be 'wicked' which stiffens it up and allows it to be placed into wall cavities without risk of sagging or, as they say in insulation speak, to 'perform well in the vertical'. Here they tend to get referred to as batts as in cavity batts or timber frame batts. Although nearly double the price of unwicked quilts, they are still good value compared to other materials.

Mineral wool

In most ways it performs very similarly to fibreglass and can also be wicked to perform well in the vertical. However, mineral wool is noticeably superior to fibreglass (and almost all other insulation materials) in terms of fire resistance. It is usually priced to compete with fibreglass though sometimes it is five to ten per cent more. The current U-value requirements for flat ceiling areas is 0.16 which requires at least 250mm of fibreglass or mineral wool. For many people that seems excessive but it still pays for itself within a few years. Production is dominated by the Danish company, Rockwool, and it's often referred to by this trade name.

Sheeps wool

The natural product on which both glass wool and mineral wool are based. In many ways it performs very similarly to its synthetic cousins but it's obviously much nicer to work with – the synthetic ones are notoriously itchy and unpleasant, especially glass wool. It's only really appeared as an option in the past few years and

it appeals mostly to people wanting to build using natural products wherever possible. They also need deep wallets because it's around five times the price of the synthetic wools.

Expanded polystyrene

Now it's on to plastics. The most familiar plastic insulation is expanded polystyrene. It gets used in buildings in two formats. The first is as a vast amorphous mass of little white beads that get blown into cavity walls from lorries. The second is in rigid boards; here two brands dominate, Jablite and Kaycell — it is often referred to by builders as Jablite. It performs very similarly to fibreglass and mineral wool in terms of insulation capabilities (but not fire protection) and is similarly cheaply priced. Used widely in cavity wall construction (in both formats) and underfloor insulation (where the regs now require around 100mm of EPS). It is much the cheapest material when you are having to build with a partial cavity fill.

Extruded polystyrene

This is a different version of polystyrene which is much denser and much stronger – expanded polystyrene sheets are notoriously brittle. In terms of insulation capabilities it lies midway between expanded polystyrene and the polyurethane family of insulants, but its big selling point is that it is resistant to water penetration. It's great under floors and below ground but it's a bit pricey to use elsewhere.

Polyurethane

The most efficient of the main insulators on the market, it is usually sold in rigid sheet format, usually foil backed. However, it is pricey even if you buy second hand, where a company called Seconds & Co is busy. The domestic market is dominated by two manufacturers, Celotex and Kingspan, though others are beginning to appear.

A big problem with polyurethane has been that its production involved the use of CFCs, now implicated in the demise of the ozone layer and therefore environmentally incorrect. This

Insulation Options

	Underfloor	Ext Wall	Flat ceiling	Sloping roof
U value requirement	0.25	0.35	0.16	0.2
Glass/Rockwool Cost/m²	INADVISABLE	75-90mm £2.20	200-250mm £2.00	INADVISABLE
Exp. Polystyrene Cost/m²	80-100mm £4.00	65-75mm £3.50	200-250mm £8.00	150mm £6.00
Extruded Polystyrene Cost/m²	50-75mm £7.50	45-60mm £6.25	INADVISABLE	120mm £12.50
Polyiso-foam Boards Cost/m²	48-60mm £6.00	35-48mm £4.50	120mm £14.00	100mm £10.00
Blown Fibre Cost/m²	INADVISABLE	c90mm £6.00	£12.00	£9.00
Reflective Foil Cost/m²	INADVISABLE	Actis or similar £12.00	£12.00	£12.00

These insulation levels meet the requirements of the 2002 Part L regulations in England & Wales. Scotland requires a slightly higher standard on walls, Ireland higher still. Standards are set to be raised again in 2005. Generally this means using thicker insulation.

Insulation in Benchmark House

Labour rate for fixing insulation	£18.00 hr
Time taken to fix 1m²	5 Min
Cost to fix 1m²	£1.50

	Area	What Used	Mats	Labour	Combined	Lab & Mats Costs/m²
Ground Floor	110 m²	60mm Celotex	£ 660	£ 170	£ 830	£ 8.00
Ext Walls	191 m²	75mm DriTherm	£ 420	£ 290	£ 710	£ 4.00
Flat Ceilings	104 m²	200mm Wool	£ 210	£ 160	£ 370	£ 4.00
Sloping Ceilings	79 m²	90mm Celotex	£ 790	£ 120	£ 910	£ 12.00
		Total	£ 2,080	£ 740	£ 2,820	

has led the manufacturers on a frantic search to find ways of making their boards with a different blowing agent, and this has produced a range of similar insulation boards made with either polyisocyanurate foam or phenolic foam. In terms of performance they are both very similar to the older polyurethanes.

Despite their cost, polyurethane (and substitutes) are being increasingly specified because their superior performance as insulators means that they are space efficient – in that you can get the desired insulation levels from a thinner sheet – and that means there are sometimes reductions in other construction costs. Basically these boards are twice as good but three times the cost of the basic insulators, expanded polystyrene and the wools.

Another application for the polyurethanes is to get blown into cavities and increasingly

under old roofs to keep them going a bit longer. It's expensive and traditionalists howl with indignation when they see it done. But it works.

Cellulose fibre

This is sometimes promoted as a green alternative to the other materials. For a start, it's made from recycled newspapers (so that's where they go) and it can also be used in timber frame walls without a vapour barrier which is reckoned, by some, to be an advantage. It has one major disadvantage in that it is not available in a sheet form so it has to be blown in by specialists. There is one main manufacturer in the UK, Exel Industries, who market their product as Warmcel.

Radiant heat barriers

There is a relatively new group of insulation

Room in the roof, 2004. The insulation used here is Actis Triso-Super 9 which has been shown to perform as well as 200mm of mineral wool. As it's only 20mm thick and is very easy to install (over the rafters), builders have been taking to it in droves. Yet despite it having achieved third party certification (from Trada BM) and being accepted by building control and the NHBC, doubts persist about the effectiveness of this and similar radiant heat barriers. There are many places in the world where this insulation assembly would not be accepted.

materials which work on the Bacofoil-behind-the-radiator principle. That is to say they have shiny reflective barriers which bounce the heat back into the room. There are three, Actis (from France), Alreflex 2L2 (from Holland) and Airtec (British) which have some body to them and therefore tend to act like conventional insulation, though none is thicker than 25mm. Industry sceptics cast doubt on what will happen to them if (or is it when) their coats lose their shiny surfaces. In any event, they mostly cost around £10-12 per sq m so they can hardly be seen as cheap substitutes for conventional insulation. They are particularly useful where you haven't much space, such as in sloping roofs. I've yet to see a convincing explanation of how exactly they work and the comparitive tests used by the manufacturers to establish their efficacy may in fact be measuring something quite different, such as good airtightness rather than any inherent insulation capabilities. But they have established a foothold in the market with third party accreditation and they are being widely specified in the housebuilding sector.

Buying tips
Generally the best place to buy insulation

materials is from the insulation specialists. Sheffield Insulation (SIG) and Encon are the best known national distributors but there are numerous local ones listed in 'Yellow Pages' under Insulation Materials. Some of the insulation installers are worth checking out for supply only. The supply and fix services offered are often a good deal; it is hard to beat them on price (or speed) except where you are not paying for site labour.

Vapour barriers
Insulation works by trapping air within its body. To continue to work well, the insulation needs to remain dry and, because of this, it has become a common practice in timber frame housing to fit a vapour barrier on the warm (room) side of the insulation layers. This vapour barrier (fancy title for polythene sheeting) stops condensation occurring within the insulation which would cause the insulation to hold water and thereby cease to be effective as an insulator.

Vapour barriers were a technical hot potato back in 1983 when an infamous 'World In Action' television programme did for timber frame construction what BSE has done for beef sales; the programme claimed that badly installed vapour barriers were leading to 'big

Obviously a house built with traditional timber windows. Wrong. These are uPVC. The house is built by Bellway Homes. Actually, these windows were so realistically woody-looking that I had to sneek up and touch them to be sure they were in fact plastic.

problems' with timber frame building which was, at the time, catching on in a big way in England.

Most leading developers immediately dropped timber frame construction methods because – even though at the time the veracity of the accusations was doubted – they couldn't afford to be selling a product which had a question mark over it. Twenty years on, timber frame has still not recovered its position in the English market and yet the debate about vapour barriers has long since died down. The fact that they are not always installed with the thoroughness they deserve is now seen as a bit of a red herring; indeed research coming out of North America is beginning to suggest that the important thing to build in is an air barrier – subtly different to a vapour barrier.

Cold bridging

Cold bridging is what happens when parts of your insulated shell are interrupted by things that don't insulate very well. What on earth am I talking about? The returns where cavity walls join around window and door openings are the best known example, but there are many others. The timber studs in a timber frame wall or the rafters in a roof, the edge of a floor where it

meets the foundation walls. All effectively leak heat rather faster than their better insulated surroundings. Even things like steel wall ties, used to tie cavities together, act as heat sinks. Now the more insulation you stuff into your fabric, the greater the relative importance of cold bridging becomes. As insulation levels rise, there are more and more products appearing which address cold bridging effects, most notably the group of products known as cavity closers which you use in the gap around window and door openings. The best known is the original one, RMC's Thermabate – but there are lots of others.

■Windows

The benchmark house has uPVC windows made by Speedframe, one of the largest national manufacturers. It's the second of my benchmark houses to use uPVC joinery and in doing so it reflects a widespread change going on in the housebuilding industry generally. uPVC first started to be used for joinery in the Sixties and it has slowly but surely spread throughout the housing market to establish itself as the No 1 material in terms of sales. In fact, new housebuilding was really the last citadel of timber windows but the relentlessly rising tide of uPVC broke through in the Nineties and it has established itself as the material of choice for developers.

The demand to switch to uPVC is coming from the customers who associate it with the magic phrase 'maintenance-free.' If builders don't fit uPVC windows, their customers will go down the road and buy a house that does and with this sort of clamour going on, they run with the crowd.

You can buy windows bespoke or off-the-peg. The housebuilding market is dominated, not surprisingly, by off-the-peg windows, made in vast numbers in a relatively small number of sizes. The off-the-peg market is dominated by a small number of national concerns who make very similar products, all fitting a series of standard window openings. In recent years, a number of uPVC manufacturers have switched their attention to making off-the-peg windows specifically aimed at new housebuilders. None has been more prominent than Rotherham-based Speedframe who have managed to re-invent the way housebuilders go about installing windows by getting them to install a subframe first and then clipping the windows into place when the moment suits them.

For years, the insurers and legislators have wanted housebuilders to fit ready-glazed windows because they are far less likely to fail. And for years, housebuilders have resisted the call because they don't like to install finished products in half-finished houses: they get broken, they get scratched, they get nicked. Speedframe's system sort of by-passed this problem by taking almost all the time (and skill) out of installing windows: you simply have to build in a cavity closer as the walls go up and you can leave the window fitting till the least possible moment. The building industry is full of innovative products but very few get taken up by professional builders: Speedframe's system has been. I was not surprised to find that Steve Baldwin, my benchmark house builder, had switched over to using it. And also not surprised to find that many competitors are

Vertical brick joints should be aligned. Here the orange line shows how the brick edges should fall. You can see how the brick edges are thrown out of alignment by the placing of a 1200mm wide window.

copying Speedframe's success. Now you can buy both uPVC and timber windows which just clip into built-in cavity closers.

Window openings

The point to grasp about off-the-peg windows, whether timber or uPVC, is that they are made to fit pre-ordained window openings. These openings thus tend to dominate the façade designs of housebuilders – it's the main reason that people complain the output of builders looks so samey. To introduce odd-sized windows is to add, unnecessarily, to costs so everyone is in the swing of producing houses with the same sized holes in.

The unit heights are easy to fathom: they are in 150mm steps, which represents two bricks courses — the height options are 450, 600, 750, 900, 1050, 1200, 1350, 1500. The width options – 488, 630, 915, 1200, 1770mm – would at first glance seem to be selected by a random number machine. It appears that the

The seven styles of British windows

Trade prices for 1200x1200mm windows

Plain Casements
£90 unglazed or
£175 factory glazed

Swept Head Style
£120 unglazed
£200 factory
glazed

Top Hung
£100 unglazed
£180 factory glazed

Horizontal Bar
£100 unglazed £200
factory glazed

Cottage Style
£120 unglazed
£300 factory glazed

Georgian or All Bar
only available
factory glazed £270

Regency Vertical Bar
£155 unglazed
£250 factory glazed

widths were changed in the early Eighties after a directive from Brussels indicated that the 300mm brick was about to take over Europe and that they'd better have joinery to suit. The joinery manufacturers all obliged but bricks remain 215mm long! This is most noticeable on the 1200 wide windows which disrupt the vertical joints on face brickwork.

It is by producing windows in this modular fashion that the likes of Boulton & Paul (now part of JeldWen) made their economies of scale that, in turn, made their product cheap. Ten years ago, you could walk into any builder's merchant and pick up window frames off the shelf but that's becoming a rarity these days and most catalogue items have to be ordered in advance. In a way, the distinction between made to measure and off-the-peg is gradually vanishing but you will still find that most of the big window manufacturers like to work to standard sizes. JeldWen, our largest timber window producer, charges an extra 20-40 per cent for non-standard sizes, not to mention a four to six week delay.

In terms of headline prices, off-the-peg

timber joinery still looks much cheaper than any of the pre-finished alternatives. There are several volume joinery manufacturers besides Jeld Wen who are turning out enormous quantities of standard-sized timber joinery – Crosby Sarek, Magnet, Abbott. Of these manufacturers, Magnet are alone in maintaining a substantial branch network of depots through which they sell exclusively. All the others sell through the established builder's merchants. There are numerous others in this business (like Howarth and Hill Leigh) who sell directly to housebuilders and the trade.

Many so-called quality window producers complain of the low standards of the volume producers. They may have a point, but it is worth bearing in mind that these standards have improved substantially in recent years. All timber is now vacuum treated with preservatives, opening casements are draught stripped and window locks and ventilation are now fitted as standard. Much of what people used to demand from a so-called high performance window is now available right throughout the ranges.

The catalogues

In days of yore, you couldn't design a cost-effective house without a joinery catalogue to hand. The joinery catalogue remains a thoroughly useful tool. And the grand-daddy of them all was Boulton & Paul's catalogue, now, of course, Jeld Wen's. Even if you don't plan to use anything from their range, it's still a useful reference because it gives you a feel for what is possible or at least what is commonly available.

The 2004 Jeld Wen catalogue has 69 pages of standard windows. At first glance the choice can seem mind-boggling, but growing familiarity shows that the choice is rather like the menu at an Indian restaurant, where every dish is available in every sauce and the length of the menu actually disguises a paucity of choices – i.e. it's really just a question of which sauce you want with your chicken, lamb or vegetables.

The backbone of their window production is the casement window, by which is meant any window that opens on hinges (as opposed to a sliding action). A window that cannot be opened is known as a fixed light, but most casement windows incorporate a fixed light or two and still get called casements. The hinging can be arranged either on the side of the casement (side-hung), from the top (top-hung) or pivoted in the middle (well-hung?), and many windows have a combination of these arrangements. Add in a varying number of glazing bars (supposedly to give a window more character) plus a swept top rail (oozes charm) and you can almost taste the poppadums.

In the current catalogue, the timber windows are available not just in different styles and sizes but with different levels of finish as well. The basic 'S' type is the raw softwood frame which was the standard fare on housebuilding sites until the end of the Nineties. The 'SG' type – stands for softwood glazed – is nearly double the price but the units come ready-glazed. The softwood styles are mostly available in hardwood as well. To get the most from the ready-glazed windows in a new build, you really want to use them in conjunction with a built-in cavity closer, à la Speedframe. Boulton & Paul have a partnership with specialist manufacturer Cavalock: their timber windows can be clipped in, just like the clever uPVC ones.

The Styles

The British window is an unusual beast, not found outside these islands. Although made by industrial methods, the styles are mostly very traditional. Work your way through a joinery catalogue and you will see Cottage Style (with cute glazing bars), Narrow Module (just so on barn conversions), All Bar (Georgian-style), Swept Head (now mercifully going out of fashion), not to mention bay windows and a whole range of sliding sash windows which are made to an entirely different set of sizes. It's really a question of matching the style of window to your overall house style. If you are working in a vernacular idiom (i.e. something olde worlde) then you'll find something out there to suit. If you want something modern, you may have to look elsewhere, though Jeld Wen have introduced a range of windows called Combis which have clean modern lines and can be mounted with reversible hinges so that you can clean them from the inside.

Sliding sash

The modern version of the Victorian sliding sash, which worked with concealed weights, has adjustable spiral balances that are a bugger to adjust and, even when well adjusted, can be very stiff to open and shut, but are in other ways superior to the original. Typically these windows offer a tilt facility so that you can clean them easily. At the top end, there are restoration specialists like Mumford & Wood who are producing a product very similar to what the Georgians built. And the sash window is not restricted to timber: there are a number of uPVC fabricators, some, such as Masterframe, producing a surprisingly convincing product.

Opening systems

There are some surprising differences in the ways we operate windows throughout the

Benchmark House - Joinery Costs

- Fitting is done by brickies and cost of fitting is included elsewhere
- Theoretical fixing costs are around £30/m²

	Width in mm	Height in mm	Area in m²	Cavity Closers	Windows	Doors
Front Door	1018	2100	2.1	£ 60	£ 350	
FD Sidelight	300	2100	0.6		£ 120	
Office Window	1200	1200	1.4	£ 40	£ 145	
Garage Car Door	2200	2100	4.6			£ 200
Garage Window	1200	1050	1.3	£ 40	£ 120	
Garage Side Door	1018	2100	2.1	£ 55		£ 380
Utility Window	630	900	0.6		£ 85	
Utility Door	920	2100	1.9	£ 70		£ 360
Shower Window	630	750	0.5	£ 25	£ 75	
Kitchen Door	918	2100	1.9	£ 55		£ 360
Kitchen Sink Window	1200	1050	1.3	£ 40	£ 130	
Kitchen Window	1770	1050	1.9	£ 45	£ 200	
D/R French Doors	1200	2100	2.5	£ 55		£ 460
Lounge Window	1770	1350	2.4	£ 50	£ 240	
Dormer 1	1200	1050	1.3		£ 200	
Dormer 2	1200	1050	1.3		£ 160	
Dormer 3	1200	1050	1.3		£ 120	
Bathroom	1200	900	1.1	£ 35	£ 210	
Bedroom 4	1200	1200	1.4	£ 40	£ 155	
Study	1200	1200	1.4	£ 40	£ 155	
Bedroom 3	1770	1050	1.9	£ 45	£ 220	
Bedroom 2	1770	1200	2.1	£ 45	£ 235	
Sun Room French Doors	2750	2100	5.8	£ 100		£ 900
Sun Room Window	2750	1350	3.7	£ 80	£ 420	
Velux in Shower Room	540	700	0.4		£ 130	
Grand Total			46.7	£ 920	£ 3,470	£ 2,660
Total for Joinery						£7,050
Cost/m²						£150

The Benchmark House was built with pre-glazed uPVC joinery made by Speedframe. It comes with a cavity closer system which simplifies the fitting. The closers are pre-formed frames that you build in. The windows and doors are clipped in later when damage can be minimised.

world. British windows tend to be side hung and open outwards using a simple stay to hold the window open: perhaps, unsurprisingly, we are at the cheap and cheerful end of the spectrum.

The French make windows in a similar fashion but they tend to open inwards (because of all those external shutters). Almost all German windows use the much more sophisticated tilt and turn mechanism which enables them to pivot open along the bottom edge (tilting) for ventilation purposes or, alternatively, along one side (turning).

North America uses both sliding sashes and outwards opening windows but their windows tend to operate on a screw thread mechanism. If you import windows, you will find these options tend to come as standard (depending on where you are importing from) but you can specify them as extras on some British designs, if you know what to ask for. However if you want to stick to traditional British looks, then you will probably want to stick with British furniture though you might want easy clean or projecting hinges (extra £10), which enable you to reach the outside of the glass from the inside or maybe coloured fittings (£7 extra) tickle your fancy.

Most timber windows are available in either a stain basecoat or a white primed finish. The default is the stain basecoat because you can paint or stain on top of that but you will be saving yourself time and money by getting the primed finish if you are going to paint over the top. Just remember that all these options will delay your delivery schedules by weeks so they are only an option if you are planning well ahead. Increasingly, we are being offered pre-finished timber windows which makes sense, especially if you are using one of the clip-in cavity lock systems.

Oh, and there's trickle vents. If you want to know about trickle vents, delve into the Ventilation section in Chapter 8.

There really isn't a lot to choose between the quality of the joinery turned out by the volume timber manufacturers, though the finer detailing does vary a little. Occasionally, you will find that one is offering much better terms than the others and you may have cause to switch horses. This is usually possible because, despite the different naming systems they use, the sizes are standard and therefore interchangeable.

Other options
Bespoke timber
Although there are many types of timber suitable for manufacturing external joinery, if you choose to have your windows supplied cheaply from a volume manufacturer then they will almost certainly be made from European Redwood, probably from Scandinavia. Although it is not particularly durable, it can be readily treated with wood preservatives; more importantly it is the cheapest type of suitable timber. It machines well and generally looks good, which makes it suitable for translucent finishes like wood staining.

There are better woods to use for external joinery but they are all very much more expensive and won't necessarily result in better (or longer-lasting) windows. Most hardwoods are inherently more durable than softwoods – oak, teak and Brazilian mahogany are particularly suitable – and there are some North American softwoods such as Douglas Fir which

are nearly as durable as the better hardwoods – certainly durable enough not to require treatment with wood preservative.

However, it must be realised that the design, installation and maintenance of the joinery is at least as important in determining how well the items perform over the long term. Specifying more durable timber will probably double your joinery costs at a stroke.

Most joinery manufacturers offer 'hardwood' alternatives in most of their ranges but you don't get any choice as to which hardwood. If you particularly wanted something like Douglas Fir for your windows then you would have to search out a small joinery shop to make them for you; this route would probably treble the cost of using a bog standard casement from a volume producer.

uPVC
Almost every window style is available in a uPVC finish. And much that I have written about the style choices for the timber windows applies equally to uPVC. If you are happy with a white uPVC finish it will generally be no more expensive than fitting a timber window – in fact uPVC is now substantially cheaper once you take into account the cost of finishing the windows.

The Speedframe windows fitted into our benchmark house cost around £150 per sq m. Timber can only be the cheaper option if you want to put a lot of your own unpaid labour into glazing and decorating. Note however that the wood-grain effect PVC windows are at least 50 per cent more than the plain white ones.

The question is, is uPVC any good? Well, uPVC windows have a stranglehold on the replacement market. What sells them is the fact that they are usually replacing clapped-out timber or steel windows which may have been in place for fifty years or more, and they are offering comfort and warmth together with the promise of being maintenance free.

It's actually too early to say if uPVC windows will be trouble-free (uPVC guttering certainly isn't), but the indications are that they are performing well. uPVC as a material may last for 30 or 40 years but it's hard to repair: in contrast, timber windows can last much longer — if they are regularly painted or stained.

Note also that Greenpeace are leading a vociferous campaign against the use of uPVC in buildings. They argue that both the production and the eventual disposal of uPVC is a toxic process involving the release of a number of unpleasant chemicals, dioxins being the most prominent. Their claims are naturally denied by the British Plastics Federation.

Composites

There are a number of suppliers who offer timber on the inside and uPVC or aluminium on the outside, thus combining the good looks of timber with a more durable exterior. They are invariably imported, mostly from North American and Scandinavia. Best known of these is Andersen Windows, an American joinery giant, who produce a huge range of timber doors and windows with an external uPVC coating. Also from North America are Norco, distributed by JeldWen, and Louwen.

The best of the Scandinavians seem to be Rationel, Nor-Dan, Sampson and Velfac though these companies are more geared towards commercial projects. Composite windows are approximately double the price of basic timber or uPVC, but note that if you want sliding sash style windows, the US designs are good value. Also note that American window dimensions are completely different to ours – they don't 'work' bricks.

Rooflights

A word about rooflights and, in particular, Velux windows. They are another form of composite window, being basically timber windows encased in an aluminium cladding, but they have revolutionised loft living by being simple to install, and near-problem-free in operation. Supply-only they cost around £200 per sq m including the essential roof flashings, very little more than the standard price for good quality timber or uPVC windows. Velux is not the only

company making rooflights but they are the trailblazers and still enjoy by far the largest market share in this specialist market: Velfac is a sister company building bespoke composite windows for external walls.

Barn conversions

Conversions usually pose problems quite different from new builds. There may be existing windows to match but more often than not you will be punching new holes in an existing wall and hoping to fit something that looks in keeping with the period of the original building. Incidentally, the expression 'punching holes' is very hip in barn converting circles at the moment, used widely by both planners and architects, so much so that you might be forgiven for thinking that the decision on where exactly to punch those holes is the be-all and end-all of barn design.

As you may have noted, made-to-order joinery tends to cost an arm and a leg and specifying it is one of the factors which makes converting barns more expensive than building new. However, if you want to keep costs down there are a number of options that may be of interest to you (or your planners) which can be bought off the shelf. First, the oh-so-modern looking 'top hung' window can actually look just-so in a barn elevation; certainly less obtrusive than the cottage or swept head styles. Also note that the narrow module casement windows tend to look better than standard-width windows in barn-type buildings.

Comparing window costs

I use square metre rates to get a shortcut method for comparing window costs. For a really lazy shortcut, I like to work with the 1200 x 1200 (double casement size) window and use that as a benchmark. It's probably the commonest size of window in new housing (certainly the commonest width) and, at 1.4 sq m, it gives you a yardstick for comparison's sake. In truth, smaller, single casement windows are much more expensive per unit area but, if our benchmark house is anything to go by, not many get used – just two installed. Sizes larger than 1200 wide tend to increase in cost in proportion to their area, so that a 1770 (three casement width) window is 50 per cent larger and 50 per cent more expensive than a 1200-wide one.

The overall window area tends to be pretty closely related to the internal floor area. For instance, our benchmark house has 24 sq m of windows combined with 17 sq m of glazed external doors (OK, I admit, adding doors makes it all a little bit dodgy but I am only looking for rough guidance): that's just over 40 sq m of openings on a floor area of 200 sq m. You won't go far wrong by sticking to this 1:5 ratio, unless you have a modern design using loads more glazing. So if you can work out the cost of a square metre of your chosen window or even just the cost of a 1200 x 1200 double casement (1.4 sq m), then you should be able to multiply that by the floor area, divide the result by five and voila, you have an approximation of what your joinery is likely to cost.

One of the things that throws people out is that the headline rates for timber windows from the large joinery manufacturers appears to be low, much lower than any of the finished windows. A raw timber window needs glazing, needs detailing around the openings and needs decorating as well: the combined costs of these items is more than double the cost of the raw timber window.

If you account for these extra items as the window table does, then you find that uPVC is now the cheapest way to build a window, by some margin.

Our benchmark house builder, Steve Baldwin, spent around £7,000 on his uPVC windows and external doors. Had he switched to a top spec window like Andersen, he would have trebled that amount.

Detailing

The Victorians set their windows and doors back into the brickwork. Not only does this decrease the effects of weathering on joinery

but it tends to look better as well. However, it is an expensive way of going about things, primarily because it requires a masonry projecting cill underneath and some form of arched lintel overhead, adding perhaps £100 per opening.

Today's volume joinery is made with integral cill sections and is designed to fit just 25mm back from the outside face of the brickwork. This is easy and cheap – but it also looks cheap, especially in brick facades. Rendered and timbered exteriors normally feature cottagey windows perched on the external face, but traditionally brickwork was associated with recessed joinery. Consider recessing your joinery if you are building in brick or stone:
■ it will be cheaper than specifying hardwood windows
■ it will almost certainly look better
■ a softwood window, set back, will probably perform better than an exposed hardwood one.

Look at the relative performance of Victorian sash windows and timber or steel casements on 20th century housing. By and large the old sash windows last about 100 years, or three-times as long as exposed casements.

If you live in an area rated severe weather exposure (and this includes all Scotland and Northern Ireland), you will have no choice but to recess your windows into the walls. Note also however that if you plan to sit your window deeper than normal, you may not be able to use some of the new cavity closers on offer and you may also have problems with exposed lintels above the window.

'Good fenestration'

Architects and planners talk loftily of something called 'good fenestration'. By this they mean that there are some ways of placing windows (and entrances) in walls that look good and others that look ugly. You'd think that what looks good and what doesn't would be a matter of individual taste, but in fact there is a surprising amount of consensus about it.

Until this century, virtually all buildings that we constructed had 'good fenestration'.

Joinery Rules of Thumb Costings

- Most houses have a window/door opening area equal to 15-20% of the external wall area
- In most house designs, external wall area is similar to the internal floor area.
- As a rough rule of thumb, you can assume that your joinery area is likley to be 20% of your internal floor area
- Thus a 200m² house will have around 40m² of joinery in its external walls.

Comparison square metre costs for joinery (say 15 windows, 4 doors)

	Typical metre square costs
uPVC Speedframe, as used on Benchmark house, inc glazing, ironmonegry and cavity closers	£ 150
Cheap uPVC	£ 100
Cheapest softwood, unglazed, unpainted	£ 60
Softwood, glazed and painted	£ 150
Hardwood, glazed and stained	£ 220
Velux	£ 300
Andersen	£ 350
Cavity Closers extra	£ 25

THINGS which will push up the basic rate

- Doors - more expensive than windows: lots of patio doors and french windows will add extra
- Small windows - the unit cost increases dramatically
- Unusual styles - sash windows, curved work, leaded lights - all extra
- Non-standard sizes - usually add between 25% and 40%

Whether we are looking at the great country houses now presided over by the National Trust or at the humble peasant's cottage or indeed at spec-built Victorian terraces, there is a general consensus that they look right.

Throughout the course of the 20th century we've gradually lost the art of fenestration, so that by the Sixties we were mostly building in ways that look all wrong to us now. Quite why this should be so is still a subject of some controversy (i.e. is it just fashion or is there something more basic?), but most designers and customers are now aware of the mistakes that have been made and in the Eighties there was a movement to build back in what developers call kerb appeal which refers to the visual impact a house makes on passers-by – what advertisers would refer to as sexiness.

The movement to build in kerb appeal has not been an unqualified success. Visit any modern housing development and you can't fail to notice what the current fashions are. Half-timbering, ornamental leadwork, rustic pantiles and cottage-style windows all suggest that developers are trying to recreate ye olde village look and yet, and yet it still all seems so unconvincing. You can get a house to look

convincingly old fashioned, but you have to avoid things like standard joinery which tends to be made out of comparatively heavy sections, which rarely looks authentic. The art of fenestration is partly to do with getting the openings in the right place but also partly to do with making sure that these correctly placed openings are filled with good-looking joinery. Much as it pains the purists, good design doesn't always equate with timber windows.

■External doors

Many of the things that I've written about windows apply equally to external doors. Furthermore, there is a polite convention that your choice of door should not clash with your choice of window – a convention that's well worth following whatever your chosen style. As with windows, the door manufacturers tend to stick to pretty conventional ideas and all produce variations on some remarkably similar themes. One of the more daring ideas is to put a little bit of stained glass in the pocket window on some of the designs. By and large, the best that can be said about the design of these doors is that 'it blends in quite well' or 'isn't that unobtrusive?' If you want a door that makes a statement about you – and, after all, the front door is the first thing visitors come into contact with – then you'll have to look to a bespoke joiner's shop or a salvage yard. Either way expect to pay.

Materials

Timber is still the most widely used material for external doors (just) but whereas it once enjoyed a near monopoly it now has to share the field with other materials. As with windows, timber doors are the cheapest to buy off the shelf but they are not universally loved by developers because they are prone to twisting and warping, entailing unwelcome call backs. Switching to hardwood doors is one option but, by all accounts, hardwood doors are almost as likely to move as softwood ones A reasonable compromise for those who want something better than a softwood door but are not keen on specifying tropical hardwood is to go for hemlock, a durable North American softwood particularly well suited to doors.

What are the other options? All are more expensive than softwood and all share the plus point that they are dimensionally stable – which no timber door will ever be. Steel is the cheapest alternative; widely used in North America, it has an aura of security about it that is perhaps unjustified, since a door is no stronger than its frame (which is usually softwood) or its locks (which are no different whatever the door). Steel takes paint well but is susceptible to bodywork damage just like a car. The market leader for steel doors is the IG Weatherbeater. Another option is uPVC – widely used in the replacement door market – which suffers visually in comparison with its competitors.

The most interesting of the alternative materials is GRP – that's glass reinforced fibre or good ol' Fibreglass. It's well established in the garage door market but is now beginning to make inroads into house doors. The wood-grained effect is far more realistic than anything uPVC can achieve and the material can be stained to match other joinery. Look out for Lindman's Fiber-Classics.

Patio doors

The idea of opening up a largish hole in the house facing the garden is attractive to most of us; it's a sort of poor man's conservatory. You have a basic choice here between sliding doors and hinged ones which we conventionally refer to as French doors (though the French, more accurately, call them porte fenêtre or window doors). There is not an awful lot to choose between them pricewise, but the overall visual effect can be very different. You see, the patio door is that rarity in new housebuilding, an essentially modern design feature, a sort of junior relative of the glass walled office block. If you are spending money (lots of it) on creating an olde worlde look, then a set of patio doors – even with leaded lights – is going to look out of place. In contrast, a pair of French terrace doors tends to add a little bit of Brideshead to the elevation; they're nothing if not old-fashioned. French doors may look the part, but the timber ones are notoriously fickle in their behaviour and are a bugger to hang well. Too tight and you'll forever be planing bits off every time it rains: too loose and the wind will whistle through them as if they were wide open.

Patio doors, whether sliding or hung, present security problems. French doors are relatively easy to force open; this can be countered to some extent by fitting sliding and locking bolts to both doors, not just the first leaf to open. They are also unusual for external doors in that they open outwards which leaves their hinge knuckles exposed and vulnerable to being cut off, though there is a little gizmo called a hinge bolt which can counteract this. Patio doors present a different problem in that they have frequently been prised, frame and all, from their moorings; very often they are secured only by three screws at either end.

Handles

Whilst in theory there are innumerable materials that you could use to make door handles from, in practice the range is surprisingly limited: aluminium, wrought iron or brass (or rather brass effect). Aluminium has the reputation for being cheap (though there are some very expensive aluminium fittings available) and brass is the preferred material for most developers, both inside and out. Its styling is usually either Victorian (plain) or Georgian (fancy scrolled edges). Black wrought iron is favoured for the country cottage look, but is out of place on anything else. If you want something a bit different, look out for modern stainless steel designs (check out Modric) or plastic (Normbau).

Heat loss

As regards overall heating costs, the role of doors is pretty negligible, largely because their overall area is small compared to other elements in the house. However since the new thermal regs came into effect in 2002, you have to consider the U-value of your external doors as well as your windows.

Timber doors don't score well, averaging well over the 2.0 figure that is anticipated in the regs. In contrast, the steel and GRP doors achieve U-values between 1.2 and 1.5 because they have hollow cores which can be filled with insulation. uPVC doors also tend to perform reasonably well; expect U values down below 2.0. Solid timber is the poorest insulator, then glazing, then insulated panels, be they steel, GRP or uPVC.

The requirement is for an overall joinery U-value of 2.0 so if you want a solid timber door with a U-value much higher than this, you can still fit it if you fit windows with a lower U-value – there is a trade-off allowed.

■ *Glazing*

Glass and glazing is one aspect of housebuilding where the changes are ringing out. Until the Nineties, most new homes were routinely fitted with single glazing. A decade later, standard double glazed units no longer meet the building regulations and we are having

to familiarise ourselves with all kinds of new energy-saving techniques, from low-e coatings to argon filling and warm edgings. We have also had to cope with new glazing techniques and new safety features.

Double glazing

The idea of double glazing is to reduce heat loss and, to a lesser extent, increase sound insulation. The work is done not so much by the extra pane of glass but by the air between the two panes, known as the air gap. The early forms of double glazing were a significant improvement on single glazing. U-values for single glazing tend to be around 5.0; in contrast a basic double glazed sealed unit is around 3.0. But the technology has kept on developing and the most advanced glazing systems available today have U values as low as 1.0. The most recent changes in our thermal building regs reflect this state of affairs and now require windows to have a U-value of no more than 2.0. What was a state-of-the-art window ten years ago now won't even pass muster. It's not exactly Pentium processor type change but it's still a lot for the dear old building industry to cope with.

In fact the building trade took a long while to come to grips with basic double glazing. There was a horribly high failure rate, usually manifesting itself in the form of misting between the panes. The air in the air gap was sealed, and was meant to stay sealed, but when the edge seals broke down, the air would mix with moist external air and condensation would take place. Hundreds of thousands of double glazed units have failed this way over the years and only recently has the industry worked out how to combat the problem. Builders were using the wrong kind of sealants and squeezing glazing units into rebates that weren't designed to take them. The results were that the units got wet around the edges and the seals disintegrated. Double glazing failure was one of the bete noirs of the warranty providers because they didn't include them in their ten year guarantees – something

Heat Loss Through Glazed Joinery

	n/a	GAP BETWEEN PANES		
		6mm	12mm	16mm+
Single Glazing	5.0			
Solid timber door	3.0			
Insulated unglazed door	1.2			
Air filled DG unit		3.1	2.8	2.7
Argon filled DG unit		2.9	2.7	2.6
Argon filled low-e DG unit		2.3	1.9	1.8
Air filled Triple glazing		2.4	2.1	2.0
Argon low-e triple glazing		1.8	1.4	1.3
Figures above are U values: the lower the more efficient				

		HEAT LOSS THROUGH GLASS			
U Value of single glazing	5.0	2.0	1.7	1.3	1.0
Extra Installation costs		regs	£250	£750	£1250
kWh heat lost/annum	177	71	60	46	35
Annual cost of heat lost	£ 82	£33	£28	£21	£16
Figures are for 30m² glazing as per Benchmark House					

which the new housebuyers never seemed to twig until they came to make a claim. But such is the confidence in the new installation techniques that both the NHBC and Zurich have, since 2000, added sealed unit failure to the list of items covered by their latent defects policies. The key change has been the uptake of drained and vented bottom rails that allow any accumulated moisture to either drain away or evaporate before it starts doing damage to the seals. Deeper glazing rebates in the joinery help matters as well and these are becoming mandatory thanks to changes in the thermal regs. Misting in units was a problem for both timber and PVC windows but the problems were worse with timber because these were often site glazed, rather badly.

Energy efficiency

Various measures improve the efficiency of double glazing. The simplest is to increase the distance between the panes. A 6mm gap was the old standard. By upping this to 16mm or 20mm you reduce heat loss by nearly 25 per cent. It's easy for the glazing manufactures to alter the gap and there is no cost penalty here. The difficulty comes in building joinery that will take deep units like this. The uPVC manufacturers didn't have any problems but the

timber window makers proved very reluctant to switch to wider glazing rebates though the new legislation effectively insists on it – the old high performance windows are now the standard.

The next trick is to fill the air gap between panes with something other than air. The inert gas argon is the common choice (though some use krypton). Argon filling tends to add about £5 per sq m to the costs of the units and it results in only a marginal improvement in efficiency, typically between five per cent and ten per cent.

Then switch to coated, low emissivity (or Low-e) glass. Low-e glass works by absorbing short wave solar heat, just like other glass, but then acting as a reflective shield to the long wave heat emanating from inside the house. In effect it introduces a layer of one way insulation into the sealed unit.

Low-e is applied as a micron-thin coating to the inside of the inner pane and, although some people claim to be able to tell the difference between low-e coated and uncoated glass – apparently it has a blue tint – I can't. Low-e coating is a developing technology and there are now hard coatings and soft coatings with varying emissivity levels. Soft coatings are better and, needless to say, more expensive. A hard coat will reduce the overall U-value by 25 per cent; a soft coat by as much as 35 per cent.

Another emerging technique is to use warm edge spacers around the sealed units. Traditionally, the spacers have been made of aluminium which is, of course, a very good heat conductor. A classic case of cold bridging. By replacing the aluminium with something less conductive (typically plastic) you get a much more even U-value across the entire sealed unit. The smaller the units, the bigger difference warm edgings make.

Beyond this, there are adjustments you can make to the frames which can have a major impact on heat loss. And ultimately, you can add an extra sheet of glass and move to triple glazing which also improves efficiency by around 25 per cent. Triple glazing is also much better for sound proofing. Add all these 25 per cents here and 35 per cents there plus the odd ten per cent and you can see how a state of the art double or triple glazed unit can get a very low U-value, far in excess of what is required by the new UK regs. In fact if you want state of the art triple glazing you will almost certainly have to import it because there isn't anyone in the UK producing triple glazed units.

Rating

Comparing glazed units and windows is a complex business. For instance glass is unique amongst building components in that it can absorb heat as well as lose it. A highly efficient window on a south facing wall is probably a net contributor of heat over a year as a whole (though of course it is never easy to measure such things). In order to try and bring some simplicity to it all, a new body called the British Fenestration Rating Council (www.bfrc.org) has plans to introduce an energy rating system for windows. It's something similar to that used by the white goods manufacturers where it is now mandatory to show the energy consumption of every machine on sale, but unlike it, the system will not be mandatory.

Renovations

The 2002 reg changes brought about another

significant change in that, for the first time, replacement windows were required to meet the new standards as well. Exactly how this is going to be policed remains something of a mystery at time of writing. But expect the glazing firms to stop selling units that don't match the 2.0 U-value figure. And expect the joinery firms to stop making windows that can't take at least 24 mm wide double glazed units.

One area that will remain exempt from the new requirements is listed buildings. English Heritage are one body that doesn't approve of the new regs – they see it as a uPVC window salesmen's licence to rip out all that is wooden and lovely with our national treasures. The exemption may also apply to properties situated in Conservation Areas though this isn't abundantly clear. The conservators' point is that thick windows (whether uPVC or timber) don't look as good as thin ones.

Safety glazing

Another important factor to consider is the regs requirement for safety glazing on:
■ any window less than 800mm off floor level
■ any window less than 300mm from a door
■ all doors and sidelights where pane width is greater than 250mm
■ internal glazed doors with pane sizes more than 250mm x 250mm.
There are two common forms of clear, strengthened glass:
■ Toughened: baked hard to about five times the strength of float glass and, when broken, shatters into (hopefully) harmless lumps. Toughened glass costs about 50 per cent more than standard float glass.
■ Laminated: consists of two sheets of ordinary glass sandwiched around a plastic film: when hit it breaks but doesn't collapse. This is now how most car windscreens are made.

Laminated glass is conventionally 6.4mm thick and it costs around double standard float glass, considerably more than toughened glass. Consequently for these applications, toughened glass is now almost universally specified, but laminated glass is preferable if you are worried about security; it's harder to break through.

Cleaning windows

Fed up with cleaning windows? Another innovation is self cleaning glass. All the big producers seem to have something on the market now. St. Gobain's is called Aquaclean. Like Low-e glass, it uses a transparent coating but this one is hydrophilic (literally 'water-loving') mineral material, so that water spreads out over the surface of the coating and causes a washing effect when it comes into contact with the window. The water then quickly evaporates, leaving no marks from dried drops of water. They don't actually claim that you'll never need to clean windows again, rather that you won't need to clean them so often.

Decorative effects

The addition of imitation leaded lights is popular in many Tudor-style developments. It can be added either as squares or diamonds. It is a relatively expensive operation (costing around £25 per sq m – that's an extra £300 on the benchmark house) and it can look awful. In fact it often does; it's another effect that rarely looks good with thick double glazed units. However, when the design is carefully handled (which usually means using it sparingly), the effect can be to simulate a much older style of window.

Georgian look

Fitting sealed units into Georgian style windows and doors can be a very expensive business, because most glaziers have a minimum charge for each unit made and small units therefore get heavily penalised. For instance, Solaglas, one of the largest of the national glazing firms, sets a minimum charge per unit of 25 per cent of the square metre rate; this means that double-glazed units do not get any cheaper when the size falls below 500 x 500mm (or its equivalent area). Now, a typical Georgian style bedroom window has 16 small panes measuring 250 x 275mm; you don't have to be a financial genius to work out that that's going to be one hell of a lot more expensive to kit out with double

glazed units. In fact it's likely to cost 16 x £9 or £144 as opposed to just £35 for a more conventional arrangement with two units.

Small wonder that a number of manufacturers like Andersen Windows offer imitation Georgian glazing bars, rather like imitation leaded lights. If your heart (or your planner) is set on Georgian-style joinery then look out early for suppliers who won't exact such a savage cost penalty.

Swept heads

The Georgian look has been drifting out of fashion in the last decade – possibly because of the high glazing costs – but it has been replaced by the country cottage look and, from the developer's point of view, the quintessential part of the cottage look is the curved head to the window. Again, there are knock-on effects to the glazing costs, but there is an important proviso here that the cost conscious should know. Whilst the real swept-head windows involve manufacturing curved glass units – adding around 20 per cent to the cost – there is an alternative, which is to stick timber swept-head inserts over the top of rectangular glass units after they have been fitted. Almost every major joinery manufacturer offers this option and it makes both the glazing and the joinery cheaper. However it is an imitation swept head at best, and though you might not be able to tell the difference from the outside, from the inside you can actually see that the insert has been stuck on top of the glass.

Obscure

People generally only fit obscure glass in bathroom windows, the reason being that they are often n-n-n-naked in the bathroom and they don't want the neighbours to have a gander. This arrangement may well suit 90 per cent of UK households, but think about you and your bathroom before blithely specifying obscure glass. You may not need privacy in every bathroom or you may not need privacy all the time, in which case Venetian blinds or curtains might serve you better. You might even enjoy

Glazing Guide Prices			
			All prices are £/m²
	MATERIALS	LABOUR	SUPPLY & FIX
DOUBLE GLAZING PRICES			
Minimum charge per sealed unit		25% of m² price	
Fixing charges for sealed units		£15	
Standard clear 4-16-4 sealed units	£25	£15	£40
Obscure 4-16-4 sealed units	£28	£15	£43
Toughened 4-16-4 sealed units	£33	£15	£48
Laminated 6.4-16-4 sealed units	£60	£15	£75
Low E glass with argon filled cavity	£35	£15	£50
Low E glass available in all options	add £12/m²		
Imitation leaded lights	add £25/m²		
Swept head glazing	add 20%		
SINGLE GLAZING PRICES			
Fixing charge for single glazing		£2/pane	
Minimum charge		£ 25	
4mm Float	£12		£15
6mm Float	£18		£20
6mm Toughened	£20		£24

Bear in mind there is a big move to get all to abandon on-site glazing and to buy all joinery pre-glazed. Double glazing has had an atrocious failure rate over the past 30 years and one of the major culprits is sloppy on-site glazing. Nevertheless, on-site glazing will continue on many sites because it's a) traditional and b) a little cheaper

lying in the bath looking out of your window, perhaps having a gander at your neighbour.

Obscure glass doesn't add much to a room from the inside and doesn't look that good from the outside. The plainer patterns tend to look least obtrusive but none of them look as good as a real window. So think whether you really need obscure before you specify it.

Daylight quality

The primary function of glazing is to let light in. Keeping heat in and not breaking when hit (either intentionally or accidentally) are lesser but more frequently discussed properties, but before passing on let's consider this primary function for a moment. Generally, the thicker the glass, the less light gets through.

Low-e glass (which saves heat) actually cuts out quite a lot of light: it acts rather like Polaroid sunglasses do in reducing glare. In rooms with lots of glazing this can be a positive benefit in itself. On the other hand, if your design keeps glazing to a minimum, remember that daylight quality is improved by

having windows in two walls of a room so that daylight arrives from more than one direction: this may be worth considering in kitchen design.

Intermediate floors

The ground floor has been looked at in the previous chapter, Groundworks. Any floors above ground level (inc floors over basements) are referred to as intermediate floors; they act as both floors for the rooms above and ceilings for the rooms below. This makes the issues we need to look at rather different. Intermediate floors only have to be thermally insulated if they are above features like garages; on the other hand, you have to consider sound insulation, which you don't on ground floors.

The structural elements of intermediate floors are pretty similar to ground floors. Obviously, the ground-bearing slab is not an option but otherwise you have the same choice to make between timber or masonry suspended floors. Timber floors are traditional and remain

First Floor Costs - Square Meter rates

	Mats	Time in mins	Labour @ £18/hr	M² rates
Joists	£ 5.70	45	£ 13.50	£ 19
I beams	£ 10.00	30	£ 9.00	£ 19
Chipboard	£ 4.20	15	£ 4.50	£ 9
Cheap Acoustic Quilt	£ 1.50	5	£ 1.50	£ 3
Acosustic Upgrades for Party Floors	£ 18.00	40	£ 12.00	£ 30
Beam and Block (above ground floor)	£ 17.00	40	£ 12.00	£ 29
Hollow core	£ 30.00	30	£ 9.00	£ 39
65mm Screed	£ 4.30	25	£ 7.50	£ 12

First Floor Options - per square metre

Timber or I beam floors to 40dB (Part E2 - for detached houses)	£30
Timber or I beam floors to Party Floor standard	£60
Beam and Block floor with Screed to 40db (Part E2 - for detached houses)	£40
Beam and Block floor with Screed to Party Floor Standard	£45
Hollow core floor with screed (all versions meet Party Floor standard)	£55

Benchmark House - First Floor Costs

	Area in m²	Mats	Lab	Total
Timber Joists with Acoustic Insulation under 22mm chipboard	106	£ 1,200	£ 2,100	£ 3,300

It's not easy making floor cost comparisons! I have ignored floor finishes altogether, although they are themselves affected by how the sub-floor has been built. I have also ignored the cost of laying services within the floor void - a task much simpler on timber floors than masonry ones, which require some sort of false ceiling below to be added on.

– timber joists or I beams, chipboard cover, single sheet of plasterboard underneath. Cost: effectively minus zero as you aren't allowed to build like this anymore.

■ New building reg requirement (E2): adds insulation in joist space and a ceiling board that is slightly heavier than what we have been getting used to. British Gypsum have launched what they call the Tenboard because it weighs 10 kg per sq m, which is the building reg requirement. Cost: zero. Hoped for decibel reduction: 40dB. You can improve this rating a little by putting in more insulation into the joist space. Don't pack it tight – 80 per cent depth is reckoned to be ideal for sound absorption.

■ Add a carpet and underlay above. Dramatic improvement in impact sound going down. Slight improvement in airborne sound coming up! If you really don't want carpet upstairs, add a resilient layer (an acoustic underlay) between the chipboard and the floor cover. Acoustilay and Ecoustic are two brand names costing between £10 and £20 per sq m, depending on your spec. Reduces sound transmission by around 5dB.

■ Use two layers of plasterboard or a heavier building board such as Fermacell on the ceiling. Added cost, maybe £5 per sq m. Sound transmission reduction: 3dB.

■ Improve this by a further 2dB by introducing resilient bars, fixed to the underside of the joists. You fix the plasterboard to the resilient bars. These metal strips, costing just 65p per linear metre, act to separate the ceiling boards from the floor joists. Isolation is one of the keys to improving sound insulation. The very best way of building isolation into a floor is to separate the ceiling joists from the floor joists, but this makes for a lot of extra work and a very deep floor void.

■ Add a floating floor above. There are numerous proprietary acoustic floor systems on the market: the insulation manufacturers all seem to make them, as do the plasterboard makers. They are rated either lightweight – aimed at impact noise mainly – or heavyweight. The heavyweight ones are usually made up of layers of heavy board products with names like SoundPlank. Overall, with attention to flanking sounds as well, heavy floating floors will add about 5dB to decibel reduction, cost maybe £5 per sq m and add 50mm to your floor depth.

Masonry floors

As a complete alternative, you can switch to a masonry floor system. You see an immediate substantial jump in airborne sound reduction between floors, of the order of 15dB, though impact sound reduction requires a bit more thought. However there is also a substantial cost penalty for switching away from timber or I-beam joists.

Realistically you can only build masonry floors if you are building a blockwork house. It's true that German timber frame builders manage to combine concrete intermediate floors with timber walls, so it's not an impossibility, but no one in Britain has a clue how to go about this so you'd be well advised not to try.

As with ground floors, the choice is either a beam and block floor or a hollow core plank floor. The planks are better acoustically but are more expensive and are more taxing to install; they require double thickness supporting walls unless the planks span between external walls. Both masonry systems can perform well but beam and block in particular is prone to catastrophic acoustic failures. Why? Because the blocks get left out. Or taken out to make a path for plumbing or soil stacks. Whatever you make a floor out of, if you start punching holes in it, it won't work.

You also have to pay attention to how best to finish a masonry floor. Underneath, you have a problem in that you need a service void in which to run lighting cables. You can either fix battens into the floor or hang the plasterboard off special clips. Above, you have a problem with the camber on the floor beams and the manufacturers want you to lay a screed. Fine, if you want underfloor heating, but expensive if you don't.

Party floors

Having gone into some detail on how to improve sound insulation levels on intermediate floors, it's worth adding that if you are involved in constructing party floors – that is floors between flats – you have to meet some very tight sound reduction standards. And you will very possibly be asked to have your floor (and party walls) tested to see if they work as designed. See the section called 'All about Noise' in the last chapter to find out more.

Also note a couple little points. First, carpet still works pretty well as a soundproofer. I know it's out of fashion but a good carpet laid over a thick underlay does wonders for keeping the noise down, at least as good as many of the other more expensive solutions I have been writing about. And downlighters. Very fashionable, I know. But making holes in the ceiling is bad news noise-wise.

Floor finishes

The lowest grade of timber floor covering in widespread use, chipboard is made out of tiny wood particles suspended in a sea of glue. At around £4 per sq m, chipboard is nearly half the price of the much stronger plywood but is not nearly as durable. The NHBC now requires that all chipboard used in new housing should be moisture resistant, but this is far from being weatherproof and it is not recommended that chipboard be built into a house before the structure is watertight – nevertheless it regularly is. One mid-priced alternative is to use Sterling Floor, a waferboard now manufactured in 2400 x 600 tongued and grooved sheets like chipboard.

Chipboard is now frequently laid as part of a floating floor: that is to say that it is laid – or rather wedged-in without any fixings at all – on top of polystyrene floor insulation sheets on the ground floor, or acoustic insulation sheets on intermediate floors. Whereas chipboard has for a long time been the standard material for covering upstairs timber floors, where it is nailed – using ring shank nails – to the timber joists, its use without any nails or screws at all is still in its infancy. Problems have been encountered with chipboard sheeting curling at the edges and with sheets getting wet and consequently expanding and cracking walls above. In theory, there is much to recommend floating chipboard floors, especially where a carpeted finish is required, and costs are no higher than the traditional cement screed topping given to ground floors. In practice it pays to use the technique with caution; lay timber battens underneath where extra support is needed such as underneath stud walls, at external doorways and at the foot of staircases.

■Internal walls & beams

The traditional routine for internal partition walls is to build blockwork walls downstairs and timber studwork upstairs. Internal studwork (at around £12 per sq m) is a little cheaper and quicker to build than blockwork (at £15 per sq m).

By the way, don't assume from this that timber frame houses are cheaper to build than block built ones: the external walls are slightly more expensive to build than their blockwork equivalents. There is a third option here, one which is rapidly gaining momentum with the major housebuilders. That is steel channel. When you have people who know what they are doing and a decent sized run of a few houses, then steel framed walling systems are cheaper than timber or block, down below £10 per sq m.

Which to choose? Well the main issues to consider here are load-bearing and sound. Do you need internal load-bearing walls? Most two storey houses with spans of more than 5 m (which is most of them) will require some way of taking the load of the first floor joists: if the span is more than 5 or 6m, then you can't run joists (or concrete floors) across the gap in one without a break and that break has to be either a load-bearing wall or a structural beam. Now you can have internal load-bearing walls built in timber — most timber frame houses do just that — but conventionally you need to add extra support down at foundation level, usually in the form of a trench foundation. So you can see that load-bearing walls are quite a bit more expensive to build than simple partition walls. At roof level, the issue is rarely critical because most roofs are designed to spread the load from side to side, across the wallplates, so no load gets transferred down to internal walls. This is why traditionally internal partition walls are blockwork downstairs and timber stud upstairs. We are beginning to go around in circles!

Sound Issues

Builders instinctively go for blockwork if load-bearing capacity is important. The other reason why they like blockwork is of course soundproofing. Generally a block wall is pretty good at soundproofing between rooms. Until 2003, the building regs didn't address the issue of soundproofing within homes but now they call for a minimum of 40dB sound resistance which, in truth, isn't very difficult or exacting. If you are building in timber or steel channel, you will have to add a little insulation into the void and use a slightly heavier than normal plasterboard (such as British Gypsum's

Although steel frame has been slow to catch on for whole houses, steel internal walling is a big seller. It's quick and it's cheap - which suggests of course that it's not any good. Wouldn't be very soundproof, that's for sure, but new regs require some measure of soundproofing between rooms now.

Internal Walls - Square Metre Rates

	Basic Mats	Acoustic Insulation	Accessories	Mats	Time in mins (inc insulation)	Labour @ £18/hr	Combined
100mm Blockwork	£ 5.00		£ 0.40	£ 5.40	35	£ 10.50	£ 16
100mm Celcon Blockwork	£ 6.70		£ 0.40	£ 7.10	35	£ 10.50	£ 18
90mm Timber Studwork	£ 3.00	£ 2.50	£ 0.25	£ 5.75	20	£ 6.00	£ 12
Steel Channel	£ 2.30	£ 2.50	£ 0.50	£ 5.30	15	£ 4.50	£ 10
add for acoustic enhancements for Timber/Steel party walls				£9.00	30	£9.00	£18

Benchmark House - Internal Walling Costs

	Area in m²	Rate	Mats	Lab	Cost
100mm Hemelite Blockwork	101	£ 16	£ 550	£ 1,070	£ 1,620
Studwork Walls	48	£ 12	£ 280	£ 300	£ 580
Total			**£ 830**	**£ 1,370**	**£ 2,200**

Tenboard). A greatly improved method is to fix double thickness boards each face of the wall. Or switch to a much heavier building board such as Fermacell, popular in any event with selfbuilders because it's much easier to finish than plasterboard.

You can go to great lengths to soundproof your bedroom walls but bear in mind that a bedroom is only as soundproof as its weakest link and that's usually the door. Unless you go to the considerable expense of fitting an acoustic doorset, then you'd probably do well not to get too fussed about the whole process. Other design tips are to place built-in cupboards between rooms you want to isolate, and to avoid placing electrical switches and socket plates in noise-sensitive walls.

Alternatives

Every year or so someone comes along with another system which will 'completely revolutionise building techniques' and make 'blockwork and studwork redundant'. We've had Stramit straw partitions, Paramount plasterboard wall units, Premaco gypsum wall blocks, Streamline system walls. All promise great savings and yet none ever really catch on. Part of the problem is that you need to have a very large site going to start enjoying real savings since the amount of initial head scratching is large; I may be doing these manufacturers a

great disservice, but I don't think the one-off house builder will be particularly interested.

Steel beams

Every designer will tell you that you can build rooms to any size that you want – 'your imagination is the limit' or some such nonsense. But they may not explain that once a room gets wider than the normal span for a floor joist you will run into extra costs because you have to fit a beam across the middle to split the loading. This width varies with the size and frequency of the floor joists, but once you get over 4 m, your costs start to rise substantially. Well, they do if you are working with timber joists: some of the alternative materials mentioned in the flooring section (i.e. concrete precast floors and timber I beams) are capable of much longer spans.

Steel beams themselves are not wildly expensive – a 102 x 178mm steel channel would cost less than £12 per lin m – but fixing them is a lot of work, no matter which method you use. If they are set inside the floor void, the floor joists will all have to be hung off the steel; if the steel is put below the ceiling then it will have to be boxed in with plasterboard.

Steel also needs looking after; it needs a coat of paint and it needs protecting from the threat of fire – usually this is achieved by fixing two thicknesses of plasterboard around it. Despite main house, which results in extra rainwater downpipes; I have seen various ways people have tried to disguise this detail but none of them look particularly convincing.

Planners permitting, you can of course forget about dormers and fit opening roof lights. Velux is the big name in this field (though there are several others) and Velux rooflights are very quick and easy to install; on a new building an opening rooflight will cost between £100 and £250 depending on size and will add virtually nothing to labour cost – it taking no longer to install than it does to fit the roof covering over the same space. In comparison, a simple dormer is likely to cost over £800. It may well be that your overall desired effect demands dormer windows in your roof and, if so, so be it. Just be aware that these types of windows (like bay windows) are not only expensive in themselves but are also heavy on management time. Unless very well planned out, they are more than likely to cause snags further on down the line.

If you are converting a barn you are likely to find that the planners will not allow dormer windows and will force you to use a rooflight. In response to this now well established pattern, Velux have produced a range of conservation rooflights which are designed to blend in with centuries-old buildings whilst still providing ease of opening and double glazing expected of modern roof windows. These conservation rooflights are however priced at a 30 per cent premium to standard rooflights.

Sunpipes

For those of you still in the dark, a sunpipe or light pipe is a highly reflective tube that allows you to pipe daylight from a roof down into the house. What you actually see is a transparent dome sitting on your roof and a translucent light diffuser – looking for all the world like an electric lampshade – fitted onto the ceiling of the room below. What you get is a credible amount of natural daylight into the darkest recesses of your home. A medium sized 350 mm light pipe will produce much more light than a 100w bulb even on a dull winter's day and will be adequate to light a room up to 15 sq m. At around £300, they are similar in cost to rooflights but they can have advantages in certain situations – you can bend the pipes round corners if necessary.

Edge details

One important detail to consider when thinking about roof designs is how to treat the roof edges. The ridges, hips and valleys will be sorted out by the roofing contractors, but the eaves and verge details are largely a matter of roof carpentry. Here, it makes no difference whether you've built a traditional cut roof or a trussed rafter one; you still have to sort out some sort of effective junction between the roof cover and the underlying structure.

Eaves

There are numerous variations on this theme, none of which is likely to cost less than about £15 per lin m (Mats £6, Lab £9) to fix (excluding decorating costs). If there is an industry standard detail it is the closed or boxed eaves. The vertical section is the fascia board: the horizontal bit under it, returning to the wall, is the soffit.

An alternative is to have open eaves. These are reckoned to look less modern and often more attractive. Some designs dispense with fascia boards altogether and allow guttering to be strapped on to the rafter feet – this is a particularly useful technique to employ with timber barn conversions where a fascia would look out of place – but the more usual method dispenses with just the soffit boards and leaves the rafter feet exposed. An open eaves detail is a little more expensive than boxed or soffitted eaves as you still have to provide a plywood plate (albeit above the rafter feet to catch the felt) and you are left with fiddly finishing details on the exposed underside.

More expensive still is to use the Georgian-style parapet. Here you build your external walls up above the eaves line and collect the rainwater draining off the roof in a hidden lead gutter behind the parapet. This technique was once common in inner-city housing terraces and large country houses, but nowadays tends to look a little bit pretentious – unless you happen to be building a large Georgian-style house.

Our Benchmark House builder, Steve Baldwin, used a different route. Having switched to uPVC windows back in 1997, he has also seen fit to switch to uPVC soffits and eaves. He subcontracted the supply and fix of his eaves details, together with the rainwater goods, for a sum of £2,400. This for 65m of eaves, 65m of guttering and 30m of downpipes. Of this total, I would expect the boxed eaves and fascias to make up around half. It's not a bad price and, of course, it leaves a fit and forget backing for uPVC rainwater gear.

Verges

Verges are only found over gable ends, so many houses without gables will have only eaves details. There are, again, two classic treatments of verge junction details. One is to lay the tiles or slates straight on to a bead of cement at the top of the supporting gable wall, the other is to oversail the wall and to finish the roof cover over a (usually timber) bargeboard. Each technique has its merits. The direct method can look horribly cheap but, equally well, is capable of being enhanced by using some fancy dog's-tooth brickwork: the bargeboard method is rather easier to install (it too can be enlivened by adding decorative effects).

Ventilation

It is surprising to many people that roof timbers do not need to be treated with preservatives (unless you live in a long-horn beetle area, mostly south of London) but you do need to consider moisture penetration very carefully.

For a conventional trussed roof where the upstairs living space does not project into the roofspace, the ventilation requirements are satisfied by the provision of a 10 mm continuous air gap all the way around the eaves. You might think that this is a very straightforward matter, but there is also concern that a ventilation gap shouldn't become an open

Roof ventilation detail

Pitched roofs must have a 10mm continuous air gap at eaves (or its equivalent). This can be achieved with either a meshed strip or a number of circular vents

If there is a "room in the roof" design, then this air gap must be increased to 25mm at the eaves and you will be required to supply some ridge ventilation as well

Also here you must keep a minimum air gap of 50mm between the roof cover and the insulation

50mm air gap

doorway to birds and insects, and therefore there has grown up a whole industry making plastic roof vents which let air in and keep bugs out. There are several different types; some are cut into the soffit boards, some are nailed on top of the fascia and some get fixed between the rafters. They range in price from £1-£3 per lin m. The roofing giants, Redland and Marley, both make proprietary ventilation systems but you will find better value from specialist producers like Glidevale and Rytons. Rytons, in particular, are geared to mail-order sales and produce a most helpful catalogue explaining the ins and outs of roof (and sub-floor) ventilation.

Ridge ventilation

When you have a room in the roof design, roof ventilation becomes a more complex problem and care has to be taken to leave a airflow gap between the roofing felt and the insulation surrounding the living space. There is also a requirement for ventilation at the top of the roof, the ridge, and this can be expensive to achieve.

One way of achieving this is to fit a ventilated ridge, a plastic extrusion which fits under the ridge tiles: this has the advantage of being visually unobtrusive but it comes at a cost of around £18 per lin m, much more than the cost of the ridge tiles themselves. Alternatively there are several formats of ridge ventilation tiles now available: they are invariably expensive – expect to pay between £30 and £50 each – and unlike the dry ridge systems they are all too obvious from the ground.

Roof or ridge vented tiles are also useful with an internal soil pipe or an extract fan that are most conveniently ducted up through the roof space. Glidevale produce the most complete catalogue of roof ventilation and also some of the best solutions for these types of problems.

If you are working with a handmade tile, Tudor Roof Tiles produces an Invisible Venting System which uses the natural camber present on most handmade tiles to provide adequate ventilation space to take the foul air away from extractor fans and soil pipes.

RedBank produce a vented ridge tile suitable for taking the exhaust from gas fired appliances: it's called a low resistance terminal and it costs around £60. Smoke from solid fuel fires has to be expelled via the more traditional chimney arrangements.

Unvented roofs

If all this ventilation seems to be more trouble than it's worth, then you'll want to know about other options. In fact, if you are building a room-in-the-roof design then you would also be well advised to use an alternative because they are likely to be cheaper and easier. The 2002 changes to the thermal building regs demand a sloping roof U-value of just 0.2 which in turn requires an awful lot of insulation (approx. 200 mm of mineral wool or polystyrene or 120 mm of Pu board). There simply isn't the depth of rafter to stuff this much insulation in and still have room for a 50 mm vent gap under the roof. But just when all seems lost, Tyvek and the breathable membranes ride in to the rescue. These materials are at once waterproof and vapour permeable and their manufacturers have convinced the authorities that if you specify one of these so-called breathable membranes instead of traditional roofing felt, then you don't need to have the 50 mm vent gap within the rafter space and you don't need to worry about eaves and ridge ventilation. Although they are expensive compared to roofing felt, you claw this money back by saving on other materials.

It's not quite true to say you don't need a vent gap at all because most designs call for counter battening under the tiles or slates – this effectively gives you a vent gap on the outside of the roof, above the rafter line.

There are many variations on the unvented roof design, sometimes known as a warm roof design. It's complicated in Scotland by the requirement for roof sarking, which is a layer of solid timber boarding traditionally nailed over the rafters, but the insulation manufactures and the breathable membrane suppliers all have details showing ways of satisfying both the U-value requirements and moisture management – every roof design has to pass what is called a Condensation Risk Analysis. The 2002 changes will have a significant impact on how we design and build room-in-the-roof but it may be some time before a clear winner emerges.

Condensation problems

A little discussed but widespread problem concerns condensation in lofts. It's a feature of cold roofs where there is unused loftspace. The insulation gets placed at ceiling level, leaving a large mass of air inside the roof but outside the heated envelope of the building. Roofs such as these require venting at eaves level – already covered – but this isn't always enough to stop condensation. The roof cover itself can get very very cold, especially on clear cold nights, and the moisture in the air in the loft finds a dew point under the felt where it proceeds to drip down onto the ceiling. It seems to make no difference whether you fit felt or a breathable membrane.

The most effective solution is to build in some form of ridge venting. Combined with the eaves venting, this creates a stack effect which keeps the air flowing through the loft. Without ridge vents, the air inside the loft frequently hangs around for a long time.

Whether this problem is being replicated in warm roofs isn't entirely clear yet. But the message is clear. It's one thing fitting ventilation in roofs: it's another getting the air to blow through it to order. Without any air movement, there is always a risk of condensation, even without a supply a warm moist air from within the house.

■Roof covers

There are many different materials you can use to cover your roof but before we go on to examine them consider first that virtually every housing estate in the country has a concrete tiled roof. Why? Simply a question of cost – concrete tiles are an amazingly cheap way to provide a roof cover and, designed well, they can look very effective. Sometimes but not, unfortunately, always.

Another plus point for concrete interlocking tiles is that they can be laid at very shallow pitches, some at as little as 14°, whereas the more traditional tiles often demand roof pitches of 35°. Low-pitched roofs have two advantages over steep-pitched roofs: their surface area is less – this makes for savings on roofing materials – and they are less visible, therefore the visual impact of any roof covering is diminished. Note, however, that if you are trying to recreate an older style of building, a low pitched roof will probably look out of place.

Concrete v clay

In contrast to concrete, a clay tile is seen as an upmarket product and people often enthuse about how much better they look but, as ever, it's a question of personal taste. Concrete and clay can look virtually identical when laid – the difference becomes apparent as they weather. After ten years a concrete tile looks washed out, the colour flat, the roof lifeless. In contrast, the look of clay actually improves with age as it develops an interesting patina. Clay tiles hold their value too – see if you can find a concrete tile in a salvage yard.

The price differential between concrete and clay used to be wide but it has been steadily falling in recent years – currently there is a 20 per cent premium for clay.

At the really cheap end, concrete has the market more or less to itself with what are known as large format or interlocking tiles – often measuring 330 x 270mm, the size of six plain tiles; you don't need very many and this fact alone makes them much quicker to lay. Large format tiles start losing their cost advantage on complex roof shapes with lots of cuts, so you tend to see them on very simple roof designs.

Small format tiles, known as plain tiles, are available from a wide range of suppliers in both concrete and clay. At the top end of the plain tile market come the handmade clay tiles: these are something else and, like handmade bricks, they tend to lend a strong vernacular flavour to any building they are put on. However, handmade clay tiles are also amazingly expensive, costing around five times as much to supply and fix as the basic concrete interlocking tile.

The roof tile market in the UK is dominated

by two giants, Redland and Marley (both recently taken over, by Lafarge and Eternit respectively). Redland sets the standards to which others aspire and if you want to get a better understanding of the possibilities with tile coverings, you should get hold of their Guide to Roofing Systems; it's free and it's an incredibly useful 46-page booklet which will tell you more than you will ever want to know about roof tiling. It's also available in Pocket Guide format – you should see it, it's a work of art. Redland tends to be more expensive than the competition (at least on single site developments) and you may find better prices if you chase Marley roofing or one of the smaller manufacturers such as Sandtoft, Russell or Weatherwell.

Most roofing contractors have cosy relationships with one particular manufacturer and you may well find that it pays you not to be too picky as to whose tile goes on your roof. Handmade tiles tend to be the province of smaller producers: if you have a deep wallet, look at Acme, Keymer and Tudor, who produce visually stunning roof tiles that are brand new yet manage to look at least 200 years old.

If you crave the look of a traditionally tiled roof but your budget doesn't stretch that far, Forticrete produce a large format concrete tile called the Gemini which simulates the plain tile look by planting a groove down the middle of a large format tile. It's this tile that Steve Baldwin chose for the roof of our benchmark house. Slightly more expensive but arguably better looking comes Sandtoft's 20/20 and HF's Beauvoise, imported from France: both are middle format clay tiles available at around £20 per sq m laid.

Slate

Slate became the preferred roofing choice of the Victorians when the railways provided access to the cheap Welsh slate quarries. The slate is still there but it is no longer cheap; indeed it is up there with handmade tiles and thatch as one of the most expensive options for the pitched roof. In rural areas, slate is unlikely to be most

people's first choice. However, planners often insist on slate roofs for the flimsiest of reasons and it is as well to be aware of that possibility.

If you want slate but are reluctant to pay the going rate for new Welsh slate there are a number of other options. You can look to source your slate from Spain: prices are much cheaper than Welsh slate but quality has been patchy and it's worth looking out for slate carrying a 30 year guarantee. Alternatively you can track down a supplier of second hand slate. Prices are similar to imported slate and quality is similarly variable but, if you know what to look for, it's relatively easy to assess the quality of a recycled slate and it can make a very good buy. There are also a number of slate substitutes on the market. The cheapest are the fibre cement slates but these are liable to warp and discolour over time.

There are also a number of interesting slate products, usually made out of reconstituted slate dust. Redland produce the best known reconstituted slate called the Cambrian and Eternit have one called the Melbourn: they are, in fact, not traditional slates at all but interlocking tiles. It is a mid-priced alternative to the natural slates and unimpressive artificials. However, many planning officers will insist on you using natural slates, even though they couldn't tell the difference when laid on a roof.

Stone belt roofing

Don't think that you can get away with just a stone facade if you live in an area where stone is the predominant building material. For sure, you will be required to lay a stone tile roof to match your neighbours. Local material prices vary from quarry to quarry but are invariably high. I was quoted 'a penny a square inch' (£16 per sq m) by one salvage yard for Westmoreland slate which puts it on a par with the other very expensive roof covers you could possibly choose. There are numerous cheaper, artificial alternatives around (e.g. Redland's Stonewold range) which will not look in the least bit convincing but using them may save you several thousand pounds. Again you face a tricky task reconciling your budget with the demands of your local planners.

Coursed stone tiling: the courses get narrower as you move up the roof. An attractive vernacular feature but time consuming and therefore expensive to achieve

Shingles

Another old vernacular stand-by is the cedar shingle. A shingle is a tile fashioned out of cedar wood and is usually supplied in random widths to give a broken up effect. It is a reasonably hard wearing material – though not as good as clay, slate or concrete – and it is used just as often to do vertical wall panels as it is pitched roofing. Cedar is a naturally durable timber which doesn't require any treatment or staining, and if you covet a genuine timber house then shingles will be your chosen roofing material.

Thatch

This is really one for enthusiasts but new thatched homes are going through a mini-revival. Not only is it very expensive, but there are numerous regulations about where thatch can go on new building. The one that used to trip people up was a requirement for thatched roofs to be at least 12 metres from another house but if you pay close attention to the internal fire proofing arrangements, using a set of guidelines known as the Dorset model, you should find that this requirement can be relaxed. Thatch is not something that can be added as an afterthought; if you are really serious about it you must design the roof around the thatch. You are more likely to come across thatch if you are involved in renovating or converting.

Turf

Turf roofing is vernacular in places like Iceland but in the UK it's distinctly organic. There have been a number of new turf roof houses in the last few years, most famously the Integer House, built for the BBC in 1999, and they always make for very interesting features. No, you don't have to mow them, not if you get your planting right. Their success depends to a large extent on having a top notch underlay and here Erisco Bauder seems to be the company of choice.

Sheet roofing

Sheet roofing is often associated with flat roofing and there is very little flat roofing being built today. There is nothing intrinsically wrong with flat roofing, but too much cheap felt got stuck on too many cheap houses in the Sixties and Seventies and the bitter taste of continual roof repairs has yet to fade away.

You might, however, be considering flat roofing for, say, a roof garden or a balcony. Be

Roof Cover Costs - Square Metre Rates

• NB In this table, the areas are take roof pitch into account

	Cost per thousand	No. per m²	Divider	Cost per m²	Accessories	Mats	Time in mins	Labour @ £18/hr	Combined rate per m²
TILES									
Concrete Interlocking	£ 500	10	100	£ 5	£ 6	£ 11	30	£ 9	£ 20
Clay Pantile	£ 430	16	62.5	£ 7	£ 7	£ 14	40	£ 12	£ 26
Concrete Plain	£ 220	60	16.7	£ 13	£ 7	£ 20	55	£ 17	£ 37
Forticrete Gemini	£ 575	19	52	£ 11	£ 7	£ 18	40	£ 12	£ 30
Clay Plain	£ 280	60	16.7	£ 17	£ 7	£ 24	55	£ 17	£ 41
Handmade Tile	£ 700	60	16.7	£ 42	£ 15	£ 57	55	£ 17	£ 74
ARTIFICIAL SLATES									
FibreCement	£ 600	13.3	75	£ 8	£ 5	£ 13	40	£ 12	£ 25
Simulated Natural	£ 1,400	13.3	75	£ 19	£ 5	£ 24	40	£ 12	£ 36
Redland Richmond	£ 600	11.1	90	£ 7	£ 5	£ 12	40	£ 12	£ 24
Redland Cambrian	£ 1,300	13.3	75	£ 17	£ 5	£ 22	40	£ 12	£ 34
NATURAL SLATE									
Spanish	£ 950	20	50	£ 19	£ 5	£ 24	50	£ 15	£ 39
Reclaimed Welsh	£ 1,000	20	50	£ 20	£ 5	£ 25	60	£ 18	£ 43
Welsh	£ 1,700	20	50	£ 34	£ 5	£ 39	50	£ 15	£ 54
SLATE/TILES									
Mini Stonewold	£ 550	9.9	100	£ 6	£ 6	£ 12	55	£ 17	£ 29
OTHERS									
Zinc				£ 70	£ 20	£ 90	120	£ 36	£ 126
Reed Thatch				£ 15	£ 5	£ 20	180	£ 54	£ 74
Cedar Shingles				£ 16	£ 6	£ 22	70	£ 21	£ 43
Lead Sheet				£ 70	£ 20	£ 90	120	£ 36	£ 126
VALLEYS & FLASHINGS									Cost per m run
Lead	£ 15		per 3m run	£ 5	£ 5	£ 10	30	£ 9	£ 19

Roofing Cover on Benchmark House

	Amount	Rate	Mats	Lab	Cost
Forticrete Gemini Roof Tiles	213m²	£ 30	£ 3,830	£ 2,560	£ 6,390
Lead sheet to dormers	2m²	£ 126	£ 180	£ 70	£ 250
Lead flashings	36m	£ 19	£ 360	£ 320	£ 680
		Totals	**£ 4,370**	**£ 2,950**	**£ 7,320**

aware that the durability of a flat roof is almost entirely dependent on how much you spend on it. Mineral felts are the cheapest covering (at around £10 per sq m, supplied and fixed, but don't expect much more than about fifteen years' lifespan); areas which are to get walked over really require something a bit stronger like asphalt (about £25 per sq m) or lead (around £50 per sq m).

Sheet metals such as zinc and copper actually make very stylish coverings for pitched roofs but their expense means that they are only ever seen on upmarket projects, usually driven by architects. Zinc is currently in vogue as it's the most neutral colour of the metal roofs, but stainless steel and copper are more durable. None of them will cost any less than £100 per sq m, supplied and fixed by specialist contractors such as Coverite.

Tile weight

Roofing materials vary enormously in weight. For example:

■ Lightweight slate   20 kg per sq m

■ Concrete interlocking tile 45 kg per sq m
■ Plain tile   90 kg per sq m

Does this matter? Well, it matters to the roof designer that the timbers holding up the roof should be strong enough to bear the imposed load but the effect on cost is surprisingly small, particularly if roof trusses are being used. The cost of using a roof truss system for a heavy roof covering will add about ten per cent to the truss cost – probably less than £100 for a detached house.

Felt and battens

Building regulations require that whatever (pitched) roof covering you decide on there should be a layer of roofing felt underneath. At a cost of less than 50p per sq m this is no great cost and it has the added advantage for quick builders of providing a temporary waterproof cover for work going on below. Felting takes place simultaneously with battening, which is necessary to provide fixings for the tiles or slates. On all but the largest houses, the whole process of felting and battening usually takes roofers no more than a day and costs around £2 per sq m (Mats £1, Lab £1).

Don't make the mistake of felting and battening before choosing a roof covering: the spacing of the battens is set by the gauge of slate or tile and the gauges are very variable. Note that the Scottish practice is to build a solid timber sarking layer on top of the rafters before laying felts: this adds significantly to the roofing costs but makes a much stronger structure.

Felts are now tending to get replaced by breathable membranes – Tyvek remains the best known but there are many others such as Klober, Monarperm 450 and Daltex Roofshield. Although expensive, two to three times the price of ordinary roofing felt, these membranes enable water vapour inside the roof space to permeate through them thus eliminating the need for other expensive ventilation gear.

Additional fittings

As most roofing is carried out by specialist contractors, usually on a supply and fix basis, there is perhaps not the need to know so much about the intricacies of roofing. However, there is a lot more to a roof than slates or tiles and on a typical detached house the actual roof tiles may make up no more than 50 per cent of the overall roofing material costs. The most visible additional element is the ridge and/or hip tiles (usually around 20 per cent of cost); the underfelt and battens (12 per cent) are the other significant costs. Ventilation gear, which is often fitted by roofers, is another expensive item.

Edge details
Hip Treatments

The hip is the name given to an external angle in a roof – an internal angle is called a valley – and the standard way of finishing a hip is to use something very similar to a conventional ridge tile, although the hipped version is sometimes slightly differently shaped. This is a cheap and quick specification, costing no more than about £10 per lin m (M £4, L £6) and it is really the only practical way of finishing a concrete interlocking tiled roof. However, if you are planning on a plain tiled roof there is an alternative which is to fix bonnets which look very rural and vernacular. However, bonneted hips are way more expensive both in labour and materials (you'll need something like ten bonnets per linear metre as opposed to two hip tiles) and the rate per linear meter works out at over £40 (M £25, L £15). An even more expensive option, which is most often seen on slate roofs, is to cut the tiles or slates to meet exactly over the hip. This is known as a close-mitred hip and it tends to be preferred by those going for neat, unfussy solutions. It is heavy on the old labour and it relies on underlying lead soakers to be effective which makes it cost in excess of £50 per lin m.

Bonnets and close-mitred hips may sound like unnecessary extravagances, but although they are way more expensive than hip tiles, the total length of hips to cover is often not that much and specifying something different here has a marked effect on kerb appeal.

Valleys

Another cost-sensitive area of roofing is the valley which is formed when two roof lines meet on an internal corner. The valley is not as visually prominent as the hip and this makes it a candidate for treating as cheaply as possible. The commonest way of doing this is by fitting a purpose-made valley gutter and cutting the tiles or slates around it. Here, fibreglass is tending to replace lead; it's quite a bit cheaper and much quicker to lay but labour costs are still

Three Hip Treatments

Hip tiles £10/m run

Bonnets £40/m run

Close mitred hips £50/m run

significant. Valley gutters cost around £20 per lin m when done in fibreglass, rising to £30 per lin m when finished in lead.

On plain tile roofs there is the alternative of using purpose-made valley tiles which are very similar to inverted bonnet hip tiles. Again, this is an expensive option – £45 per lin m (M £25, L £15) – but it is worth considering around features like dormer windows where the valleys are visible from the ground.

Verges

If you are roofing up to a gable wall, you will need to form some effective junction at the verge. The simplest method is to lay a mini-soffit board (known as an undercloak) on top of the brickwork (or timber bargeboard if one is specified), run the roof cover up to the edge of the undercloak and then fill the void between with cement. Such an arrangement costs no more than £3 per lin m to execute and is no different whether the roof cover is slate, tile or stone. There are alternatives – Redland make a concrete wrap-over tile that can be used with certain tile covers and there is even a plastic verge system. However, these other methods all cost around double the cement undercloak technique and they add nothing to the look of your roof edge.

An interesting innovation in this field is a product called Roofblock, marketed by Forticrete. This is a masonry alternative to fixing fascias, soffits and bargeboards – i.e. all the roof edge details which drive builders mad. With Roofblock you simply lay a special shaped block on top of the wall and the detail is sorted. It does equally well for eaves and verges.

Decorative accessories

Whilst most fittings are purely functional, occasionally a decorative touch can make a very plain roof exciting. Caught by the general trend for all things vernacular, roofing manufacturers have been busy reproducing Victorian embellishments like cockscomb ridge tiles and fleur-de-lys finials. Handle with care; in the right place these can look fantastic but on

Roof Edge and Rainwater Gear Costs - per Linear Metre

	Mats	Time in Mins	Labour @ £18/hr	Combined Rates
Timber Fascias & Soffits	£ 5	45	£ 14	£ 19
uPVC Fascias & Soffits	£ 8	45	£ 14	£ 22
uPVC Rainwater Gear	£ 5	15	£ 5	£ 10
Metal Rainwater Gear	£ 16	15	£ 5	£ 21

Benchmark House Costs for Fascias, Soffits and Rainwater Gear

All in uPVC	m	Rate	Materials	Labour	Combined
Boxed Eaves	65	£ 22	£ 520	£ 900	£ 1,420
Guttering	65	£ 10	£ 330	£ 300	£ 630
Downpipes	30	£ 10	£ 150	£ 150	£ 300
		Total	£ 1,000	£ 1,350	£ 2,350

most roofs they look plain silly. Similarly, two-tone effect roofing (either with contrasting tile colours or accentuated ridge tiles) is invariably very striking – but that doesn't always mean it works. If you see a roof you like, photograph it and show it to your roofer for quotation. Chances are it will be out of your price bracket!

Dry tech systems

The parts of the roof most vulnerable to weather damage are the perimeter areas like ridges, hips and verges. The traditional way of fixing ridge, hip and verge tiles is to bed them in cement. For some time now the tile manufacturers have been trying to persuade us to use dry systems, which clip together with a series of mechanical fixings, but there is a general reluctance to take up their offers partly because of the higher prices charged for these fittings and partly because the look is even more modern and nondescript than the conventional roof. In Scotland, dry verges are the norm and that housebuilders seeking a low maintenance finish are also specifying them – cement fillets on roof edges are notoriously brittle.

▋*Rainwater*

Getting rainwater off roofs and down into the drainage systems is one of the small but very important details that can make or break the appearance of a house. Done well, with appropriate materials, it can add a little to the overall visual appeal of a house. However,

done badly, it can ruin a fancy facade. The key to getting the look right is the placing of the downpipes and, as a general rule, the fewer the better.

Plastic

The low maintenance, low budget option is plastic (uPVC). There are around half a dozen manufacturers in the UK and they all sell through the builder's merchants. Note that there is a compatibility problem here: even though the designs are very similar, the rival manufacturers' products rarely fit each other, so don't mix and match your guttering. Generally uPVC guttering is available in four colours: black, brown, grey and white, though Hunter Plastics have a range with additional colours. There are also a range of sizes and styles: both half-round and square-box are common plus there are a few more ornate sections such as ogee.

When designing rainwater systems, you have to bear in mind the likely flow rates which naturally tend to vary with the area of roof being drained: if your roof areas are large you may find yourself having to fit more downpipes than you wish and one way around this is to use a larger guttering and downpipe. The manufacturers all hold data to help you specify appropriate sizes. For instance, Osma produce an Amazon gutter section which will drain over 100 sq m of roof area, as opposed to the 57 sq m maximum specified for their standard RoundLine section. Now, the Amazon

Downpipes, inspired by the Richard Rogers school of Architecture

is over twice the price of the RoundLine, but specifying it can sometimes actually save money by cutting down on both the number of downpipes and the length of underground drainage work.

Fixing uPVC guttering off scaffolding is at best a semi-skilled job easily mastered by a competent DIYer – the manufacturers all have concise installation guides. But note that whilst it is a relatively easy task to do from scaffolding, it can be a very dangerous and difficult thing to undertake using just a ladder. Also you need to pay attention to the brackets used to hold the gutters and downpipes in place.

There is quite a choice available, designed to cope with the whole range of materials that you may have to fix into or around. Note that there are adjustable brackets available which can accommodate situations where you are unable to fix into your preferred location – very useful when working with uneven surfaces that you might expect to find on barn conversions or stone buildings.

There are two drawbacks to using plastic guttering. One is that, as discussed, it all looks rather naff; the other is that it isn't actually any good. uPVC guttering generally, and the rubber jointing gaskets in particular, seem to break down under the effects of bright sunlight and the effective lifespan of a uPVC rainwater

system is probably only about 15-20 years. Expect to start replacing bits after this time.

Other options
All the other options are more expensive but all promise greater durability. The traditional British material used for guttering before the advent of plastic was cast-iron and this is still widely available in a range of period details. It is now mostly used on conservation work and listed buildings. With proper maintenance (which means repainting every five years or so), cast-iron guttering does last a long time – there are many examples of Victorian rainwater systems still in good working order.

Copper is another material, widely used on the Continent. It's very resistant to the elements and doesn't need any painting. Copper of course changes colour over time to eventually achieve a lime-green patina which will suit some properties better than others. Copper is also used with chain pipes, an interesting technique which does away with the conventional enclosed downpipe and allows the rainwater to run down a chain to the ground – only to be recommended when you have a good overhang on your eaves.

Aluminium and plastic-coated steel are also used. Aluminium now tends to be the province of specialist suppliers who provide seamless welding. Both these systems are available in a wide range of colours and promise many years' maintenance free service.

Rainwater harvesting
There is no reason to stop you putting some of this mildly acidic rainwater to good use before pouring it all away. Many people will be interested in building in rainwater butts and these can be made much more useful and more productive if they are designed in from the beginning. For around £10, you can add a rain diverter to your downpipes which will not only redirect your rain into a tank but is also intelligent enough to know when the tank is full and then redirect the rain back down the downpipe. If you want to use the rainwater for

domestic purposes – and there's good money to be saved here – you are talking more serious underground storage tanks and pumps. May I refer you to the section called 'Saving water' in Chapter 13.

heats water to 80°C and this water is then
pumped through the primaries (large copper
pipes) and thence to the cylinder and radiators.

Cylinder

Placed in the airing cupboard, this acts like a
giant (bath-sized) kettle for heating domestic
hot water (DHW). It starts to empty every time
a hot tap is turned on; it is simultaneously
filled from a tank of cold water in the loft space
which, in turn, is filled from the water main.
The cylinder is indirect which means that the
water inside never passes directly through the
boiler but is heated at one stage removed by
the boiler water passing through copper loops
inside the cylinder.

Radiators

These are fitted and connected by two copper
pipe circuits: one – the flow – takes the hot
water from the boiler around the circuit, the
other – the return – takes the cooler water
coming out of the radiators back to the boiler.
A small plastic tank (feed and expansion tank)
is placed in the loft which gives the hot water
in the circuit space to expand – which it does as
it gets hotter. Note that the current benchmark
house eschews all tanks in the loft and uses a
mains pressure hot water system instead. Mains
pressure systems are rapidly replacing gravity
for delivering hot water around the house.

Controls

The system is electrically pumped to supply
even heat around the house. There is a
programmer and a couple of thermostats
which turn the system on/off and also switch
motorised valves so that the hot water pumped
from the boiler can be switched between
heating the water in the cylinder or circulating
around the radiators.

Labour content

In a new four-bedroom house, the pipework
and control cabling will be 'first fixed' in
three to four days; first fixing needs to take
place after the structure is up but before the

plastering starts. The 'second fix' (including
hanging radiators) will take five to six days.
Conventionally, the heating engineer also fits
the sanitaryware, does the kitchen plumbing
and the above ground waste runs, and all this
work tends to get lumped into one quotation
and carried out together.

Cost summary

The table Benchmark House Heating Installation
shows the costs for a 20kW, 15-radiator
installation of the type that was fitted into
our benchmark house. Materials are at prices
which non-plumbers should be able to obtain
at specialist merchants like Plumb Center. The
grand total figure is derived from quotations
and so includes an element of profit which a
small plumbing firm would charge.

Open fires

Most large family homes are still built with
an open fire in the living room. Despite
modern central heating being quite adequate
to provide warmth in the most extreme winter
conditions, housebuilders are still apparently
happy to pay £1,000 plus for an open fireplace
with accompanying chimney. Whereas central
heating is regarded in entirely functional terms
(fuel efficiency, programmed control, water
pressures, etc), the open fire is altogether much
more of a romantic dream – and a very potent
one. So what if 70 per cent of the heat goes up
the chimney and it needs daily cleaning? To the
average British household, a fire in the living
room is as fundamental as sex in the bedroom.

Because fires are both expensive to install
and largely unnecessary, the current trend is to
only see them specified on upmarket homes.
Open fires are dealt with in their own section
in this chapter and any heat given off by open
fires will be treated as free background heating
in the same way that we treat winter sunshine,
heat from electrical appliances and, of course,
body heat. Solid fuel stoves and kitchen ranges,
together with other non-standard forms of
heating are looked at in another section of this
chapter, 'Alternative heating'.

▄*Which fuel?*

When considering which fuel to use to provide space heating and domestic hot water (DHW) there are a number of considerations:

■ Availability
■ Installation and storage costs
■ Capabilities of each fuel
■ Fuel costs
■ Environmental impact.

Availability

Piped gas from the North Sea reserves is currently available to over 70 per cent of UK households, which includes almost all urban areas. However, large tracts of rural Britain and Ireland are deemed too remote to justify laying gas mains and most of these areas will never have the option of a piped gas supply. If in doubt, a phone call to the local office of British Gas will illuminate the situation in your area. Sometimes an initial enquiry will trigger the offer to extend a gas main along a side road.

The other fuels touched on here are available everywhere except the remotest corners.

Installation
Electricity

Installation to a new site is charged on a time and materials basis. Even when it's straightforward it is unlikely to be less than £300. However, as its use in modern housing is universal, when considering electricity as a heat source it is effectively there for nothing. An Economy 10 (two-rate) meter can be installed at no extra cost and is generally worth doing even if you don't plan to use electric heating.

Gas

British Gas subsidises the installation costs because they want new customers. If gas supply is adjacent then connection is usually free. Longer distances are possible, subject to negotiation with British Gas new supplies. Beyond a distance of a couple of hundred metres or so, it becomes prohibitively expensive unless the cost of connection can be borne with neighbours.

Oil

The costs are solely to do with onsite storage. Storage tanks are available in steel or plastic. The usual sizes are 300 gallons (1,365lt) and 600 gallons (2,730lt). Steel is much cheaper (£220 for a 2,730lt tank compared to £400 for an equivalent in plastic) but plastic is guaranteed for ten years and everybody seems to have switched to plastic now. If you are building for a largish detached house you would do well to get the large tank size that should be enough to last a year at a time – buy in the summer when oil prices are low. Steel tanks have been known to start leaking after five years and are meant to be painted every year (nobody ever does). Add to this figure building up supporting piers (Mats £25, Lab £50), initial placement (L £50), measuring gauge (M £40), filter (M £40), fire check valve (M £30) and microbore connection to boiler (M £10, L £30), and budget around £450 for a steel tank, £600 for a plastic one. The tank can be placed up to 2m below the boiler, but then a tiger loop will be needed as well (extra £40). Attention must be paid to placing oil tanks; they must be outside and they must be 1.8m from any openings. Recent upgrading of the regulations means that ideally an oil tank should be placed 1.8m from the house and 760mm from a boundary, though if you build a reasonably fireproof structure these distances can be relaxed. If there is a danger of leaking into watercourses, then a catch pit or bund must be constructed. Oil tanks are also ugly and their careless siting can spoil an otherwise attractive elevation. They can be buried underground (like a petrol station) but the cost here soars to more than £2000. Camouflaging with trellis and climbers is a cheaper option but allows access for tank replacement.

Liquid petroleum gas (LPG)

Storage tank needs to be 3m from any buildings or boundaries so there are comparatively few sites that it is suited to. Calor Gas are the biggest supplier and they take on full responsibility for installation and maintenance of tanks. They usually charge around £300 to install a tank:

Fuel: Raw Costs Compared

	STREET COST	CONVERSION	COST /kWh	ANNUAL TARIFFS
ELECTRICITY				
Standard Rate	6.5p/unit	none needed	6.5p	£ 25
Economy 7 - daytime	6.5p/unit	none needed	6.5p	£ 38
Economy 7 - night time	3p/unit	none needed	2.5p	
MAINS GAS	1.5p/unit	none	1.5p	£ 35
LPG (Calor Gas)	17.7p/lt	Divide by 7.1	2.5p	£ 55
OIL (28-second)	19.5p/lt	Divide by 10.2	1.9p	£ 0
House Coal	£150/tonne	Divide by 8300	1.8p	£ 0
Anthracite	£220/tonne	Divide by 9370	2.3p	£ 0

this includes pipe laying to boiler. Occasionally they are prone to doing special offers at around £100. Note that alternative suppliers such as Shell supply tanks for free – but you are then bound to use them as suppliers. Bulk gas tanks are even more of an eyesore than oil tanks and their placing is a matter that the planners will want to consider – don't plump for an LPG supply as an afterthought, you may be letting yourself in for big problems. Note that, like oil tanks, LPG tanks can be buried underground but this is likely to cost £400 extra plus excavation costs.

Solid Fuel

This all-embracing term includes just about everything you can burn which isn't a liquid (oil) or a gas: housecoal, anthracite and the processed coals (coalite, fernicite, coke) wood, peat, you name it. Solid fuel can be stored anywhere under cover (the bath?) but purpose-built coal bunkers would cost a minimum of £200 (M £80, L £120). Plastic ones are available from £90. If you use wood, it is important to have somewhere dry to store it; this takes space but can be an attractive feature in its own right.

Capabilities
Gas
Gas is the preferred fuel for most people and gas is at the leading edge of heating technology. Nearly 80 per cent of central heating systems run on mains gas and, where it is available, it is the overwhelming choice in new developments. The market responds to this by making far more

Fuel: Effective Costs Compared

	Fuel Cost/ kWh	Appliance or Boiler efficiency	Effective Cost
ELECTRICITY			
Daytime Peak Rate	6.5p	100%	6.5p
Off-peak Rates	3.2p	100%	3.2p
MAINS GAS			
Elderly Cast Iron Boiler	1.5p	60%	2.5p
New Boiler	1.5p	78%	1.9p
Condensing Boiler	1.5p	90%	1.7p
LPG			
Elderly Cast Iron Boiler	2.5p	60%	4.2p
New Boiler	2.5p	80%	3.1p
Condensing Boiler	2.5p	90%	2.8p
OIL			
Elderly Cast Iron Boiler	1.9p	70%	2.7p
New Boiler	1.9p	85%	2.2p
Condensing Boiler	1.9p	95%	2.0p
COAL			
Open Fire	1.8p	35%	5.0p
Stove	1.8p	65%	2.7p
ANTHRACITE			
Open Fire	2.3p	35%	6.6p
Stove	2.3p	65%	3.5p
ALL FIGURES INCLUDE VAT at 5%			

gas-burning products available – and at keener prices. Another plus for gas is that it is, arguably, the best fuel for cooking.

LPG
Despite having a tiny fraction of the market (around two per cent), LPG versions of many gas boilers are available, though usually around 10 to 15 per cent more expensive – LPG boilers can be converted to mains gas. Note that LPG can also be used for cooking.

Oil

Oil-fired systems account for around ten per cent of the market overall, and are much the most popular choice in rural areas where mains gas is not an option. There is a much smaller range of boilers available and prices are 20-50 per cent more than gas equivalents, though this is partly because they use the more efficient pressure jet burner which reduces running costs. Oil cannot be used to cook with (unless using an oil-fired range).

Solid fuel

Solid fuel heating systems are available as kitchen ranges, living room stoves or utility room boilers. Anything that the other fuels can do, solid fuel can do; compared to the other fuels, though, solid fuel heating is unresponsive, inefficient and plain hard work. Wood-burning stoves do not generate enough heat for DHW and wet heating systems combined.

Electricity

Using electricity as a main heat source invariably means latching on to one of the off-peak tariffs. This, in turn, means restricted hours of use, which is the biggest limitation. In other respects electricity is the most capable of all fuels because it can be used for just about every household function requiring power.

Green power sources

There is always a healthy interest in non-fossil fuel sources and there are some interesting, if experimental, houses being built which hardly use any fossil fuels at all. The problem with all of the green alternatives is that they don't provide an all round energy solution: they'll give you some of your hot water, some of your electricity but you will still need some form of fossil fuel backup. For instance, warm water solar panels are, at best, a top-up source that can provide most of the hot water for a UK house in summer and less than 15 per cent in winter. Using solar power is unlikely to save more than 10 per cent of overall fuel bills, whichever system you use for your main heat source.

There are also green heating systems around such as heat pumps which take energy from the ground. But these require electricity to run.

Fuel costs

Prices in the Fuel Costs Tables are for the Cambridgeshire area, where the benchmark house is located, during 2004. There is inevitably some regional variation in prices but these tend not to be greater than ten per cent up or down, and so these figures give a reasonable guideline to likely charges. The tables show the apparent cost of each fuel and gives a method for converting these costs into kWh for easier comparison. I have only covered the main fuel choices and if the fuel you are planning to use is not listed, get in touch with Sutherland Associates who publish a very comprehensive guide to comparative fuel costs. The Effective Costs' table shows the cost of the heat after it has been converted from the raw fuel by your boiler; this effective cost is dependent on the efficiency of your appliance.

Electricity

Electricity is charged by the kWh and so price comparisons are straightforward. Also, electric heating is virtually 100 per cent efficient so what you pay for is what you get. Electricity suppliers (RECs) are free to set their own tariffs and there is some variation between them. And since 1999, domestic customers in England, Wales and Scotland have been free to buy their electricity from a range of suppliers – currently over 30 and rising. A current list can be found on OFGEM's web page at www.ofgem.gov.uk or check one of the comparison websites such as UK Power. Not only are there more suppliers but each has its own tariffs and its own payment options. Your electricity bills can be reduced by careful shopping about, by using as much cheap-rate night-time electricity as possible (look to use Economy 10 tariffs or similar) and by paying your bills by direct debit — usually worth a five per cent reduction on its own. You can increase your bills by between five per cent and seven per cent by opting for an Eco

Tariff which promises to match your demand with a similar amount of electricity generated by renewable sources such as solar panels and wind power. To get prices contact Bill Enquiries at your local electricity supply company who are – much as it perplexes them – obliged to give you a list of alternative suppliers as well.

Note that one of the alternative suppliers is British Gas who promise great savings simply by combining the two utility bills. It seems almost fatuous, but apparently something like one hour in four spent working for a utility company is spent collecting the monies it is owed, so there is certainly logic in offering to combine the billing.

Gas

Gas is also billed in kWhs which makes comparison with electricity easy — again, phone your Bill Enquiries for local rates. How much of the gas you consume actually ends up heating your house depends on the efficiency of your boiler, hence the variable efficiency ratios suggested in the accompanying table. As with electricity supply companies, British Gas also offers a favourable tariff to customers offering to pay monthly by direct debit; doing this should save you more than five per cent on your gas bill. The comments about combining utility bills apply just as much to the gas industry as the electricity industry and you can now

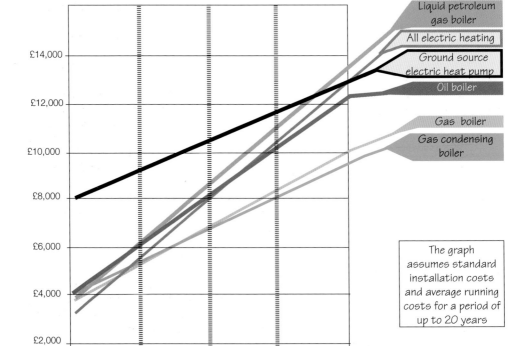

Comparitive heating costs

The graph assumes standard installation costs and average running costs for a period of up to 20 years purchase your gas from a number of suppliers, including electricity companies.

LPG

Although there is no tariff as such, Calor Gas – the main supplier – make a charge of around £50 per annum for tank maintenance. For local prices, check Yellow Pages under Gas Suppliers or Bottled Gas.

Oil

The most common fuel of this type is known as 28-second burning oil. The modern generation of pressure-jet oil boilers are more efficient than non-condensing gas boilers but only if regularly maintained (which means replacing the burner every year or so). Otherwise, the same general principles of boiler efficiency still operate – although note that oil-fired condensing boilers are very expensive.

For best local prices, check Yellow Pages under Oil fuel distributors & suppliers. Oil prices have been fluctuating wildly for the past few years: in the Nineties oil was cheaper than gas but now it's usually a little more expensive. There is also usually a significant seasonal fluctuation, and having a tank large enough to allow buying once a year – in summer – will lower your fuel bills.

Solid fuel

More complex to price because of the variety of different types of fuel and the enormous variation in boiler/stove efficiencies. I am not aware of anyone having built-in coal or coke heating into their new home for…well I can't remember it happening at all actually. Which isn't to say that many people don't install wood burning stoves, but that's a bit different. One area that is growing (but slowly) is the use of pellet fuel, burned in special boilers. It's solid fuel (compressed wood pellets) and it's pretty clean but there are very few suppliers in the UK.

Environmental impact

There are two particular areas where concern focuses: firstly how clean (or dirty) any particular fuel is and secondly how much carbon dioxide (CO_2) each fuel releases into the atmosphere. CO_2 is the gas readily associated with the greenhouse effect and is therefore seen as the principal cause of global warming.

■ Solar power is generally a very green power source. As yet its impact on the environment is limited because it's too expensive to install.

■ Gas is the cleanest of the fossil fuels in that it produces very little sulphur dioxide or nitrous oxide (the acid rain gases). It's also efficient in that little is lost in transmission from source to end user and so its combustion produces comparatively little CO_2.

■ Oil is a slightly dirtier fuel than gas (acid rain wise) but tends to produce even less CO_2 than gas. Transporting oil around the world is cheap but occasionally hazardous when tankers run aground.

■ Electricity is a form of converted energy so it is much processed before it enters the home. It is generated in a number of ways – by burning coal, oil, gas and other fossil fuels, by hydroelectricity, by wind and solar power and, most controversially, by nuclear fission. Some of these are clean, some are not, whilst nuclear power is, paradoxically, both the cleanest major energy source available and potentially the most dangerous. Whatever the merits or demerits of electricity generation, much of its energy is lost in transmission along the national grid, which adds to its expense and reinforces its poor environmental rating.

■ Coal, British Coal in particular, is a dirty fuel which contributes loads of sulphur to the atmosphere. Despite cutbacks in coal-mining, it remains the one British fossil fuel with long-term reserves. Anthracite and the smokeless fuels are much cleaner than housecoal, but do still not compare well with gas or oil.

And the winner is..

There is actually remarkably little in it.

The graph summarises the comparative costs of using different fuels on the benchmark house. The three main fuel choices, gas, oil and LPG are each assessed in two different ways, firstly with a new but conventionally-fired boiler and next with condensing boilers – more on these anon. Electricity is also assessed as both storage heating and using a heat pump – I have ignored solid fuel. The table looks at space heating and hot water costs in a house built to the new thermal standards which came into effect in 2002. In addition cooking costs are added to the blend. It is assumed that where gas is available it will be used for both oven and hob. Actually the fuel used for cooking has quite a significant impact on the whole equation, enough to make mains gas look about £50 a year cheaper than oil. If you chose to have electric cooking instead, the running costs would be almost identical. The condensing boilers are more expensive to install but do pay for themselves by lowering running costs.

The option that does surprisingly well is electric heating. It's so cheap to install that even though its annual running costs are nearly double that of mains gas, it takes between five and ten years before the aggregate cost of installation and total running costs overtakes mains gas and oil. This is looking at a fairly conventional electric heating system, either storage heaters or underfloor elements. Switch to an electrically powered ground source heat pump and you'd have a heat source that is a) the most expensive to install and b) the cheapest to run.

There are of course many other factors at play. The more insulation you build into the structure, the less heat you require. There is more on this in the 'Green Issues' chapter. And of course I have ignored things like solar panels, which give you some free heat.

■ *Boilers*

Boilers are rated according to the power they can produce. Manufacturers still work in BTU (British Thermal Units); I'm trying to be metric, but in the section, for clarity's sake, I'll use both. Just remember:

■ 1kW = 3410 BTU.

A small application – like a one-bedroom

flat – might use a 20,000 BTU boiler (6kW); a large Victorian vicarage would require something in excess of 100,000 BTU (30kW). A new four-bedroom house built to the latest thermal regulations will need – well read on, it's a bit controversial.

Conventionally, boilers are sized by totalling the radiator output (worked out from the heat calculation) and adding a bit for heating domestic hot water (DHW), and then going to the nearest size above. This is a bit hit and miss, to say the least. For a more detailed explanation of heat calculations, see Chapter 13.

The industry standard is to design heating systems capable of keeping the house around 21°C warmer than the temperature outside. Now in a new house, built to 2002 building regs, the amount of heat needed to keep the structure 21°C warmer than outside is surprisingly small. As a rule of thumb, you need no more than 15 watts per cubic metre of living space. The benchmark house, with a floor area of 200 sq m has 460 cu m of heated living space and this means that the heating requirement is 6,900 Watts (15 x 460) or 6.9kW (24,000 BTU). However, the Boulter Classic oil boiler fitted into the house is rated at 20kW. How come the discrepancy? Are U values (the basis of heat calculations) meaningless or is there some conspiracy to sell us bigger boilers and radiators than we really need?

One little known reason for apparent oversizing is that radiators are usually only 70 per cent efficient: outputs claimed in manufacturers' brochures apply to radiators connected at the top corner on one side and at the bottom on the other: these days radiators are usually connected bottom to bottom and this dramatically lowers their output. Mears calculators and various rules of thumb, used by plumbers to carry out heat calculations, take account of this discrepancy without ever explaining it. However, whilst radiators should arguably be oversized by as much as 50 per cent, boilers themselves do not have to be 50 per cent larger to deliver the anticipated heat from each radiator.

Plumbing Systems Compared

TRADITIONAL BRITISH METHOD
Tanks in the loft and a hot water
cylinder

COMBIS
No water storage involved at all. The
cold feeds all come off the mains. The
hot water is heated instantly as it
passes through the combi boiler

Another factor to take into account is that a central heating system has to be felt to be working and that means that it must be able not only to keep a house warm, but to heat it up from cold within a reasonable (say one hour) time-scale. This obviously requires extra heat but not that much extra – the benchmark house requires just 2kW extra heat to raise the temperature 10°C in one hour – and a 12kW (40,000 BTU) boiler really ought to handle background heating, boost heating and hot water needs. Such a boiler will be £100 cheaper to buy and cheaper to run. However, if you insisted on a 12kW boiler, your plumber would probably want you to sign a disclaimer in event of it being underpowered! I know of plumbers who have been sued by clients – albeit ones living in uninsulated old houses – because the system they installed didn't make the house warm enough, so perhaps it's not surprising that plumbers tend to view these things conservatively and to err on the side of caution.

The Plumb Center catalogue routinely refers to 30,000 BTU boilers as five-radiator ones and 40,000 BTU boilers as seven-radiator ones. In the replacement market, ideal but the 15-radiator benchmark house doesn't even need

a 30,000 BTU boiler to keep the place warm. It could get by on something a lot smaller. However, the reason boilers don't get much smaller is that they have another job to do, which is heating up the hot water for the taps. The really low output boiler couldn't do that job in an acceptable timescale.

How size affects price

Typically, each model will be produced in six or seven sizes ranging from mini 15-30,000 BTU (4-8kW) up to 80-100,000 BTU (23-30kW). Plumber's merchants will regularly knock 30 per cent off list for trade customers – more for regular clients. The price difference between sizes is not great; however that difference increases with the boiler sizes. The difference between the smallest and the next smallest is just £40, whereas the difference between the largest shown and the next size down is £100.

Boiler heat exchangers

The older type of gas- and oil-fired boilers use cast iron heat exchangers and work by heating this cast-iron, which holds heat well and, in turn, transfers the heat through to the hot water. They are characterised by being easy to install, reliable and inefficient. The cast iron takes a comparatively long time to heat up and a correspondingly long time to cool down – hence the inefficiency of heat transfer.

The more modern style of boilers – which includes the combi and condensing boilers – are made with copper or other lightweight metal heat exchangers and operate with a much lower water content. Some of them have two heat exchangers, made of different materials. They are more efficient but have to be much more carefully commissioned, and it is vital that the correct corrosion inhibitors are present. They also need more servicing.

Combination boilers

A combi has a second heat exchanger in the boiler, which works as an instantaneous water heater, in the manner of the once popular Ascot water heaters, used to heat water bound directly for the hot tap. This second heat exchanger adds 50-80 per cent to the price of the boiler but this cost penalty is clawed back by the elimination of hot water storage (in cylinders), and tanks and associated pipework in the loft. All in all, it is cheaper to install than a conventional system. Combi boilers are now well established in the UK – they account for around 50 per cent of all new boiler sales – and the market is dominated by continental manufacturers like Vaillant and Vokera. Low flow rates mean they are not that wonderful for applications such as showers but they are good choices for households with erratic lifestyles, coming and going at all hours. The relatively low water content heat exchangers also mean they need rather more careful commissioning by the plumber and, even so, the heat exchangers scale up in hard water areas. Hard water scaling isn't a terminal problem – you can get the boilers de-scaled – but it won't do any harm to fit some sort of scale-inhibiting device as well.

Condensing boilers

Condensing boilers, also known as energy efficient boilers, work by having extra large heat exchangers (or, in some designs, a second

one) that extract a much greater proportion of the usable energy from the fuel; consequently, the exhaust fumes are much cooler and this causes condensation inside the boiler (hence the name), which in all other boilers would spell disaster. The exhaust gas comes out at a surprisingly low temperature, usually around 50°C to 60°C as opposed to 250°C on a conventional boiler and as a result the flue from a condenser can be plastic. They also give off a mildly acid condensate which should be piped into the soil stack or to an outside gully. To cope with the condensation, the heat exchangers are made of aluminium or stainless steel – one of the main reasons for their extra expense. Condensing technology isn't specific to one class of boiler: they can be stand-alones, combis or all-in-one system boilers, wall mounted or floor mounted, gas or oil fired.

The overall market share for condensers is expanding rapidly thanks almost entirely to the changes in the building regs in 2002. Before the change, condensers were down at about three per cent by market share. Since 2002, this has jumped to nearly 20 per cent: a proposal to tighten CO_2 emissions even further in 2005 may well force out non-condensing boilers altogether. There are now hundreds of models of gas condensers available and an increasing number of oil-fired ones as well: you can check out models and their efficiency ratings on www.boilers.org.uk

Modulation

A new technology only available with condensing boilers is a modulating burner. This is capable of altering the amount of fuel burned in the boiler: instead of being either on or off, a modulator self-adjusts the fuel input in order to increase efficiency still further.

The plume

One problem that is present with condensing boilers is the plume of water vapour that issues from the waste flue. Its chemical composition is no different to waste gas coming out of conventional boilers but because the gas has been allowed to cool below 54°C, the large amount of water vapour present condenses and appears as a white cloud known as a plume. For each kilogram of natural gas burnt, approximately two kilograms of water vapour is produced and a condensing boiler, when working in full condensing mode, can produce about a pint of liquid per hour. Some of this emerges in the plume, some needs to be piped away to the drains. There are certain situations such as flats where the plume has caused problems for neighbours, but in a detached house this should be of minor importance, though it may well be worth locating the flue well away from windows – many condensing boilers allow you to duct the waste gas quite a distance.

Boiler efficiency

In the 2002 building reg changes, minimum standards were set for newly installed boilers in both new build and in the replacement market, these being a 78 per cent efficiency for gas, 80 per cent for LPG and 85 per cent for oil boilers. At a stroke many old tried and trusted boilers were rendered obsolete. And whilst these efficiencies don't require condensing technology in order to comply, the U value trade-offs allowed in the regs, the so-called Target Method of compliance, meant that housebuilders could get away with less insulation in the fabric of the structure in exchange for fitting a condensing boiler.

The key to understanding all this is to be found on the web at www.boilers.org.uk where the efficiencies of hundreds of boilers is listed — the list is updated monthly and is growing all the time. When I put together the first edition of The Housebuilder's Bible in 1995, there was just one oil-fired condensing boiler on the market (very expensive it was too): my last trawl through the site showed up 46. Gas condensers there are by the hundred. Here is a technology that is lifting off.

The key factor which the government is concerned about is boiler efficiency. This is measured as a percentage, being the percentage

of fuel turned into hot water. So a 78 per cent percentage means that 78 per cent of the fuel turns into heat in the home and the other 22 per cent gets wasted. Like GCSEs, boilers are now banded from A (excellent) down to G (terrible – suitable for the Albanian export market only). D is the pass mark for gas boilers – i.e. over 78 per cent in gas, 80 per cent in LPG or 85 per cent for oil-fired. The best, most efficient boiler in the SEDBUK charts at time of writing was the oil fired Grant Vortex with a 97 per cent efficiency rating. The best gas boiler was the brand new Potterton Promax in its small, 15kW version – it was rated at 91.3 per cent. Most commercially available boilers are now SEDBUK rated but a few smaller boiler manufacturers don't seem to have got around to it at time of writing. Note that the boiler efficiency rules do not apply in Scotland – a cynical sales ploy to get rid of old boilers that no longer cut the mustard south of the border?

Flue choices

Where you have a boiler, you must also have some form of exhaust pipe to get rid of the fumes. The flue, as it is known, is actually

1460 high x 550 wide x 600 deep, the Potterton Powermax HE is an all-in-one gas-fired condensing boiler and unvented hot water system. Its SEDBUK rating is right up there in Band A (90.5% efficiency); its hot water output is very fast and my local plumber's merchant had 'never heard of it.' The drawback is the price – £1,875.

radiators into fashion accessories.

Traditional cast-iron radiators are still around and available from an increasing range of suppliers. In period bathrooms and the like they are just the ticket but they do not come cheap. Expect to pay around £180-£200 per kW output – and that's just for rads supplied in grey primer that need painting.

Skirting radiators

Sometimes preferred because of their low visual impact. Leading name here is Myson's Wallstrip. It goes where you would normally fit skirting board – now there's a saving. Like skirting, it can go around bends and it tends to get priced by the metre and so it's a little difficult to compare with conventional rads. Look to pay around £30-£35 per metre run (depending on the number of bends, ends, etc). Heat output depends very much on water temperature. A conventional 75°C would give off about 0.5kW/m; a condensing boiler, working at 55°C, about half that amount. However you look at it they are not going to be less than £70 per kW, about twice the effective cost of standard radiators.

Heated towel rails

These specialist radiators, usually hung in the vertical, are now becoming an item in the contemporary bathroom. Zehnder are the most elegant, complete with dinky little collapsible towel rails, but they cost between £140 and £250 (about £170 per kW). Myson and Worcester are around half that price. All can be coloured to match your bathroom suite (add £40) and all are available with an electric immersion heater option for summer use (add £100 plus).

Underfloor heating

Available as either water-based (wet) or electric, underfloor heating (or UFH) is very popular in Germany and Switzerland and is now widely specified in the UK selfbuild market. It's just beginning to take off with developers as well. Overall, its market share in the UK is still

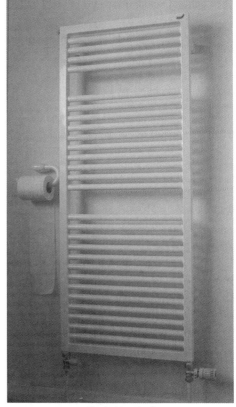

Heated towel rail

minute (of the order of two per cent of central heating installations) but this is expected to grow dramatically during the next ten years. With an underfloor heating system, the floor itself becomes the emitter and, so as you don't burn your tootsies, the wet systems need to work at lower temperatures than ordinary wall rads and they are often used in conjunction with condensing boilers (which are designed to work at lower temperatures), otherwise temperature reducing equipment is needed. They are mostly laid under a cement screed which is used as a heat reservoir (like an electric storage heater); this means that the heat is released slowly throughout the day – it is pleasantly draught free and the heat stays close to the floor. Electric underfloor heating is touched on in a following section in this chapter (Alternative Heating). There are now many businesses offering varying levels of service and most can be found at the selfbuild exhibitions.

Underfloor heating is not a homogeneous product: every system is different and the quotations need to be deconstructed carefully to see whether you are comparing like with like. Watch out to see if significant extras are included – insulation, heating controls, mesh to attach the pipe to. Note that whilst UFH does away with radiators, you still need to find somewhere to fit the manifold – these are large and ugly and are best concealed in a cupboard or a utility area. In cost terms, UFH tends to work out about £1,500-£2,500 more than a standard radiator system in a largish house, pretty similar to using skirting heating or unusual radiators.

UFH under timber floors

Whilst there is some debate about the suitability of UFH under timber floors – wood is regarded as an insulating material – virtually every supplier offers it as an option. There are several methods of installing UFH under timber floors. Some use aluminium plates to spread the heat across the floor: some require a mortar 'pug' to be built as an extra layer in the floor, some use nothing at all, the pipes being clipped to the underside of the floor after it is laid. Generally the aluminium plate system is rather more expensive than the other systems in terms of materials supplied but the mortar pug system requires a fair amount of extra building work. Some suppliers quote for installation using alternative designs: the mortar pug system usually appears to be significantly cheaper but bear in mind that it will involve other significant construction costs.

Pipe issues

People naturally fear pipe failure with UFH. Suppliers go to great lengths to ensure that the pipe is up to the job, but as it is still a relatively new technique there is some justification for at least being worried about it. Most warm water UFH is run in PEX pipe, now widely used all over Europe and reckoned to be the safe choice.

There are many methods of fixing underfloor heating pipe. An increasingly popular one on ground floors is to use a plastic backing board into which you press home the pipe, to a designed layout. Pictured right is a NuHeat system

An alternative is to use one of the polybutylene pipes like OsmaGold or Hep₂O. It's best to specify one with an oxygen barrier as this reduces the risk of rust getting into the system.

Energy saving

Many suppliers claim that UFH is inherently energy efficient and will save you money in the long term. I have my doubts. Just because it works at low temperatures, compared to radiator-based systems, doesn't necessarily mean it will cost less to run – you are after all heating up a much larger area, using much more water. When placed in a cement screed, UFH is a very slow response system: it takes a long time to heat up and a long time to cool down. It is therefore best suited to lifestyles where people are around all day, otherwise you end up heating an empty house. Under timber floors the response times are quicker but the efficiency is reduced because of the insulating qualities of timber. Ditto when placed under thick carpets.

One common route taken by selfbuilders is to run UFH downstairs and radiators upstairs. It makes a lot of sense because a) it's a bit cheaper and b) radiators are not quite such a problem in bedrooms.

■ Domestic Hot Water

The standard system, used in Britain for most of the 20th century, uses a copper cylinder, fed by a tank overhead or in the loft, and heated by copper tubes inside. These tubes transfer heat from the boiler primary circuit to the water in the cylinder: the domestic hot water (DHW) never passes through the boiler at all and thus it is known as an indirect system. All cylinders these days come ready insulated (lagged).

Cost

Fitting a regular cylinder (inc. backup electric immersion heater) costs around £200 (Mats £100, Lab £100). Quick recovery cylinders (which heat cold water to 60°C within half an hour) cost around £50 extra.

Plus

Cheap, easy to install and well understood by the average plumber. Replacement is straightforward; facility for electric immersion heating if the boiler is out of action.

Minus

Having water tanks and pipework in the loft. Poor flow rates achieved from hot water taps due to inadequate head (or pressure) of water – this poor flow rate only really matters where a powerful shower is valued.

Loft Plumbing

In conventional systems, there are two tanks in the loft: one (usually 227lts) feeds the cylinder, the other (usually 18lts) supplies the central heating system. Having to put a tank in the loft – avoiding this is sold as a big plus for other systems – actually costs around £220 (M 100, L £120) for the water storage tank and around £80 (M £40, L £40) for the feed and expansion tank (aka the Jockey Tank). Therefore, any system that does away with all loft plumbing is going to save you around £300.

Instantaneous hot water

Small instantaneous hot water heaters are still sold but in a new house the normal way of achieving this is by fitting a Combination Boiler (or combi). Although combi boilers are 30-50 per cent more expensive than conventional boilers, the savings in avoiding cylinders as well as loft plumbing combine to make this system as cheap and possibly cheaper to install than the standard DHW system.

Plus

No cylinder; no loft pipework or tanks; hot water on demand, 24 hrs a day; simplified controls; no switching valves needed.

Minus

Poor flow rate remains the big problem — anything below 15lts per minute is not adequate for a family home and many combis produce as little as 10lts per minute. Also problems with scaling (in hard water areas) in the hot water heat exchanger which reduces flow rates still further.

Mains Pressure Hot Water

These systems use unvented (i.e. no loft pipework for expansion) hot water cylinders which are strong enough to withstand storing hot water under mains pressure. They answer the problem of low flow rates to showers but at a cost of around £500. To operate to full effect they need at least 2.5 bar of mains pressure and a mains flow rate of 35lts per minute. Unfortunately, UK water companies are only obliged to provide mains water at 1 bar pressure so many situations will not benefit at all. Phone your water company to determine your local pressure. Despite being a British invention which went on to be the most popular hot water delivery method in the rest of Europe and North America, mains pressure hot water cylinders were actually prohibited by our water bylaws until 1987. On grounds of safety. Not that they are particularly dangerous. They are now available with a whole raft of safety features attached (which is partly responsible for their comparative expense) and a requirement that they be installed by a qualified person. Despite all this, they have been rapidly taken up and account for around one in six all new cylinder sales and as much as 50 per of cylinders going into new homes.

Plus

No loft pipework; mains pressure hot water delivered to all parts of the house, particularly valued by shower users; a small saving on being able to use smaller bore pipework throughout.

Minus

Expensive (extra £200 on standard): need certified installers (also likely to be expensive). Don't use with cheap taps: leaks, when they do occur, are much worse when under mains pressure. No back up storage if supply is cut off. It's worth paying extra for a stainless steel or enamel version if you live in a hard water area.

Variations

I have outlined three approaches to delivery of DHW. Needless to say there are a number of other options that sort of mix and match these three approaches.

Thermal stores

A variation of the unvented hot water cylinder is the thermal store. These systems work by reversing the logic of the standard setup and use a cylinder of hot water to heat cold water channelled through it at mains pressure. Result? Hot water at up to 30lts per minute comes straight out of the hot taps. As hot water is not actually stored under mains pressure, it doesn't have to be installed by a qualified plumber. Thermal stores also usually work without the need for tanks in the loft; instead they come with integral feed and expansion tanks. For a four-bedroom house, expect installation costs of around £300 (including mixing valves), about midway between using the standard route and using mains pressure unvented systems.

Thermal stores were first developed by British Gas in the early Eighties and are produced by a number of small British manufacturers. They are particularly good when you want to combine different inputs; e.g. if you have a solar panel or a heat pump supplying hot water as well as a boiler. You can get thermal stores made to order to fit your particular application from a couple of thermal store boutiques, Chelmer Heating and DPS Heatsave.

All-in-one units

Another approach is to combine both boiler and cylinder in one box, a systems approach if you like. A piece of kit such as Potterton's Powermax HE has a mains pressure condensing boiler and a stainless steel mains pressure cylinder plus a pump and a programmer all in a box just 550 wide by 600 deep – the height varies with the size of the water tank but the biggest, the 150lt tank version, is still only 1460mm high. All the installer has to do is fit six copper connections and the flue. All you have to do is fork out £1,800 for the kit.

Shower pumps

When all is said and done, the main reason for having mains pressure hot water is to enjoy decent showers — that's the place you really notice the difference. If you want to stick with a gravity system but value a good shower, then you will need to fit a shower pump. There are single impeller pumps which boost the water after the mixing valve, and double impellers which boost both hot and cold before they enter the valve. There is also an increasing number of all-in-one pump and valve shower units like the Triton Aquasensation (£170). Which you choose is partly dependent on the layout you have. Prices are largely dependent on the power of the pump. They can be purchased for just over £100, but a pump delivering 30lts per minute (equivalent to a good mains pressure system) will cost £180 plus. Most work on a timed switch. Add the costs for extra wiring and fitting and you can see that a shower pump is not a very clever option in a new building, where you would be quids in by starting off with a better DHW system. Leading manufacturers: Mira, Aqualisa.

Background

■ A bath takes about 70-80lts of hot water and so water storage needs to be above this level (or instantaneous) to be adequate. Hot water cylinders usually hold around twice this amount.
■ A typical household of four uses between 200 and 250lts of hot water a day, conventionally heated to 60°C.
■ It takes 12kWh to heat 200lts of water through 50°C (the difference between the temperature of the cold water and the hot water) and the average cost of water heating (by gas or oil-fired boiler) is £100 per annum.
■ Just under half of all water consumed in the home is heated.

Showers and flow rates

■ A good power shower needs a flow rate of 25lts per minute. This will not be achieved by the conventional system where the flow of hot water is determined by the height of the loft tank above the outlet. A pump will be required (or else feeble showers endured).
■ In an unvented mains pressure system (or a thermal store), the flow rate is dependent on the mains pressure supplied by the local water company.
■ With a combi boiler, which produces instantaneous hot water, the flow rate depends on the design of the boiler. It is unlikely to be much better than 10lts per minute.

Recovery rates

The time taken for cold water from the mains to get to 60°C inside the cylinder is referred to as the recovery rate. This rate is dependent on the size of the boiler or the cylinder heat exchanger, whichever is smaller. For instance, a typical cylinder for a four-bedroom house needs 8kWh of energy to heat its 140lts of water from 10°C to 60°C; an 8kW heater will accomplish this feat in one hour, whereas a 16kW heater will take just half as long. In theory a 32kW heater would achieve the same feat in 15 minutes, but in practice this would not happen unless the boiler was also rated at 32kW, which is unlikely. Here the boiler size becomes the limiting factor in the recovery rate. Unlike boilers, cylinders are not advertised by the size of their heat exchangers; however, most manufacturers sell a 'standard' version (Cost £80) which takes about one hour to heat up and a 'quick recovery' version which takes 20 minutes (Cost £130). The latter simply have larger heat exchangers.

Efficiency/heat loss

All new cylinders are insulated to reduce heat loss to less than 3kW of heat during a 24-hour period. Effectively, this heat loss can be ignored for six months of the year as it is simply transferring heat from water to space heat; during the summer you might leak something like 500kWh of heat – value £10-£15. Many new cylinders (like the Megaflo) are encapsulated by 50mm of polyurethane which reduces heat lost over a 24hr period to under 1kW — nothing to all intents and purposes.

Annual DHW costs using an average 225lts per day should be about 5,000kWh or £100 for a gas or oil system. A super-lagged cylinder will save around £10 per annum.

Dead legs

The hot water piping running between the cylinder and the hot water taps is effectively an extension to the cylinder; water sitting there loses its heat very quickly. An efficiently designed installation would have around 5lts of water sitting in the hot pipes. This may sound insignificant, but bear in mind that every time a hot tap is opened some of this water is replaced and so if every hot tap is turned on just three times a day, then 15lts of extra hot water has to be heated (cost per annum 300kWh or £6-£10). An inefficient design with much longer dead legs – i.e. bathrooms and kitchen all at opposite ends of the house – might use four or five times the length of hot water pipe. Not only does the cost of supplying hot water to the dead legs then become significant (£30 plus per annum) but you start getting 20-30 second lags between opening the hot tap and getting hot water. Avoid long dead legs if possible.

There is a way around this problem which is to create a pumped hot water loop around the house so that there is always hot water at each hot tap. However you have the added cost of installing and running a circulation pump and, to be effective, you have to insulate the hot water pipes to a high standard otherwise you will gain very little.

■Heating controls

Before the days of central heating (c.1950), heating controls consisted of putting (or not putting) coal on the fire or, at best, an on/off switch on an electric heater. Here is an industry that has grown at a prodigious rate and there is now a bewildering range of options open to the householder. Yet the purpose of controls is quite simple:
■ to increase comfort
■ to decrease fuel consumption

■ safety.

This section concentrates on wet heating systems; other heating systems (warm air, electric, solid fuel) tend to have different control systems which will be touched on in the following section, Alternative Heating. The logic behind them all remains the same.

Programmers

Timers to the layman. These are basically the on/off switch for the whole heating system and, as such, override all the other controls (except safety features like frost thermostats). Digital display has brought big improvements to programmers and now for little more than £30 you can get separate control for hot water heating and space heating which you can switch on and off 21 times a week. Changing the setting is about as easy as recording a film on the video – i.e. it helps to be young. Also, plumbers just love being called back to find out why the heating isn't coming on, only to find that you've been messing around with the programmer.

Look for ones with a boost (or 'Extra Hour') facility which allows you to turn the system on at odd times – mostly a standard feature now. A basic electronic programmer is now considered an absolutely essential component of a central heating system. Digital displays are now almost universal, although it hasn't made them easier to use or understand than the older ones with plastic knobs.

Thermostats

Known by plumbers as just stats, these provide a secondary level of on/off switching, controlled by temperature. So if the air or water temperature is higher than the thermostat setting, these controls will switch the heating system off, even though the programmer says 'run'.

■ Room stats: cost £12. Will cut off hot water to radiators when the set temperature is reached. Placing them requires care. To some extent being replaced by TRVs and programmable thermostats – see below.

The thermostaic radiator valve – or TRV. Very common on new systems – but their operation remains problematic

■ Cylinder stat: cost £9. Does much the same for hot water cylinder. Some are integral with the cylinder, some are strapped onto the copper walls.

■ Boiler stats: Usually integral with the boiler, these set the temperature of water passing through the boiler, which is the hottest part of the system.

■ Frost stat: cost £20. A safety device which turns on heating if there is a danger of any components freezing – e.g. boilers in garages or other unheated spaces. It can of course take precedence over a timer which says the system should be off. Malfunctioning frost stats can be expensive to run and difficult to pinpoint.

■ High limit stat: cost £30. A safety device to stop sealed system boilers overheating (or boiling). Ask if your preferred boiler needs one.

Motorised zone valves

These are what the programmer operates; they are used to switch the flow of hot water around different parts (or zones) of the system. The cheapest systems use a 3-port valve (£40) but it is better to use two 2-port valves (2 x £30). The simplest valves switch all water either this way or that and therefore give rise to something called hot water priority, which means that the hot water stops being pumped around the radiators when the domestic hot water is being

heated in the cylinder. There are more costly valves that are capable of opening in a middle position which allows a flow of hot water both ways.

A standard set of heating controls (excluding TRVs) for a four-bedroom house would cost around £200 (Mats £100, Lab £100). These controls are often sold in packages which usually include a pump, motorised valve, a programmer, a room stat and a cylinder stat. Note that wiring must be provided between all these components.

TRVs

Thermostatic radiator valves (TRVs) are apparently simple little gizmos fitted on to the bottom of the radiators that can sense the air temperature and switch off supply to the radiator when satisfied. They are cheap (£7); they increase comfort levels by stopping overheating and they reduce fuel bills. They are becoming almost standard – they are fitted throughout the benchmark house.

Minus

There have been problems with the operation of TRVs. Many people do not understand the principle of thermostatic control and, when feeling cold and seeing a dial, turn the TRVs on fully, thinking this will make the radiators hotter. It won't. Furthermore, because they require manual operation, there is no way of knowing (other than learning from experience) how high to set them to achieve comfortable space heating in any given room – though note that the latest versions allow you to limit the highest/lowest settings.

Another minus
TRVs have been prone to sticking (usually in the off position) and many people have reported radiators not working at all at the beginning of the heating season. Drayton TRVs had a particularly poor record; I know of someone who took all their TRVs off because they appeared to stop the radiators working at all. Manufacturing controls now appear to be better and this problem should be eliminated, but only time will tell. Honeywell TRVs are said to be among the more reliable.

Yet Another Minus
TRVs don't reduce fuel bills by as much as you might think — or that their manufacturers might claim. Although they can stop supply of hot water to the radiator to which they are fitted, they have no way of letting the boiler know this fact. In some systems which replace the room stat with TRVs, all radiators can be satisfied yet the boiler will continue to push hot water around the flow and return runs controlled only by the timer and the boiler thermostat. Don't be talked into doing away with the room stat just because you've fitted TRVs. They really only offer fine adjustments to the heating in each room.

Underfloor systems
If you want underfloor heating controlled on a room-by-room basis, you have to use wall mounted room stats, which is an expensive option when compared with TRVs.

Programmable thermostats
These combine the functions of the ordinary programmer (time switching) with that of the room stat (temperature switching). They also allow you to pre-select different temperature maxima for different times of day: very clever but even less user-friendly than the ordinary electronic programmers. A potential energy saver and a potential comfort increaser and no more expensive than a programmer and room stat separately. Whereas ordinary time-only programmers can be placed anywhere that's convenient, once you introduce a thermostat you have to think very carefully about its location and which temperatures it will be measuring.

Boiler managers
(aka optimisers or weather compensators). Currently the most upmarket controls option available, the use of these is slowly filtering down from large industrial buildings to housing. The price reflects the variety and complexity of controls from relatively simple systems like the Honeywell AQ 6000 (costs around £170 – around double the basic controls) to multi-zoned systems like Landis & Staefer's RVP 75 or the DCD Heating Controller which cost around £300.

They aim to stabilise room temperatures whilst reducing the fuel consumption of boilers. You programme the manager to have your home heated to the temperatures you choose at the times you select and the manager decides the most efficient ways of achieving this. A microprocessor is fed data, monitoring outside air temperature and heating water temperature, and it is able to independently switch the boiler and the pump on or off to maximise efficiency. Their use is particularly recommended with condensing boilers where they are able to maximise the length of time that the boilers can work in condensing mode (which increases fuel efficiency).

Minus
There have been problems to do with rusting heat exchangers when boiler managers have been coupled with a cast-iron boiler. Check with your boiler manufacturer to see if it is compatible with a boiler manager running a

low temperature heating system.

Another minus

The controls are even more difficult to understand than programmable thermostats; many people are likely to be flummoxed by them, which partly accounts for their slow uptake in domestic situations. This is particularly true of the more upmarket systems like the Landis & Staefer's. If you lead an erratic lifestyle, in and out at all hours, the supposed efficiencies of a boiler manager will be wasted on you, but for homes with regular occupation patterns, a boiler manager should produce tangible savings.

Two-zone heating systems

An energy saving idea which splits the space heating into two heating zones – typically upstairs/downstairs – in addition to heating the hot water. It involves using a three-zone programmer such as the Horstman Channel Plus. Again, the benefits very much depend on lifestyle – i.e. whether you really use your house in a predictable way. If, for instance, you hardly ever went upstairs before 9.00pm then you could have upstairs heating off all day which could conceivably save 10-15 per cent of space heating bills. You could achieve similar results with TRVs but these would need daily manual adjustment. Zoning more complex than upstairs/downstairs is possible, but would probably involve longer and less efficient pipe runs which would tend to cancel out any advantage. The 2002 energy efficiency regs suggest that a building larger than 150 sq m should be split into heating zones: it is not quite a requirement, the wording in the Approved Document is a bit woolly.

Are they worth it?

The savings achieved by superior heating controls are extremely difficult to estimate because they depend to a large extent on how the house is lived in. Often manufacturers will claim 15 per cent or 20 per cent savings on running costs but these are usually comparisons with systems with no automatic controls, which are most unlikely to be fitted today.

A more reasonable assumption would be that any one of these extra levels of heating control might save five per cent on fuel costs for heating. At the present time you cannot run a boiler manager covering more than one heating zone unless you pay around £370, so it's either/or but not both.

On a detached four-bedroom house, fitting a cocktail of sophisticated heating controls might save around £50 per annum. However, had you already decided to spend extra money on super insulation and condensing boilers your prospective fuel bills would be halved, so your 15 per cent saving would also be halved, down to something like £25 per annum. Even so, the cost of more effective heating controls should not be more than £300 and so they are what you might call a moderately attractive investment.

■Alternative Heating

Electric Heating

The electricity supply companies would be horrified to learn that they are an alternative heating supplier, but a scan of comparative fuel costs (see Which Fuel? earlier in this chapter) will show you why I have placed them in this category. The popularity of electric heating with developers is due almost entirely to its low installation costs. At peak rate it is a prohibitively expensive fuel to run (7p/kWh); off-peak is less than half this price, but still twice the price of gas. Off-peak night-storage heating is also about the most uncontrollable, unresponsive heating system ever designed, delivering the bulk of its heat when it's hardly needed.

To counteract these failings, the supply companies have tariffs with off-peak rates in the afternoon and evenings. Also, they recognise that night-storage heaters are not everyone's idea of beauty and so they currently recommend underfloor heating topped up with ceiling heaters, which are designed to run on the new Economy 10 tariffs. These developments represent a big improvement in the outlook for electric heating – the pluses that apply to wet underfloor systems apply just as strongly to electric heating – yet as long as oil and gas remain half the price, electricity is unlikely to be many people's first choice. It will also remain a relatively uncontrollable heat source as long as the effective hours of use are limited to ten per day.

A night-storage heating system for a four-bedroom house would cost just under £2,000. This would involve fitting seven or eight night-storage heaters and providing convector radiators for the rest of the house. An electric underfloor/ceiling system would cost around £1,500 for underfloor heating downstairs and ceiling heating to both downstairs and upstairs; adding an underfloor system upstairs (which would necessitate a beam and block first floor) adds £250 to the whole system. Electric underfloor heating is now controlled automatically as standard in ways not dissimilar to how boiler managers work; both outside temperatures and screed temperatures are monitored to adjust the levels of heat input needed.

This under and over system, as it is known, is by some margin the cheapest form of central heating to install. Electric heating systems have come on in leaps and bounds in the last few years and it is certainly worth considering as an option, particularly if you're interested in underfloor heating.

Your local electricity supply company will have a New Homes Dept which will design and cost (and arrange installation of) a suitable system for your house. Other underfloor/overhead specialists are ESWA and Devi. One of the areas where electric heating systems fall down is that they don't give you any hot water and for that you need to either fit a cylinder with an immersion heater or use a wet boiler such as the Amptec Boiler.

Plus
No additional connection charges; available everywhere; cheap installation costs; low maintenance costs as the 'boiler' is located at a distant power station; doesn't leak; no radiators with underfloor heating; underfloor heating coupled with convector booster heaters are actually a very good team, the first giving comfortable heat, the second giving quick response.

Minus
Expensive to run; generally unresponsive; underfloor heating concept does not work so well upstairs; not very green; when comparing quotations don't overlook the fact that electric heating makes no allowance for domestic hot water; Economy 7 cylinders are expensive and limited.

Ground source heat pumps
A very different approach to electric heating is to use a heat pump. They've been around for decades but have never really caught on in the UK, mostly because they are expensive to install, up to double the cost of the main alternative options. However, recently a number of small companies have begun offering ground source heat pump solutions. Heat pumps work on the principle of gearing, a concept more commonly found in financial circles: they draw a little bit of heat into a large amount of liquid – typically pipes laid under the garden – and then transfer this heat into a much smaller amount of water so that you turn a 10°C uplift in the garden pipes into a 30-40°C uplift in the house, at which temperature there is enough output to run a hot water underfloor heating system (which run at cooler temps than radiators). Indeed, it's enough to run baths and showers as well: the requirement to store water at 60°C is solely to do with preventing the legionella bacteria which like warm water.

Warm air
Warm air or forced air heating systems work by blowing heated air around the house in a series of ducts. All you see of it are inlet and outlet grills, usually a pair per room. It's the most

Heat pumps

Adrian Thurley's Cambridgeshire house, built in 2003, is heated entirely by an Ice Energy heat pump. The heat pump is located in the basement; it's connected to two 200m long pipes that run under the front garden and it is capable of providing 18.5kW of heat, using less then a third of this amount of electricity to do so. It heats the water up to 55°C, to be stored in a large pressurised cylinder. 'It's been fascinating to see it working,' said Adrian. 'I was led to believe that it drew its heat from the ground, which remained at a constant 10°C all year around. But in fact the temperature in the garden loop has changed dramatically through the year, peaking at 21°C in summer and going as low as -1°C in winter. Yet even at -1°C, the heat pump still manages to extract 3° or 4° of heat from the pipes. For every one kilowatt of power used in running the system, we get between three and four kilowatts of heat out of it. That's the magic of heat pumps.' It wasn't cheap, costing around £8,000 to install, but part of this cost was offset by a Clear Skies grant of £1,200. 'It's a government initiative to encourage us to install green technologies (check out www.clear-skies.org). I think I am the first person in the country to get a grant for installing a heat pump.'

common form of heating in American homes but in Britain it's fallen right out of favour after many systems fitted in the Sixties and Seventies proved to be noisy and ineffective.

I don't think any private developers have fitted warm air heating systems into new homes since about 1985. Johnson and Starley are the only firm left producing warm air units in this country, mostly satisfying the retrofit market. They work with a conventional flued, floor-standing gas-fired boiler. The system must be installed by a CORGI registered installer and would cost around £4,000 for a four-bedroom house. This would include a gas-fired boiler and all the ducting to push the hot air around the house, but domestic hot water (DHW) would have to be supplied by other means. It's not a completely bleak outlook. A recent entrant into the market is Schrag, a warm-air system from Germany, which comes with the very upmarket Huf Haus. I am told it's marvellous.

Plus

Very responsive – heat house quickly; no radiators; air can be filtered; possibilities of being combined with heat recovery systems and air conditioning.

Minus

Warm air is arguably the least comfortable form of heating; lacks any radiant heat and, despite air filtering, tends to throw up dust particles. Not well understood in UK; poorly designed and installed they have been known to be noisy. However, recent users have reported high satisfaction rates.

Heat recovery

See next section on Ventilation.

Underfloor heating

See previous section on Emitters.

Solar power

Solar power now splits between two options: panels for heating water and panels (or cells) for creating electricity. Neither option comes cheap. For a water heating system, a standard installation on a family house would cost over £2,000 for the flat plate collector and about £3,500 for a vacuum tube collector. The vacuum tubes are a considerable improvement; they are sensitive to light rather than sunshine and they are not as affected by wind chill. However, even when working at full whack the output is only going to be around 3kW: this would easily be enough to provide DHW in the summer and provide some DHW in the winter.

The problem is that the cost of DHW heating with a well-insulated cylinder and a gas-or oil-fired boiler is remarkably small – just £100 per annum in the benchmark house. Getting £40 or £50 of 'free' hot water each year is paltry when compared to installation costs; the payback period is as much as 70 years. The electricity-producing panels, known as photovoltaic cells, are even more expensive to install though you can – with difficulty – connect these to the grid which enables you to sell electricity back to your regular supplier (albeit at a miserly rate).

Having said that, there are signs that solar panels will become cheaper as they become much more widely installed in places with warmer, sunnier climes than ours. If you are interested in alternative energy production generally (and I've overlooked a number of other options), you should point yourself towards the Centre for Alternative Technology in North Wales. They have carried out much excellent pioneering work in this field and they also have a good bookshop. Also consider joining the Association of Environment Conscious Builders (AECB) who will put you in touch with dozens of very useful contacts.

The most significant recent change in this field has come via the deregulation of the electricity supply industry. Now several of the major suppliers are offering EcoPower options which allow you to buy your renewable electricity over the grid.

For a small premium (usually between five per cent and ten per cent), the supplier will match any power you use with power created by some distant wind farm or photovoltaic solar panel.

Green energy for £30 or £40 a year sounds like an inviting option and a lot less hassle than installing and maintaining your own power plants on site – maybe this will prove to be the catalyst which will really get renewable power sources off the ground.

Solid fuel

Solid fuel stoves exist which can handle heating for the largest houses. This means that they can be harnessed to provide hot water to be pumped around radiators and through the hot water cylinder as well as giving off more than a pleasing glow in the room where they sit. They come in three basic styles; the decorative cast-iron finish to go in the living room, the kitchen range which adds cooking capabilities, or the utilitarian box to be hidden out of view.

They are never going to win on the convenience stakes as in order to perform the task equivalent to a gas/oil boiler they will have to be kept going all through the winter, which means frequent stoking, riddling and emptying. Attempts by manufacturers like Charnwood to market automatically loading and emptying stoves have been abandoned because of high cost. And in the semi-cold seasons (September-November and March-May) you'll never be quite sure if or when to fire up and so you'll need some sort of backup system (probably electric), which rather defeats the purpose of spending all the money in the first place. There is still a place for them as whole house heat sources, but realistically only in homes permanently occupied. Many remote locations still suffer regular power cuts and the ability to heat the home without recourse to electrically controlled components remains important yet, like other wet central heating systems, solid fuel systems are nowadays designed with electric pumps and valves to distribute the hot water so even this potential advantage is largely lost.

Living room stoves

The Coalbrookdale range (made by Aga Rayburn) are well known and readily available. There are four sizes and each size is available

with or without a boiler. Without a boiler,
the stoves are really just efficient room fires;
the boiler (which absorbs around 60-70 per
cent of the stove's heat output) is essential if a
wet whole house heating and DHW system is
wanted. The benchmark house would require
at least the second largest Coalbrookdale, the
Severn, which belts out 10kW of hot water as
well as 3kW of room heat. It weighs a quarter
of a ton and costs around £900. There are a
number of other manufactures, both British and
European, who produce variations on the same
theme, some with highly individualist styling
(Euroheat, Waterford's Erin, Morso), but prices
are remarkably similar.

Kitchen ranges
Another approach is to use a cast-iron cooker
as a centre piece in a kitchen. The Aga is the
best known and, at around £5,500 to buy, the
most expensive. However the Aga only has a
small boiler, capable of supplying DHW but
not further space heating. There are a range
of good-looking stoves which can cook, heat
and do DHW – e.g. Rayburn, Stanley, Wamsler,
Hergom. Strictly speaking, we're moving away
from solid fuel because these cooker/heaters
can be (and most frequently are) fired by gas
or oil.

In its solid fuel version the top of the range
Rayburn would be big enough (16kW) to
provide for the benchmark house – but it would
require refuelling every two hours! Overnight
its output would drop to just 2kW, which
would make those January mornings a bit too
nippy and would necessitate electric backup
heating. At around £3,000 plus installation costs
it's an expensive but stylish option. Wamsler
produce a solid fuel central heating cooker
that looks more basic (as you might see in a
restaurant kitchen) which is about 25 per cent
less than Rayburns and Stanleys. All these ranges
can be run in summer, thus doing away with
the need for separate cookers, but then they belt
out more heat than you'd really want.

To find out more, check out dealers in the
Yellow Pages under Heating Eqpt – solid fuel.

Plus
Style; reliability; doesn't pack up during power
cuts (although central heating at least is usually
electrically pumped); many stoves are 'multi-
fuel' which means they can burn virtually
anything, which may be an attraction if you
own a wood or a peat bog.

Minus
Initial price is high; need backup heating; extra
housework; fuel not especially cheap; inefficient
(unlike gas or oil the boiler can't be turned off
at the flick of a switch); unresponsive; fuel
needs storage; need open flue (and probably
chimney); room stoves get hot and are not child
friendly.

Cooling
Air conditioning and cooling had always been
thought of as unnecessary in UK homes because
our summer climate never got that hot. But
in recent years we have experienced one or
two summers which were nothing short of
sweltering. Plus we are seeing the widespread
adopting of air conditioning in our cars – it's
now almost standard on new models, having
only recently been considered a luxury. There
are home air conditioning systems available
in the UK but whilst new housebuilders
show increasing interest in more and more
sophisticated ways of staying warm during
the 20-odd week annual heating season, there
remains approximately nil interest in staying
cool during the 10-week high summer period.

Why? Well for a starter, it is expensive
to install. An air conditioning system for a
detached house would set you back in the
region of £5,000, rather more than the most
elaborate heating systems on the market. A
one-room system would cost around £1,500.
The existing models are all electrically powered
and a whole house model would consume
around 3-5kW of power when going at full
blast – typically it would run for only 50 per
cent of the time, even on the hottest of days,
providing you remember to keep the doors and

windows shut. The units also tend to be noisy, though this problem can be reduced if the design of the installation is good. Like boilers, air conditioning needs to have exhaust ducting and this means that the system has to be built in permanently and is connected to an outdoor unit. To my knowledge, there are no portable air conditioners that you could move around the house with you. There is a new system on the market called Idrosplit that piggy-backs on to a radiator central heating system, available from Plumb Center, clever but pricey. Alternatively, some of the heat recovery units offer an air cooling facility; the Villavent 4 unit provides something called comfort cooling – it will not turn the house into a fridge like the ones in American homes, but will be able to drop incoming air temperature by several degrees.

■Ventilation

Buildings need to be ventilated. Trapped water vapour in particular can be very damaging, causing condensation and encouraging mould growth and wet rot. It's a potential problem in both the external structure of a house – especially under ground floors and in roofs – and the enclosed living space.

The building regulations deal with the need for ventilation in both areas. Underfloor ventilation (only applicable with suspended ground floors) is by way of air bricks; roof ventilation is by eaves or soffit vents and occasionally air bricks too.

The building regs dealing with internal ventilation specify that habitable rooms must have opening windows fitted with trickle vents (more on these later) and that kitchens and bathrooms must have extractor fans (or 'adequate means of extraction'). A cooker hood ducted to the outside is acceptable in a kitchen or else there must be an extractor fan capable of shifting 60lts/s (litres/second); the bathroom fan must be capable of shifting 15lts/s, equivalent to a small bathroom full of air in about ten or fifteen minutes. A separate toilet can make do with an opening window or a small fan.

Standard solutions

Fit trickle vents in the windows. Extractor fans in kitchens and bathrooms.

Trickle Vents

These slimline plastic inserts have now become nearly universal on standard joinery – indeed it is a problem to find windows without them. Trickle vents, which can be open or closed from inside, are slotted into a hole drilled out of the head of the window. Some manufacturers still charge £6 extra for fitting them, some supply windows with just the slots cut out and supply the vents separately at around £6 each.

Cooker hoods

Normally fitted as standard in kitchens, although they don't have to be ducted outside – they are said to 'recirculate' if they don't. It makes very good sense to make sure your cooker does duct directly outside as it works much better and saves the cost of a second, more powerful extractor fan. Cooker hoods are usually sold as part of a package with hobs and ovens. They start at around £50: automatic versions with humidity controlled switching are available at around £100, but the current fashion if for rather grand stainless steel ones which typically cost £300 upwards.

Bathroom fans

A basic, 15 litres per second, fan can be controlled by a pull switch, or linked to a room light switch. Bathrooms without windows have to have models fitted with automatic overrun timers, and where ducting is required a centrifugal fan is recommended. Higher up the range, the fans have humidistats which can automatically switch fans between off, low and high settings dependent on humidity in the bathroom. And at the top of the range are a small number of heat recovery fans which do all these things as well as recycling some of the heat normally pumped out by the fan.

Not included in the above prices for fans are exterior wall grilles (£5) or any ducting (£12 per 3m run). Fans can be ducted horizontally through external walls or vertically into the roof space and then out through the ridge via a ridge vent tile (£50) or through a roof vent tile (£35). Fitting is normally done by the electrician and budget charges will be around £20 for the switch (Mats £5, Lab £15) and around £25 labour for fitting the fan, more if there are complex ducting routes involved.

The total cost of these measures on the benchmark house was around £500, made up as follows:

■ Trickle Vents   18 @ £6   £108
■ Cooker Hood and Ducting   £100
■ Bathroom Fans   3 @ £100   £300

Note that trickle vents are installed as the default option when you order joinery. If you choose to specify something else you may, or may not, be able to save a bit of money by cancelling the trickle vents. Speedframe, the uPVC window manufacturers who worked on our benchmark house, actually build their trickle vents into the subframes so you don't see them protrude through the windows.

Whole House Systems
Mechanical Ventilation

The building regs allow for radically different approaches to ventilation. One is to do away with trickle vents and to provide both extract and inlet ventilation via a series of ducts controlled by electric fans. A number of manufacturers produce units which will recapture some of the heat being sucked out of the house, mixing it with fresh air being brought in through the loft. A new house has such high insulation levels that the fabric (i.e. walls, roof, floor) lose comparatively little heat. If careful attention isn't paid to airtightness and ventilation, then much of this saved heat will just trickle away. Between a third and a half of the space heating bill goes on replacing unwarranted ventilation – in the benchmark house, that would amount to £100 per annum. Worth saving. Unfortunately, a heat recovery system will cost at least £1,500 to install and as much as £50 per annum to run because it is powered by two electric fans on continuously;

in addition there will be occasional servicing costs. In terms of power saved v power used (known as the efficiency ratio), heat recovery systems perform reasonably well, but when costed it turns out that the power saved usually costs about 2p per kWh, whereas the electricity to run the unit is costing around 7p per kWh. The evidence suggests that, in our temperate climate, airborne heat recovery systems are not good value. In response to these criticisms, manufacturers have been introducing systems powered by low wattage fans (such as VentAxias HR200V) which improve the overall returns.

When pressed, most manufacturers will admit that the economic return is negligible but will still insist that there are benefits in increased comfort levels. This may well be true but it will have to be taken as an act of faith because it is notoriously difficult to predict how an as yet unbuilt house will behave: most people find warm, well insulated housing remarkably comfortable and free of condensation without

Installation layout for whole house mecahnical ventilation. There are four extracts and five inlets, enough for a small house.

recourse to mechanical heat recovery systems.

Passive stack ventilation

This is another option that can be used if you are interested in whole house ventilation. Passive stack ventilation also uses ducts to extract stale air from the house but there the similarity ends. Trickle vents are fitted in all the dry rooms (i.e. living rooms, bedrooms) whilst ducts run from the wet areas (bathrooms, kitchens) up to a vented ridge tile; air pressure does the rest, drawing air in through the house and away through the roof. A simple concept, essentially no different to a chimney stack (hence the name). Each extract duct has to be connected to its own vented ridge tile via an insulated flexible pipe and will cost £120-£150; in certain situations (bathrooms with no external walls) this will be cheaper than using a centrifugal fan with ducting. A whole house system (with four passive stacks) would cost around £800 (Mats £400, Lab £400). Add a cooker hood (which is recommended) and the overall cost will be around 60 per cent more than the standard route.

There are currently two passive stack suppliers, Passivent and Johnson & Starley (Aereco). Passivent have a couple of variations on the basic module including a system which introduces humidistats on both the inlets (trickle vents) and the extract grilles. This effectively cuts down excessive air-changes as the vents close below a certain level of humidity. Strictly speaking, this would seem to be contrary to the building regs standard that half an air-change per hour should take place throughout the house, but humidity levels are a good indicator of the level of use a room is getting (people produce water vapour) and no one seems to be complaining. The 'intelligent system' with humidistats costs around £250 more than the ordinary stack system, by now nearly double the standard route – though still half the price of mechanical heat recovery. For around £400 above the standard solution, you get a system that works without anything mechanical to go wrong and introduces an

element of heat saving. Passive stack systems are still relatively new and many architects and designers are unaware of their existence. However passive stack ventilation took a huge step forward in 1998 when Wimpey Homes, the UK's biggest housebuilder, started using it throughout their range, though for first floor bathrooms only. Their kitchens and downstairs WCs are vented with conventional fans; this arrangement is now known as the Wimpey option.

Plus
Quiet; no running cost; nothing to break down; no filters to change; the 'intelligent' systems reduce overall heat loss in well sealed housing.

Minus
Doesn't suit every situation – the taller the building the better they will work; because there is so little to them, many people simply don't believe they work; they want fans! It's also difficult (verging on the impossible actually) to configure when you are building into the loftspace – it doesn't work so well when you start angling ducts into the rafter space.

Comment

The subject of ventilation is intriguing because it is as yet very poorly understood. There is a general consensus that ventilation needs to be planned into modern buildings but there is no agreement on how much ventilation is really needed. If it were a question of just replacing oxygen used by the inhabitants, the ventilation rate would have to be no more than 1lt per second per person: some authorities think a minimum figure should be about 2.5 times this level, others think it should be no less than 40 times this level. Our current building regulations suggest that 0.5 air-changes per hour is sufficient – this equates to around 65lts per second in our 460 cu m benchmark house which puts it bang in the middle of the range of assumptions.

Both mechanical and passive stack ventilation systems work on the assumption that, without their intervention, houses would be inadequately ventilated and would suffer from:

■ excess water vapour
■ condensation
■ smells
■ stuffiness
■ lack of oxygen
■ build-up of toxic gases like radon, formaldehyde or volatile organic compounds given off by synthetic carpet and the like.

However, it is worth emphasising that before spending good money on fancy ventilation systems, you should ensure that you have a reasonably airtight structure. The 'air-leakiness' of your house may make the installation of such fancy ventilation schemes quite redundant. Even with trickle vents all sealed, it would appear that many UK homes will 'self-ventilate' at a level of around two air-changes per hour just through leaks in the structure – for instance, where there is imperfect draught sealing around doors, windows, skirting boards, pipe holes and loft hatches; an unsealed chimney alone extracts 20lts of air per second.

A cursory glance at heat-loss calculations for the benchmark house (see Chapter 13) will show what a large part heating air-changes plays in the overall heating costs. At half an air-change per hr (65lts/s), the benchmark house will lose about a third of its heat through ventilation. However, if the house is built 'leaky' – at say two air-changes per hr – then this heat-loss figure will multiply fourfold to around £200 per year. In comparison, the so-called building fabric (walls, roof, ground floor, windows) ships no more than £100 of heat during the course of a year, so you can see what an important place ventilation has in the scheme of things.

So if you are interested in installing something more advanced than the standard ventilation requirements, you should pay careful attention to draught proofing beforehand. To this effect, you should fit a damper on your chimney to shut it off when not in use, you should seal all cracks, holes and joints with a flexible silicone sealer – dry-lined plasterboard walls have a particularly bad reputation in this respect – and you should consider fitting a proprietary sealed loft hatch (like Marley's, cost £50). Pay attention to door furniture so that you do not have open keyholes, and note that French doors and stable doors are particularly difficult to draught proof.

Pressure tests

If you want to take this process to its logical conclusion, then you can have a pressure test carried out on your house for around £200. They attach a giant vacuum cleaning-type device which puts the house under pressure (up to 50 Pascals, which sounds like a lot but it's not noticeable if you are inside) and then measures the rate the device draws air in through it to replace the air being displaced through all the cracks in the structure. At 50 Pascals, the leakage rates are five or ten times more than you would get under typical atmospheric conditions. This may seem an expensive and unnecessary test to put your house through, but if you are about to pay out a great deal more than this for a whole house ventilation system, not to mention an elaborate heating system, it's possibly worth ensuring that it's at least going to work as planned. Contact Retrotec.

■Fires & chimneys

Functionally, central heating has made the fireplace redundant yet the fireplace lives on in most new family homes. If you want to save money building your home and you want a 'green', low-running-cost style of house, then you will be doing yourself a great favour by cutting out all plans for room fires of whatever type. Trouble is – what do you put in the middle of the living room wall? Without a fireplace something is missing. It's like a church without an altar – it just doesn't look right. A living-room fire on a cold winter's night feels so good because it strikes a chord with the caveman or woman inside us all, whose control of fire was the very thing that separated us from the wild beasts roaming outside. In

The benchmark house is typical of most contemporary homes. Despite not requiring a fireplace, Steve Baldwin wouldn't have dreamed of building the house without one. Note the large beam over the fire opening, sometimes called a bessemer (usually by upmarket estate agents)

other words, we are in the land of the adman's 'aspirational purchases.'

Feeding this aspiration is now seen as a bit of a luxury and the majority of smaller homes being built do without the open fire altogether. Some plump for a gas fire, some for nothing at all. Actually, chimney spotting is an interesting exercise – take a look around and see who is building them and who isn't; the results can be quite surprising.

Fire options
Open fires
If you want an open fire, the simplest option available is to form an opening using a fireback unit. Ventilation is provided by an airbrick somewhere in the vicinity of the fireplace, and you decorate the opening with some sort of simple mantelpiece. For just over £100 more you can fit a purpose-made fire basket complete with ventilation and removable ash can – the Baxi Burnall is the best known – and if you want a regular fire this is a worthwhile addition.

Stoves
Another approach is to take the fire out into the room space and contain it in a metal surround

– the stove. This is a much more efficient way of heating a room (though even the most efficient cast-iron stoves are no match for a new oil- or gas-fired boiler) and is much favoured by hippies living in isolated cottages. However, in a new house it probably represents the worst of both worlds in that a) you don't actually need a stove for room heating and b) you lose the sexiness of having open fire in your living room. Most solid-fuel stoves are very traditional in appearance and they are not cheap. For more modern designs, you need to look to the Continent and a price tag of £3,000 plus.

A more detailed discussion of the merits of stoves appears in the section Alternative Heating a few pages back.

Gas fires
For those who cannot be doing with the hassle of solid fuel but still want a focal point, then gas fires may be the answer. You can buy a student digs style gas fire such as Valor's Firelite for around £80, or you can get gas fires which can be inset into a fireplace (£200 upwards). Of more interest to new housebuilders will be the balanced-flue gas fires like the Canon Coalridge and the Valor Flamenco (£280 plus) which can be set on any outside wall and don't need a

chimney at all, which makes for a very cheap way of getting a focal point fire into a living space. There is also a range of decorative effect gas fires – what I have learned to call Loggy-Glows – which heat up ceramic coal and logs. By the time you've fitted them with decorative fire baskets and decorative fire surrounds you won't have much change from £250 and you still have to fit a chimney to take away the exhaust gases.

Electric fires

Ever keen to compete with gas, there are a number of electric Living Flame effect fires. As these are a poor imitation of a gas fire making a poor imitation of a coal fire I can't see them being hugely fancied by new housebuilders but, in this business, choice is king and it would be ungracious of me not to mention them in passing. Prices range from £70 for a free standing 2kW (bar) fire with plastic logs stuck on top, to £300 for ones which have a flame effect glow going on in the background. Naff as you like.

Chimneys
Masonry

The standard way of evacuating smoke from fires is via a brick- or block-built chimney, the higher the better. The standard way to do this is to use concrete or clay flue liners set into an insulated cement screed, built up with the masonry work. It makes little difference to cost whether this chimney is built against an internal or an external wall – though there is a small cost penalty when building a masonry chimney in a timber frame house. In many traditionally styled homes, a large fireplace and chimney are designed to be the very heart of the house; for instance, Potton Homes, who specialise in creating Tudor style interiors, indicate that the construction costs of an inglenook fireplace and chimney suitable for one of their Heritage range would cost around £4,000; this figure could be quartered if you specified a simpler style of chimney but you would of course lose the splendour of the timber-beamed, brick-faced fireplace.

Feature chimneys, as opposed to feature fireplaces, are another money soaker. The old English (or Jacobean) chimney is enjoying something of a revival. On a steeply pitched roof with a handmade roof tile it can look fantastic, but it is likely to take a week or two to build and will add a minimum £500 to the chimney costs. If your budget doesn't stretch to ornamental brickwork, you might be interested in just an ornamental chimney pot. Salvage yards usually have stacks of them and Redbank produce a wide range at costs between £10 and £700.

Stainless Steel

There are a number of outfits producing stainless steel flues which can be used instead of a conventional chimney. Check out Selkirk and Brefco. A stainless steel insulated flue is not cheap: it would cost more than £500 to purchase an 8 m-long system for the benchmark house, which is about twice as much as the materials for a conventional chimney — but there are a number of plus points worth examining as they:
■ allow total flexibility as regards siting
■ are quick and easy to install
■ work rather better than regular chimneys
■ need very little cleaning
■ are particularly well suited to timber frame construction.

The biggest downside to using these systems is the look of the flue terminals. Instead of a

Chimney Costs on Benchmark House				
		Mats	Lab	Combined
Chimney brickwork	8 m²	£ 180	£ 180	£ 360
Extra blockwork	5 m²	£ 30	£ 50	£ 80
Flue Liners (300hx225)	24 N°	£ 170	£ 60	£ 230
Chimney Pot	1 N°	£ 30	£ 20	£ 50
Vermiculite Insulation	0.05 m³/m	£ 30		£ 30
Lead roof flashings	1 m	£ 20	£ 10	£ 30
Timber beam	1 N°	£ 30		£ 30
Tiled hearth	1 m²	£ 50	£ 30	£ 80
Firebasket	1 N°	£ 80		£ 80
	Totals	£ 620	£ 350	£ 970

traditional brick chimney you get an industrial looking stainless steel flue terminal; this can look fine in modern designs of housing but if you aspire to the trad then it looks pretty awful. Having said that, many barn conversions sport these aluminium flue terminals because planners are dead set against building masonry chimneys into a barn because it is not seen as being in keeping.

Prefabricated chimneys

Very popular in Scandinavia, the best known names in the UK are Isokern and Anki. They produce a pumice stone chimney lining system which fits together like Lego and has the advantage of being pre-insulated. One of the problems with conventional, flue-lined chimneys is that the temperature of the escaping smoke drops substantially as it rises up the chimney, causing both condensation and tar deposition; this is a noted problem when relatively high temperature stoves are being used. Ideally, the chimney linings should be insulated as constructed but this is frequently not done and specifying a pre-insulated lining such as Anki or Isokern (or one of the stainless steel ones) should alleviate the problem. These prefab chimneys are typically around £300 more expensive in materials than traditional flue liners and blocks, but they save something in construction time.

■Plumbing

Plumbing and heating, together with roofing and electrical work, is conventionally undertaken by specialist subcontractors who usually supply materials as well as labour. In analysing the labour costs, I've subtracted from quotations the amount a general contractor would hope to spend on materials: this leaves a labour rate of £30 per hr which is rather more than a plumber would charge in most areas of the country. The difference is explained by the mark-up a plumber would normally put on materials, so that though he would expect to be buying somewhat cheaper than a rookie builder,

Stainless steel flue terminals can ruin a traditional roofline. Despite this, the planners are implacably opposed to masonry chimneys in barn conversions

he would price the job as if the materials were list price. The difference is perhaps academic but it explains why the rate per hour looks so high. You should be able to hire a one-man-band type plumber for nearer half this rate but he might not be happy for you to buy materials. However, if you are working on a zero-rated job (new build and barn conversions) and you hire a non-VAT registered plumber (or for that matter any other tradesman), you should insist on buying the materials yourself otherwise you will not be able to reclaim the VAT.

Conventionally, plumbers are hired to fit heating and sanitaryware; this includes all above-ground waste fittings, but rarely underground drainage or rainwater goods. Traditionally, plumbers also undertook sheet-metal work on roofing, but now this is tending to be carried out by roofers. There are a couple of grey areas that it is good to be aware of. The first concerns the wiring of heating controls (which is sometimes carried out by the electrician) and the second concerns the installation of kitchen sinks and dishwashers, which is sometimes undertaken by specialist kitchen installers. Be clear, when you are hiring, who is to do what. The table runs through the heating tasks on an hour and cost basis; one of the plumbers who've checked over this, commented simply 'I wish it was always that quick!' The other main area covered by the plumber, fitting bathrooms, is covered in Chapter 11.

Benchmark House Heating Installation	Mats	Lab Hours	Lab @ £30/hr	Combined
Oil fired Boiler	£ 600	10	£ 300	£ 900
Oil Tank	£ 250	6	£ 180	£ 430
Megaflo Hot Water Tank	£ 500	4	£ 120	£ 620
Primaries, Valves, Pumps	£ 200	8	£ 240	£ 440
15 Radiators with TRVs	£ 800	23	£ 690	£ 1,490
Heating Controls	£ 200	6	£ 180	£ 380
Commission system		8	£ 240	£ 240
Totals	**£2,550**	**65**	**£1,950**	**£ 4,500**
Devi Heat Pads	£ 170	2	£ 60	£ 230
Devi Room Controls	£ 180	6	£ 180	£ 360
Devi UFH Total	**£350**	**8**	**£240**	**£ 590**

Check the spec

Many contractors have only the vaguest understanding of the ins and out of heating and plumbing systems and are more than happy to let their plumber design, price and install whatever system they like, and plumbers have become quite used to acting almost autonomously, as long as the kit works and the price is about right. Comparing quotations between plumbers is consequently a very difficult business because the specifications of the competing heating systems are almost bound to be different unless a professional has been employed to design the system beforehand, something which hardly anyone bothers with on smaller residential construction jobs.

Points to watch out for when comparing quotations are:
■ Are the design considerations identical? What temperature is each room to be heated to? How many air changes an hour have been assumed in the calculations?
■ What fuel is being specified to run the system? Have the costs of connecting to or storing the fuel been fully taken into account?
■ What controls are being provided? How efficient will the system be? How easy will it be to service the system? Will pumps and cables be concealed? What insulation is being provided to the hot water pipes?
■ What sort of emitters are being specified? If standard panel radiators, where will they be

sited? Will they have TRVs fitted as standard? If so, will these be in addition to or instead of a whole-house thermostat?
■ What provision has been made for towel radiators? Heating airing cupboards?
■ What arrangements will be made for hot water storage? What will hot water flow rates be like?
■ What sort of pipework will be used? Where will the overflows run to?
■ What sort of guarantee is offered? Does the business offer any form of regular servicing contract?

Plastic waste pipes

Slowly but steadily, plumbing is going plastic. There are still many plumbers who wouldn't be seen dead using anything other than copper for their water feeds but you will search high and low to find one who uses anything other than plastic for waste fittings.

The whole subject of plumbing in the waste for bathrooms, loos and kitchens is surprisingly complicated and is covered at good length in the building regs (part H, if you must). The problem is that you need to stop smells getting up into the house from the drains: this is (usually) achieved by designing in water traps separating the appliances from the drains below.

There are several different trap designs around, usually named after letters of the alphabet – P and S figure prominently. Were that all there was to it, it would be the end of the story but unfortunately these water traps have a habit of failing, often through induced siphonage sucking the water down the pipe. What has evolved is a series of rules dictating how we should lay out our waste runs and where and when the runs should be joined together. The ones which tend to catch people out are the maximum length of basin runs – 1.7m – laid at a fall of between 18 and 22mm per metre run. It seems ridiculously precise; it's borne out of many years analysing just why basins gurgle and loose their water seals.

You can cheat: there are now non-return valves that don't require a water seal — the best known is Hepworth's ingenious HepVO valve.

The main waste runs also cause problems. The general rule is to run the appliances, such as basins, baths and showers, in small pipe sections (typically 32, 40 or 50 mm) into a 110mm pipe, called a stack, which drops vertically down to the underground drain system. Stacks need to be ventilated and at least one stack on every drain run needs to be ventilated to the outside, usually done through the roof.

If you have more than one stack, you can use a short version, known as a stub stack, on the subsequent stacks: these can be topped off with air admittance valves, also known as Durgos. These act in a similar fashion to the smaller HepVO valves used in small bore drain runs – letting air into the system but not letting any out. The HepVO valve actually has a lot going for it and deserves to be better known because it effectively rewrites the way that you are meant to plumb in bathroom wastes. It's been around since 1997 but few plumbers are aware of its existence.

At ground floor level, it's usual to run the waste pipes together into an external gulley and thence to the drains. The principle remains the same: to prevent smells from the drains escaping into the house. It's one part of the house fit out which is routinely tested on completion of the job – the air test usually involves putting a bung into the drains at the highest manhole and another bung somewhere short of the air outlet and then seeing if the system between holds a given air pressure.

Indoor waste pipes have migrated across to plastic almost exclusively now but there is a choice of plastics and a choice of working methods. The DIY route is to use a push-fit system based on either uPVC or polyproplylene. Serious plumbers often prefer to use a glued system, known as solvent weld. These are typically made of ABS or uPVC, two rather more rigid plastics. The average spend in a house on above ground waste fittings is around £200 so it's not a budget buster, whichever system you opt for.

Water

Indoor plastic plumbing has been kicking around since the late Seventies and in its time it's come in for a fair amount of stick from the professionals who were content to look at it as just a DIY product. It's also resulted in numerous floodings resulting from duff joints or, more often, lazy installers. However, it's very easy and quick to install; it's mostly push-fit and it comes on a roll so you don't have to bother with soldering joints as you do with copper. So quick and easy that, at long last, it's really taking off in professional plumbing circles as well. Partly it's because it's used exclusively for underfloor heating (where it seems to perform fine) and partly because new building techniques such as I beam floors are becoming widespread and it's difficult to get copper tube through an I beam floor. The product itself has matured. Hepworth, the originators, have redesigned their joints to make them hopefully idiot proof and there is now competition from other big names in the field like Osma and Marley. Other big names in this field are John Guest's Speedfit, and Polyplumb.

It's hard not to come to the conclusion that copper plumbing is on the way out, although it will continue to be used extensively for many years to come. Gas plumbing, for instance, has to be done in copper. One area where plastic plumbing really wins out is when you are specifying I beam floors: you can't notch I-beam floors (you can actually, but the results are disastrous) so the ability to uncoil the pipe through holes in the webbing is almost indispensable.

Chapter 9
Wiring

Introduction
House wiring
Lighting
Built-in vacuums
TVs phones and cables

■Introduction

The housebuilding industry's standard for electrical provision is some way in advance of the minimum requirements. This will surprise many who automatically assume that professional developers always try and get away with the bare minimum, but in fact the NHBC standards for power supply to any new house are absolutely basic: the building regs don't even require power provision. Most house buyers – and selfbuilders – will expect at least double the number of outlets required by the NHBC. Certainly, the power and lighting specifications for the benchmark house are way above these standards – you could hardly have less than one light per room.

The benchmark house has a rather superior electrical specification and, without going over the top, the builder has spent rather more than most developers would. It's worth bearing in mind that even if you chose the NHBC minimum standard for lighting, you would probably spend a lot more money on lampshades, table lamps and fittings, all of which would attract VAT at 17.5 per cent, whereas built-in light fittings are zero-rated in a new house. It's probably a fair estimate to assume that you won't be leaving naked bulbs hanging for more than about five years and that

in the long run you'll spend an additional £500 on shades and separate table lamps.

You may feel that the NHBC minimum requirements are a red herring but, be warned, costs derived from these standards are widely used by businesses selling the bits of houses that don't include the wiring, to illustrate how much (or how little) it will cost to finish off the house. So it is as well to be aware that by current market standards the minimum requirements are unrealistically low.

The tables in this chapter shows just how each element of an electrician's quotation would be made up and how this translates into a whole house quotation – in this case the one used on our benchmark house.

More than most aspects of construction, electrical fittings vary enormously in quality. For many years, the market has been dominated by two British businesses, MK and Crabtree: indeed many specifiers indicate that fittings should be by either of these two firms. But there is a huge gulf between MK/Crabtree prices and some very cheap imported gear that you can get hold of. The current TLC catalogue has MK Logic Plus 13amp double sockets at £4.37 each; however, they also have their own brand version (Telco) at £1.90 each. If you want a mid-priced alternative, I can recommend MEM who produce a comprehensive catalogue.

House wiring

Connection fees

Regional electricity companies (RECs) are free to set their own connection fees and, being monopoly suppliers of an indispensable power source, they tend to charge a lot. Even a straightforward connection is likely to cost in the region of £300. If you are considering electric heating in your house, you may find that the REC offers to halve or even waive the entire connection fee as a sweetener. Long cable runs (say in excess of 50 m) can be prohibitively expensive, costing thousands, and should be carefully costed when assessing the plot. Each REC has a New Supplies Department, which is where you should look for quotations; you don't need to own the plot before getting a quotation.

Temporary supplies

Some builders manage without temporary electricity supplies, relying on generators and diesel-powered mixers; indeed most of the house superstructure can be easily erected without power tools. However, plumbers, electricians and second-fix carpenters are big users of power tools and you can't have your permanent supply turned on until they're finished so, for most builders, a temporary supply makes good sense.

Current regs insist that the temporary supply board is adequately housed; on most sites this

A temporary electrical supply box needs to be waterproof and secure

NHBC Minimum Standards

Power Sockets
(NB Double sockets count as two)
Kitchen/utility: 6
Dining room: 2
Living room: 4 + TV coaxial outlet
Master bedroom: 3
Other bedrooms: 2
Landing: 1
Hall: 1

Other Provisions
• electric cooker must have 30amp switched outlet
• electric immersion heater to hot water cylinder (optional)
• extract fans to kitchen and bathrooms
• provision for boiler electrics
• power laid on for smoke detectors
• sockets must be protected by RCDs (residual circuit breaking devices)

Lighting Standards
The NHBC minimum standard is as follows: "Every room should have at least one lighting outlet. There should be provision for lighting in halls, landing and staircases. Two-way switching should be provided to staircases." IEE regs state further that bathroom lighting should be encased and pull switched. Two-way switching means that a light can be switched on/off from two different places (typically at the top or bottom of the stairs); it should not be confused with 2-gang switching which means that there are two switches on one switch plate, each controlling a different light.

means building a blockwork box with at least a paving slab roof and a lockable door. Budget a day's work and £100 materials to build an adequate shed with consumer unit and sockets on a backing board inside. Care should be given to locating the temporary supply so that long cables are not left trailing over the site where they could be run over by diggers, dumpers or lorries. Discuss your requirements with the REC's new supplies estimator; there will be an extra charge for temporary supply but it's usually not large, provided there are no major cable detours.

Meter boxes

The industry standard is to install white plastic boxes built into the external wall. The RECs like them because they can access the meter without entering the house; builders like them because the RECs supply them free (as they do lengths of underground ducting) and they can be built into the outer skin brick wall without a lintel. Only problem is that they are ugly, ugly enough to ruin a fancy period facade. If this bothers you then either look to locate the plastic meter box where it won't detract from your kerb appeal or insist that the company supply comes into the house where it can be concealed in a cupboard.

Gas supplies have the same problem but they offer an alternative meter box concealed in the ground; however, this is felt to be unsafe for an electrical supply. Water meters are always concealed in the ground.

Consumer units and RCDs

The consumer unit – what used to be known as the fuse box – is the place where the REC's supply is split into a number of separate circuits for distribution around the house. There are conventions on how these circuits should be arranged, although the exact design will depend on each particular layout. A 10-gang unit will suffice for all but the largest houses and it is recommended not to economise too much on this item. Miniature circuit breakers (MCBs) have now all but replaced the traditional fuses; instead of fusewire blowing, a little button pops out and reconnection is never more complicated than pressing the button in again.

Another recent development is the advent of residual circuit-breaking devices (RCDs) – now mandatory – which provide increased protection against electrocution in event of contact with live wires. One drawback of RCDs is that they are very sensitive and can be triggered by thunderstorms or faulty

Electrical design is often undertaken thus. You get your electrician to walk around the house with you and you mark it up as you go. The trouble with this approach is a) you are quite likely to forget something and b) there may be better ways of achieving your aims.

Electrics - Key rates

ITEM	COST	ITEM	COST
POWER CIRCUITS		SAFETY	
Double Socket	£ 8	Smoke Detectors	£ 30
Single Socket	£ 7	LIGHTING	
Fused Spur	£ 8	1-gang Switch	£ 4
5-amp Socket	£ 8	2-gang Switch	£ 6
Cooker Switch	£ 13	3-gang Switch	£ 8
Cooker Outlet	£ 5	Pull Switch	£ 6
Shaver Point	£ 25	2-way Switching	£ 2
Immersion Point	£ 8	3-way Switching	£ 4
External Sockets	£ 15	Central Pendant	£ 4
Consumer Unit	£ 30	Fixed Ceiling Light	£ 3
Residual Circuit Devices	£ 40	Halogen Downlights	£ 15
Each Fuse	£ 4	Wall Light	£ 2
TV/TELECOM WIRING		Extra for Light Fittings	£ 25
Coaxial Point	£ 8	External Light Points	£ 5
Telephone Point	£ 5	FANS	
Loft Aerial	£ 20	Bathroom Fans	£ 50
Door Bell	£ 5	Kitchen Fan	£ 75

Electricians Charges

LABOUR charged at	£ 30 per hour	
Sockets	30 mins	£ 15
External Sockets	75 mins	£ 38
Door Bells	60 mins	£ 30
Light Outlet	30 mins	£ 15
Each Switch	20 mins	£ 10
External Lights	60 mins	£ 30
Extra for Light Fittings	45 mins	£ 23
Fans (inc Kitchen Extracts)	120 mins	£ 60
Smoke Detectors	45 mins	£ 23
Basic Consumer Unit	30 mins	£ 15
Extra for Each Circuit	10 mins	£ 5
Electric Ovens and Hobs	180 mins	£ 90

Prices are for reasonably basic kit and the times allowed are for straightforward runs

equipment. This in turn may cause problems with things that must not have their power supply cut off – chiefly freezers and smoke detectors. An RCD-inspired power cut-out could have very messy consequences if it occurred during your two weeks in the Algarve, and for this reason it is recommended that freezers are run off separate circuits not protected by an RCD. The net result of all this is that you'll be spending around £100 on your consumer unit whereas in the bad old days it might have cost only £20.

Sockets

If you've got deep pockets, fit lots of sockets – but at £20-£25 per outlet this can rapidly become a prohibitively expensive option. If you know how you are going to arrange beds and furniture in each room you can minimise the number of sockets needed; if you want to retain flexibility for each room then you'll probably need a minimum of three sockets per bedroom and four sockets in living rooms. It will cost alot more to add sockets in the future and not having them where you want them when you've moved in is very frustrating. Also, don't think that you are saving money by fitting single sockets instead of doubles. The work

involved in installing them is identical and the materials price is only pennies different. You can step-up to brass-fronted sockets for an extra £3 per outlet.

Safety issues

Britain is one of the few countries that allows unqualified people to install wiring. A new installation is routinely checked over by the REC before final connection is made, but the inspections are often rather cursory and often they only check that the earth bonding is in place. There are a number of areas where DIY housewirers – and professional electricians come to that – are prone to make untraceable errors and you would be well advised to steer clear of house wiring unless you have a thorough knowledge of the tasks in hand. Even if you are just supervising a subcontractor, you should be on your guard for the following pitfalls.

Cables in walls

Cables buried in walls must be set either vertically or horizontally from the outlets they supply. The idea is that the follow-on trades have some idea where not to drill holes. However, this requirement is frequently ignored in the rush to get jobs done and sometimes even to try and save money by using less cable. Even if you know where the cable is buried and, therefore, think it doesn't matter, don't forget that the cable will still be there long after you've moved on and some poor sucker thirty years hence could be in for a nasty surprise. Technically, you are allowed to run cables within 150 mm of internal corners and wall and ceiling junctions, but this habit cannot be recommended.

Earth bonding

It is a requirement that exposed metalwork should be earthed to prevent it becoming 'live.' This is normally done with 10 mm earthing cable (it's green and yellow). What exactly needs to be bonded?

■ Water and gas mains as they enter the house
■ Any exposed structural steel and oil tanks
■ All services must be bonded together
■ All metal in bathrooms must be bonded together.

Note that if you are plumbing with plastic pipe (such as Hep2O or Speedfit), the requirement to earth bathroom radiators and steel baths is dropped.

Circuit lengths

Many electricians do not realise that there are prescribed maximum circuit lengths for any given cable size. For instance, a normal ring main run in 2.5 sq mm cable should not be longer than 66 m. There are several guides available explaining the regulations but they are

Benchmark House - Wiring Schedule

	Sockets	Lights	Switches	Light Fittings	TV & Phones	Power unit & RCDs	Smoke Detectors	Fans	Shaver Points	
Room by Room						1				
Master Bedroom	4	5	2		2	1				
En-suite Showerroom		2	1					1	1	
Airing Cupboard	1									
Bathroom Cupboard										
Family Bathroom		2	1					1	1	
Bed 4	3	3	1		1					
Study	3	3	1		1					
Bed 3	3	3	1		1					
Bed 2	3	3	1		1					
Landing	1	3	2				1			
Sun Room	2	4	1				1			
Lounge	4	1	2	1	1					
Kitchen	8	17	2	2	2	1		1		
Stairwell/Hall	1	2	2			1	1			
Shower Room		2	1						1	
Utility	3	2	1					1		
Office	3	3	1		2					
Garage	1	1	1			1				
Externals	1	6	2			1				
Totals	41	62	23	3	11	5	3	4	3	**Totals**
Labour in hrs	21	31	8	2	6	1	2	8	2	81
Rounded Cost of labour	£ 630	£ 930	£ 240	£ 60	£ 180	£ 30	£ 60	£ 240	£ 60	£ 2,400
Typical material costs	£ 8	£ 15	£ 6	£ 100	£ 8	£ 40	£ 30	£ 50	£ 25	
Rounded Cost of materials	£ 330	£ 930	£ 140	£ 300	£ 90	£ 200	£ 90	£ 200	£ 80	£ 2,400
								Wiring total labour and materials		£ 4,800

not pretty nor easy going.

Electric heating

If you are interested in electric heating
– and it's a much improved product – then
your best bet is to contact your REC's New
Homes Department. They are rather more
entrepreneurial than British Gas – their product
is harder to sell – and they are keen to suggest
and quote for different types of electric heating
(for example underfloor, night storage, electric
boilers). These can be installed by specialists
or by your own electrician. The power supply
to your house is likely to be uprated – in some
cases to three-phase – but you are unlikely to
have to pay excess for this. Off-peak electricity
is what it's all about and your off-peak usage
will be metered separately and controlled by
a separate consumer unit. For a more detailed
assessment of electric heating, refer to the
section, 'Alternative Heating', in Chapter 8.

Off-peak electricity

Even if you don't choose to install electric
heating, you can still have an Economy 10
meter fitted at no extra cost and enjoy the
savings of using half-price, off-peak power at
night.

Frequently overlooked

When designing electricity supplies to a house
there are a number of points to watch out for
– and easily forgotten at the first-fix, cable-
burying stage. Many electricians are used to
doing what they are told and no more and will
be of little help in designing a better system.
Here is a bulletted list of commonly forgotten
wiring details:
■ Loft lights, cupboard lights – do you want
them?
■ Separate freezer circuit – preferably not
protected by RCD
■ Separate garage supply if garage is external
■ Outside power points, security lights,
welcome lights
■ Kitchen unit lighting – usually fixed below
wall units

■ Check the rating of your electric cooking
gear – 30 amps may not be enough
■ Wiring for electric showers and power
shower pumps
■ Wiring and installation of fans in bathrooms
and kitchen
■ Separate circuit for immersion heater
■ Outlets left for smoke detectors (now
mandatory)
■ Doorbell wiring
■ Heating controls wiring: boiler, programmer,
thermostats, pump and valves all need to be
connected. This work is often undertaken by the
plumber but the electrician must leave at least a
fused spur to power the controls. If the plumber
does this wiring, then a separate test certificate
will be needed from him
■ Fused spurs for waste disposal units and/or
water softeners
■ Wiring to sewage treatment plants or for
any external water pumps (water features,
swimming pools)
■ Wiring for electric garage door operators:
needs an accurately placed single socket, not
really a problem if power is in the garage
■ Burglar alarm first-fix.

Lighting

The best light is natural sunlight. Lux is a
measurement of light density and whereas 500
lux is the generally accepted level of electric
light needed for reading, bright sunshine
delivers 100,000 lux and even a cloudy overcast
day will produce 5,000 lux of light.

The older you get the more light you need. A
60-year-old requires ten times more light than
a 10-year-old. Apart from brightness, there are
two qualities of light that are important.

Colour rendering

Some light sources show colours close to their
natural daylight colours and are said to have
good colour render. Other sources – notably
orange street lamps – are incapable of showing
any colour variations at all. Fluorescent lighting
(including low-energy light bulbs) tends to

give a washed-out, faded look to colours. This bothers some people more than others, but before you install energy-saving lightbulbs everywhere in your house, make sure you can live with the light quality.

Colour appearance

Or 'How white is your lamp?' The bog standard tungsten lamp which we all know and love is said to be orange white – others say warm; halogen is, like Daz, a whiter white – or crisp white; fluorescents give off a milky, cool white, though there are warm-coloured fluorescents available.

This may seem all very technical and uninteresting but the quality of the light source is an important feature of how a room looks. Some lighting designers will actually recommend that a multipurpose room (say an office by day and a living room by night) has two different lighting schemes – fluorescent for business, tungsten or tungsten-halogen for pleasure. The feel of the room is then transformed at the flick of a switch.

Central pendant lighting

This is the basic standard lighting scheme much loved by penny-pinching developers. It provides adequate ambient (background) lighting and it will always be the most efficient way of distributing light into a room but it is, generally, a very poor source for reading by or carrying out intricate manual operations because you will tend to be in the shade. It is really only a very good light source when the light is wanted directly beneath it – e.g. dining tables – but most other light sources require multiple outlets in each room to work well and so pendant lighting will remain a cheap and cheerless option.

Spotlights

Back in the Sixties the appearance of spotlights on the scene was a breath of fresh air and they became the first popular form of directional lighting. They are still immensely popular but there are often better ways of achieving the required results. Because the entire fitting is fixed and visible, spotlights have the ability to completely ruin the look of a room, especially when mounted on tracks in the middle of ceilings.

Downlighters

Light sources concealed in the ceiling have the big advantage of being stylistically neutral – i.e. they can blend in with any type of decor. They have the disadvantage of only being able to light a rather limited area and a large room lit entirely with downlighters might need as many as ten – which is expensive. Despite their name, downlighters do not have to point straight down: there are 'eyeball' versions which beam the light off at an angle – in effect sidelighters.

Low-voltage halogen downlighters, which supply a very bright, good quality light, are now the height of fashion and some lighting specialists specify them almost exclusively. The low voltage is achieved by the use of transformers and, whilst installation is not particularly difficult, incorrect wiring can be dangerous – there are still a few electricians who know nothing of low-voltage work. If you are fitting low-voltage, then make sure that yours does.

Uplighters

These work by reflecting light off another surface (usually the ceiling) and many people assume that the light quality will therefore be low. However – provided the room has white or near-white ceilings – they are actually a very efficient way of providing ambient light and the light cast down from the ceiling is usually very good for reading under. Uplighters are normally fixed slightly above eye level to conceal the light source and they come in many shapes and forms; one particularly popular one is to fit unglazed ceramic bowls (cost £15-£25) and then to paint them with the same emulsion used on the surrounding walls. This provides stylistically neutral lighting that blends well with natural wood finishes and off-white walls.

Lightbulbs

Tungsten
Ordinary lightbulbs (or GLS bulbs): cheap (30p), average life 1,000hrs, power-hungry, good colour rendering, slightly orange light, easily dimmable; available in a huge choice of shapes and sizes (reflectors, tubes, pygmies, candles) which all cost a good deal more than 30p.

Mains-Voltage Halogen
Also known as Halogen A: cost £2.50, average life 2,000hrs, power-hungry, good colour rendering, pure white light, dimmable, fully interchangeable with tungsten bulb fittings.

Low-Voltage Halogen
Come in specialist fittings (spotlights, downlighters) which vary enormously in cost from under £5 to £40 plus. Replacement bulbs costs around £3.50. Average life of bulb, 2,000hrs; consumes around half the power of tungsten bulbs, good colour rendering, pure white light, dimmable with a appropriate electronic switch, now widely available. Best LV halogen lights are dichroic with reflectors and they require transformers.

Fluorescent
Usually fitted as tubes; miniatures (as used in shaver lights or as kitchen surface lights) costing around £2.50; available in tubes up to 2.4m long (cost around £7). Average life 8,000hrs; consumes around 25% of power of tungsten, cold flat light with poor colour rendering. Tends to be used in utility, garage spaces

Compact Fluorescent
Better known as energy-saving lightbulbs: cost £5-£15, performance similar in every way to long fluorescent tubes but compact shape makes them much more versatile when it comes to positioning. Interchangeable with GLS lightbulbs, but do not fit easily inside average lightshade and can look cumbersome. Note that they cannot be dimmed by regular methods and so don't try and replace dimmed GLS lights with compact fluorescents. Which? carried out a somewhat damning survey of them in Jan 2004: they all claim to last 6,000 hours but 25% of those tested didn't. They also tend to dim over time and don't work too well when it's cold. However, they do continue to improve as a technology and they do save a lot of electricity. Most reliable makes were Osram and Philips.

LEDs
LED lighting has been around since the 1960s (think of red digital clockfaces) but only in recent years has the technology developed so that green and blue and now, white light can be made from LEDs. They use very low currents and therefore promises very low energy consumption but at the moment LED lighting schemes are still a rarity in the home because the actual lighting units are expensive. There are a number of other light sources readily available — metal halide, sodium, neon — but their use is rare in the home and is unlikely to be specified by anyone other than a specialist lighting consultant.

Sidelights and table lamps
People habitually refer to their sidelights as 'reading lights' which suggests that the central light is good for vacuum cleaning and not much else. There is an enormous variety of shapes and styles to suit every taste: table lamps from £5 upwards, floor (or standard) lamps from £30. The one big advantage of independent lights is that you retain the flexibility to arrange your room in any fashion you choose, as long as you've got a socket nearby.

5-amp plugs
A handy idea for living rooms where you want to have a number of sidelights is to fit a series of 5-amp lighting sockets (usually with small round-pin holes to distinguish them from 13-amp mains sockets). These can be linked together and all switched from one point. It's convenient not only because it gives you a master switch to control all the sidelights plugged into the 5-amp sockets, but it also gives you the ability to dim. By arranging the

switching next to the door, it gives you the
option of doing away with the central pendant
lighting altogether. Budget £20-£30 per outlet
plus a similar amount for the switch.

If you know nothing about the art of good
lighting and you are in a hurry and don't want
to waste a small fortune, you won't go wrong
by specifying a handful of 5-amp sockets. You
can create quite sophisticated lighting effects
by using side lighting and, without spending a
fortune on fittings, you can get pools of light
wherever you want them whilst retaining a
flexibility to change it all if you get bored and
want something different.

Dimmers

Dimmer switches give you the ability to
control the amount of light given off by a bulb
and thus set the mood for a room. They are
particularly useful in living rooms where you
may want to relax in front of the TV, watching
the fire, and don't want to do it under the
glare of 100 watt bulbs. Furthermore, dimmed
lights save energy, and if you use dimmers
which don't have a push on/off capability, you
increase the length of your bulb life by having
a 'soft start' – most bulbs blow when you turn
them on.

As regular dimmers can be bought for around
£5 (compared with £3 for an on/off switch),
there is an argument for fitting them just about
everywhere. You can dim just about any kind
of light but the very basic dimming switches
will only work on the standard GLS tungsten
lightbulbs.

There are now electronic dimmers widely
available from around £10 which will handle
either mains or low voltage halogen. Other
kinds of bulbs require special dimmers which
cost upwards of £30 for one-gang switching.
Contact Home Automation.

Alternative lighting

If you wanted to improve on the basic
developer's specification at the design stage,
there are two other routes which you may be
interested in.

The green approach

An energy-efficient lighting scheme is looked
at in some detail in Chapter 13, Green Issues. I
estimate this would add around £300-£400 to
building costs (but would cut furnishing costs
by perhaps £150-£200) and could easily save
£50 per annum on electricity bills.

The 2002 energy efficiency building regs
address lighting for the first time. They want
you to fit some energy efficient lightbulbs. But
where? And how many? They are a bit vague
about where, merely suggesting 'where lighting
can be expected to have most use.' And the
number required is dependent on the number
of rooms built. More than seven rooms, it's
three. More than ten rooms, it's four.

The high-tech approach

In this low-voltage light scheme, the emphasis is
on quality using ultra-bright tungsten-halogen
downlighters. Because of the comparatively
narrow light fields of low-voltage downlighters, a
bedroom would require a minimum of three and
a living room probably eight or more. In fact,
our benchmark house builder, Steve Baldwin,
was positively gung-ho on low voltage halogen,
fitting nearly 50 of them. The cost of lighting the
benchmark house was around £2,400.

One stage on from this comes the concept
of scene lighting. Here you programme banks
of lights to come on together to create moods
or scenes. It's something which is commonly
seen in places like conference suites and lecture
theatres but is beginning to migrate towards the
home (via the USA). Products such as Lutron's
Homeworks works with most types of bulbs
and allows you to create and recall lighting
arrangements, including dimming. Not only can
you switch banks of lights on and off with one
button but you can also do vacation settings for
security. But I'm straying off here. This stuff really
belongs in the Home Automation section coming
shortly.

Room by room
Kitchens

Central pendant lighting is particularly inept

at providing light for kitchen worksurfaces, and this is one area where task lighting is now considered essential. The conventional place for this is under the wall cupboard units, hidden from view by the decorative downstand known as the pelmet. There is a choice of tungsten or fluorescent fittings; tungsten gives better light rendering but gets hot and tends to 'cook' the contents of the overhead cupboard; fluorescent stays cool and is generally preferable, particularly if you choose a warm, white type like Sylvania Homelight de Luxe. An alternative is to fit downlighters in the ceiling over the kitchen surfaces, but placement has to be extremely accurate and you risk getting unlit areas under the wall units. If you have an extractor hood, make sure it has a light as well. Lumiance have introduced a range of low-voltage halogen downlighters which are only 20 mm deep and are specifically designed to fit into a cupboard shelf. If your kitchen design doesn't want or need pelmets under your wall cupboards and you don't want exposed lights, then this is the answer for you.

Dining tables

A pendant light hanging over a dining table works very well, but make sure that the bulb is well concealed by the shade or fitting. Lighting from the side is much more difficult because of the shadows cast by the diners. As an alternative to a hanging light, go for a cluster of low-voltage downlighters – the way they do it in fancy restaurants. Avoid fluorescent lighting if you are of the gourmet tendency and like to see what it is you're eating. And if you are the type who goes for candlelit dinner parties, it's very useful to be able to dim the ambient lighting.

Living rooms

There are no set rules for lighting living areas. Chandeliers, spotlights, uplighters, wall lights, downlighters, table lamps, sidelights – all have a role to play and it's very much a question of taste. Most developers and selfbuilders will be planning fairly conservative interiors, particularly in their living rooms, and an awful

lot of the high-tech lighting schemes would be completely inappropriate here. However, the use of concealed fittings, such as downlighters, is compatible with virtually all settings.

Lighting a room with downlighters is generally pleasing to the eye but it is expensive because of the numbers needed. Pendant fittings and wall lights may be preferred but considerable time and expense may go in selecting the right fittings for the room; downlighters actually require less thought. Another option is to go for three or four uplighters or wall lights, which will generally be enough to provide all the lighting needs (including reading) for a largish room; this presents a stylish mid-priced alternative between the expense of downlighters and the poor light quality offered by a central light.

Feature mirrors need to be set where they do not directly reflect lights. A traditional effect like a mirror above an Adam style fireplace will be ruined by a chandelier directly in front of it. Picture lighting is another problem area which you can ruin if you don't get it right.

Bedrooms

For most people, bedroom lighting will be a mixture of an ambient central pendant and table lamps for reading. Although a central pendant light source will be cheaper to install, when the cost of task lighting is included, the alternative options of uplighters or downlighters look more pocket-friendly, though you must pay attention to switching from the bed as well as by the door.

Bathrooms

The regulations require that bathroom light fittings should be concealed to prevent direct contact with water. Conventionally, this is done by placing a central light inside some sort of glazed casing. There are some extremely naff bathroom light fittings around and finding a good one can be difficult. An alternative approach is to use sealed downlighters.

Task lighting is also very useful around bathroom mirrors. The standard method is to fit

The 500W halogen floodlight is the bane of external lighting. Fine if you are running a prison but do you really want this on your home?

a tungsten strip light (combined with electric shaver socket) which is adequate but rarely beautiful. Mirrors with integral lights are a stylish solution but they are very expensive.

Hallways/stairwells

■ Don't be tempted to hang lights where you can't change the bulb without a ladder.
■ Don't fit uplighters at the foot of stairwells where you can see the bulbs from above.
■ Bear in mind that the building regs now require some energy efficient bulbs in new homes. Fitting them in to the halls and stairwells is probably the easiest way of complying, if you don't particularly want them throughout the house.

External Lighting

The bane of external lighting is the 500 watt halogen floodlight. In the last few years these have become very cheap (under £20) and very common, yet their effect is blindingly unpleasant, unless well concealed.

Security lighting need not be unattractive. It is worth giving a bit of thought to external lighting; unless you are building next to a well-lit road, you will find that some form of external light is essential just to negotiate the front path. By all means arrange to switch it on a timed Passive Infra Red (PIR) detector, but that doesn't mean you have to blast people in the face with 500W bulbs. PIR switches can

be purchased on their own for around £25 and can be adjusted to trip on at different light levels and for different lengths of time – from a few seconds to several minutes. As alternatives to tungsten halogen floodlights, consider wall-mounted lanterns (about £30), outdoor spotlights spiked into the ground (about £10), free standing bollards (about £60) or even brick lights (which replace a standard brick in your external wall) (around £30).

The 2002 energy efficiency regs brought external lighting into their ambit for the first time. They demand that external lights should either be fitted with daylight detectors and timed switches or not use more than a 40W bulb – ideally a compact fluorescent lamp.

■ Built-in vacuums

Why bother to fit a built-in vacuum cleaning system? The big plus with central vacuums is that what gets sucked up stays sucked up. With a portable vacuum, efficiency depends on how well the filter works. Small particles of dust go through the filter and get re-circulated which is why a house often smells a little bit different after vacuuming. By removing the motor to somewhere like a utility room or better still a garage, you are shifting all this dust out there, though it may not do much for the look of your shiny new car. And, by locating the motor out of the way, you also get another plus which is near-silent vacuuming.

The biggest minus seems to be finding somewhere to stash the pipe. The fewer inlets you have the cheaper and easier to install but the longer the external pipe needs to be. Many people fit one inlet downstairs and one upstairs which means you need up to 10 m of pipe to be able to get to the far corners of the house. Coiled up this makes a considerable heap – much bigger than a portable vacuum. The solution is to build in a rack, like a hosepipe rack, somewhere handy to get to but easy to conceal. A pipe cupboard no less. Canada is the spiritual home of central vacuuming; it gets fitted into the majority of new housing there.

If you ever visit one of the selfbuild shows, you can't fail to notice the displays of the built-in vacuum sellers. They habitually suck up the odd duster and you can watch it travel all around the transparent tubing at breakneck speed. It's not quite Alton Towers but it never fails to impress.

The Candians build homes which are nearly airtight and one of the side effects of living in near-airtight housing is that people become very concerned with indoor air quality. They take planned ventilation very seriously, they avoid possibly toxic materials in construction and they pay close attention to things like vacuuming to ensure it does the job it should.

There are a number of small manufacturers moving into this market in the UK, though note that the two most significant players, Beam and Smart, are both owned by Electrolux, the household appliance giant. Most advertise heavily in the selfbuild press and can be regularly found making pitches at the selfbuild exhibitions. If you are interested, most will quote from floor plans you send them. They aim particularly at the new build market because the system is most conveniently fitted at the first-fix stage so that the ducting is easily concealed. Put another way, it's more trouble than it's worth to fit the pipes into an old house but building into a new home is relatively straightforward. Prices for a built-in vacuum cleaner installed on a four-bedroom detached house are around £500 (excluding labour). Some businesses actually give away the wall ducting with timber frame

kit homes, hoping this will create a sale later.

■ *TVs phones and cables*

Of all the sections in 'The Housebuilder's Bible' that have required rewriting over its ten-year history, this one stands out because it has changed the most. As recently as 1995, this was a fairly short section: you stuck a phone line in, you put a couple of TV points in, an aerial in the loft, maybe a satellite dish and you were away. For many people this will still be a fine solution, but the intervening years have seen the arrival of home office working, the internet, and digital TV, and suddenly the basic house wiring doesn't look quite up to the mark anymore. Now you have to make an educated guess as to what to put in and what to leave out, not only for your own requirements but for any possible future buyers as well. Time to knuckle down and take a hard look at what's in and what's out in home cabling.

What are the key changes in home wiring?
The twentieth century saw the widespread introduction of three different wiring systems into the home: electricity, telephones and

television, with a few homes opting for a fourth system, wiring for burglar alarms. Of these, only the first, electricity, has conventionally been cabled all over the house. Telephones initially came into the house at just one socket, more recently two or three and likewise TV outlets have been restricted to one, two or three outlets.

Whilst the electric cabling routes around the house remain largely unchanged, the demand for more complex phone wiring and TV cabling is causing these other systems to grow and converge. Phone wiring is changing because we want more outlets and because we are using phone lines for more than just conversations. TV wiring is changing because the methods of delivering TV signals are changing. Over and beyond this, the actual cables used for phones and TVs are changing and people are starting to cable for additional reasons: things like security and lighting control.

What do I need to watch digital TV?

The government has let it be known that it wants to stop analogue TV broadcasts (i.e. terrestrial Channels One to Five) in order to auction off the airwaves but there is much doubt as to whether this will ever happen, at least for another generation, especially as these frequencies no longer seem to be quite as valuable as once imagined. So first point is that you needn't feel hustled into turning digital. There is however more to digital TV than Sky's £35 per month subscription services; there are an increasing number of free-to-air channels that are available only via digital means.

At present (and this is unlikely to change), TV signals are delivered to the home by three different methods, rooftop aerial (known as terrestrial), satellite dish and fibre optic cable. If you live in or near to a big city, you will have a choice of all three but this is not the case in many rural districts so you need to find out what is available and what works well in your area.

Analogue TV signals (the ones we have all grown up with since the Fifties) have

conventionally been fed around the house in brown coaxial cable from the rooftop or loft aerial. The standard signal is usually adequate to service three or four TV sets – if you want more you need to add a small amplifier to the system.

Digital TV works rather differently. The signal needs to be decoded in the house, something usually achieved in a box of tricks called a digibox, although it can also be done inside a digital TV (that is a TV that has a built-in decoder). So you need to consider where your decoder should sit. Digiboxes are about the size of a video recorder and, like VCRs, are usually fitted around the main TV. Whether you receive your digital signal by aerial, satellite dish or cable, there must be a direct cable connection to the decoder and this then sends the signal to the TV or TVs.

Digital decoders struggle to handle more than one channel at a time (though they can now record one whilst simultaneously showing another via the SkyPlus and TIVO systems) and if you link TVs in series they will all have to watch the same thing unless you purchase additional decoders and pay additional subscriptions.

So at present, if you want, say, three TV outlets in your home and you want to receive both analogue and digital at each outlet, you need two different cabling systems in place – unless you go for a structured cabling system. More on this later.

What are the options for phones?

Phone cabling around the house has traditionally been a simple affair. Your service provider (traditionally BT) installs a master socket and you can run a small number of extensions out from there. If you started running a business from home, you would install a second line with a fax cum phone on it. It rarely got more complicated than that. And then came the internet.

The internet. I guess that's made it more complicated...

It rather depends on how you use the internet.

If you are just an occasional surfer who likes to perhaps do a bit of home shopping and send the odd e-mail, then the typical phone arrangements we already have works just fine. But if you are a heavy user – and increasingly people working at home are heavy users – then a second line becomes almost essential because once online, the phone line is engaged and this becomes inconvenient to the rest of the household. Now that flat rate internet charging structures are becoming the norm, many people will stay online during the entire working day so a separate line for this becomes essential. If you work from home you have the prospect of a household with three phone lines — and it's beginning to get a bit silly. There are better ways of managing the situation.

Most people now will be looking to get a broadband connection. There was a competing technology called ISDN but it was never as fast as broadband and looks like it may soon be consigned to history. The only reason to fit ISDN is if you can't receive broadband but, having dragged its heels for years, BT has suddenly started rolling broadband out across the country at remarkable speed and I anticipate that during the lifespan of this edition, broadband will be an option for 95 per cent of new households.

Broadband connections cost around £200 to install and thereafter £25 per month for permanent unmetered internet access at speeds eight to ten times faster than the current crop of modems. In addition, you can install broadband on a phone line and still use the line to make voice calls as well, even when you are surfing on the internet. So in many ways, broadband makes life simpler for people working from home who previously would have had to install multiple phone lines. However, broadband is still a maturing technology and there are homes where it won't reach, largely because they are more than a few miles from the broadband-enabled exchanges.

To find out if you can get broadband, visit www.btopenworld.com and do a search by postcode. Broadband should be available to most during the lifespan of this edition.

Cable modems, an alternative way of getting broadband, are available to customers of the two cable networks, NTL and Telewest, who between them cover 50 per cent of the UK population. The deals are broadly similar to BT's broadband offerings though cable modems do require an additional cable to be run into the home. If you can't get either, broadband is shortly going to be available over satellite.

The whole telecoms and internet industry is watching anxiously to see how things pan out. But perhaps the most important thing to bear in mind, if you are planning to wire up a new house, is just what facilities you might want where. If your needs are predictable and fairly conservative, you don't need to put dozens of outlets around the house. If, for instance, you know which room you plan to use as a home office, and you suspect that you may need an extra phone line there, then it is a simple matter to wire it up conventionally at the outset. But if you want to retain maximum flexibility so that any room could be used as an office or a TV lounge, then it's time to consider a structured cabling system.

A structured cabling system? What's that?

It's a way of wiring houses with high speed data cable, known as Category 5 or Cat 5 cable. It has migrated from offices where it is now as common as electric wiring. Instead of haphazardly running cables from the various input points to the various output points around the house, you designate a place in the house as a central hub (known as the wiring closet) and you bring all the incoming cables to this point and then distribute them around the house to wall mounted data sockets which look very much like electric sockets.

A wiring closet doesn't have to reside in its own purpose built room – unlike the other kind of WC.

The essential element in a wiring closet is a patch panel, a wall hung box the size of a small suitcase. The patch panel plays a similar role to an electrical fusebox in household electrical wiring where the power coming into the house is split up and sorted into different circuits. It is in here that the phone lines and TV cables are all connected. Rather than being connected up in series (or daisy chained) as many TV and phone outlets are in conventional set-ups, each outlet throughout the house is connected directly back to the patch panel. That means a double data socket will have two cables running next to each other back to the patch panel where each will terminate with its own unique number which corresponds to a number etched on the data socket.

What's the advantage of installing structured cabling?

It really comes into its own if you want to gain a degree of flexibility in your home. A well designed system will allow you to plug TVs and phones in wherever you want to, not at the limited number of outlets you otherwise specify. You will also be able to set up small phone and computer networks which would allow you, for instance, to share printers or modems between computers or to back up your essential data without using disc drives or other media. Useful stuff in an office but arguably not quite so compelling in a typical home. But you only have to see how the numbers of electrical sockets have proliferated around the home over the past few decades to see that our attitudes to sending and receiving data will probably change substantially in years to come. Structured cabling gives you the built-in flexibility to do that.

What else can you do with structured cabling?

The Cat 5 cable is capable of carrying all kinds of data. It's become the industry standard cable for computer networks – known as Ethernet – and yet it can be used for sending all manner of other signals besides voice calls and computer data, giving you remote control capabilities which only recently people would have thought were pure science fiction. You can pipe high quality sound signals along Cat 5 thus giving you the ability to have multi-room sound systems. You can use it to control lighting scenes

Mains electricity, FM radio, digital TV, phone, computer networking, CD jukebox. The two sockets to the right are numbered: the numbers correspond to positions on the patch panel

around the house. You can use it to control motors which could open or close gates or windows. And you can use it for closed-circuit TV, security features and panic buttons. Provided you have built in enough outlets, you have the capabilities of building an intelligent home and enough flexibility to add to the intelligence levels as and when you see fit.

Just about the one major weak point with Cat 5 cabling was that it didn't deliver a very compelling TV signal. Because of this it has been conventional to run CT-100 coaxial cable as well as Cat 5 around the house and back to the patch panel. But techniques have been developed to send video signals through CAT 5 without any loss of quality: check out Kat5 TV, IP Homenet and Extron. This is a considerable breakthrough because it greatly reduces the amount (and type) of cable needed.

What does a structured cabling system cost?

The Cat 5 cable itself is not expensive, typically no more than electric cable. Similarly the patch panel and the RJ45 outlets are commodity items. The materials to fit out a four-bedroomed house would typically cost around £800 to £1,200 pounds, depending on the number of outlets that you require. This compares very similarly with the cost of electrical wiring. For many selfbuilders, the cabling is seen as just another DIY task to be completed along with the underfloor heating and the central vacuum system. There are now many companies offering to supply and fit structured cabling systems and prices start from about £2,000 for a basic fit out, though many of the more esoteric uses of structured cabling such as lighting control and multi-room sound systems are expensive extras costing many additional thousands.

Are there any alternatives?

There are two main competing technologies for intelligent homes. The original one is mains-borne – that is using the existing electricity cables to move data around the house as well as electricity. There is a well established system called X10 which does just this. It's nothing new – in fact it's been around since the Seventies – and you can get a simple starter pack for no more than £50. X10 is the province of the dedicated home automation enthusiast who wants to be able to do things like closing the blinds remotely. It's never really developed into a whole house data system because it doesn't handle phones and data.

The other technology is wireless. We have become used to using mobile and cordless phones, and the latest generation of digital cordless phones (known as DECT phones) enable you to do clever things like transferring calls between handsets. What is newly emerging is the capability for computers to send data between each other and to their peripherals using radio frequencies.

Apple Computers has a system up and running called Airport which does just this and great hopes exist for another similar technology called Bluetooth which works with all manner of appliances. There are now a number of heating controls that work without cables – usually referred to as RF – so it may be that all the switching signals which lie at the heart of the intelligent home may end up being done using radio waves and not cables. Honeywell have developed a remote control unit for home heating, the CM60RF; this enables you to control the heating from a handset anywhere in the house which is moderately useful but not as useful as being able to turn the heating on with a phonecall from the airport, one of the holy grails of home automation: it can be done but it's not easy and it's not cheap. And wireless communication still can't yet handle TV, video and audio signals but in five, ten or twenty years time these technical problems may have been overcome. So you could just do nothing and hope that technology will catch up with your future needs, but there is a risk that without a structured cabling system your house will begin to look very dated very quickly.

Chapter 10
Finishes

Internal wall finishes
Floor finishes
Second fix carpentry
Painting and decorating
Curtains and blinds
Driveways and pavings
· Fencing and turfing

Traditionally, the second-fix stage of housebuilding begins with the internal plastering, even though these days the majority of new houses never get to see any traditional plastering. Up until this time, everything going on inside the superstructure of the house has been first-fixing – constructing walls, roofs and floors, burying pipes and cables. The key difference between the two stages is that the first-fix works will remain hidden in the structure, whilst the second-fix items will be there for all to see when the house is completed. Hence this chapter, entitled 'Finishes,' covers everything from the second-fixing stage onwards.

▮ *Internal Wall Finishes*

Plastering is the cheapest way of providing good internal wall and ceiling coverings. There are different systems of 'plastering' but they all come within spitting distance of £8-£10 per sq m in price. There are alternatives which can be used when you know exactly what you want – exposed brickwork, tongued and grooved matchboarding – but they are considerably more expensive than a plastered finish and are

normally only built as features.

The big question facing housebuilders is whether to go for a wet or dry system of wall coverings. The wet techniques use wet-mixed cement renders and gypsum plasters: the dry systems use dry-lined plasterboards. The wet techniques are traditional British building – the dry techniques are imported from countries where timber frame is prevalent. Ceilings are almost invariably fixed with plasterboard, but here there remains a choice about whether to cover them with a wet Thistle Finish plaster, to dry-line or to comb on Artex. Pricewise, there is very little to choose between the systems – though I estimate dry-lining is a little cheaper.

Wet plastering
Plus
It is well understood by builders and favoured by most plasterers; a well-skimmed plaster finish looks fantastic – at least initially.

Minus
It's wet. Something like one cubic metre of water (equals12 bathfulls) is being built into the fabric of the house if it is wet plastered and this must in time dry out, which will take

a summer at least. This drying out results in movement which causes cracking in the top coat plaster which looks naff and gets builders called back on site to carry out cosmetic repairs. This problem is particularly bad when plasterboard ceilings are skimmed with a plaster finish; here the movement in timber behind the boards causes hairline cracks around all the plasterboard joints. None of this cracking is in the least bit dangerous – it doesn't mean subsidence is occurring – and many people live happily with it knowing that these bedding-in problems can be filled in at the first redecoration. However, for many unsuspecting souls it is a source of genuine grievance and complaint.

Dry-lining

Plus

It's dry – avoiding problems outlined above. It is relatively easy to correct out-of-plumb blockwork – you just adjust the thickness of the adhesive dabs. It also gives a comparatively soft wall with enough give for small children to bounce off unharmed, whereas a hard, plastered wall would bring forth tears.

Minus

Dry-lining is not particularly difficult to learn – the plasterboard manufacturers all run cheap two- or three-day training courses – but it can be badly applied, leaving a ridged effect on walls and ceilings. Plasterboard has to be fixed

Plastering - Key Material Costs

	Unit	Price	Divider	Metre Rate
12.5mm Plasterboard	1200x2400	£ 3.75	2.8	£ 1.30 m²
12.5mm Fermacell Board	1200x2400	£ 11	2.8	£ 3.80 m²
12mm Render	Cubic Metre	£ 48	80	£ 0.60 m²
Thistle Skim Finish	25kg bag	£ 3.25	9	£ 0.40 m²
Artex	25kg bag	£ 9	25	£ 0.40 m²
65mm Screed mixed on site	Cubic Metre	£ 66	15	£ 4.40 m²
Coving 100mm	3m length	£ 3.60	2.5	£ 1.40 m

Plasterers' Key Square Metre Rates

	Charged rate £20 hour	Labour	Mats	Total
Render and Skim	30 mins	£ 10	£ 2	£ 12
Render only (scratch coat)	15 mins	£ 5	£ 1	£ 6
Render top coat	20 mins	£ 7	£ 1	£ 8
Tacking (Nailing) Plasterboard	12 mins	£ 4	£ 2	£ 6
Dot and Dab (Sticking) Plasterboard	10 mins	£ 4	£ 2	£ 6
Skim Finish on Plasterboard	16 mins	£ 6	£ 0.50	£ 7
Dry Lined Finish to Plasterboard	12 mins	£ 4	£ 0.50	£ 5
Artex Finish on Plasterboard	12 mins	£ 4	£ 0.50	£ 5
Fixing External Mesh for Render	12 mins	£ 4	£ 8	£ 12
Two-coat External Render	40 mins	£ 14	£ 2	£ 16
Floor Screed, 65mm Thick	25 mins	£ 9	£ 5	£ 14
Basic Coving (in linear metres)	10 min/m	£ 4	£ 2	£ 6

Benchmark House Plastering Costs

	Area	Rate	Mats	Lab	Total
External Render	None	£ 14			
Internal Render & Skim	208 m²	£ 12	£ 420	£ 2,080	£ 2,500
Plasterboard and Skim	406 m²	£ 13	£ 1,020	£ 4,060	£ 5,080
Floor Screeds	110 m²	£ 14	£ 550	£ 990	£ 1,540
Coving	164 m	£ 6	£ 330	£ 660	£ 990
		Total	**£ 2,320**	**£ 7,790**	**£ 10,110**

more carefully than is normal trade practice so as to keep the number of cuts to a minimum. The wall finish is similar to what you would get if painting on to lining paper (which is basically what you are doing) and this may not be glossy enough for some tastes. Plasterboard walls are not as damage-resistant as traditional plasters, though repairs can be easily effected.

Another problem with dry-lining is that it can be draughty. In theory the backing walls should be airtight – why do you have to put in all those expensive trickle vents in the windows? – but in practice air sneaks through the most unlikely joints. The solution to this problem is to seal all the joints between sheets and around openings prior to taping and jointing. However this is both expensive (Gyproc's sealer costs around £10 per litre) and time consuming. This air leakiness problem occurs with all forms of construction that use dry-lining, but its significance is greatly reduced when you build in timber-frame, incorporating a vapour barrier in the external walls.

Blockwork v studwork

You can only apply wet render on to a masonry background and it is, therefore, not an option for timber framers. Those using studwork walls will have to fit a wallboard, usually plasterboard – though, as already noted, plasterboard will take a 3mm wet plaster finish. On the other hand, if a dry method is desired in a brick and block house, then the favoured method is to stick plasterboard on to the blockwork using the dot and dab technique which uses specialised gypsum plasters as adhesives. This is the method currently in favour with over 70 per cent of professional house builders – just goes to show how much they value not being called back because 'there's cracks in me walls.'

Plasterboard

What is it? Gypsum plaster sandwiched between two layers of paper. It is characterised by being easy to cut, fairly easy to handle and it provides a good backing for paint and plaster. Note that wastage can be high when using plasterboard –

up to 30 per cent on small rooms and ceilings, 10-15 per cent on walls. It is available in several different formats: square edged (for wet plaster skimming) or tapered edge (for dry-lining); 12.5mm thick for 600mm spaced studwork and 9.5mm thick for 400mm spacings; foil-backed for providing an integral vapour barrier (it's cheaper to use a separate polythene sheet); small boards measuring 1800x900mm as well as the more normal, room-height, boards which are 1200x2400mm. Since the sound regs were beefed up in 2003, there is a big take up of heavier boards to get studwork partitions up to the required 40dB sound reduction rating. Sound deadening boards at 12.5mm are what to look out for. None of these formats is expensive: rates vary between £1.20 per sq m and £1.80 per sq m depending on what you want the board to do.

There are also now a number of plasterboards which are laminated to insulation. Make sure you get the right format for the job and make sure that you've used metric spacings on your wall studs and ceiling joists as imperial-sized plasterboard is no longer made.

Plasterboard is a very competitive business with three companies (BPB aka British Gypsum, Knauf and Lafarge) slugging it out for the European market. Consequently, the price hasn't really changed much in 20 years – amazing value if you think about it. There is little to choose between the rivals either on price or quality.

Alternatives
Fermacell

Widely used in Germany, Fermacell is, in some ways, very similar to plasterboard and, in others, rather superior. It has a much higher racking strength than plasterboard and is therefore particularly useful when you want to hang radiators and bathroom furniture off timber stud walls and you don't know where the studs are. Fermacell also makes for better soundproofing. However, it is pricey in comparison with plasterboard, costing over £3 per sq m, nearly three times the price.

The benchmark house sun room, indulges in both exposed internal brickwork and a pine matchboarded ceiling

Consequently, it is mostly being used in the UK as a backing board for kitchens and bathrooms. It is usual to glue the boards together and simply paint over them for a finished surface. Another board worth seeking out is Knauf's Aquapanel, a cement particle board which is completely waterproof and can therefore be specified in shower enclosures.

Exposed Brickwork

Costing between £20 and £30 per sq m – depending largely on your choice of brick – using exposed brickwork internally can be surprisingly cheap. With block and stud walls costing between £6 and £10 per sq m, plaster finishes costing around £7 per sq m and painting costs of around £1 per sq m, exposed brickwork from £20 per sq m doesn't look an expensive option. On internal walls, with both sides exposed, the arithmetic looks even more favourable. However, please note that £20 per sq m buys a pretty basic 'developers brick' and that a 'character brick' (i.e. second hand or handmade) will cost 50 per cent more to lay. Also note that a masonry sealer (at around £4 per lt) should be applied – and this is more expensive than emulsion work. More significant problems are encountered with fixtures like

door and window lintels and electric cables which would normally be concealed behind the plaster. These problems mean that feature brickwork is most often seen in small areas such as fireplaces. Used adroitly, exposed brickwork can be an effective feature at a cost little more than conventional plastering.

Pine matchboarding

Finishing walls and ceilings with timber matchboarded panels would cost around £20 per sq m (Mats £10, Lab £10). This price is made up of timber at £6 per sq m, fixing at £6 per sq m, sanding and filling at £2 per sq m and varnishing at £6 per sq m. Pine panelling used to be very popular but is now rarely seen over whole walls, though its use as a stained boarding, fixed vertically between skirting and dado rail, is a currently fashionable effect. It is also an effective way of creating decorative service panels behind which can be run pipework and cabling, though this is a complex matter which ideally needs designing into the building from the beginning.

Glass blocks

One of the most intriguing trends in home interiors recently has been the re-emergence of glass block walls. They were widely used in the Thirties, mostly on public buildings, but then fell completely out of fashion. You simply didn't see them until about five years ago when the TV interior shows rediscovered them and suddenly glass blocks are everywhere. You can't get through B&Q without tripping over them. Many firms like Luxcrete, Shakerley and Vitra offer glass blocks together with everything you need to lay them – it seems to be a popular DIY job. Ballpark materials costs come in at around £60 per sq m.

Plastered fancies

Coving is used to mask the joint between walls and ceilings. It used to be almost ubiquitous in new housing but it's beginning to fall out of fashion. It's not particularly expensive – including adhesive, it works out to around £1.60 per lin.m and is fixed for around £2.50 per lin.m. Providing coving throughout the benchmark house cost around £700 which includes an elaborate profile in the lounge but plain, simple coving everywhere else.

Artex produce a range of four classical styles which cost around £3 per lin.m and are harder to fix than standard coving but do add a certain grandeur to a room that you might like. They can be combined with fancy ceiling roses (at around £10). There are a number of other specialist companies producing all kinds of plaster mouldings – arches, dado rails, corner details, wall plaques. Check Yellow Pages under Plaster Ware.

Decorative panelling

British Gypsum produce a number of decorative fielded panels out of a material called Glasroc which, as its name suggests, is gypsum plaster reinforced with glass fibre. They can be combined to provide a very smart looking interior wall detailing that would, in truth, look better in a shop or a restaurant than a home. They would be normally fixed on top of a wall finish (instead of replacing it) so the cost, at around £10 per sq m to buy, makes it similar to pine matchboarding.

Ceramic tiling

Tiling is not strictly speaking an alternative to plastering because it is usually applied on top, so 'addition' might be a better word. Its use is often entirely functional when applied as a splashback behind sinks, basins and baths, but visit Italy or Portugal and you'll be amazed to see ceramic tiling in living rooms and bedrooms as well. In the UK wall tiling is seen in more functional terms; our benchmark house is unusual in this respect in that there is 56 sq m of ceramic tiling, far more wall tiling than you would normally expect in a house of this quality.

Whether you pay under £5 per sq m for some unadorned and unnamed import or £80 per sq m for some top of the range, handpainted tile out of the Fired Earth catalogue, the fixing costs remain remarkably similar. The adhesives which you use to stick the tiles down with and the grouts which you spread between the tiles tend to work out together at between £3 and £4 per sq m depending on the thickness and specification. The laying costs depend on the intricacies of the task in hand, but on fairly straightforward work, it takes a tiler around one hour to fix a square metre of tiles and about 15 minutes to grout them up later. Big straight runs will be faster than this but most tiling work in new housing involves a fair amount of cutting and this takes the time.

Buying tips

Ceramic tiles vary enormously in style and quality from the cheap, mass-produced output of large factories to the exotic and individual handmade styles, often produced in the third world. The UK market is dominated by two big names, Pilkington (the glass makers) and Cristal. Their ranges are widely available at all kinds of outlets – DIY sheds, builder's merchants and tiling specialists – and their ranges are also largely complementary; at their simplest they have several earthy and pastelly coloured floor and wall tiles priced below the £10 per sq m mark. They both have acres of largely nondescript kitchen and bathroom motif tiles either with inoffensive patterns or odd adornments like wheatsheaves or dolphins. Very homely but not going to win any design awards. However, both Pilks and Cristal have some much more interesting designs that you might have to visit a tiling centre to gen up on. And, of course, there are any number of lesser known producers – check out Marlborough, Sphinx or any of the Italian imports.

The revived interest in all things handmade has produced a rash of simulated handmade tiles like Cristal's Linda Beard collection. Though nothing like the authentic ones, these tiles do represent a reasonable compromise between looks and price. For the real thing, you can do no better than phone Fired Earth for a catalogue.

■ *Floor finishes*

Nowhere else in building is there such a great variety of materials at such a huge variation in price. You could carpet a four-bedroom house for less than £1,000 (inc. VAT); equally you could spend over £10,000 and not risk being accused of extravagance. Normally, floor finishes are not included in building budgets unless

they are an integral part of the construction; developers rarely fit floor finishes although they occasionally offer to carpet houses as a sweetener to encourage a sale.

Carpet

Even when glued down, carpet is regarded by Customs & Excise as a movable item and therefore subject to VAT as a furnishing – all other types of floor finish are zero-rated and therefore effectively exempt from VAT when built into a new house. Even so, carpeting still provides potentially the cheapest form of floor covering available – especially the bonded cords which also happen to be reasonably hard wearing. Beware offers of free underlay and free laying; obviously these services are not free and the charge for them is included in the price. Usually priced by the yard, carpet laying can be subject to enormous wastage because of the limited roll sizes. The DIY builder might be happier to lay carpet tiles, but if price is the only consideration, then it will still probably be cheaper to look out for the absolute basic ranges supplied and fitted by one of the carpet warehouses. Some of these carpets sell for a good deal less than a decent underlay (which

Floor Finishes - Key Square Metre Rates

Charged Rate	£ 18.00 per hour						
All costs are £/m²	PRICE	WASTE	EXTRAS	MATS TOTAL	Time in Mins	Labour @ £18/hr	TOTAL
Cheap Carpet	£ 5	£ 1	£ 2	£ 8	15	£ 5	£13
Decent Carpet	£ 20	£ 4	£ 2	£ 26	20	£ 6	£ 32
Axminster Wool	£ 50	£ 10	£ 2	£ 62	20	£ 6	£ 68
Cheap Vinyl Tile	£ 5	£ 1	£ 2	£ 8	40	£ 12	£ 20
Expensive Amtico-like Vinyl	£ 55	£ 11	£ 2	£ 68	60	£ 18	£ 86
Cork	£ 14	£ 3	£ 2	£ 19	40	£ 12	£ 31
Red Quarry Tile	£ 12	£ 2	£ 4	£ 18	60	£ 18	£ 36
Chinese Slate	£ 25	£ 5	£ 4	£ 34	80	£ 24	£ 58
Cheap Ceramic Tiles	£ 7	£ 1	£ 4	£ 12	60	£ 18	£ 30
Mid price Ceramics	£ 20	£ 4	£ 4	£ 28	60	£ 18	£ 46
Expensive Ceramic Tiling	£ 50	£ 10	£ 4	£ 64	60	£ 18	£ 82
Softwood T&G boards	£ 9	£ 2	£ 7	£ 18	80	£ 24	£ 42
Junckers-style Beech Floor	£ 45	£ 9	£ 4	£ 58	80	£ 24	£ 82
Reclaimed Boards	£ 25	£ 5	£ 8	£ 38	80	£ 24	£ 62
Wood Block	£ 16	£ 3	£ 8	£ 27	80	£ 24	£ 51
Oak	£ 32	£ 6	£ 7	£ 45	80	£ 24	£ 69
Hardwood/MDF Floors	£ 30	£ 6	£ 4	£ 40	60	£ 18	£ 58

can cost £3 per sq m) so you can imagine what the quality is like.

For the novice, buying carpets is a bit of a minefield with enormous price variations for apparently similar products. The Carpet Foundation runs a grading scheme as follows:

■ Grade 1: suitable for areas getting low use (bedrooms)

■ Grade 2: average use areas (dining rooms, studies)

■ Grades 3/4: heavily used areas (halls, staircases). This grading scheme would be more useful if every retailer stuck by it but they don't. Some use their own grading systems and others blithely ignore the whole procedure. It can all be a particularly taxing affair for the selfbuilder who is often under great pressure to move in quickly. There often isn't time to make an informed decision and rash choices here can be expensive and hard to live with. Key buying points to watch out for are:

■ Don't be misled by incredibly low area prices quoted in newspapers and magazines. Get written quotations with details of underlay, fitting charges, and any extra that might get charged for gripper, door bars, delivery, etc. There are plenty of hidden costs for the unwary.

■ Material. Wool is the traditional and natural material for carpets; it also tends to be the most expensive. Synthetics like nylon and acrylics are now commonplace and much carpet sold these days is a cocktail of wool and synthetics – and people walking on them would not know the difference. The very cheapest material is polypropylene which looks synthetic but may be fine for your needs, especially in bedrooms.

■ Comparing prices over the phone is difficult because a lot of carpet is not branded and there are so many varieties on the market that very often no two outlets sell the same thing. Sticking to an established name like John Lewis will ensure that you are not ripped-off, but they are unlikely to be selling carpet below £10 per sq m, which is higher than many people's budget will allow.

■ Bear in mind this rule of thumb when estimating cost: you should double the advertised price of a fitted carpet to get an idea of what it will all cost when laid on your floors. This will allow for offcuts, underlay and laying costs.

Bathroom Carpeting

Avoid woollen carpets in bathrooms as they will tend to go mouldy, especially if they have a hessian backing. Polypropylene carpets with foam backings are cheap and durable and will survive many years of bath time frolicking.

Tiles

There are many different materials used to tile or sheet floors and there is not space to cover them all here. In particular, there are any number of synthetic rubbery plastic type floor coverings which are generally more at home in an industrial or commercial setting than a house. If you want to know more, check out your Yellow Pages under Flooring Services. Here I look at just the three most popular tiled finishes.

Vinyl

The very word vinyl sounds cheap but don't be misled, it's not. Either in sheet or tile form, this can vary between the very cheap marble effects (like Polyflex) costing less than £5 per sq m – these tiles usually have only a small percentage of vinyl in them – to Amtico floor tiles costing over £80 per sq m. The best results are to be had when the immediate sub-floor is covered either with a 5mm latex screed or hardboard sheeting. Adhesive adds around £1.50 per sq m, laying costs between £2.50 and £5.00 per sq m.

Cork

Cheap cork tiles can be purchased in the DIY sheds, but they do not last very long. In any area receiving reasonably heavy wear, use vinyl covered and backed tiles. Wicanders is the main producer: their top of the range Cork Master costs around £25 per sq m. Best laid on board; if laid on a cement screed ensure that it's completely dry – this takes around eight summer weeks. Adhesive adds £2.50 per sq m, laying costs around £5 per sq m.

The floor finishes are
amalgamated with the wall
tiling in this table because
the tiler doesn't really make
any distinctions between
floors and walls

Benchmark House - Floor Finishes & Wall Tiling

	Area in m²	Rate	Mats	Lab	Totals
Floor Tiling	65	£58	£2,210	£1,560	£3,770
Oak Floor Boards	46	£69	£2,070	£1,100	£3,170
Oak Laminate	69	£58	£2,760	£1,240	£4,000
Flooring Total	**180**		**£7,040**	**£3,900**	**£10,940**
Wall Tiling	**56**	**£46**	**£1,570**	**£1,010**	**£2,580**

Ceramic/Quarry Tiles

Laying costs are higher when specifying
ceramic tiles because it is a more involved
process, requiring time-consuming cutting and
a second pass to grout up the results. Adhesives
and grouts add around £1.50 to £2 per sq
m to prices. The very cheapest floor tiles are
usually imported from Italy or Portugal and
are displayed under little known brand names
in the DIY sheds and discount tile shops at less
than £5 per sq m. The cheapest British quarry
tiles – which are made from reconstituted stone
rather than baked clay – are available in red at
around £10 per sq m, whilst Cristal, Pilkington
and Wooliscroft produce popular floor tiles
from around £9 per sq m upwards. At the other
end of the scale, Fired Earth and numerous
imitators sell a dazzling array of terracotta floor
tiles, many of them reclaimed, from around
£35 per sq m upwards.

Another popular option is to fit a stone floor.
I have seen a lot of Indian slate laid recently – it
looks good and it's very cheap but it seems to
suffer from varying thicknesses which makes
a pig of laying. Paving stones or flagstones
are conventionally laid outside but they can
also make stunning interiors as well; Classical
Flagstones produce convincing replica York
stone from £25 per sq m which is often used
indoors.

Timber flooring

The rise and rise of hardwood flooring is
notable trend in contemporary home design. It
was always thought of as an aspirational feature
but people used to get put off by the price. It's
not got any cheaper but all of a sudden people
seem to be quite happily paying £40 - £80

per sq m for hardwood floor planking and are
being increasingly daring as to the choice of
wood – current top of the pops seems to be
bamboo which sounds like it might be cheap
but ain't. Slightly cheaper options are to use
a veneered floor which has a 4-5mm layer of
hardwood stuck onto a composite backing. If
anything, a veneer floor is going to be more
stable because of the backing. However, every
time you sand a hardwood floor you strip at
least 1mm off the top surface so in the long
term maintenance stakes, a solid floor wins out.
But how many times are you actually going to
sand a hardwood floor? Cheaper still is to use
a wood look-alike floor cover but this is really
cheating now.

Our benchmark house builder, Steve Baldwin,
fitted lots of oak into his house. Downstairs he
sourced some oak laminate board at £37 per sq
m. Upstairs he went for solid oak which was
actually marginally cheaper. There are an awful
lot of options and a wide range of prices; oak
planks can be anywhere between £17 per sq
m and £80 per sq m, a huge range of prices
for what you might imagine are very similar
products. Of course, they're not. One of the key
points to watch if you buy a solid hardwood
floor is that the moisture content is right
down at around eight per cent when you lay
– this is especially important if you want to fit
underfloor heating.

How about a softwood floor? You can lay a
new tongued and grooved pine floor; materials
can be bought from as little as £7.50 per sq m
but these need sanding and sealing after laying
– allow around £5 per sq m for this – and will
almost certainly shrink dramatically, opening
up unsightly cracks between the boards. This
shrinkage problem is a feature of all wood

floors – though it is insignificant when using well-seasoned hardwoods – and the only way to ensure it doesn't happen is to let the timber dry out in your centrally heated environment before laying – rather impractical for most builders. But if you are prepared to source better quality pine planking from slow growth timbers in north Scandinavian latitudes, then you can match the performance of many hardwood floors at around half the price. You do, however, have to know what you are buying – don't just pitch up in a timber yard and buy tongued and grooved flooring.

Another approach is to use a reclaimed board which has been stored undercover and is, hopefully, dimensionally stable. These vary in price from around £6 per sq m up to £30 per sq m and will almost certainly involve you in a lot of extra work (de-nailing, sanding, hole filling, more sanding, sealing). The huge variation in prices for reclaimed boards is of course an indication that there is a huge variation in quality as well. If you go to one of the better salvage yards, such as Machell's, near Leeds, you'll find good quality board but prices to match new planks. Another option is to use wood blocks – reclaimed oak can still be picked up from salvage yards for less than £15 per sq m – but again be prepared to have to carry out a lot of extra preparation work. However, a wood block floor (sometimes known as parquet) has to be laid on a solid backing, which will generally involve laying some form of extra screed or decking beneath, especially as floor insulation is now mandatory.

Matwells

It's always a nice touch to see people thinking ahead and building in a sunken matwell is usually a sign that someone has been. Now that the disabled access regs require level access, usually at the main entrance door, a sunken matwell becomes even more important, as the door now opens just a few millimetres above the floor cover. There is an industry standard matwell (which may surprise some) which is 760 x 460 x 40mm. If you stick to this you

can buy galvanised steel surrounds for around £40 and these will take industry standard sized coconut matting (costs around £8 per mat). If you are putting down a timber floor, you can of course create your own surrounds.

■*Second Fix Carpentry*

Second-fix carpentry is a bit of a rag-bag of different activities that covers just about everything that carpenters get up to after the plasterers are finished. It usually includes door hanging and staircase fixing, as well as fixing skirtings and architraves and pipe boxings; often it also includes fitting kitchens, and vanity units in bathrooms, and putting up shelves.

Internal doors

The world of the internal door is split between the hollow and the solid. The hollow doors are like sandwiches; the casings are layers of board and the filling consists of a material very similar to egg boxes. Where you would normally place the handle and latch, they put a solid hunk of wood called the lock block and foolish would-be chippies (like me) have been known to hang these doors in a hurry, only to find that the lock block is on the hinge side of the door. If you are observant, you will hang the door on the correct side – there is only ever one lock block in a hollow door and if you look on the bottom edge you will see which side the lock block is located.

This all sounds very cheap and tacky and, generally speaking, eggbox-style doors are, but they can also be purchased with hardwood veneers, usually from some environmentally incorrect species like sapele (pronounced sa-pee-lee), and this pushes the price up to levels at which you can buy solid softwood doors, around the £25 mark. Sapele is in fact by far and away the most popular veneer in this country: the doors have 2.5mm chipboard facing onto which the veneers are ironed or steamed.

The very cheapest doors you can get are eggbox-filled doors which are encased in, wait

Second Fix Carpentry - Key Rates

Carpenters and Joiners charging rate		£ 18.00	per hour			
Item	Unit	Cheap	Mid Price	Fancy	Time Taken in mins	Labour @ £18/hr
Windowboard	m run		£ 3.50		20	£ 6
Door Linings	5.1m set	£ 8	£ 10	£ 20	45	£ 14
Internal Doors	ea	£ 30	£ 140	£ 210	120	£ 36
Double Glazed Doors	pr		£ 210	£ 450	300	£ 90
Door Furniture	per door		£ 10	£ 30	inc in hanging	
Skirtings	m run	£ 0.65	£ 1.25	£ 2.00	12	£ 3.60
Architrave	m run	£ 0.55	£ 0.90	£ 1.80	8	£ 2.40
Cupboard Fit Out	m³		£ 20		180	£ 54
Matchboarding	m²	£ 6	£ 7	£ 15	40	£ 12
Loft Access Covers	ea		£ 30		45	£ 14
Loft Ladders	ea	£ 30		£ 120	120	£ 36

for it, hardboard. Expect to pay around £12 for one of these but don't ever kick it. A popular variation on this theme is the embossed or moulded door; they are no stronger but they imitate the fielded panels found on timber doors and some of them imitate wood grain texture. The simpler ones cost between £30 and £40 each and they look quite acceptable when painted, which is what they are designed for. Some superior ones use a type of fibreboard for the casing and they are strong enough to take glazing, although doors with glazing panels are much more expensive – around £70. All the major joinery manufacturers have a selection of these doors and, if you want to select a door, get hold of one of their catalogues. Premdor Crosby and Magnet both have good ranges. Most designs are also available in bi-fold format for use as sliding cupboard doors.

Solid wood doors

For people who like their doors to go clunk rather than thwack when they shut. Not that these doors are that much heavier than their eggbox counterparts; indeed there are a number of incredibly cheap (i.e. less than £30) imported timber doors available in the DIY sheds which look as though they might actually disintegrate if you shut them too hard. They are usually stored about ten feet above ground level and when you get to see them close up you realise why.

Generally, internal timber doors fall into two categories; stainable and paint-only grade. The paint-only ones are made from inferior timbers that may well have dead knots – which are given to working loose – and are frequently made up of short sections of timber which are finger-jointed together. If you are planning to paint the doors you might just as well settle for a paint-only grade door costing around £40; the better quality, stainable doors are more than twice as much.

Hardwood is an option as well. Oak and meranti are widely available but expensive at around £150 per door. The hardwood veneered hollow doors are about half this price and are solid enough for most people's demands.

Cottage style doors

An increasingly popular option is to fit ledged-and-braced doors to all internal openings. This style of door used to be exclusively associated with back doors and outbuildings, but with the fashion for all things cottagey, they are beginning to move indoors. External doors are manufactured with a moisture content of around 18 per cent whereas the ideal moisture content for internal doors is around half this amount. Hanging an external door inside tends to result in them twisting out of shape.

The joinery majors such as JeldWen now carry internal cottage doors (in their case known as an FL&B for Framed Ledged & Braced) but they cost twice as much as the ones designed for exterior use. Alternatively, seek out one of the small specialist suppliers such The Real Door Company; they will tend to charge between £140 and £200 for softwood doors.

MDF doors

Another approach which is gaining in popularity, especially as regards fitted cupboard doors, is to make them on site using MDF (medium density fibreboard). MDF is a manufactured timber board which has no grain but can be worked like natural timber; the finish can be sanded to accept paint or even, at a pinch, stain.

Mouldings can be either routed into the board or stuck on to the surface. This is obviously rather labour intensive and the doors tend to be a bit on the heavy side but it is cheap. If you have nonstandard sized doorways, which often occurs with alcove cupboards and the like, then MDF is often a good solution. You need a board that's at least 25mm thick or else you won't be able to hinge it; alternatively, you can stick two thinner boards together and cut bits out of the top one to make decorative panelling effects. A good timber merchant will be able to dimension MDF for you, a facility not to be sniffed at.

Door furniture

Door furniture is the phrase used to describe just about everything to do with doors excluding the door itself. That usually means all the bits made of metal, and door ironmongery would be a much easier to understand expression, but the building trade likes the word furniture to be used here. I really don't know why. Perhaps it adds to the mystique of the whole thing or maybe they are just being pig-ignorant. Anyway, I digress.

The point to cotton on to here is that some door furniture is purely functional in that you don't see it or, if you do, you don't notice it; however other bits are very visual and – wait for it – tactile. Yes folks, door handles are sexy. Developers know this and consequently are prepared to spend above the bare minimum to create an impression on the would-be house purchaser. Door handles may indeed be the only part of the house that the viewer actually touches during an inspection and female purchasers are thought to be impressed by something strong and solid which responds readily to their grasp.

Style

Most developers fit brass-plated furniture to their doors. There are two basic styles: Victorian

Don't hang external ledged and braced doors internally! When initially hung, these cupboard doors were absolutely plumb with one another. Yet within a few weeks, the twisting is so severe that the only way of correcting it is to start again with new doors. The reason is to do with residual moisture content, likely to be around 18 per cent on external doors whereas internal timber dries to below 12 per cent.

Benchmark House Second Fix Carpentry Costs				Materials	Labour	Combined
	Range					
Door Linings	Mid	15.5 sets		£ 160	£ 220	£ 380
Architraves	Mid	141 m		£ 130	£ 340	£ 470
Skirtings	Mid	154 m		£ 190	£ 680	£ 870
Internal Doors	Mid	13 no.		£ 1,820	£ 470	£ 2,290
Int Double Doors (x2)	Fancy	2.5 pairs		£ 1,130	£ 230	£ 1,360
Door Funiture	Mid	16 sets		£ 160	inc above	£ 160
Matchboarding	Fancy	20 m²		£ 290	£ 240	£ 530
Loft Access Cover	Mid			£ 30	£ 10	£ 40
Loft Ladder	Cheap			£ 30	£ 40	£ 70
Air Cupboard	Mid	2 m³		£ 40	£ 110	£ 150
Stairs - two turns	Softwood			£ 1,000	£ 580	£ 1,580
			Totals	£ 4,980	£ 2,920	£ 7,900

(or plain) and Georgian (frilly bits added). Both styles are catered for by builder's merchants and DIY sheds who sell shrink-wrapped pre-packs at fairly reasonable prices.

These pre-packs have one big advantage going for them in that they've got all the bits you need in the pack; you may be able to buy at keener prices but you risk a) forgetting vital bits, b) having to overbuy on items like screws and c) buying the wrong bits – classic one here is to get the wrong-sized hinges. If your tastes veer away from these mainstream choices you'll have to brave it and go and order your very own door furniture.

Our benchmark house is fitted out with brass furniture on its internal ledged and braced doors. The external doors, in uPVC, all came ready-furnished as part of the all-in price.

Door Security

Door security features are dealt with in the Security section in this chapter. To summarise, current NHBC guidelines recommend fitting 5-lever locks to all external doors but also recommend that the main exit door should be protected by a Yale-type night latch which can be readily opened from inside without a key; this is to make escape easier in case of fire.

5-Point Locking Systems

These are fancy multi-point locking systems that are fitted, as standard, on uPVC doors, but only because the basic material is so flexible

that it would not be secure without bolts top, middle and bottom. The use of 5-point locking systems is creeping into the world of timber joinery and you can fit your own to any timber door simply by routing a slot down the closing edge. They cost around £90; they have an integral handle but they don't replace the 5-lever lock necessary on any external door.

Buying tips

As already mentioned, the door furniture pre-packs are a moderately good deal if you are happy to stay within a limited range. If you want more unusual fittings then the DIY sheds have a surprising variety; if you want wood or ceramic knobs this is a good place to look. More specialised still are the Architectural Ironmongers: check the Yellow Pages in your area. A very useful 'Bible' for door furniture is published by Ironmongery Direct.

Another tip well worth pursuing is to order all your external door locks 'to pass.' This means that all your 5-lever locks are adjusted so that they can be opened with the same key. It's not exactly the automated house but it's a big improvement on lugging around identical looking keys, each of which will open only one of your doors. A good merchant will be able to sell you locks to pass at no extra cost though they will take an extra day or two to sort it out.

Knobs

Sorry to bring up this sordid subject again but

Stairs - Key Rates				
	Softwood	Hardwood	Time Taken in hrs	Labour @ £18/hr
Straight flight + landing balusters	£ 400	£ 700	16	£ 300
One turn + stair & landing balusters	£ 800	£ 1,300	24	£ 440
Two turns + stairs & landing balusters	£ 1,000	£ 1,500	32	£ 580

the observant amongst you may have noticed that there are two distinct styles of door opening levers, otherwise known as handles and knobs. Whatever the merits and demerits of the two, there is one painful little trap to watch out for if you go for a knob – you need to fit a longer latch otherwise you will scrape your knuckles every time you open the door. For the technically challenged, the latch, in this instance, is the metal tube that fits inside the door and the hole in the latch determines exactly how far the handle or the knob sits from the edge of the door. The standard tubular latch is 63mm long and it's designed for handles; when fitting a knob on an internal door, fit a 75mm latch and an external door knob will require an even longer latch – say 95mm. The pre-packed knobsets normally include 75mm latches, but if you are buying independently then watch out.

Stairs

By far the cheapest staircase you can specify is the straight-flight with 13 steps and a total rise of 2600mm, which is the industry standard distance between floors. Timber staircases like this can be picked up off the shelf for as little as £180; they are also much quicker to install and, generally, have far less in the way of newel posts and balusters. A straight flight staircase with all the trimmings is going to take a good chippie no more than two days to put in, and so anticipate a cost (without decoration or carpeting) of just £600 (Mats £350, Lab £250). The cheapest source of straight stairs is the Magnets of the joinery world; for more complex arrangements, a local joiner may well be very competitive, though note that Jeld Wen's bespoke staircase production is often excellent, though note the cautionary tale from the

benchmark house, noted in the accompanying photograph.

Half-Landings

The commonest alternative is to split the staircase into two halves connected by a half-landing. This arrangement is better when you want a more open stairwell design and often makes it much easier to design the internal layout of the house. Half-landings (and the related quarter-landings) tend to double the overall staircase costs.

Winders

Winders (pronounced wine-ders, not win-ders) is the name given to steps that turn corners whilst still climbing; a spiral staircase consists of nothing but winders but a more conventional arrangement uses three winder steps (usually at the top or the bottom of the flight) to navigate a 90° turn. They are space efficient and so are normally used in situations where space is tight. These days they are most commonly used with loft conversions, precisely because of this reason. They are not cheap – the staircase alone will cost £800 plus – and in many ways they are best avoided, especially when you want to move furniture up or downstairs.

Spirals

The ultimate in winding-staircases is the fully fledged spiral staircase. Usually done in steel, they are expensive and enormously impractical. The logic behind spiral staircases is that they save space but in reality the amount of space saved is minimal. They do certainly impose a style and in certain, modern looking interiors, they are just so. But the average UK housebuilder is going to find them far too ostentatious. Expect to pay over £2,000 for a simple steel spiral unit. Supply and fix prices for curved staircases are invariably over £3,000.

Fittings

At least as significant visually as the shape of the staircase is the specification of all the little bits that go with the stairs; the banisters, the handrails, the newel posts. These days banisters tend to get called balusters which is, perhaps, something to do with European integration, but the details remain wedded to the turn of the century (last time around). As with so much else in UK housebuilding, the standard options all hark back to our dearly beloved bygones: Georgian, Victorian, Colonial, Fluting, Rope Twist, etc. Easily the least fussy – and the cheapest – are the peasant variety known as Plain Balusters. The plain arrangements cost around £30 per lin.m whereas the fancy turned timber balusters start from around £45 per lin. m. Even on a relatively straightforward staircase, the fittings will often cost as much as the stairs.

Galleries

A surprising number of otherwise very conventional new homes incorporate an open-plan gallery area which links the two floors with a grand staircase arrangement. Typically there will be an area of hallway around the front door that is open right up to the upstairs ceiling or even the underside of the roof, lit by a Velux rooflight. It makes for a very impressive entrance with dramatic overtones of minstrels' galleries and the like. In a way it's pure theatre; it is an extremely impractical arrangement and it doesn't owe much to traditional housing styles that we British seem so keen to ape in other respects. Done out using acres of glass, white walls and chrome staircase, we would say "It's far too open plan for us." However, dress up the same idea with pile carpeting and traditional looking balustrading and we react quite differently – 'Gosh! Isn't that just like Gone With The Wind'.

However you finish it, the gallery/open-plan stairwell arrangement is space hungry and is, therefore, a luxury. In itself it's not a particularly

Benchmark house staircase – it's a quarter landing supplied by JeldWen from their plant in Melton Mowbray, which produces over 1,000 staircases a week, around 30 per cent of the UK total. This one was made-to-measure and it was measured wrong, so the first version had to be returned and replaced.

expensive detail (unless you start curving the staircase and the balustrading) but before you embark on a maximum impact entrance, first consider whether you wouldn't rather have an extra room or two instead. Chances are that if you want that kind of entrance then, frankly, you don't give a damn.

Skirting and architrave

The amazing thing about skirtings and architraves is that we don't really need them at all. Indeed, many countries have already done away with them. Yet a glance at the building costs of our benchmark house reveals that, in common with all the major UK housebuilders and just about every selfbuilder, Steve Baldwin spent good money (around one per cent of the total building costs) on fixing largely superfluous bits of timber to the base of all the walls and around all the internal door openings.

There is (or rather was) a logic behind fitting skirting boards. It used to be standard building practice to leave a 50mm gap between the floor and the bottom of the plaster on the wall so as not to breach the damp-proof course placed in the wall; however, damp-proofing techniques have changed and now floor membranes are lapped into wall membranes and the rising damp never (in theory) penetrates the room space at all. It still leaves the problem of filling the unsightly crack between wall and floor but the widespread incorporation of fitted carpets has made even this problem a thing of the past.

Not that I've anything against skirting boards; I love 'em – the wider the better. They look great and any room without them will look cold and, worse still, European. Both skirtings and architrave are available in a range of styles varying from the very plain to the thick moulded sections beloved by the Victorians. Fixing times don't vary much (prices usually hover around £2.50 per m) but as regards material costs, the fancy sections are two to three times more than the utilitarian versions which are around 40p per m.

If you are in a hurry you can use prepainted MDF sections, which are now becoming widely available at builder's merchants. These are best nailed into the walls but, alternatively, can be stuck on with an adhesive like Gripfill, a mastic glue which can be used to bond all kinds of materials. Not only could you use it for all your skirtings and architraves, but it's fantastically useful for sorting out little problems like squeaky stairs. A true friend to the bodge merchant.

Dados and picture rails

You may find it hard to believe that skirtings and architraves are purely cosmetic, but even the most sceptical amongst you will have

to agree that dados and picture rails are not essential. However, they were regarded as essential in polite Victorian parlours. The dado rail was placed at waist height, the picture rail just a few inches below the ceiling. Their chief function was to provide a visual break in the eye feast that was the Victorian living room, whose walls consisted of two different kinds of wallpaper as well as (starting at the bottom) skirtings, dados, picture rails and plaster covings. Despite the fashions for all things Olde Worlde, this level of detail in new housing is now extremely uncommon. Nevertheless, good timber yards still keep these sections, mostly for restoration work, and you may choose to fit them in a new house if you are looking for a bit of style.

Loft hatch

Every house has one (unless you have a room in the loft) and they are not the most demanding of features. But take a little care in fitting a loft hatch as it is frequently a weak point in your home's battle against draughts. Furthermore, being an outlet for draughts rather than an inlet, you are never likely to be aware of just how much warm air you may lose through the loft hatch. Many an otherwise fastidious greenie (myself included) has insulated the top of the loft trap door – Gripfill is brilliant for this job as well – but neglected to effectively draught proof the strips of wood on which the hatch door sits. In terms of heat loss through loft hatches, effective draught proofing is ten times more important than the insulation. You don't have to do anything dramatic; just make sure it sits tight. If you are particularly fussy, you can buy proprietary loft hatches made from uPVC which clamp shut: they cost around £50.

Loft ladders

Not essential but nevertheless incredibly useful, even if you only go up there once a year. A decent aluminium sliding loft ladder will cost around £50 and take a competent DIY boffin around two hours to fit. However, if you are interested in making your loft hatch

Torus skirting, costs £1.30 - £2.50/lin.m, depending on quality

Moulded architrave, costs around 75p/lin.m

Dado rail, costs around £1.30/lin.m

Moulded picture rail, costs £1.60/lin.m

still very commonly fitted. There is one major drawback to the contemporary airing cupboard and that is that with the new generation of super-lagged hot-water cylinders, you no longer have a creditable heat source in the airing cupboard; hence, perpetually soggy towels. Well, that's not quite true; any new house will enjoy a much higher ambient temperature than an old wreck and this will tend to dry damp clothes, albeit rather slowly. You can, of course, just put fully dried clothes in the airing cupboard, but this rather defeats the purpose of having an airing cupboard in the first place. Alternatively, you can fit a mini-heater or a 150W light bulb inside. It all seems a bit futile when the cause of your problem is the fact that you've wrapped up the hot water cylinder so well that it no longer gives off any heat.

What's really needed is an effective way of lagging and unlagging your hot water tank, controlled automatically by the relative humidity of air inside the cupboard. But this sounds very expensive and surely the world is full of more pressing problems. Still it's one to ponder on during those long sleepless nights.

Boxing in

Boxing in the pipes is a new facet of housebuilding that now forms a significant bit of a second-fixer's work. In the good-bad-indifferent-Olde days the pipes were left naked for all to see. The stench pipe in particular was usually run down the outside of the house.

Current fashions are for internal stench pipes – concealed internal stench pipes – and this means boxing is de rigeur. Now, depending on your disposition, this type of job can seem like an incredible almighty drag or a marvellous opportunity to show the world just how creative you can be with a bit of dead space.

Whichever camp you fall into, it helps to plan your pipe runs and attendant boxings well ahead so that the boxing can be incorporated into the overall scheme of things rather than sticking out into rooms like an ugly carbuncle ('monstrous', I hear you saying).

Bathroom boxings are often best tiled

draught-proof, it is really worth carrying out the installation of a loft ladder first because it usually leads to you having to make significant adjustments to the trap door housing.

Whilst we're on the subject, it's worth installing a permanent light in the loft just to make life easy when fixing a loft ladder. You won't regret it.

Airing cupboard

Airing cupboards are not actually required in houses with central heating but they are

over, but you must allow at least some of
the panelling to be removable – a trick that's
accomplished with mirror screws and flexible
mastic joints. If you are painting the finish,
then MDF is probably the best material to use,
but if you plan to stick ceramic tiles on, then a
waterproof 18mm plywood would be a better
choice.

Boxing is also widely used in bathrooms to
create a fitted vanity unit effect. There are a
range of basins (known as semi-countertop)
that are designed to sit over a boxed unit, and
there are also concealed cisterns which will be
proud to flush behind your mini-wall. The usual
choice of wall finish will be ceramic tiles but
pine matchboarding is becoming fashionable
once again, albeit painted not varnished.

Shelving
The only quotation that The Duchess of Windsor
is remembered for is 'you can't be too rich and
you can't be too thin'. Had she been a keen
builder, she might have added 'you can't have
enough shelves' because it is an axiom that,
however many shelves you put up, you will still
need more. I can discern three approaches to
shelving:
■ Buy some: go out and buy some ready made
up units. DIY sheds have some pretty basic ones;
IKEA has some basic ones which are a little
better designed. Department stores like Habitat
and John Lewis have some very nice expensive
shelving systems. Free-standing shelving units
are not especially cheap but they are removable.
■ Bash them up: utility shelving can be
extremely cheap to fit. If you use one of the
proprietary steel bracket systems like Spur or
Element 32 you pay a lot more but you get a
system that's very quick to install and easy to
alter. It is also readily removable. Materials for
a steel bracket shelving system work out at
around £30 per lin.m which is cheaper than
almost any ready made system.
■ Labour of love: design your shelving to fit
a particular alcove or sit at a certain height.
Think a little of the finished look; perhaps add
some sort of pelmet and possibly some lighting

as well. This sort of detail does not have to be
expensive but it does require a certain amount
of forethought. If you know what MDF is and
know how to wield a router, you should be
able to erect bespoke shelving (with no metal
brackets showing!) for less than £20 per lin.m
(materials only).

■ Painting and decorating
Exterior Work
You can avoid exterior decorating altogether
by specifying pre-finished materials like uPVC.
Indeed, many are doing just that: our current
benchmark house being a prime example,
Steve Baldwin having used uPVC not just for
the external joinery but also for the fascias
and soffits as well. There are other options,
if you really don't like uPVC. Windows and
doors are available with composite finishes:
there are masonry alternatives for fascias and
soffits and even timber boarding is available in
cementitous replica or in species like cedar that
doesn't require any paint or stain.

But if regular timber is your thing, then you
have to provide some form of protection for it
if it's used externally. The main choice is now
between traditional paint and woodstains. Even
though woodstains are more expensive to buy,
the cost difference between the two systems
is negligible because there is such a high
labour content in decorating and, if anything,
stains are slightly quicker to apply. What really
causes decorating costs to tumble is reducing
the number of coats needed to get a decent
finish. Many builders do this with stains by
dispensing with the third coat, which would be
difficult with conventional paint, but there are
now a number of one-coat paints (e.g. Crown
Solo) which enable you to dispense with the
undercoat – at a price.

Wood paints
The traditional way of finishing external timber
is with oil-based gloss paint. This is applied in
a three-coat system: primer, undercoat, gloss.
If you want to use a traditional paint finish you

Painting & Decorating Key Rates

		Coverage/coat	Divider	Cost/m²
General Labour rate worked on	£ 14 /hr			
Emulsion	£ 10 / 5lt tin	12 m²/lt	60	£ 0.17
Gloss	£ 14 / 5lt tin	16 m²/lt	80	£ 0.18
Stain on sawn timber	£ 32 / 5lt tin	5 m²/lt	25	£ 1.28
Stain on planed timber	£ 32 / 5lt tin	10 m²/lt	50	£ 0.64
Thick stains/varnish on joinery	£ 18 / 2.5lt tin	15 m²/lt	35	£ 0.51
Masonary paint	£ 20 / 5lt tin	5 m²/lt	15	£ 1.33
Wallpaper	huge variety of prices. £2/m² is a mid price.			£ 2.00

Painting v Staining: Time and Metre Rates

	Time in mins	Labour @ £14/hr	Cost of Paint	Cost of Stain
Emulsioning Walls and Ceilings	5 mins/m²/coat	£ 1.20	£ 0.20	
Masonary Paint to External walls	12 mins/m²/coat	£ 2.80	£ 1.30	
Painting/Staining/Varnishing Options				
Floor covers (with some sanding)	12 mins/m²/coat	£ 2.80		£ 0.50
External Wall Claddings	12 mins/m²/coat	£ 2.80	£ 0.60	£ 1.30
Windows (each face)	30 mins/m²/coat	£ 7.00	£ 0.20	£ 0.60
Doors (each face)	15 mins/m²/coat	£ 3.50	£ 0.20	£ 0.60
Balusters (both faces)	30 mins/m²/coat	£ 7.00	£ 0.20	£ 0.60
Strips	4 mins/linear metre/coat	£ 0.90	£ 0.10	£ 0.20
Wallpapering	20 mins/m²/layer	£ 5.00	£ 2.00	

Benchmark House Decorating Costs

	Area/Length		Rate		Materials	Labour	Total
Internal plasterwork	634	m²	£ 4.20		£ 380	£ 2,280	£ 2,660
Stain Internal Doors (opening area)	30	m²	£ 25	both faces	£ 110	£ 610	£ 720
Stairwell balusters (each side)	7	m²	£ 46	both faces	£ 30	£ 290	£ 320
Timber lengths							
Stain Door Linings	83	m	£ 3.30		£ 50	£ 220	£ 270
Stain Architraves	141	m	£ 3.30		£ 80	£ 380	£ 460
Stain Skirtings	154	m	£ 3.30		£ 90	£ 420	£ 510
Stain Windowboards	19	m	£ 3.30		£ 10	£ 50	£ 60
				Total	£ 750	£ 4,250	£ 5,000

Decorating - Metre Rates (inc Lab & Mats)

	Each coat	Cost of 3 coats
Emulsion to Int plasterwork	£ 1.40 m²	£ 4.20 m²
Masonary paint to ext render	£ 4.10 m²	£ 12.30 m²
Stain to ext cladding	£ 4.10 m²	£ 12.30 m²
Varnish to hardwood flooring	£ 3.30 m²	£ 9.90 m²
Paint one face of a window	£ 7.20 m²	£ 21.60 m²
Stain one face of a window	£ 7.60 m²	£ 22.80 m²
Paint one face of a door	£ 3.70 m²	£ 11.10 m²
Stain one face of a door	£ 4.10 m²	£ 12.30 m²
Paint balusters & stair supports	£ 7.20 m²	£ 21.60 m²
Stain balusters & stairs	£ 7.60 m²	£ 22.80 m²
Paint strips	£ 1.00 m run	£ 3.00 m run
Stain strips	£ 1.10 m run	£ 3.30 m run
Wallpaper	£ 7.00 m²	

can save money and time by specifying that your joinery arrives on site primed with paint instead of the current industry standard of a basecoat of honey-coloured stain.

Which paint to use? There is a bewildering array of paints available: traditional oil-based gloss, non-drip gloss, one-coat gloss, microporous paints, acrylic paints to name but a few. Coupled with the fact that every manufacturer seems to use a different naming system to describe their product and it's no wonder the poor consumer gets confused. Which? magazine carries out an annual review of exterior paints (and stains) but it only scratches the surface of the paint market; their survey is just not comprehensive enough to provide a complete picture and, in any event, the canny manufacturers are forever reformulating their products and giving them new brand names so that the chances are, even if you went around B&Q armed with the latest Which? survey in your hand, you'd still not find their recommendations. Or if you did, how would you know it was the same as it was five years ago when Which?'s test started?

Water-based acrylics

Two factors have combined to increase the sales of water-based paints and they are both to do with user friendliness. Firstly, they are very easy to apply – afterwards the brushes can be washed out under a cold tap; secondly, there are increasing concerns over the health risks of using the traditional oil-based gloss paints. The people most likely to benefit from both these factors are the professional painters and decorators yet, paradoxically, they are the ones who are most resistant to using water-based paints, reckoning them to be useless. Expensive more like. Though they are still a comparatively new system (first introduced in the Seventies) the indications are that water-based paints perform rather better than many oil-based alternatives. What they won't give you is a high-gloss sheen finish, but then the matt look is preferred by most people these days.

Masonry paints

As if to emphasise the last point about the durability of water-based paints, standard masonry paints, which are used to cover external render and masonry, are mostly water-based and many will claim to last for 15 years before needing recoating. They are easy to apply but their application should not be rushed; the underlying cement render must be allowed to dry out thoroughly. This is a drag because many builders are itching to strike the scaffolding by the time the external rendering is done and waiting for render to dry can take forever. Take the scaffolding down and it'll take you three times as long to paint the house. The moral?

Only build houses with external painted panels when the sun shines.

Stains

Woodstaining is one of the very few continental ideas to have really caught on in British housebuilding. The habit of applying woodstains has been a hit with the wood-stripping Habitat generation because the stains enable you to see the natural grain of the timber. Generically, stains are divided into two subgroups, low-build and medium-build, but you are unlikely to hear these terms bandied about on a building site where they are known by their brand names. The build rating refers to the thickness of the stain and the higher the build the better the protection but the less you see of the underlying wood. The biggest names in this business are Sadolin and Sikkens, now both part of Akzo Nobel, though the British manufacturers are at last getting their act together (Ronseal, Dulux, Hicksons, Cuprinol). Sadolin's low-build stain is called Classic and is most widely used on sawn timber which drinks it like a Dublin bar on St. Patrick's night; their medium-build stain is called Extra and this is much more oily – treacly almost – and you use this for covering timber joinery. All these stains are available in a range of woody colours but the really jazzy colours are usually restricted to the low-build ranges.

Conventionally, stains have been spirit-based but, as with paints, you can now buy water-based acrylic stains. Sikkens' Cetol BL range is reckoned to be one of the best. The use of woodstains seems to have peeked, as the Habitat generation gives way to the IKEA one. In the mid-Nineties, 60 per cent of timber windows fitted into new homes were getting a stain finish: today, that's fallen back to 40 per cent.

Interior work
Walls and ceilings

Most interior walls are finished with emulsion paints, which are very cheap and very easy to apply, being water-based. The standard choice you need to make is between a matt finish and a silk finish. Matt finishes are characterised as being thicker (more opaque) and softer; silk finishes produce a harder, glossier look that has the added advantage of being more readily washable. There is no difference in price. Satin finishes are a halfway house between matt and silk. One tip for new housebuilders is to apply your emulsions immediately after plastering or dry-lining is finished. You can get in and have a relatively free run at bare walls without having to fiddle around with skirtings, architraves, socket boxes, switch plates and radiators.

Another tip, this one for the stylistically challenged housebuilder, is to slap magnolia on everything. White is a bit too clinical for most people's taste; in contrast magnolia has enough cream in it to soften the overall effect without making any loud statements that will clash with furnishing choices made later on. If you are in a hurry and don't want to be bothered planning colour schemes, then magnolia is the answer. It's also a boon in homes shared with small children where walls have an endearing habit of getting drawn on. Dull but true.

Woodwork

Interior woodwork gets very similar treatment to exterior woodwork. Traditionally, that meant a three-coat gloss paint system. Increasingly it means that woodstains are used instead.

Floors

I'm tempted to say that varnishing is vanishing but I wouldn't be so daft; its use is, however, much more limited than it used to be. Externally – where it is prone to blistering and flaking – it has been replaced by the woodstains. However there is still a place for varnishes indoors on any exposed timbers, most notably hardwood floors. Some you can buy pre-lacquered, which is easy, but most require some form of surface treatment. The quickest route is to apply as hard a sealer as you can find – Dulux's Diamond Glaze is often chosen as it's as hard as they come. The problem with this approach is that, given time,

even the hardest coatings wear through and then you are faced with a re-sand. The other approach is to use an oil and to be prepared to re-apply it regularly. This is fine in rooms like bedrooms but it's an almighty drag in kitchens and hallways. Actuallly, the truth is that hardwood floors require maintenance if you want them to continue to look fantastic, whichever surface treatment you choose.

Specialist finishes
Artex textured ceilings

Don't think that Artex is a replacement for painting as well as plastering. It has to be painted to stop the smell, and emulsioning Artex is a good deal more time-consuming than going over a flat surface. Many of the big housebuilders still specify Artex on their ceilings throughout, presumably because of problems they have experienced with cracking in plastered ceilings. Dry-lining, which is now prevalent on internal walls, can of course be applied to ceilings as well but the taping and jointing work needed to finish it is more complicated because there is always a much higher number of cuts and joints on ceilings than on walls.

Wallpaper

It's not so very expensive but wallpaper is right out of fashion at the moment. You could wallpaper the benchmark house throughout for around £800 over and above the cost of slapping on a basic emulsion.

Paint effects

There has been a considerable revival of interest in near-forgotten painting techniques like stippling and rag rolling. If you are at all interested you will probably already have a book by Jocasta Innes and there's really nothing more to add. However, if you want to dip your toes in it but are afraid that you might get stoned on scumble glazes then you can cheat and use one of the new proprietary two-tone paints like Dulux's Duet. However, I don't think Jocasta would approve somehow.

Shingle and gravel

This is the cheapest option and, in many rural situations, the most attractive. It's particularly suitable for long drives. However, note that the better gravel driveways are actually labour intensive as they involve laying three or four layers of stones, each rolled and then left for a day or two between coats. Edgings need to be placed – treated timber strips are adequate – and the success of the drive overall depends on good hardcore beneath.

Top coat materials shouldn't cost much more than £1.00 per sq m but laying costs are likely to be high, especially if there's no mechanised plant available.

Quotes to supply and lay a gravel drive often specify a simpler two layer application as this keeps the price down to around the £7 per sq m mark (excluding foundation works).

Resin-Bonded Driveways

Available from specialist firms, these work by sticking small stones into a rigid sheet to give a shingle-look driveway which is as hard and durable as concrete or tarmac. Fantastic product if it's done properly but can be a disaster if not. Prices tend to start around the £30 per sq m mark (excluding hardcore foundation work).

Fancy paving options

There are many other materials available to lay paths and, in particular, patios. Labour costs for laying vary widely (£5-£15 per sq m) depending on whether they can be laid wet or dry and whether they need pointing-up afterwards. Wet laying involves using cement (albeit usually a dryish mix) and tends to be very much more labour intensive. Some hardcore backfill is usually advisable though when it is designed for foot traffic only it does not need to be laid as deep as it is under driveways. Materials choices include:
■ Plain paving slabs: £4.00-£5.00 per sq m
■ Riven paving slabs (textured surface): £6.00-£7.00 per sq m
■ Heritage paving (simulated natural stone): £15 per sq m

■ Natural York stone flags (the real McCoy): £50 per sq m
■ Granite setts: £40 per sq m
■ 75mm Beach Cobbles: £15 per sq m
■ Reconstituted stone: £25 per sq m.

Marshalls of Halifax are the largest supplier of manufactured pavings (and garden walling effects). Their brochures, which are widely available at builder's merchants, are a good starting point in assimilating some possibilities. They also have a wide choice of block pavers (both concrete and clay) and paving slabs.

Natural stone slabs, setts and cobbles are widely available though you have to search them out from smaller suppliers and quarries: try Harris & Bailey. Blanc de Bierge produce an attractive honey-coloured range of reconstituted stone slabs and sets which cost around £20 per sq m. Be aware that prices are usually quoted ex-works and that transport costs are likely to add between £100 and £250 to the total depending on amount and distance.

Specialists

Laying a drive should not be beyond the competence of a good builder yet many people prefer to subcontract the whole process to a specialist, typically found in the Yellow Pages under Asphalt and Macadam or Paving Services.

Before you do this, I would like to draw your attention to a 1995 Which? report which revealed a staggering range of prices as well as some uncompromising high pressure selling tactics associated with national companies advertising through magazines and usually (but not always) selling patterned concrete or resin-bonded driveways. In this Which? report, prices for one 60 sq m driveway varied from £329 to £6,210! The table gives a flavour of the middle range of driveway prices. I would tend to steer clear of both the very cheap quotes and the very expensive ones.

Finally a plug for www.pavingexpert.com, a website maintained by paving guru Tony McCormack, where you can find out more than you possibly ever wanted to know about the black art.

External Works - Key Rates

Labour charged at		£ 18 /hr			
	Mats	Time Taken in mins	Labour @ £18/hr		Combined
150mm Hardcore base	£ 2 m²	20	£ 6 m²	£ 8	m²
100mm concrete slab	£ 5 m²	25	£ 8 m²	£ 13	m²
2 coat tarmac	£ 5 m²	30	£ 9 m²	£ 14	m²
75mm Gravel	£ 1 m²	30	£ 9 m²	£ 10	m²
Paving slabs	£ 7 m²	30	£ 9 m²	£ 16	m²
York stone	£ 40 m²	40	£ 12 m²	£ 52	m²
Simple kerbs	£ 2 m	30	£ 9 m	£ 11	m
Plain Block pavings	£ 8 m²	30	£ 9 m²	£ 17	m²
Fancy Block setts	£ 20 m²	30	£ 9 m²	£ 29	m²
Block kerbs	£ 6 m	30	£ 9 m	£ 15	m
Turfing	£ 2 m²	12	£ 4 m²	£ 6	m²
Post and 3 Rail Fencing	£ 5 m	20	£ 6 m	£ 11	m
Palings	£ 4 m	20	£ 6 m	£ 10	m
Picket Fence	£ 8 m	20	£ 6 m	£ 14	m
Close Boarded Fence (1.8h)	£ 20 m	45	£ 14 m	£ 34	m
9" brick wall with piers (1.8h)	£ 120 m run	360	£ 110 m	£ 230	m

Benchmark House - Externals

	Area/Length	Rate	Lab	Mats	Total
Base Preparation	150 m²	£ 8	£ 900	£ 300	£ 1,200
Block Paving Setts	100 m²	£ 29	£ 900	£ 2,000	£ 2,900
Tarmac	50 m²	£ 14	£ 450	£ 250	£ 700
Close boarded Fencing	50 m	£ 34	£ 700	£ 1,000	£ 1,700
Turfing	130 m²	£ 6	£ 520	£ 260	£ 800
		Total	**£2,600**	**£3,500**	**£6,100**

■Fencing and turfing

Fencing

If you just want to mark a boundary and are not too bothered about privacy or security, then the cheapest permanent option is the timber post-and-rail fence. This arrangement shouldn't cost more than £10 per lin.m (Mats £4, Lab £6); it looks fine and is easily maintained. If you have longish (30m plus) lengths to erect, then the cheapest suppliers are to be found in the pages of Horse & Hound (down below £8 per lin. m). Alternatively, a chain link fence will cost a similar amount and, though less attractive, is more secure and should stop dogs and children straying to boot.

Another cheapish option are 1.2m-high chestnut palings (costing around £5 per lin.m) which, being vertical, are much harder to get over. They are easily fixed – just whack posts in

every 2m or so – but have a temporary air about them which may not appeal to all. The picket fence is similar in design but altogether more permanent in appearance but it costs around £15 per lin.m (M £9, L £6).

If you require privacy and security then you will have to go for a solid or near solid fence with a height of 1.8m (above head height). The traditional way of doing this is to erect something similar to a post-and-rail fence and then to cover it with vertically fixed, featheredge boarding. This is known as a close-boarded fence. Expect it to cost around £25 per lin.m (M £15, L £10). It is a little cheaper to use ready-made panels of the type you see in garden centres but the result is very flimsy in comparison. There are many variations on the theme of boarded fences; you can set the boards horizontally or diagonally, or alternate the boards between the inside and the outside

Post and rail £8/ lin.m

Palings £8/lin.m

Picket fence
£15/lin.m

Close-boarded
fence
£25/lin.m

of the fence posts (called hit and miss fencing). You can achieve quite stunning effects very simply and they don't have to be stained dark afterwards. If you want to investigate further, I recommend you get Jackson's Good Fencing Guide – it's free from Jacksons. They also deal with wire fencing which, I am assuming, is of lesser interest to would-be housebuilders.

Brick walls

Whilst timber fencing is getting expensive at around £30 per lin.m, you are not going to get even a whiff of a brick boundary wall under £100 per lin.m and, if you use a nice brick and build up to head-height, the cost will be around £200 per lin.m. This is a different animal altogether and ideally should be erected along with the main house so as to combine economies of scale – not to mention getting JCBs into the back garden. A 1.8m-high brick wall is actually a rather vulnerable construction, prone to blowing over in howling gales, and best practice advice now recommends that all unsupported walls over a mere 650mm high should be built two brick skins thick (225mm). In exposed locations, a 1.8m-high brick wall should be built 330mm thick. Whether your

wall is freestanding or is being built as a retaining wall against some high ground, your building inspector will advise you as to the exact requirements needed. Dry stone walls are, needless to say, even more expensive, costing around £300 per lin.m for a waist-high one.

Turfing

A detailed look at landscaping lies beyond the scope of this book, but I feel I must cover turfing at least because most developers consider it part of their remit to make a garden look acceptable, if not exactly inspired. Indeed, as with fencing, the VAT office allows you to reclaim VAT on purchases of turf when erecting a new house: unfortunately for keen gardeners, the VAT line is drawn at turf.

Of course there's more to it than just laying the turf. After the builders have done their bit, the average plot resembles a World War One battle ground (hopefully without the bodies) and the site has first to be cleaned of debris. Usually, it is then rotavated, levelled and rolled, and normally a selective weed killer is applied to prevent thistles taking over. Turf itself usually costs around £2 per sq m to purchase; the preparation work and the laying will cost around £3 per sq m, more if the work is particularly arduous or if there are slopes involved. If extra topsoil is needed, this costs around £10-£20 per cu m. You can halve the cost of turfing if you seed the area instead but this can be a bit hit and miss: seeding is best carried out in September, though you can often get away with it in springtime as well. You need to be lucky with the rain or else you will have to water for about eight weeks.

Chapter 11
Room by Room

Kitchen design

Kitchen units

Sinks

Kitchen worktops

Kitchen appliances

Kitchen waste

Bathrooms

Bedrooms

The home office

Conservatories

Garages

■ *Kitchen design*

The kitchen is the most expensive part of the house to build. Whereas unfurnished spaces (such as bedrooms and living rooms) cost around £600 per sq m and bathrooms around £800 per sq m, the spend on the kitchen area is likely to be in excess of £900 per sq m.

This is perhaps a slightly misleading statistic because only the kitchen and bathrooms are finished at the building stage; everywhere else has to be furnished by the homeowner. But even so, if insurance company figures are anything to go by, the average home has just £20,000 of stealable fittings and, looked at on a pounds per sq m basis, that only adds £250 per sq m to floor area costings. So, whichever way you look at it, kitchens remain the most expensive item in the contemporary house.

Benchmark kitchen

The kitchen in our benchmark house occupies a huge slug of the ground floor. The main kitchen area is a rectangle, 7m long and mostly 5.5m wide, save for a chunk taken out by the stairwell. In addition there is a utility/laundry area between the hall and the attached garage. This is one aspect of the overall house design that doesn't work so well – having to cross the hall to get from the kitchen to the utility. Combine the two areas and you have 40 sq m of kitchen, 20 per cent of the overall living space. Of course, compared to kitchens of old, the room is much more of a living room. The family will eat in there and doubtless congregate there before and after the day's work is done.

What prominence you decide to give to the kitchen is the most difficult internal design decision that you will be faced with. The two extremes to opt for are:

■ the kitchen as utility area (hidden from view and servicing a separate dining room)

■ the kitchen to be the main living area of the home, typically called an open-plan arrangement.

The trend is towards the open-plan kitchen; this suits the kitchen suppliers as it means a) bigger kitchens and b) consumers are more conscious of the way their kitchens are going

Benchmark House - kitchen costs		Unit price	Mat cost	Labour	Combined
Rigid Kitchen Units	13 m³	£ 550	£ 7,150	£ 650	£ 7,800
Slate Worktops	10 m run	£ 250	£ 2,500	£ 300	£ 2,800
Fix Sinks into Worktop	2 no			£ 80	£ 80
Range			£ 1,200	£ 90	£ 1,290
Washing Machine			£ 350	£ 60	£ 410
Dishwasher			£ 350	£ 60	£ 410
Kitchen Sink			£ 100	£ 150	£ 250
Belfast Sink			£ 100	£ 150	£ 250
Utility Sink			£ 60	£ 150	£ 210
Total			£ 11,800	£ 1,690	£ 13,500

to look. If you accept the notion that you want your kitchen to be the most important room in the house, then you are probably prepared to spend a much larger sum on making it beautiful. On the other hand, if you want to keep costs down, design your kitchen more as a utility area and have a separate dining room where you eat.

Mud rooms and larders

Many designs relegate the utility area to little more than a laundry room, but for many people, particularly country dwellers, a proper mud room would be far more useful; somewhere warm and light to take off wellies and wet coats, to air clothes, for dogs to sleep in. It's the natural place for a back door, but to do it properly requires a surprising amount of space. They are not called mud rooms for nothing; for as much as six months every year, just going out into the garden is a seriously mucky business and the interface between inside and outside needs thought.

The separate larder is an old idea coming back into fashion. This can be a small room and doesn't need any daylight but to work well it needs to be easily accessed from the kitchen preparation area. Ideally you locate it against an outside wall that doesn't face south and you exclude it from the insulated shell of the house – that way it stays cool. You may want to give some attention to airflow (strategically placed airbricks) and to draught proofing around the door. If your design can't handle all this, then even an internal, heated larder is useful if only to store dried food and crockery: it's

much cheaper than fitting it all into expensive kitchen units.

Grasping the kettle

When you've come to some conclusion about how you want your kitchen to work with the rest of the house, you can then get down to the nuts and bolts design matters of what goes where. It is usual to start with a list of household appliances. If you have opted for a separate utility area, this will be the natural home of washing machines and tumble dryers and, possibly, freezers. The kitchen proper must have a sink, some sort of cooker and a fridge. Dishwashers are now almost ubiquitous and are conventionally placed close to the sink. The positioning of your appliances around the kitchen becomes the skeleton on which the kitchen furniture is hung. There are some conventional dos and don'ts to consider:
■ DO locate sinks and plumbed-in appliances where waste pipes can get to the drains. Usually this means placing them against an outside wall.
■ DO locate cooker hoods against an outside wall where exhaust fumes can be evacuated. You can run ducting to get around this problem but it is a fiddle best avoided.
■ DO leave worktop space either side of both the sink and the hob (or cooker top).
■ DO keep the sink, the hob and the fridge reasonably close to each other. Simply for the sake of convenience. Some kitchen planners will go on at length about the importance of the work triangle in the kitchen. Politely ignore them.
■ DON'T place a hob or a sink in a corner

unless you consider an angled corner arrangement (expensive); corners tend to make poor working/storage space.

■ DON'T place a fridge or freezer next to or under a heat source (hob, cooker, radiator).

■ DON'T forget to consider the boiler if it needs to be in the kitchen. Not only will it be hot but there are rules concerning just where you can and can't place boiler flue terminals (see Chapter 8, section on boilers).

■ DON'T put wall cupboards over the sink; conventionally, sinks go under windows and for most small- or medium-sized kitchens this will always be the most practical location.

If you're a neat, logical kind of person, having got this far you should be able to draw a layout plan on some graph paper and begin to get an idea of the number of units you will need. Congratulate yourself because you're the kind of client any kitchen supplier would be pleased to have – you actually know what you want!

■Kitchen units

The fitted kitchen is an invention of the late 20th century. In the Sixties, a kitchen cabinet was thought of as something to do with Harold Wilson's unique government style. But shortly thereafter, the fitted kitchen arrived in the home in a big way. And, bit-by-bit, we have learned to spend more and more money on our kitchens. There are several procurement routes, each with its own pitfalls. Whilst the bulk of the new kitchen market now goes into replacing existing kitchens, a significant chunk gets accounted for by the 150,000-odd new homes built each year. And whilst a penny pinching spec housebuilder may spend as little as £2,000 on fitting a kitchen on a starter home, you only have to open a Sunday newspaper to realise that some people are happy to spend over £100,000 on a fitted (or perhaps an unfitted) kitchen. Bigger of course, better undoubtedly, but not fifty times bigger or better.

Just shelves with fancy doors
When we think of fitted kitchens, we think of

how the door fronts look. The kitchen dream sellers are well aware of this and, although the actual units may make up only 25 per cent of the final bill, these are how kitchens are sold to us. New fashions have come but they've never really gone so kitchen design continually expands to incorporate new ideas whilst simultaneously recycling the old ones. The basic manufacturing process is relatively simple and cheap so that no new idea can ever be free from imitators for more than a few months.

The kitchen business is fully metricated and works in modular units which increase in 100mm intervals. Thus any given range of floor units or wall cupboards will be available in widths of typically 300mm, 400mm, 500mm and 600mm; 600mm is the key one, this is the building block of the fitted kitchen – appliances are conventionally made to fit into 600mm gaps. The other sizes tend to get used to fill awkward gaps between the 600mm units. By twiddling the plan about a bit, you can fill any space on any wall to the nearest 100mm – and they sell blanking-off pieces to cover any little gaps left over. So give a kitchen designer a space that's 3600x2400mm and they will tend to think of it as six units long and four across.

All but the most expensive kitchen unit carcasses are made from a wood pulp board like chipboard or MDF, usually covered with a melamine veneer which serves both to make them stronger and moisture resistant. The cheaper doors, which are hung over these carcasses, are made of similar materials, though here the melamine covering is usually decorated with some trim. Solid timber is a more upmarket door option and there are more adventurous designs using materials such as stainless steel and plastic.

Flat pack DIY kitchens
There are several ways of getting fixed up with a kitchen. About the cheapest is to go to one of the giant DIY retailers such as B&Q, MFI or IKEA and buy yourself a flat pack. The cheaper kitchens tend to be supplied flat packed and need assembling on site, a feat which in

Kitchens - Key Rates

	Unit	Cheap	Mid	Fancy	Time Taken in hrs	Labour
Kitchen Fittting Labour	£ 18	hr				
Plumbers/sparkies	£ 30	hr				
Kitchen Units - Flat Pack	m³	£ 300	£ 500	£ 700	3.5	£ 70
Kitchen Units - Rigid	m³	£ 340	£ 700	£ 3,000	2.5	£ 50
Worktops	m run	£ 20	£ 80	£ 250	1.5	£ 30
Kitchen Sinks	ea	£ 60	£ 100	£ 300	5	£ 150
Hob	ea	£ 100	£ 300	£ 800	3	£ 90
Fit Elements into Worktops	ea	-	-	-	2	£ 40
Washing Machine	ea	£ 225	£ 350	£ 800	2	£ 60
Dishwasher	ea	£ 200	£ 350	£ 700	2	£ 60
Extractor	ea	£ 50	£ 150	£ 1,200	2	£ 60
Oven	ea	£ 200	£ 300	£ 800	3	£ 90
Range Cooker	ea	£ 600	£ 1,200	£ 3,000	3	£ 90

theory is straightforward but in practice can be damned difficult, especially when it takes you two days to realise you haven't got all the bits. Which? magazine surveyed six major flat pack outlets in Jan 2002, namely, B&Q, Focus, IKEA, Jewson, MFI and Wickes, which is owned by Focus but continues to trade independently. On price there wasn't much to choose from, as you might expect. They concluded that the two key things to look for were adjustable legs, to take account of uneven floors, and drawer quality. Only the most basic units didn't have adjustable legs but the drawer quality varied considerably from inadequate wooden runners (MFI) to poorly designed metal runners (most) to three rollers (IKEA). Pretty much on this count and this count alone IKEA came out tops in their survey. 'The best quality units we tested,' they wrote, adding the barb, 'provided you can follow the instructions.'

They might have added a few more barbs because as any experienced IKEA shopper knows buying things from IKEA is often a fraught experience. My old mucker, Robin Gomm, fits a lot of IKEA kitchens these days and he reckons his main problem is in getting hold of all the right parts. 'Always allow for at least two visits to the store, sometimes three,' he says. Apparently, IKEA's service is nothing short of excellent in most of the many other countries they operate in but not so in the UK where pre-ordering is a no-no but items are routinely out

of stock. Per head of population, the British are the world's largest consumers of IKEA products so the Swedes who run the operation have obviously worked us out to a tee. Some suspect it's a deliberate ruse to get us to go back time and time again because we can't stop spending money in the stores.

If you have seriously set your heart on an IKEA kitchen, get hold of their kitchen catalogue which is distinct from the main IKEA catalogue. There are items in the former which don't appear in the latter.

Another point well worth garnering about flat pack kitchens is that you are buying the materials, not the fitting out. Consequently, they look much cheaper than all the other options, which come on a supply and fix basis. Now B&Q may well have a few trade cards stuck at the back of the store with names of recommended installers but tread with care here. Installing a kitchen is a complex multi-task of a job involving co-ordinating fitters, plumbers, sparkies, tilers and fitters all over again. It's not just a question of getting hold of some bloke handy with a screwdriver, he must be bloody useful with a mobile phone as well.

The Continentals

The more innovative and interesting designs are the preserve of the upmarket kitchen. The Germans were the first into this pond in the Seventies when names like Wellman, Allmilmo

Benchmark Kitchen: note the Butler's sink and the granite worktops. The units are from Pineland Kitchens.

and, most notably, Poggenpohl came to the UK. Like all things German, they have built up a reputation for superbly crafted kitchens. In terms of style however they've been left in the slow lane. The high-tech, Continental look is now led by the French and, especially, the Italians – look out for Boffi's futuristic designs from Alternative Plans.

Smallbone, etc.

Despite exporting barely any kitchens at all (we import about 20 per cent), the British have responded to the threat of mainly upmarket invasion by inventing a whole new romantic theme – sometimes known as the English Revival style or, more often, doing a Smallbone. Smallbone – which started as an antiques business in Wiltshire – led the way in creating a new vernacular kitchen, which managed to strike some chord in the English middle-class psyche and led people to pay vast sums to recreate a past that never existed. Using many revived techniques and idioms (rag rolling, marbling, Welsh dressers), they created a magnificent, seductive illusion. To purchase the actual Smallbone marque is now expensive – though not necessarily poor value – but the style has spawned hundreds of imitators. This school of kitchen design has grown away from providing modular boxes towards what has

become known as the unfitted kitchen – an Aga here, a beech block table there, terracotta tiles on the floor, wicker baskets hanging on rails, you can almost smell the garlic and olive oil.

Some of these upmarket companies must be approached directly, many have just one UK outlet. The nearest thing to a directory exists in the back of 'Kitchens, Bedrooms and Bathrooms' magazine which will give you an overview of the market's top end.

Kitchen boutiques

Another approach is to ignore the plethora of manufacturers and concentrate on your local kitchen specialists. Most small towns have at least one, and a regional shopping centre will have several – check Yellow Pages. Most will stock only three or four manufacturers' products but as manufacturers offer sometimes hundreds of options (especially in door colours) this can still be quite bewildering. Typically, they will stock a mass-produced British flat-pack product (like Ram Kitchens or Symphony) which they will use to try and compete with MFI and Co, but the bulk of their showrooms is given over to displaying a more upmarket Continental range. They make more money on the more expensive kitchens so it is understandable that it is these that they promote.

Many people are rather reluctant to set foot inside a kitchen specialist as they think it would be a) too expensive and b) involve high-pressure selling. By and large, this is not the case; though they probably cannot compete with MFI on kitchen unit price alone, they are usually owner-managed and tend to give a high level of personal service without resorting to any pressure tactics. Unlike the major retail outlets, prices are usually negotiable and this makes it hard to compare on a like for like basis.

The builder

If you are fitting a kitchen as part of a much larger project (i.e. building a house) then it may make sense to keep the work in house and ask your builder to fit it. That's if you are still on speaking terms by the time you have reached the kitchen fitting. There are several outlets (principally builder's merchants and joinery centres) that aim to sell mainly to builders and they have kitchen catalogues available to browse through and sometimes showrooms to visit.

The major joinery firms – Jeld Wen, Premdor, Magnet – all produce fitted kitchens though, stylistically, they tend to be the most conservative of all. Their catalogues are easy to get hold of and clearly priced. The builder can buy these units (and the accessories) at discounts of between 20 to 40 per cent off list price and many will be happy to negotiate to share at least some of the discount with you – see section on Contracts in Chapter 5, 'Project Management', in particular find out what a PC Sum is. Even so, the prices from the volume joinery majors, even with full discount, will be slightly more than the cheapest available from the likes of MFI; but there is one big advantage if your builder fits the units and that is that he will remain responsible for sorting out any snags. If, on the other hand, you supply your own units to your builder and, say, the hinges work loose or there are unsightly gaps here and there, then you'll have your work cut out trying to convince him it's his fault: indeed you'll have fallen into one of the contractual traps placed along the route.

Bespoke kitchens

Before the advent of Smallbone, getting a joiner to make up a kitchen for you was always thought of as the most expensive option. If you choose to have doors made up out of gale-blown timbers, etc., this can still prove to be expensive enough but, with the advent of MDF, simple handmade and handpainted kitchens can be surprisingly cheap. Almost all kitchen carcassing (i.e. the bits you don't see) is made up of chipboard or MDF. You can buy 18mm thick MDF board in 2.4x1.2msheets for as little as £15 per sheet and get it machine cut for under 50p per cut. A sheet will make up an averaged-sized kitchen carcass and door; add a little for ironmongery and knobs, paint or varnish, design a simple trim and plinth detail and – lo and behold – you've got all the materials for our standard kitchen at less than half the price of MFI's cheapest. Get hold of the Hafele catalogue and you suddenly have access to all the same ironmongery as the kitchen manufacturers do (because they use the same catalogue). Carousels, fancy pedal bins, you name it, they are all in there.

Even though a competent joiner would take little longer to assemble this kitchen than he would a flat-pack, there are still remarkably few takers for such a design. This is probably a result of marketing failure as much as anything else. There are many economies in fabricating on site but most people are simply unaware what they might be. There are substantial design limitations – glass doors, friezes, fielded panelling and other complicated motifs are best carried out in factories – but there is, however, undoubtedly a niche for kitchen designers to create simple made-on-site kitchens which will accommodate the limited budget. This would be much closer to the ideal of the Shaker kitchen than those maddeningly expensive ones that carry that currently fashionable title.

Costs

Strange as it may seem, you can quite easily compare kitchen unit costs by the cubic metre. It's actually quite helpful because it gives you

In 1999, IKEA joined the ranks of the unfitted kitchen set with a range called Varde. All the units are free standing, making it easy to alter, renew or add on to. The birch worktops are placed on top of the work units. There are matching wall units from a range called FAKTUM.

a handle on both basic cost and quantity. You need to carry out a few measurements: basically the length, depth and height of the units. You don't have to measure individually – work in blocks of units.

Floor units are conventionally 700mm high and 600mm deep. Over-worktop wall units are also 700mm high but only 300mm deep. A small starter kitchen will typically consist of around 2 cu m of units: in contrast, our benchmark house has 13 cu m of units (made and fitted by Pineland Kitchens). Down at the MFI flat-pack end of things, unit costs are £250 per cu m. The upmarket bespoke options can be ten times this amount, supplied and fitted.

■*Sinks*

Stainless Steel

Stainless steel sinks now represent the cheap and cheerful option, which is perhaps surprising because in many other contexts stainless steel is regarded as an expensive material. Steel is actually a very good choice of material for a sink; it's strong, lightweight and easily cleaned. However, it is something of a victim of its own success because stainless steel sinks became so ubiquitous in the Sixties and Seventies that people started to choose other materials just to

be different. It also suffered from the fact that it was a one-colour product at a time when kitchens were becoming colour coordinated.

The very cheapest kitchen sinks now tend to be stainless steel; single bowl/single drainers can be picked up for less than £30, a set of taps for less than £20. However, the products from the big names in kitchen sinks (Fordham, Leisure, Carron, Franke, Blanco) can be every bit as expensive as coloured ones. Expect to pay £120-plus for something as good as a Franke one-and-a-half bowl sink.

Asterite

Asterite (which is made by ICI) is just the best known of many resinous silicone-based materials, all of them revolutionary and all with names that sound like bit players from Star Trek: Resan, Sylaca, Silquartz, Silacron, Novean, Astracast. Every sink manufacturer seems to have developed their own material (mostly made in conjunction with ICI). Whilst steel became stigmatised as being downmarket, these synthetics, typically coloured white, brown or something in between (usually christened Mocca or Cappuccino to add sophistication), took off in a big way. In terms of performance they offer no advantages over steel – in fact they are a damn sight harder to clean – but they do look good in kitchen showrooms, particularly with colour coordinated taps.

Asterite sinks are most commonly sold in packs. What this means is that you'll get a bundle of extras like sink racks, drainers and (maybe) a hardwood chopping board thrown in along with taps and waste fittings. If you don't mind obscure brands, then expect to pay around £135 for a one-and-a-half bowl sink pack. Generally it's worth paying an extra £15 to get taps with ceramic discs which, it is claimed, never drip.

Butler's sinks

The old fashioned butler's sink also tends to look a wow in the kitchen showroom, particularly when it is inset in a hardwood surround with drainage grooves. It's not changed from the original Victorian design (i.e. a large white rectangular box) and this adds an air of authenticity to it which nothing else in a modern kitchen can touch, not even an Aga (which hails from the Thirties). Consequently, it's become an item in all Smallbone-inspired kitchens and its very size and weight stand as statements of contempt for the standard mass-produced fitted kitchen. Butler's sinks, such as the Armitage Shanks Belfast, cost between £110 and £150 depending on size. Taps and waste are extra: these sinks are most definitely not sold in packs.

■ Kitchen worktops

The worktop is the name given to the main shelf in a kitchen where all the action happens — the food preparation, the cooking and the cleaning. Everything else is just storage. Getting the worktop right is a crucial part of kitchen design and, though it may not be the first thing you think about when selecting a kitchen, it will be the single most important element in your kitchen. The standard width for worktops is 600mm, which is sufficient for most kitchen configurations. Peninsulas, islands and breakfast bars may all require wider surfaces; there are a few extra-wide sizes available with two good

edges, designed for these types of applications. The cheapest option is 28mm thick white or near-white laminate which costs around £20 for a 3m length, available at DIY sheds or trade outlets like Magnet. However, if you want irregular shapes or fancy trims then you will need to go via a kitchen specialist and probably have to buy a more expensive laminate.

Expensive laminates

The patterned varieties are what the kitchen showrooms push. There are a few well known names like Formica, Polyrey, Resopal, Duropal and Beaumel; the showrooms often try to sell their own versions. They are usually sold in 40mm thicknesses which gives them a beefy feel — though provided the front is supported every 600mm the extra thickness is unnecessary. There is a far wider choice of colours and patterns but prices will be around three times the cheapest options — i.e. they start at around £60 for a 3m length or, if you prefer, £20 per linear metre.

Hardwood

These usually appear as thick strips of woods such as beech or oak which are glued and laminated into a solid board, usually available in two thicknesses, either 26mm or 42mm. You can either have them shaped up as a series of thin strips all bonded together or as wider planks, maybe 150mm wide, so that a 600 worktop would consist of four glued planks. Costs start at under £100 per lin m for beech, the cheapest hardwood, up to nearly double that for oak. Iroko is a popular mid-priced alternative. Ideally hardwood worktops need a little looking after — occasional oiling — and they also have a nasty little habit of staining if they get persistently wet, such as awkward spots behind sinks.

Granite

Granite has come from nowhere to become Britain's favourite worktop surface in the space of a decade. It's bloody expensive, rarely costing under £150 per linear metre run. Normally this supplies a 30mm thick slab which is sometimes fitted on to a timber sub-base for extra support. Holes can be cut for sinks and hobs (at around £100 per hole) and intricate moulded edges can be applied at £10 per lin m; drainage grooves can be cut at around £20 each. The benchmark house has used granite, cut and fitted on site by an interesting business called affordablegranite.co.uk. They turn up on site with the granite in the back of the van which doubles as a workshop. The granite is cut and finished on site. They fitted around 10 linear metres of worktop for under £2,500

Corian

Corian is a product that is used to make both worktops and sinks. It is best known for making it possible to 'weld' sinks seamlessly into the worktop so they appear to be one and the same item. It remains a bit high-tech for many people's tastes and a bit high priced for many people's pockets. What is it? Well, it's an inert mineral filler fixed in a matrix of methyl methacrylate polymer. Nuff said? It's a synthetic panel product but unlike the regular melamine laminates (which are actually just thin coverings stuck on chipboard) these boys are solid, heavy and smooth. Every kitchen specialist showroom boasts a Corian (or Corian look-alike such as Shock) sink-cum-worktop but they don't actually shift very many. There are an increasing number of alternative makes and some are beginning to get very much cheaper than original Corian. Look out for Silkstone which looks very similar but costs something akin to a mere £100 per m run, about half the price of Corian.

Trim options

The standard edge detail for laminate worktops is what is called Postform, which gives a curved finish to the front edge. You can get square-edged finishes but they are not recommended unless you are going to add some sort of trim to it. An otherwise cheap and cheerless laminate top can be made to look very much more attractive with the addition of an edge trim.

These can be applied by hand but it is difficult to do a professional job on site; if factory applied, it will approximately double the cost of a laminate worktop (budget £50 per lin m). Even more expensive trims are available – like Corian – which would push the price up by over £70 per lin m.

Jointing options

One of the problems in specifying laminate worktops, particularly ones with curved, postformed edges, is how to get around corners. The cheap option is to use metal jointing strips which stand up proud of the worktops and cover the gap where the two worktops meet. They are cheap, at around £3 each, but seamless they are not. Worktop fabricators offer various options for jointing worktops so that they appear to be one piece; straight runs are butt jointed from about £10; angles get a mason's mitre for around £15. If you are not going through a kitchen specialist then a useful contact is Allied Manufacturing who supply a wide range of kitchen fittings besides worktops.

█ *Kitchen appliances*

All prices quoted in this section will include VAT. Trade prices invariably exclude it whilst retail outlets invariably include it. Whichever way, new housebuilders in the UK cannot reclaim VAT on kitchen cookers or appliances with the sole exception of cooker hoods, which are regarded as a ventilation item.

Cooking

The standard practice today is to buy a built-in oven with a separate hob and a hood, often sold together in a package. Every supplier offers a choice of gas or electricity for your hob without any effect on price, but a gas oven is more expensive than an electric one. The budget developers' packages (Ariston, Whirlpool) are priced at around £300: you can buy similar packages from MFI or Comet for even less. Note that IKEA, such good value on kitchen units, is actually quite a rip-off on appliances, their best deal for a Whirlpool cooker/hob/fan package being £565. You can pick up a better-regarded brand name like Neff from one of the suppliers like Arrow for less than £400.

Appliances are mostly made to modular sizes so that they slip easily into any kitchen unit assembly so there is no compulsion to source your appliances from the same place as your units. Neither of course is there any compulsion to stick to the same brand of appliances throughout the kitchen, though for convenience many people do.

Stand alone/slot-in cookers

Go into Currys or Comet and you will still find a range of very Fifties style gas and electric stoves. I don't think very many go into new homes (unless you are specifically going for that Fifties retro-look) but they are very cheap. However, 21st century housebuilders all go for fitted ovens and hobs. The question is which oven, hob and hood? In recent years the choice has multiplied alarmingly making this once simple task extremely taxing.

Ovens

At the basic end you get a single electric oven with a timer clock and two or three functions. That is enough for 90 per cent of us. It'll cook a Christmas dinner, what more can you ask? Well, a lot. What's happened with ovens mimics what's happened with computers. They have grown more functions and controls. Take a top of the range Miele single oven. It comes with ten functions: true fan heat, top heat, conventional heat, bottom heat, intensive bake, fan grill, automatic roast, defrost, full grill, economy grill. It also has ThermoClean plus pyrolytic cleaning with Air Clean catalyser. Don't yer luv this stuff? You need to go on a course just to see how it works and, not surprisingly, Miele, along with a handful of other manufacturers, run cookery demonstration courses.

You can opt for a double oven which gives you a second cooking chamber, useful if you

want to cook things at different temperatures but for many people the top oven gets used as an eye-level grill – you don't really need any other functions.

Gas ovens

Built-in gas ovens are widely available but much less common than electric ones (though note that MFI stocks them); they tend to be more expensive and don't have many of the features of an electric oven. Their main selling point is low running costs – around 25 per cent of conventional electric cooking. The extra cost of a gas oven will pay for itself within five years if burning mains gas, and ten years if burning LPG. Only Stoves make a true gas double oven: more usually you get a grill compartment set over a separate oven but the grill chamber cannot be used to cook conventionally.

Specialist ovens

The relentless rise of the microwave has seen it elevated from being a countertop accessory to being a built-in second oven in its own right. Most people find it far more useful and flexible than having a double oven. Despite being limited in their uses, microwaves are excellent in a number of areas (e.g. cooking casseroles and fish, boiling vegetables, reheating, defrosting) where conventional cooking is cumbersome. They are quick, clean and energy efficient.

As an alternative to fitting a separate microwave unit, most manufacturers now make multi-function or combi ovens that include a microwave function. You can use these as either conventional only, microwave only or both functions at once which allows you to halve the cooking time for something like a joint or a chicken or roast potatoes but still get an element of crispy browning. However operating them in combined mode is quite complicated – it requires a whole new set of cooking skills.

Steam ovens sell themselves as healthy alternatives to microwaves. They tend to be quite small, not much bigger than a microwave, and they work by boiling water and blasting steam into the cooking chamber (some of them do this under pressure). Like microwaves, they are surprisingly versatile and can do much of the cooking undertaken on a hob as well as useful little jobs like defrosting and sterilising bottles. Again, it's a whole different approach to cooking which has to be learned afresh. Steam ovens are still quite a specialised item and they are not cheap, prices starting from about £600 from de Dietrich or Miele.

Hobs

Where they have a choice, most people go for a gas hob. Gas is fast, responsive and cheap to use: its drawbacks are that they are hard to clean and they have a dislike of pans boiling over. If mains gas is unobtainable, then consider having bottled gas just for the hob. A 19kg gas tank costs around £12 and should last about six months if it's only being used for a hob. If you use it for oven and grilling as well, you can switch to 47kg tanks with lower unit costs. Gas cooking has another big, often unspoken plus going for it in that it continues to work in power cuts, something many rural areas still suffer from frequently.

Whilst electric hobs have been seen as the poor relation, there are a number of developments that make them more interesting. First the ceramic hob came along which was easier to clean, if nothing else, but they perform only slightly better than conventional electric plates. They do, however, make a pleasing orange glow. More recently we have seen induction hobs which work via a magnetic field rather than an element. When magnetic pans are placed on the surface, a field is created which produces heat. The field is only generated where the pan touches so induction cooking is efficient and extremely quick – faster even than gas. Induction hobs are also horribly expensive – expect to pay around £750 for one of these beauties. And buy new cookware – it has to be magnetic.

The more upmarket suppliers can also fit you out with specialist hoblets where you can mix and match your cooking surfaces and include griddles and fryers as well as the more usual plates. Most manufacturers also give you the option of having extended hobs if you find the standard 600mm width a bit limiting.

Be aware that the standard electrical supply for electric cooking in the kitchen is a 30amp cable. This is only capable of supplying 7.5kW of power (you need 4 amps for each kW). Double ovens will use as much as 6kW with everything on and an induction hob or a five or six plate ceramic hob can take as much as 8kW with every ring in action. You can elect to either uprate your supply to 45 amp or run separate circuits for the oven and the hob.

Cooker hoods

In a new, draught-free house, condensation and cooking smells will not easily disperse without opening windows, so a cooker hood is nigh-on essential, especially as you have to have some form of extractor fan in a kitchen in order to satisfy building regs. You can have cooker hoods that merely 'recirculate' the air back into the kitchen but these are really nothing more than glorified grease filters. It's accepted as far better practice to enable your cooker hood to extract to the outside which obviously involves knocking a whole in the wall and connecting ducting to it. However, if you have a whole house ventilation system, you may want to hang onto some of the usable heat you are extracting and here a recirculator may make sense.

Cooker hoods now seem to come in four flavours. The standard version is a rectangular box which sits between 650 and 750mm above the hob: you get a three speed fan and a light (actually very useful) but they are cheap and usually noisy. There is an 'integrated' variety which gets concealed in an overhead wall cupboard and is activated by pulling the top-hung cupboard door open. Next a slimline or telescopic version which is typically no more than 25mm deep and these are turned on just by a gentle tug towards you; the fan itself sits in a dummy cupboard above.

The most upmarket option is to go for a canopy cooker hood which acts more like a conventional chimney: usually finished in stainless steel, look to pay north of £350 for this type. If you want to study how basic functional items have morphed into high fashion items, then the cooker hood would be a good subject. You can get one for £30 if you look carefully. You also pay more than £1,500 if you want, as much as a basic chimney costs.

Which make?

There is an awful lot of snobbery about kitchen appliances. Classy kitchens need white goods with German (or at least German sounding) names like AEG, Bosch, Neff or Miele (it's pronounced like Sheila). Very classy kitchens need classy German makes like Gaggenau. British manufacturers like Hotpoint, Tricity Bendix, Creda have reputations based on price rather than quality, as have Philips Whirlpool and most of the Italian manufacturers with the exception of Smeg (yes, they are Italian) who have levered themselves up to Premiership status. The very cheapest appliances often come with little-known brand names and obscure East European origins.

Getting confused? It gets worse. White goods branding is an extremely complicated area. There is much cross-manufacturing of parts and 'country of origin' labelling should more correctly read 'country of final assembly.' As an example, most European cooker hoods are made in Italy and perform to much the same (rather noisy) standard whether they are branded Candy, Neff or Creda. Much of the upmarket German kit is actually assembled in Turkey or Portugal.

No wonder purchasers often subcontract the decision making as well as the installation. Broadly speaking, if you want to create an impression then the brand names have to be German. The very best cookers tend to be German, but don't assume that a German brand name is necessarily a sign of quality. Also, if you want anything unusual like a built-in griddle you will need to seek out the high quality brand names. However, if low price is your main concern, then you should check out

Curry and Comet own brands or alternatively, if you want integrated appliances, look at MFI or specialists selling to developers – phone Arrow, Allied, BDC or Crangrove.

Agas

The Aga remains the item for the complete country kitchen. Despite their exorbitant cost (nothing less than £5,000 to purchase new plus the need for adequate foundations, suitable chimney arrangements and £300 fitting costs) and their exorbitant running costs (nothing less than £7 per week in fuel and annual servicing costs of £200), otherwise rational people still salivate at the thought of having an Aga in the kitchen. They can't do chips, they can't grill and boiling a kettle takes forever but, to quote the sales blurb: 'An Aga transforms even the most functional kitchen into a warm and welcoming gathering place for all the family. It becomes the heart and hub of your home.' The fact that this description is often spot on usually says more about the state of the rest of the house than any unique attributes of the Aga. Any large radiant heat source will be immensely attractive on a bitingly cold day and it's this aspect of the Aga – over half a tonne of hot cast-iron – which fuels its seemingly unending popularity. A large storage heater would fulfil the same function at a fraction of the cost but, I'm afraid, it would completely lack the necessary style.

If you are contemplating an Aga for your home, you must plan for it from the ground upwards. Though not designed as water boilers, for an extra £200 you can go for an Aga with a boiler capable of heating not less than 400 litres of water a day (i.e. enough for about eight people) and – provided yours is a new house qualifying for VAT zero-rating – you can reclaim VAT on the purchase which instantly saves around £500. Customs & Excise are usually happy to accept this distinction and they cannot insist that the boiler is ever connected to your hot water cylinder. Agas come in gas-fired, oil-fired, solid fuel and electric (Economy 7) versions. There are a number of cast iron stove makers besides Aga and they are usually quite a

Over the past ten years, the range cooker has become near ubiquitous in detached housing. Our benchmark house is no exception, fitted with a Rangemaster Elan, costing around £1,600 and fuelled by an LPG gas bottle in the passageway outside.

bit cheaper. Many of them incorporate boilers so that you can use them as both cookers and house heaters but although this sounds economical, it can be a mixed blessing when it's your only heat source – it's not so much a case of being warm in winter as boiling in the summer.

Ranges

There are alternatives between the splendour of the Aga and the industry standard 'tin boxes' which are sold as part of a fitted kitchen. When the first edition of this book came out in 1995, hobby cookers were unheard of. Now every kitchen showroom has them on display at prices starting at around £800, even less at Currys. They are now referred to as range cookers and they are about half as wide again as the industry standard 600mm so you get six rings instead of four. You can get them dual fuel so that you get an electric oven and a gas hob: indeed this is the most popular option. Which? road tested 12 ranges in Feb 2002 and was rather sniffy about them all. It's best buy was the dual fuel Flavel Cookmaster, costing around £850. But there are quite a few that cost over £2,500. The benchmark house got a Rangemaster Elan, pictured above.

Dishwashers

If you want a dishwasher, the big decision facing you is whether to go free standing or integrated. If you are buying a fitted kitchen you will come under a little pressure to go for an integrated one which will slip behind a kitchen-unit door so that you wouldn't know there was a dishwasher there at all.

Now, despite the integrated ones having less in the way of metal casing, they invariably cost more though sometimes it can be hard to compare because the models are not directly equivalent. But take a good, solid German make like Miele whose basic 638 model is available as both a free standing and an integrated unit. Free standing costs around £350, integrated – you'll do well to get one for less than £450. The divergence in costs is even more clearly illustrated at MFI where they sell a freestanding dishwasher (under their own Hygena label) at £199 but their cheapest integrated one (also badged as Hygena) is £399. Incidentally, if you want white goods with recognisable brand names like Bosch or Smeg, MFI is not the place to get them. Buy direct from a trade outlet or over the internet.

If you succumb to the allure of an integrated

dishwasher, you have a further choice to make. Whether to hide the entire machine behind your chosen kitchen unit door – that's known as fully integrated – or to let the control panel peep out at you in a way referred to as semi-integrated by some and as drawer line by others. Just as girls wearing tight Lycra cycle shorts are prone to exhibit an elastic knicker line, so kitchen units are said to have a drawer line, conventionally located at 200mm below the worksurface. The semi-integrated or drawer line units have the control panels located above the drawer line (same as the free standing dishwashers) and leave an infill space below designed to take a matching door panel. In contrast, the fully integrated dishwashers engineer the control panels so that they are actually located on the top edge of the door. You can only get to them by opening the dishwasher.

If you find the distinction between fully and semi integrated dishwashers all a bit too precious, then save yourself a couple of hundred quid and bung a free standing one in. And avoid stainless steel and save yourself another couple of hundred quid. Stainless steel looks good, photographs well but as anyone who has lived with one will tell you, they don't half show the fingermarks. If you want the stainless steel look to stay looking clean, then you need aluminium, which is even more expensive.

Laundry

You can get integrated washing machines and tumble dryers but generally these items get placed in a separate utility room and they are therefore normally purchased as free standing items. Hotpoint remain the biggest name in washing machines, accounting for 50 per cent of the UK market. Their basic stand alone models start at around £280; their Aquarius range starts at £400 and incorporates a number of green features (less water, less power, less powder). Hoover are one of the very few to offer a machine with a delay timer. The last time Which? surveyed washing machine reliability

in May 2002, Hotpoint and Hoover scored down near the bottom of 16 brands. The most reliable? Miele.

Tumble dryers

You don't have to get a tumble dryer to vent outside but it makes good sense. Full-size, air-vented dryers cost around £180 whereas the alternative option is to have a condensing dryer which are getting on for double the price. Tumble dryers are notorious energy guzzlers and one way you can save on running costs is to fit a gas tumble dryer. They are made by Crosslee under the White Knight brand name (though note that White Knight also do electric tumble dryers) and though they cost around £300 they will dry a drum of wet clothes for 10p, as opposed to 40p or so on an electric dryer. Whilst they may cost an extra £50 to plumb in, they will save that in running costs within two years. However, the truth is that gas tumble dryers are much slower than electric ones: the market for them is tiny.

Washer-dryers

The trend towards separate utility areas in larger houses has meant that there are few built-in washing machines and no built-in tumble dryers. Instead there are a large number of extremely expensive washer dryers costing from £500 upwards. They do save space but they are not as convenient as you might hope – they are only capable of tumble drying half a wash load at a time so they need unpacking between programs. They are also the most unreliable of all kitchen appliances.

Cold storage

There are numerous options of above- and below-freezing point storage and there are also numerous arrangements for their housing. You have the same decisions you get with cookers – whether to integrate or go free standing. Free standing is invariably cheaper. Or was until the arrival on our shores of the giant American fridges which you haven't a hope of integrating into any MDF kitchen unit. Now a

Plumbers Rates		
Labour rate used for calcs	£ 30 hr	
Fix Bathroom Suite (Bath/Basin/WC)	6 hr	£ 180
H+C Plumbing to Same	4 hr	£ 120
Waste from Suite to Stack	2 hr	£ 60
Fit Waste Stack (Ground to Roof)	4 hr	£ 120
Shower Fitting (inc H+C, Waste)	8 hr	£ 240
Bidet Fitting (inc H+C, Waste)	4 hr	£ 120
Fix Cloakroom Suite	4 hr	£ 120
H+C Plumbing to Same	2 hr	£ 60
Waste from Cloakroom to Stack	2 hr	£ 60
Fit Kitchen Sink (inc H+C, Waste)	5 hr	£ 150
Fit W/M or D/W (inc H+C, Waste)	2 hr	£ 60
Fit Outside Tap	2 hr	£ 60
Bathroom fittings - basic rates		
Toilet		£ 80
Basin plus taps		£ 60
Bath plus taps		£ 200
Shower Tray		£ 150
Shower Door		£ 100
Shower screen (door and side)		£ 200
Shower		£ 150
Copper pipe (m run inc fittings)		£ 3
Plastic pipe (m run inc fittings)		£ 4
Waste pipe (m run inc fittings)		£ 8
100mm Soil pipe (m run in fittings)		£ 4

claim that the effective standards are those imposed by the housebuying public, which seems to be about thirty years ahead of the building regulations in this instance.

Costs

The bathroom is a multi-trade zone. Do not be fooled into thinking that bathrooms are all about plumbing-in sanitaryware: that's just the beginning. Ventilation, wall tiling, mirrors, accessories, obscured glazing, enclosed light fittings, pull switches, towel rails (heated or otherwise) and specialised floor coverings all combine to make bathroom fitting a complex and elaborate process – and one that is easy to neglect in the hurry to finish a house. Bathroom planning is even more important in timber frame buildings because timber bearers should be present in the walls to secure all the fittings.

Bathrooms are expensive. The accompanying table shows costings for the two bathrooms plus downstairs cloakroom in the benchmark

house. This is a typical installation with a bath in the family bathroom and an enclosed shower in the en-suite bathroom. Bear in mind that it's not the size of the bathroom that is expensive but the fittings in it. Big bathrooms are becoming very popular; many people want to fit cupboards and furniture in them and the en-suite bathroom, in particular, seems to be getting bigger and bigger, eating chunks out of its attached bedroom.

Of the overall floor area of our benchmark house eight per cent (15sq m) comprises bathrooms and it's an expensive eight per cent; the combined bathrooms cost £200 per sq m more to fit out than bedroom space – the comparison is approximately £600 per sq m for regular living space and £800 per sq m for bathrooms. Only the kitchen is more expensive.

Shower cubicles are three times the price of a basic bath. Don't think you are saving water (and therefore money) by showering; an enclosed shower space is a luxury, and the extra £250-£300 over and above the cost of a cheap bath will not be paid for out of water saved, especially if you fit a power or mains pressure shower which uses a bath-load of water in three minutes.

Bathroom suites

Budget bathrooms are most usually sold as three-piece suites. Normally a bathroom suite includes:
■ Bath, bath taps, plug
■ Bath panels (to conceal the fact that the bath is plastic)
■ Basin and supporting pedestal
■ Basin taps and plug
■ WC, cistern, seat, handle.

If you don't buy a suite, you'll have to remember to get all these items separately – items like cistern levers are easily overlooked. If you want to opt for a separate shower instead of a bath you may be able to find a two-piece 'cloakroom suite' (be warned: cloakroom basins are often minute).

A very basic bathroom suite will cost £200-£250. You won't get high style at this price

Benchmark House - Plumbing Costs					
3 Bathrooms: ensuite and shower room are identical		Mats	Labour hrs	Lab our @ £30/hr	Combined
Toilet		£ 80	4	£ 120	
Basin		£ 60			
Shower		£ 150			
Shower Tray		£ 150	8	£ 240	
Shower enclosure		£ 200			
Pipes	12 m	£ 40	2	£ 60	
Waste	6 m	£ 50	2	£ 60	
Shower Room		£ 730	16	£ 480	£ 1,210
En-suite bathroom		£ 730	16	£ 480	£ 1,210
Family Bathroom					
Toilet/Bath/Basin		£ 340	6	£ 180	
Pipes	20 m	£ 60	4	£ 120	
Waste	12 m	£ 100	6	£ 180	
Family bathroom		£ 500	16	£ 480	£ 980
Totals		£ 1,960	48	£ 1,440	£ 3,400

but you will get a choice of six or seven pastel colours, which can be coordinated with tiles to at least suggest that you've tried. Most bathroom outlets have a range of four or five suites going up in price to around £400; after that, you get into more upmarket designs where all items come priced individually.

Prices tend to get softer as they get higher and trade discounts of 'no more than ten per cent' on budget lines suddenly rise to 30 per cent or more when your spend rises above £1,000.

Taps

To date, baths and basins have been available with all manner of tap arrangements. The old British standard of hot tap on the left and cold tap on the right has gradually been superceded by various mixer taps which are often extremely unintuitive. The government, in its wisdom, announced in 2004 that it wanted to make thermostatic mixer taps compulsory when it revises Part G of the building regs, probably in 2006. This is to prevent around 20 deaths and 600 serious scaldings which occur every year because of hot water in baths, in particular. The problem is that hot water is routinely stored at 60°C in order to prevent legionella bacteria from multiplying and 60°C is about 18°C hotter than you want a bath or a shower. Thermostatic taps premix the hot and cold water and include

temperature limiters to stop water going above a preset tempertature.

Accessories

Most suites offer a wide range of matching accessories (shelves, soap holders, loo roll holders, toothbrush holders, toilet brush holders, towel rails) at prices well over the odds for what you would pay in a DIY shed. Even on a fairly basic suite, you could easily spend over £100 on buying matching fittings, adding another 20 per cent to your suite price. If you want a bidet, expect this to add around 30per cent to the basic three-piece suite price.

Styles

There are currently two discernible streams of bathroom styling, mirroring the fashion in contemporary kitchens. One is towards modern looking, built-in fixtures; the other is harking back to Victorian and Edwardian times. The more money you spend, the greater the divergence of styles become. The major UK producers (Armitage Shanks, Ideal Standard, Shires, Twyfords) all plough this well-worn furrow. If you want something that transcends these styles, you'll have to look at continental brand names like Sottini or Roca or, if you want to get thoroughly minimalist, check out Vola UK who import all manner of weird and

Visit any bathroom showroom and it immediately becomes apparent that there is a style war in progress. Top: the Continental look, all sleek lines and curves. Bottom: Ancient British look, profoundly Eurosceptic.

wonderful sanitary sculptures like glass sinks. Sales literature is available at most plumber's and builder's merchants; also check out the growing number of bathroom boutiques – try looking in the Yellow Pages under Bathroom Eqpt. If you want something out of the ordinary, be aware that it may take many weeks for it to be delivered.

Period styling
Up till fifteen years ago, people were still stripping out period porcelain and nothing new had been produced since the Fifties. The return to fashion of these styles (always white or off-white) has been the one big success story for sanitaryware producers in the last few years and now every manufacturer produces sanitaryware to fit the period. The cheaper suites are priced at

£350-£400 but they don't look very authentic (Plumb Center's Bramham Suite is as good as any). Ideal Standard have produced suites in four period styles (Victorian, Edwardian, Art Deco, Country Cottage).

Authenticity comes at a price; the Victorians never had mahogany bath panels nor glazed shower screens. To get the full period effect, attention must be paid to the detailing throughout the bathroom. A roll-top, cast-iron bath that can stand on its own will cost £500 plus; a Dorchester heated towel rail £400. There are small craft producers, like Sanitan and Vernon Tutbury, producing authentic designs but such a bathroom can cost £3,000 just for the sanitaryware.

The modern look
This is the other dominant style in contemporary bathrooms. The porcelain styling is all curves and pastel colours, the taps look like mushrooms and lavatory cisterns are concealed. Basin vanity units can be purchased from the merchants (from £70) but a more pleasing alternative is to build tiled work surfaces on to which you place a semi-countertop basin (like Ideal Standard's Tulip, £70 plus taps). The essence of this style of bathroom is, not surprisingly, to match colours. If you want to do this, check that the British Standard colour numbers are the same – don't assume that 'Ivory' or 'Misty Peach' is the same colour for tile producers as it is for bathroom suppliers. You can also have your heated towel rails spray-painted to match bathroom suites (costs about £40 extra).

Whirlpool baths like the Jacuzzi will cost £2,000+ though the plumbing-in is relatively straightforward. Other ideas that you may come across are building in saunas or gyms; all of which will cost a great deal of money and good luck to you.

Showers
A rapidly growing market, showers are popular both as attachments to bath taps (known as shower mixers) and in their own right in stand-

alone shower cubicles. Apart from style – and there are showers to fit every style – there are two things to look out for: thermostatic control and adequate flow rate.

Thermostatic control

Thermostatic control automatically adjusts the balance of hot and cold water flowing through the shower head as other taps in the house turn on and off. It is expensive, usually adding around £70 to the cost of a shower. A cheaper alternative is to have a shower with a high-temperature limiter which will avoid scalding but may still leave you drenched in cold water when a hot tap opens somewhere else. Note that from 2006, thermostatic control is likely to be mandatory.

Shower power

There are many routes to getting a good pressure through your shower head. The most effective are to install a mains pressure hot water system or a thermal store (see section on Domestic Hot Water in Chapter 8, 'Services'). The least effective are to install an electric shower or a combination boiler, both of which heat water instantaneously and therefore suffer from low flow rates. In between these extremes come a whole gamut of power showers which aim to add whoosh to feeble pressure from tanks in the loft. There are single impeller pumps, which boost the water after the mixing valve, and double impellers, which boost both hot and cold before they enter the valve. Which you choose is partly dependent on the layout you have and prices are largely dependent on the power of the pump. They can be purchased for just over £100, but a pump delivering 30lts per minute (equivalent to a good mains pressure system) will cost £180plus. Leading manufacturers: Mira, Aqualisa.

There are a also number of integral pumped shower valves like the Triton AS 1000 . These tend to be a cheaper option (the styling is naff) and you end up with an unsightly box of tricks in the shower cubicle. There are also electric showers which work entirely off the cold main

and don't need a hot water supply, and electric showers like the Triton T90 (£300) which heat, pump and make thermostatic adjustments. The most ingenious (and probably the cheapest option) is the Croydex H20 shower (around £80) which uses the pressure from the cold main to force the hot water flow rate up. Alone of the power showers it doesn't need a power supply, but there's no thermostatic control and you can't use it with a combi boiler.

If you want a power shower in a new house, you would be well advised to avoid all these products and go for a mains pressure or near mains pressure hot water system. Having taken us decades to accept mains pressure hot water systems in the UK – they weren't admitted until 1987 – they have now pretty much swept the field in new housing : the days of water tanks up in the loft appear to be numbered.

Shower trays

Acrylic trays can be had for under £50 but they are not recommended because of problems with leaking caused by the trays flexing. The most popular option is the ceramic stone trays: Matki's is good (cost £75). For another £15 you can buy them with an undertile upstand which will minimise any possibility of leakage. The standard size is 760mm square (which suits the standard pivot doors). There is a significant (100 per cent) cost penalty if you want a larger tray.

Shower doors

You have a choice of building the shower into an alcove (with three side walls tiled), into a corner or free-standing against one wall. Pricewise there is little to choose – the cost of a tiled wall being similar to the cost of a glazed side panel. The alcove option usually looks the most professional; you finish the opening with either a pivot or a bi-fold door which will cost anything from £80 (Elbee, Laconite, Ram Niagra) to £200 or more (Matki, Daryl, Showerlux, Nordic). Matching side panels tend to be 60-80 per cent of the door price. If your shower is incorporated with your bath, then you have a choice of a simple shower curtain hung from a rail (from £30) to a glazed shower screen (£50 upwards).

Open Showers

What price open showers running into a floor drain? It's a detail regularly seen on the Continent and has been widely specified in this country in special needs bathrooms. You dispense with the tray and your enclosure need only be a shower curtain. The key component is the floor drain which has to be able to sit inside a floor void, to be able to cope with the 30 litres per minute which a power shower will throw, to include a trap and yet be readily cleanable which means that the grate and the assembly must be removable. In consequence, shower drains are relatively sophisticated and good ones cost over £100.

Manufactures include Harmer (part of the Alumasc group) and Caroflow and designs allow incorporation with either regular floor tile sizes or sheet materials such as Altro Safety Flooring. Altro's main shower product is Marine 20 which is a 2mm covering laid over floors and can be continued up walls as well. At just under £15 per sq m (material only), it is no more expensive than ceramic tiling.

The key to getting a floor shower drain to work well is to build in a fall of 1:40 for a metre around the floor drain. In masonry floors, this can be achieved relatively easily with a 25mm depression in the screed – the Harmer floor drain requires only a 25mm deep screed. However, you can rarely shave 25mm off the top of a timber joist without seriously weakening the floor so the usual solution is to build a fall up with firrings laid across the tops of the joists; this leaves you with a 25mm threshold at the bathroom door which needs to be addressed.

Open showers are not without their problems. Like it or not, you end up with a wet floor after using the shower and subsequent bathroom users don't really appreciate wet floors, especially if they are wearing shoes or socks.

Avoiding leaky showers

In theory, this is no problem; in practice, tiled shower cubicles often ship water where they shouldn't and tiled floors will tend to fare even worse. It really is worth paying a lot of attention to the construction of shower enclosures generally because their failure is one of the commonest faults in new buildings. Don't skimp on the linings – use a waterproof plywood or a waterproof board like Knauf's Aquapanel rather than regular plasterboard – and use the best adhesive you can afford to fix ceramic tiles with.

The key failure point, however, is the joint between the walls and the floor (or more likely tray) and with most designs you are dependent on a bead of silicone mastic to stop water finding a route through the defence. Your silicone sealant will stand a much better chance of success if the joint is tight and even, something which usually depends on how good your carpentry is. But failures can also occur in the tile grouting and around the shower fitting itself.

One ingenious way around the problem of leaking showers is to install an all-in-one moulded cubicle. Advanced Showers produce a range of elegant, stand-alone enclosures which, whilst not cheap (costing upwards of £600), are very quick and easy to install and will be valued by all those who have experienced the frustrations of shower leaks. Another option is to avoid timber joists in your first floor: it's the shrinkage in these joists (often as much as 8mm) when the house is drying out that causes most shower leaks. Specify either a beam and block first floor or something like a Trus Joist floor (see Chapter 7, section on Floors).

▉ *Bedrooms*

For developers, bedroom space is cheap space. All that really has to be provided is enough room to fit a bed and an item of furniture plus enough space to manoeuvre about between them – the technical term for this is swinging a cat.

The master bedroom in the benchmark house is built into the roof using attic trusses. Looked at in plan, it looks like a huge room but the raked ceilings give a cottagey effect, accenuated by the dormer windows

Design considerations

You can of course give far more consideration to the whole issue. It's worth visualising the layout of the bedroom furniture so as to work out where to place radiators and power sockets. Also it's a nice touch to arrange light switching so that it can be reached easily from the bed. On the other hand, if you want to maintain maximum flexibility, then fit power sockets on every wall so you can accommodate various layouts. In reality there may only be one sensible place where a bed can go, but there may be other considerations. What is appropriate as a nursery for a toddler is unlikely to suit a teenager and you should consider how the uses a bedroom gets put to will change over the years. Don't always assume that a bedroom will remain a bedroom.

Size

It is conventional to rank bedrooms by size. Now, you might think that in a four-bedroom house you would provide a double bedroom for mum and dad (or whoever tickles your fancy) plus three smaller but similar sized rooms for the children. But no; the British way of doing it is to build bedrooms in ever decreasing sizes. It's also the British way of doing things to rank houses according to the number of bedrooms they have. Almost all developers switch to four bedrooms when the overall floor size creeps over 110 sq m. I am pleased to say that the benchmark house we are using for this edition bucks this stupid trend and builds three bedrooms of similar size, only funking out on the study (aka fifth bedroom) which is substantially smaller. The ranking look like this

- Master bedroom   8.2 x 3.3   27 sq m
- Bedroom two   4.0 x 3.5   14 sq m
- Bedroom three   4.0 x 3.6   14 sq m
- Bedroom four   3.6 x 2.7   10 sq m
- Study (bed five)   2.7 x 2.6   7 sq m

Looking at it like this, in table format, you can see that strictly speaking they aren't similar size and that the occupant of Bedroom four is short-changed by 4 sq m. But if you take a look at the floor layout (in Chapter 2) you can see the logic that dictates the bedroom size. Everything upstairs in the house is located in the main aisle, excepting the master bedroom, which is built into the extension roofspace, using attic trusses. The main aisle is a 10 x 7.5m rectangle, dominated structurally by the load-bearing wall running across the aisle: it's not shown as such on the floor plan but it's the wall that divides bedrooms two and three from the stairwell and the study. This effectively splits the main aisle into two blocks, one 4m wide, the other 6m wide. The 6m wide block has to incorporate the stairs and the landing (whose dimensions are effectively fixed) and so the remaining rooms wrap around the landing. Given a 10 x 7.5m block and working to maximum spans of 4 m, this is a very logical design.

If you don't require so many separate rooms, you could easily leave out the odd partition wall here and there. For instance, bedroom four and the study could quite easily be reconfigured as one room.

Wardrobes

Not usually included by developers and not usually included in any summary of building costs, the wardrobe is, nevertheless, a near essential item in any bedroom. There are basically three approaches to creating bedroom storage space:
■ Use free standing furniture: it costs but you can take it with you
■ Use specialist bedroom fittings
■ Make your own.

The last method has one major advantage, recently agreed by Customs & Excise, in that it is regarded as zero-rated for VAT purposes. Typically you would design your bedroom wall partitions with various strategically placed kinks into which you slip a hanging rail and a few open shelves and then hang a door or two in front. It's probably the cheapest option for new housebuilders as the cupboards can be created as you go rather than being added on afterwards. Actually, Customs & Excise go into some incredibly complicated definitions of what constitutes a zero-rated wardrobe and I can't resist repeating them here, if only to convince you that this country is run by a committee of numbskulls. You can claim VAT back on wardrobes in your new home IF:

a) The wardrobe encloses a space bordered by the walls, ceiling and floor. But units whose design includes, for example, an element to bridge over a bed or create a dressing table are furniture and cannot be claimed.

b) The side and back use three walls of the room (such as across the end of a wall), or two walls and a stub wall. But a wardrobe installed in the corner of a room where one side is a closing end panel is furniture and cannot be claimed.

c) On opening the wardrobe you should see the walls of the building. These would normally be either bare plaster or painted plaster. Wardrobes that contain internal panelling, typically as part of a modular or carcass system, are furniture and cannot be claimed.

d) The wardrobe should feature no more than a single shelf running the full length of the wardrobe, a rail for hanging clothes and a closing door or doors.

PLUS Wardrobes with internal divisions, drawers, shoe racks or other features are furniture and cannot be claimed.

Now whether the Customs & Excise unit in Birmingham, dedicated to dealing with selfbuild reclaims of VAT, has enough time to check the details of how its selfbuild wardrobes are constructed is not considered. Of course they don't.

The kinked bedroom wall creates wardrobe space and satisfies the VAT office. It also adds to sound-proofing between bedrooms

Budget between £100 and £250 per fitted wardrobe, depending on the size, finish and complexity of the design; this would include shelving, hanging rails and a door or two. Magnet and the DIY sheds sell melamine wardrobe fitting kits, complete with hanging rails, at around £35 each.

The home office

Pick up any paper or magazine and you're likely to find articles about working from home, as if it had just been discovered as the panacea of all modern ills. This is completely daft. Working from home is what most of us always did, long before they invented factories and offices, and there are still loads of trades and businesses which have always worked from home. What is new is that there is a whole host of office workers who would previously have commuted some distance to work now padding a few feet down the passageway. Journalists in particular are able to work from home which is, just possibly, why you read so much about it in the newspapers and magazines. But my farming friends just scratch their heads and wonder what everyone is talking about.

What's the upshot of all this? Well, what most people think when they think of working from home is that they need an office, or at least some office space. The physical requirements for all this are remarkably small, usually satisfied by a few shelves and a working space serviced by a couple of power outlets and a telephone socket (two if you are greedy). There really isn't much designing to be done, you just take over the box bedroom and have done with it. Even if you are inclined towards the hi-tech office with PCs, faxes, printers, scanners, copiers, modems and the like, you still don't really need anything more in the way of infrastructure – though extra power points and phone sockets would certainly come in handy.

Planning issues

However, for many others, working from home will need considerably more thought. You may require meeting space or consultation rooms which are best kept quite separate from the rest of the household in order to maintain a professional atmosphere: sometimes this can be quite neatly achieved with an additional ground floor room which has its own external entrance. On the other hand, you may need workshop space which will create dust or noise or smell and which is ideally situated in a separate building. These are specialised concerns and really no one is going to understand them better than yourself, so it is pointless me wittering on. What I should point out though is that the more specialised and separate your workspace becomes, the more problems you are likely to encounter at the planning stage.

These problems are likely to hinge on whether you can extend the terms of the planning permission to include non-residential uses. Solo home office working is frankly not going to be an issue but anything that a) makes a lot of noise or smell or b) attracts a lot of visitors is not going to be passed through on the nod; in fact, it's probably unlikely to get passed at all if the area is zoned purely residential. However the buzz word of contemporary planning, sustainability, is on your side here. For decades the planning system has worked to separate the residential zones from the industrial zones on the premise that the two don't mix well, but as much of our working activities have become cleaner and quieter, the wisdom of this zoning has been called into question. Now the boot seems to be on the other foot because the car – more particularly the car journey – has become the bete noir of planning departments. Anything which can be done to reduce the number of car journeys is said to be sustainable, which is planning speak for a good thing.

Dedicated office?

Spec housing is still being built without dedicated office space though this is changing quite rapidly. Our benchmark house has a room upstairs designated as a study and another downstairs designated as an office and there are now many examples of developers building in a far more sophisticated level of home working so that the whole house resembles dedicated office space. Within 10 or 20 years, I expect this level of sophistication will be as standard as electrical power cabling has been, though there are difficulties in knowing just which standards will end up being adopted. More elaborate specifications are touched on at the end of Chapter 9.

If you are designing a one-off house and have no need for an office-level data infrastructure, should you be concerned? Probably not. Any future developments in home cabling systems will have to be capable of being retro-fitted into existing houses so you can afford to sit and wait and see what the future may bring.

It would be as well to bear in mind that, though you may not want a dedicated home office, future purchasers are likely to have such space high on their wish list. If there is a lesson to be learned here, it is to plan a little flexibility into the scheme you are designing. If you definitely want a home workspace then you should fit it out accordingly, but many people are not altogether sure that they do: instead of fitting one out from the word go, identify which room you think would be best for this purpose and at least specify a couple of extra power sockets and maybe first fix an extra phone line in.

■Conservatories

Adding a conservatory is big business in the home refurbishment market (200,000 new ones built each year) but comparatively small beer in the world of new building – only about one per cent of new homes are built with conservatories. Why should that be? Well, for one thing, a conservatory is usually more expensive to build than an ordinary extension. The substructural works are no different but both glass walls and glass roofing are more expensive than traditional building methods, and these combine to make the costs of conservatories range from around £500 per sq m to over £1,000 per sq m. In comparison,

the basic cost of an extension would be less than £400 per sq m (before fitting out). The reasons for this are not hard to fathom; whereas a developer might spend around £50 per sq m on external walling and £80 per sq m on roof carpentry and coverings combined, the cost of toughened double-glazed units alone is £50 per sq m and normally a conservatory's glazing costs are much less than the cost of the surrounding frames.

Conservatories also cost a lot to keep warm in winter and require specialised (i.e. expensive) blinds and fans if they are to be kept cool in summer. You can, of course, choose to not use your conservatory when it's either too hot or too cold or too dark, but that's an awful lot of times for a room that's so expensive to build, and it makes little sense when you consider the size of the initial investment. Furthermore, conservatories add little if anything to house values – not everyone loves them.

Alternatives

Adding a conservatory on to a new house is often a sign that the original design work is not what it might have been. Conservatories are expensive and problematical, and whereas they may make stunning and effective extensions to existing houses, their role in a new house is not at all clear. If you feel you need a conservatory to add that certain panache to your dream home, then you may just have under-designed the house in the first place. A rethink on the basic layout would probably save you money and give you a better house to boot.

If you want more living space, think of incorporating a south-side summer room (with lots of windows and a french/patio door) and a north-facing winter room designed for cosy dark nights around the fireside. If you really want glazed roofing, consider fitting two or more large Velux rooflights in a lean-to section. Veluxes are much easier to clean and are easily openable, making ventilation a doddle; this way you can achieve some of the benefits of a conservatory without the drawbacks.

New homes tend to work better with integral sun rooms, rather than out-and-out conservatories. To add on a conservatory is to indicate that the house was poorly designed in the first place.

Aspirations

Despite my reservations I must admit that there are certain situations where a conservatory comes into its own: Sunday lunch in April, reading the newspaper on a sunny winter's morn, sundowners on long summer evenings among the potted plants. Rather like an Aga, the conservatory forms part of many peoples' dreams of stylish living and, however inappropriate in a new house, some people cannot be without them. In advertising jargon, conservatories are another 'aspirational purchase' for romantics and who am I to decry their pleasures? Shame on my puritanical self.

Though not fundamentally different to any other types of building, conservatory construction has evolved into a specialist trade. Many glazing firms have branched out into designing and building conservatories, and many of them offer an all-in-one design and build service. Styles range from utilitarian greenhouse to ornate Victorian complete with fancy ridge pieces; structures are commonly built from timber, aluminium or uPVC. Budget conservatories can be picked up from the DIY sheds and Wickes, whilst the more upmarket structures are dominated by the likes of Amdega and Portland who advertise heavily in the

national press.

If you are interested in designing and building your own conservatory there are a number of specialists who produce the structural aluminium channel sections to order. Check BACO (British Aluminium) or Pilkington.

Polycarbonate sheets

One of the extra expenses incurred with a conservatory is the glazed roofing panels. If double-glazed, the spec on these is usually one skin laminated and the other skin toughened glass = mucho expensivo. One way of greatly reducing costs is to use polycarbonate sheeting at around £25 per sq m. However it's a somewhat threadbare alternative to the real thing and it does get incredibly noisy when there's a hailstorm about.

Building Regs

Conservatories are problematic when it comes to energy efficiency. At times they can contribute just enough solar gain to heat the entire house; at other times they can be a huge heat sink, sucking heat out of the house; and at still other times they can provide so much heat that you need air conditioning to stay comfortable. How do our energy efficiency regs get to grips with them? They make a crucial distinction between conservatories which are separated from the rest of the building, and open-plan ones. Separation is defined as being built outside the heated envelope so the division must be done with either external walls or doors, built with the appropriate U values and draught stripping. If you choose to build your conservatory as an open extension to the rest of the house, then it has to comply with the 2002 Part L regulations, one of which is that glazed areas should not exceed 25 per cent of the total floor area. That could be tricky.

■ Garages

Before you commit yourself to spending good money on garage space consider for a moment whether it is really necessary. Although current fashions in house styles tend towards the traditional, there is absolutely nothing traditional about a garage. Its nearest equivalent in pre-20th century housing is the stable or, perhaps, the cowshed; but the housing of cars is an altogether different affair. Furthermore, whilst thirty or forty years ago it was a good idea to keep vehicles undercover to facilitate winter starts and to stop rust, cars these days are made to very much higher standards and it is really not necessary to keep them undercover. Nowadays, security is often cited as a reason for building garages – but does this really justify spending as much on a garage as it costs to buy a small car? And for many practised car thieves, a locked garage doesn't really represent much of an obstacle in any event, especially as people tend to be much less security conscious on outbuildings.

Other functions

Of course, garages have many other uses besides providing undercover car parking, as is shown by the numbers of people who have them but never park their cars inside them. Solid fuel, tools, lawnmowers, gardening equipment, bicycles, golf clubs, baby buggies, deep freezes, paddling pools, paint, you name it, it gets

stored out there, and very useful it is too. But if you are designing a house from scratch, you may come to the conclusion that what you need is a larger utility room or a basement, not a garage. Garages are obviously valued by a great number of people otherwise speculative developments wouldn't include them as a matter of course, but don't just fall into the trap of assuming that a house must have a garage because it's not a proper house without one.

When to build it?

You can, of course, decide to leave the construction of a garage until an unspecified later date, provided that it's not integral to the house. If it is included on your planning permission drawings, then the right to build it cannot be taken away once you have started the main house. NB This ruling goes for conservatories, swimming pools and any other fancy accoutrements that you aspire to but can't afford. Therefore just drawing the plans in might represent a good compromise solution for those who don't really need a garage but worry that the house might be difficult to sell without one. Against this, you should be aware that any building work that takes place after you move into a house will not be exempt from VAT, so it will cost you 17.5 per cent more to construct. Also, it is worth pointing out that many people find it very useful to build the garage before the rest of the house as it provides a useful and secure store cum site hut whilst the main construction forges ahead. Indeed, with a bit of adaptation, you could just about live in a garage for a few months – certainly not much worse than the average caravan.

Siting

By and large, house designers do not like garages. They are difficult. On most sites, access demands that they are located somewhere prominent near the frontage and yet, by their very nature, they are more akin to outbuildings and sheds. Now, polite architectural convention dictates that you don't put a humble shed in the front garden and so you are left with the problem of having to make the garage look good without costing too much.

Integral

One way around this conundrum is to have an integral garage, that is, one that is built into or at least attached to the main house.

For

■ It makes for a more effective utility room type garage if that's what you have in mind
■ You can use it to house boilers and freezers
■ The arrangement fits better on narrow fronted sites (under 15m wide).

Against

It doesn't usually do much for the look of a house. Most garage doors are better suited to largely unseen parts of your estate – i.e. they are naff – and placing one prominently in your front elevation can be very ugly. The problem of the garage door is particularly acute when you are building in a traditional style. One way of alleviating it is to have an 'L' shaped house and to tuck the garage into the bit of the L that projects forward towards the road. This softens the impact of the integral garage on the all important kerb appeal. This is the arrangement used on the benchmark house.

Detached

Given a site without space constraints, most builders will plump for a detached garage. The main attraction of this arrangement is that it maintains the integrity of the house design but, even so, this can still be overwhelmed by the siting of the garage. Ideally, this will be well away to one side but most plots these days are not large enough to make this a viable option and so very often the house is half-hidden by the detached garage in front of it. Effectively, this means that the garage plays a crucial role in people's initial views of a house, and developers have responded to this by spending more and more money on external appearance, commonly including fancy roofing effects not seen on the main house.

The basic problem for garage designers is encapsulated with these two pictures. The cart shed (Weald and Downland Open Air Museum) is almost exactly the same shape as the four-bay garage, pictured below. Functonally they are also pretty much the same, too. However, I don't see many people paying to look at the garage pictured below in years to come. The main difference, visually, is of course the garage doors.

Building Costs

Many of the costs of building a garage – whether integral or detached – are no different from the costs of building the main house. Garages do not have to meet the standard building regulations as regards insulation and damp penetration and this allows them to be constructed with thinner, single-skin walls. However, groundwork costs and roofing costs are basically identical, and despite the fact that garages are rarely fitted out with all the paraphernalia of a finished house, the construction costs of a garage are still as much as 60 per cent of those of a finished house when compared on a floor area basis.

Alternatives

Car ports

One alternative approach is to build just a

lean-to car port or undercover car parking bay. You need some form of hard standing for the car and then the rest is up to you. The finished result could be anything from a flimsy timber construction which might look better as a garden pergola to a fully-fledged garage without a door.

Prefabricated

There are several small manufacturers who produce prefabricated garages at prices way below standard construction costs. But what you are buying is probably little different in quality to a garden shed. That may be exactly what you are looking for of course. They are very utilitarian and would probably be best sited away from the main house.

Underground

Budget costs for a fully submerged basement (shell only) are £430-600 per sq m, around double the cost of an above-ground structure. Consequently, an underground garage is unlikely to be a cost-effective option unless space is at a premium. Access ramps (budget £8,000) and potential drainage problems make the totally underground garage an expensive luxury. However, the economics look far friendlier when sorting out sloping ground. There are instances where burying car parking below ground can actually free up ground elsewhere for more cost-effective uses (like building extra houses), but this is unlikely to be relevant to many single housebuilders.

Garage Doors

For many designers, the problem with garages begins and ends with the garage door. Until the Seventies garage doors were strictly functional and utilitarian, often made of steel with no attempts at embellishment. Since then, a large number of imitation traditional door styles have sprung up, aping the move back to other traditional forms. The trouble is, that whilst a window or a front door can be made in styles copied from old doors, there are no old garage doors to copy from. Hence a mock Georgian

or mock Tudor garage door looks more than faintly ridiculous. Double doors, over 4m wide, look particularly strange and attempts to mould classical patterns on them merely emphasise how strange and out of place they look.

If there is a traditional British garage door it is the side opening style that you see on houses built in the Twenties and Thirties, made from solid timbers and lit by small square frosted glass panels. Magnet still produce such a door and it is remarkably good value at around £150 for a pair large enough for a single garage (though these need glazing and painting). The current trend is to go for doors which open vertically and there are a number of manufacturers producing especially for this market, e.g. Cardale, Henderson, Garador and Hormann. As with front entrance doors, there is a choice of different materials, the main ones being timber, steel and glass fibre (or GRP as it gets called in this business).

Garage doors are large and therefore tend to get pricey. It's a specialist business and your best bet is to trawl through Yellow Pages to 'Garage Doors' and seek quotations from there. Steel is much the cheapest material but also the least attractive. Timber and GRP are around twice the price. GRP doors are usually produced to look like timber – in fact they can look incredibly realistic. They can also be stained; their main advantage over timber is that they are (hopefully) maintenance-free, yet many people will prefer to stick with timber.

If you don't like any of the commercially available doors yet still crave the convenience of an up-and-over door, then check out Hormann's sub-frames which you can fill in with your own designs at your leisure. They are called Open-for-Infill doors.

Opening mechanisms

As already stated, most garage doors these days open vertically. But it's not quite that simple. There is vertical and vertical.

■ The simplest type of opening is the canopy or up-and-over door; when open, about a third of the door protrudes outside the frame, forming a canopy. They are usually hand operated and canopy double doors are something you could live without as they can get very heavy and awkward to lift.

■ As its name suggests, the fully retractable door glides all the way back into the garage on a set of tracks. These are much more suitable for double doors and for remote operators.

■ The North Americans like to fit sectional garage doors. These split into, typically, four horizontal sections which slide up a set of vertical tracks and then, one section at a time, turn through 90° and end up under the garage roof. The advantage of this is that the door doesn't protrude when opening so that you can park hard up to both the inside and outside face and still open the door.

■ Finally, there are various makes of Roller Doors around which perform in much the same way as sectional doors. However instead of turning through 90°, these doors roll up like a carpet. They look like steel shutters, which is what they are, and so kerb appeal is limited.

How wide?

The traditional width for a single garage door in the UK has been 7 ft (2134mm). It's mean. There are an awful lot of cars around that will struggle to get through such a gap, particularly so if the entry angle isn't dead straight. If you have the room, go for doors which are 7 ft 6 in wide (2286mm). If space is very tight, you can usually gain a crucial few inches by locating the supporting frame behind the walls rather than between them. Height is also an issue. Some big cars won't fit under a 7 ft doorway.

If you are planning a double garage, you have the choice of a double door or two singles. Two single doors usually work out cheaper; although you have to build a dividing pillar, the cost of this is offset by the extra cost of a 4.5m lintel to cross the gap above a double door opening. Opening double doors by hand can also be quite a hassle, particularly if the spring mechanism works out of adjustment. On the other hand, if you plan to use an electric door operator you save yourself the cost of installing a second one.

Remote control operators

An increasingly popular item which allows you to open and close your garage door automatically from both a switch inside the garage and a remote control unit which you can keep inside the car. They are not cheap – coming in at around £250 which includes just one operator (extra ones cost £45 each) – but they do make a lot of sense when you consider the hassle involved in opening garage doors manually. All the garage door suppliers sell these and they come in varying levels of sophistication. Hormann and Bosch market multi-function ones which can switch on welcome lights and open entrance gates as well. However, even the most basic ones come with timed welcome lights that come on whenever the door is opened: this is very useful.

Electric operators also come in different flavours. Most work with a geared chain but there are some (Hormann's Supramatic) which work on a Kevlar belt which promise virtually silent opening. They tend not to work on the basic canopy up-and-over doors although Cardale's Autoglide is an exception: in fact it can be retrofitted onto existing doors. If you are going to spend £6,000 plus on a garage, then it's probably worthwhile spending the extra £350 on an operator so that you actually get to use the garage for its intended purpose.

Chapter 12
Shopping

Taking off quantities
Entering the bazaar
Hiring in plant
Trucking
Concrete
Steel
Mortars
Timber
Joinery

If you love shopping, it's a given that you'll love housebuilding. One of the secret joys of building homes is that you can indulge yourself on the grea——test shopping trip of your life. But successful housebuilders are always canny shoppers, not spendthrifts, and there are a few basic lessons to be learned before you launch into it all. Firstly, do not get carried away with the thrill of it all and choose items way beyond your budget. Secondly, know where to look. And thirdly, know how to shop, how to strike a bargain. It's well worth studying the whole buying process. This is the logic of this chapter. It doesn't cover everything but it does cover many of the important areas that have been otherwise ignored up to this point.

■ *Taking off quantities*

A bill of quantities is a fancy, construction professional's term for a shopping list. Making a comprehensive one is fundamental to controlling costs and is one of the major

benefits to derive from having a properly designed, properly specified job. Many times in the past I have measured off plan to estimate a cost and then gone and measured again on site to order materials. I must also admit to having measured three or even four times when the bit of wood I write the measurements on gets nailed into some studwork or gets painted over. If I had taken the advice that I'm offering now I'd be a little bit richer and a little bit fatter. It may just be that you have built so inaccurately that your house does not resemble the plans that were drawn up, but if this is the case then you're playing in a different orchestra to me and there's no help to be proffered; go ahead and skip the rest of this section.

Now, serious construction professionals will engage the services of a quantity surveyor (known on site as 'the QS') to work out what is needed. However, QSs don't come cheap and many small builders work on their own rules of thumb for estimating the right quantities. These are not usually as accurate as a QS would get them but they are much better than nothing.

Free take-offs

If you've no experience of this sort of quantification work, then I would tend to steer well clear unless you have loads of time and patience, particularly as many builder's merchants now offer a free take-off service ideally suited to the needs of rookie builders.

Much of the repetitive grind of measuring and recording is carried out by computer and, provided the job is relatively straightforward, they are pretty accurate. The closer you stick to industry standard solutions, the better the outcome and they are quite capable of generating accurate results from a basic set of plans and elevations. The materials-buying sheets generated for the benchmark house included amounts for foundations, masonry work, joinery, lintels, roof covers, carpentry, rainwater gear and sanitaryware; not exhaustive but a good start.

Traditional route

Let's compare it with the traditional way of doing a take-off. Traditional here means that your source document is a written schedule of works (often known as the spec), not the plans. You use the plans to calculate the areas and volumes but you work methodically down the written list so as not to miss anything out. To give you a flavour of what I'm on about, here is a clause taken from the spec of a previous benchmark house.
■ External (house) walls of 275 - 280mm 3.5N clinker blockwork cavity work incorporating 75mm Rockwool or similar full fill cavity insulation and 200mm s/s butterfly brick ties at max 900mm horizontal and 450mm vertically and at every block course adjacent to openings. Additional 105mm skin of face brickwork (bricks to client's choice) forming plinth wall and tied to blockwork with s/s butterfly ties as described above. Plinth wall extends 10 courses above DPC.

Hardly a riveting read, but it's clear enough. The job of the QS is, if you like, to rewrite this

specification with the quantities added in so that it might read:
■ 158 sq m double skin external (house) walls of 275 - 280mm 3.5N clinker blockwork cavity work incorporating 145 sq m x 75mm Rockwool or similar full fill cavity insulation and 580No. 200mm s/s butterfly brick ties at max 900mm horizontally and 450mm vertically and at every block course adjacent to openings. Additional 55 sq m x 105mm skin of face brickwork (bricks to clients choice) forming plinth wall and tied to blockwork with 130No. s/s butterfly ties as described above. Plinth wall extends 10 courses above DPC.

You don't need any specialised equipment. All you need are your finished plans, a decent ruler, a calculator and a pen and pencil (rubber would be handy). And bags of common sense. If you've got a computer and you know your way around a spreadsheet you'll save yourself a bit of work, but not that much.

Measurements to take

Take your measurements from your detailed plans (which are now conventionally drawn in metric scale which makes scaling up a damn sight easier). If the distance you want is referred to on the drawings then use it, otherwise you must measure off plan in millimetres and scale up to get actual sizes; thus, if drawings are 1:50, then you multiply your measurement by 50 to get the actual measurement.

Many of the dimensions you need will be written in on the plan so you won't need to measure. Where an area is needed you multiply the two sides together, but when this area is not a simple rectangle you must split the overall area into a number of smaller rectangular boxes and add these together. Remember that the area of a triangle equals half base x height.

For all but the very largest houses all this measuring should take about four to six hours. Complicated building details like split levels, curved work, dormer windows or raked ceilings make the measuring much more complex too and it is well worth double-checking as a mistake here will have costly ramifications on down the line. Oh, and don't forget to write the answers down where you won't lose them.

I also find it incredibly handy to make little notes next to the calculations, which remind me what assumptions I have made when doing the calculations. Typically these read as 'have assumed no skirtings in conservatory' or 'have allowed for three courses of face brickwork below DPC.' It's a good idea to decide whether your derived quantities are 'as measured' or whether you have added an allowance for waste. It really doesn't matter which method you employ but you must be consistent otherwise you will end up adding 15 per cent to the quantities several times over and you will over-order by miles.

The further your house gets away from the good old box shape, the more complicated it gets to measure out and, if a feature like a bay window or a fancy chimney is difficult to quantify, then you can bet that it will also be difficult to build.

Working through the spec

You work methodically through the spec quantifying everything that is quantifiable. You then have to sweep through the whole thing a second time to generate a shopping list; some of the things you have quantified will have to be amalgamated with other sections, others will have to be broken down still further.

Blockwork is a good example. I've already dealt with the bulk of this house's blockwork under the subheading 'Traditional route' on the previous page, but there is more blockwork in the garage, in the internal walls downstairs and around the chimney. All these have to be totalled to get an overall total for blockwork. And then consider that blockwork includes not just the blocks themselves, but the sand and cement making up the mortar, not to mention the labour to lay them with. These totals have to be extracted from the blockwork total and added to the brickwork total which, to add to the confusion, will have different square metre labour rates and uses different volumes of mortar.

Written specifications

Well, that's the traditional route. It's time consuming but it works. If you plan to do your own project management it may even be worth going through this exercise to familiarise yourself with the job in hand. However, many housebuilders never bother with anything so elaborate as a written specification of works but just make do with plans on a couple of A1 sheets. This is fine if you know what you are doing, but using a set of plans without a written spec can be a bit like trying to cook a new dish for which you have a list of the ingredients but no instructions on how they go together. Arguably it doesn't matter which order you measure quantities in but the danger is that if you don't work methodically through a list, you will miss whole chunks out. If you have skimped on this stage of the design process, then this is where your chickens come home to roost.

Applying measurements

From all these measurements plus various details drawn in on the plans you should be able to construct a reasonably accurate bill of quantities. You may not actually want to make up a shopping list for paint at the planning stage, but the point is that by having taken all these measurements you shouldn't have to keep taking them throughout the job. You have the figures. From these figures plus a little close scrutiny of your house plans you can work out quantities for:

- Excavation
- Concrete (approximate)
- Flooring materials
- Walling materials
- Roofing materials
- Insulation
- Plasterboarding and plastering
- Decorating materials
- Skirting and architrave
- Covings
- Scaffolding
- Guttering and downpipes
- Whole house heat-loss calculations.

Joinery is treated rather differently. If you've got a pukka written spec, there will be a joinery schedule attached that will list all the opening sizes and the window and door styles which will fit in the openings. I find it helpful to start with the joinery: I work out the overall areas and use this sum to subtract from wall areas. The joinery schedule can also be used to calculate approximate quantities for glazing, lengths for lintels and cavity breaks and a subsidiary schedule for door furniture.

Average prices

The rates I quote throughout the book are all rates current for building work in southern England in 2004, especially around my home town of Cambridge. The key rate is £18 per hour, equivalent to £140 per day, £700 a week, or just over £30,000 per annum, typical wage for good tradesmen. Your area may (almost certainly will) have different prices in operation by the time you start building, but bear in mind that Cambridgeshire is close to the national average on building costs. Early editions of this book (it first appeared in 1994) were able to neatly summarise both material and labour costs right across mainland Britain – only Ireland diverged significantly. But the decade since has seen that change. Labour rates in boom areas seem to be up by 50 per cent to 100 per cent whilst slack areas are little changed from the Nineties. London in particular is very expensive but there are other parts of the country where labour can be just as difficult to get hold of, let alone wring sensible prices out of. It's certainly not exclusively a South East of England problem – Edinburgh appears to be almost as expensive as London – but the result is that many of the labour rates will have to be adjusted up or down by 30 per cent or more – I have tried to pitch them somewhere in the middle. In any event, my prices are intended only as a guideline by which you can compare your own quotations.

The current benchmark house was built in 2003 using tradesmen working at between £15 and £18 an hour. My impression is that the wage increases have more or less slowed down and that during the next year or so I don't anticipate any dramatic labour cost increases, though note the chart in Chapter 1 which suggests a link between house prices and labour rates. Materials price increases are generally pretty subdued, especially if you stick to basic building materials.

Wastage

If you manage to work out the theoretical quantities of just about everything you need, you are still faced with the problem of knowing how much extra to order to cover wastage. Wastage is a wonderfully vague term that covers just about any and every mishap that can occur on a building site from defective materials being delivered to perfectly adequate materials apparently walking off site. There's really no way of knowing in advance what your wastage rate will be, but experience suggests that you'd be wise to over-order by between eight and ten per cent on heavyside materials like bricks, blocks, sand and cement and also plastering materials. You should be able to work out timber quantities exactly, but here you will probably be blighted by timber quality not being what you require and again you would do well to add extra lengths to your totals. Buying more than you actually need is, of course, expensive but so are the frequent shopping trips which happen when you buy too little.

Entering the bazaar

The British consumer is used to being able to see what something costs. Visit any high street or supermarket and the price you pay will be clearly labelled on the goods or, at least, on the shelf underneath. Haggling over the price is something that you might do on holiday in Morocco or Turkey but it's thought not to be part of the British way of life.

This is far from the truth. Step off the high street and into the world of commerce (or house buying or even car purchase) and we Brits are out there haggling with the best of them. Generally speaking, when there are three or more zeros on the end of the price tag, the gloves come off and any pretence at civilised shopping goes out of the window. Anyone responsible for purchasing building materials would do well to bear this in mind because a well-organised buyer can achieve savings of 20 per cent or more over the unprepared novice.

It helps to be an established builder. To have a proven trading record stretching back over some years and, better still, to have had a record as a prompt payer will stand anyone in good stead with their suppliers. But, these days, merchants are keen to attract any custom (except the doubtful payers) and if you can establish your credit worthiness and the fact that you might be a substantial customer, if only temporarily, then you will have a strong bargaining chip.

Inside a builder's merchant

Like any business, builder's merchants and all the related building trade suppliers are buying in goods and selling them on at a mark-up. The services that a merchant provides for this mark-up are:
■ accessibility
■ delivery (usually free)
■ advice.

After a round of take-overs and mergers, there are only three national chains left: Jewsons (which took over Harcros in 1997 and Grahams in 1999) is now the largest, Travis Perkins (which swallowed Keyline in 1999), and Builder Center (part of the giant Wolseley group). In addition there are around thirty regional operations (typically with five to ten outlets) and still a fair number of small independents, one- or two-branch outfits which may well turn over less than £1million per annum. In addition, there are specialist trade outlets dealing with plumbing (e.g. Wolseley's Plumb Center), electrics, roofing, joinery, ironmongery and glass. Whether they are any good or not depends an awful lot on the quality of the staff working in any particular branch and, especially, the branch manager. Needless to

say, the smaller operations tend to give a more personalised service but can't always match the prices offered by the large chains.

A general merchant will hope – indeed need – to make an average mark-up in excess of 50 per cent to stay in business. Thus, if they purchase some paint for, say, £100 then they will need to sell it for £150. An awful lot of their business is conducted with preferred clients at mark-ups much lower than this 50 per cent and so to balance this out they must sell a great deal at mark-ups of 70, 80 or even 100 per cent. So, one of the keys to getting good prices from a builder's merchant is to become known as a preferred client. Step one is to open an account.

Trading accounts

To set up an account with a builder's merchant, you would normally be asked for a bank reference and two trade references. The bank reference shouldn't be a problem (depending on your relationship with your bank, of course) but trade references could prove difficult if you've never had a trading account. Instead, write a letter of introduction saying who you are and what your project is. This will carry far more clout if you include a copy of the plans, which they may well offer to quote on.

If you've never had a trading account (and if you are not in business on your own account there is no particular reason to have had one), they operate under a very simple code. When you pick goods up or have them delivered you get a dispatch or delivery note. The tax invoice arrives a few days later by post (this is the one you must keep for VAT records) and every month you are sent a statement of account which summarises all the invoices you have run up on your account in the previous calendar month. Normal terms are that you must pay off the outstanding balance on your account at the end of each subsequent month; i.e. if you spent £500 on account with Jewsons during April, you would be required to give them a cheque for £500 at the end of May. In effect you get between 30 and 60 days' credit depending on whether your purchase happened at the beginning of the month or the end of the month. Sometimes postponing a purchase by a day or two – so as to avoid the month end – can get you an extra 30 days' credit. Builders merchants know all about these tricks and they consistently get more sales in the first week of a month than they do in the last week.

Don't just open an account and start purchasing materials as and when you need them – you'll pay top whack this way. If you've get the whole job priced up you know that you will have some serious prices back because they suspect you will have got prices from the competition. You may well be able to improve on these quoted prices. A question you occasionally get asked over the phone by a builder's merchant is 'Is this a job you are actually doing?' Probably sounds rather silly but they are sounding you out: if you're just estimating you get one price, if you are buying you get a better price. They quite expect you to go the rounds of local suppliers and they want to have a bit of fat they can lose on the next call.

This practice of haggling over prices is common to almost all areas of building supplies except the DIY sheds (Homebase, B&Q, etc.). It's partly volume driven (that is, if you buy 150 sheets of plasterboard you'll get a better rate than if you buy just one), but it also has much to do with the cosy understanding that exists between builders and their suppliers, which goes to make builders' rates look cheaper than they actually are – or to put it another way, to discourage the DIY enthusiast from getting out of bed. The levels of discount vary from product to product and just to make it complicated some merchants operate two, three or even four levels of discount off the retail price. Some products are sold with a list price from which you have to negotiate the biggest discount you can get; other products have no list prices and the prices paid for them just come down to negotiation. Purchasing well is an art. Get too pushy and the merchants will get annoyed and shut up shop. Too relaxed and they'll squeeze whatever extra they can get out of you.

Now, as recently as the Eighties what I have just written would have practically barred me from ever setting foot in a builder's merchant again. But slowly the worm is turning and the trade merchants are far more aware of a) the competition from the DIY sheds and b) the growth of the selfbuild market. Most merchants I talk to are only too willing to supply one-off builders at somewhere near their best prices. They have had too many cosy relationships with 'trusted trade customers' turn horribly sour and now the order of the day is to do any business which pays. So even if you are a coven of Bangladeshi single-parent lesbians, don't feel you'd not be welcome – although you'll probably still get funny looks in the cement shed.

A new development is the arrival of selfbuild buying clubs that promise to cut right through all the delicate negotiations of trying to nail down best prices. Clubs isn't strictly speaking what they are; they are businesses just like any other but in exchange for you offering to put almost all your business their way, they promise unbeatable prices. You trade flexibility for price. There are currently two competing businesses in this market, Buildplan (part of the Buildstore group which also does land and finance) and HousebuilderXL. Both will undertake take-offs as well as quotes for materials.

One further point. Don't assume that your work is done after you have agreed some good prices. You have to check that you are invoiced correctly: builder's merchants, large and small, have an annoying little habit of ignoring agreed prices and invoicing you at top whack. Keep your quotes somewhere handy and cross check against them when the invoices arrive. To hazard a guess, I would reckon that ten per cent of invoices from builder's merchants come with prices higher than agreed – never lower!

Buying direct

This whole question of who supplies whom is still a pretty murky area. Most manufacturers take the view that they should support the established distribution channels (i.e. the general merchants) and consequently you will have to shop there for the product. For instance, you can't buy plastic drain ware direct even if you are Barratt Homes. On the other hand, there are manufacturers like Rytons (who produce roof ventilation) who readily sell via mail order to all comers but who, consequently, tend to get blackballed by builder's merchants so that their product is little known.

As a general rule, manufacturers do not deal direct with end users except where they set up their own distribution channels, such as Magnet. To make the whole picture thoroughly confusing, you will find that some distributors (notably Jewsons) will have own brand items on sale, which suggests that they are manufacturers. Just like Sainsburys are farmers. But this doesn't mean you are buying direct. What really matters is not which brand or where you bought it from but was it cheap and was it any good?

B&Q and Homebase

One of the reasons for the success of the edge of town DIY sheds is the perceived unfriendliness of the builder's merchant to non-trade customers. The Saturday afternoon patio-building brigade have long felt that they have been treated as second-class customers at trade outlets and, what is worse, have been forced to pay over the odds for this dubious privilege. How much more convivial to shop at a place where the prices are actually displayed, even if they aren't particularly cheap, and where the staff probably know even less than you do – "ere, Sharon, do we sell rawlplugs?" 'I dunno, tell him to look in lighting.'

As a rule the DIY sheds are not very competitive on heavyside, bulky materials but tend to be pretty good on the finishes, provided you are not looking for anything fancy.

The one exception I've found is Wickes, whose prices are keen right across the board. Wickes is a hybrid between a builder's merchant and a DIY shed; the prices are close to (and sometimes better than) a regular builder's merchant's trade prices but they are also on full

display – a big advantage to rookie builders. Wickes are now a near-nationwide chain and, though they don't operate credit accounts like the trade outlets, they are well worth looking out for. Wickes tends to work on the EDLP principle – EveryDay Low Pricing – as opposed to offering discounts and special offers. The one area where it switches tack is in kitchens where it finds that people only ever buy if it says 50 per cent off. Silly, but true.

Specialists

The general builder's merchant is to the building trade what a convenience store is to the high street shopper. You can get just about anything you want there and the prices are reasonable. However, for the serious shopper, intent on sniffing out bargains, there are any number of specialist suppliers who can usually undercut the general merchants in their own areas. The trouble is they take some hunting out, and often they don't want to be bothered by small fry, one-off housebuilders, let alone amateurs. You could spend an awful lot of time tracking down specialist suppliers and not save more than a few hundred quid overall, and it may well be that you decide the convenience (and often helpfulness) of a local builder's merchant is worth hanging on to.

However, I would not be doing my duty if I weren't to make you aware of how the professionals do it. Where do they go shopping? Well you could do worse than let your fingers do the walking and look in the Yellow Pages; this is where you will find many of the best local contacts, and subcontractors too for that matter. The general builder's merchants do still get a look in. They are conspicuously strong when it comes to supplying cement, drains, timber, plastering materials and joinery, but they tend to be out-priced by specialists in most other areas. However, do bear in mind that whilst the general merchants are to some extent geared to Wallies asking stupid questions, the specialists usually expect you to know what you are talking about. Ask a steel stockholder what you should use to reinforce your garage floor

Wickes is neither straight builder's merchant nor DIY multiple. It sells own label goods to the trade but doesn't offer credit. The prices are keen and their catalogue is worth having on shelf, even if you don't shop there.

and you'll probably get told some crap mother-in-law joke.

Sand and aggregates

Straight from quarries or via specialist hauliers. Check Yellow Pages under Quarries.

Cement, lime

General merchants are usually the best place to buy unless you want one of the speciality limes in which case you want either a local producer or an eco-merchant.

Bricks, blocks, pavings

Besides the general merchants there are a number of specialist brick wholesalers (or factors) who specialise in supplying full loads direct to site. Look out for Brickability1, particularly good for sourcing block paving. Also check Yellow Pages under Brick Merchants.

Building stone

Either direct from quarries or via brick or stone merchants. Check Yellow Pages under Stone Merchants.

Readymix concrete

Direct from Readymix outfits. Check Yellow Pages under Concrete – Ready Mixed.

Drainage

General merchants do well, though there are some specialists who are worth checking out. John Davidson Pipes are good for Osma and Burdens are good all round groundworks suppliers.

Joinery

Mass-produced joinery is usually best sought out via the general merchants. Magnet joinery, which is characterised by being 'good value', is alone amongst the major producers in being only available from its own depots – and for not making any deliveries. For workshop joinery, look in the Yellow Pages under Joinery Manufacturers.

Timber and timber boards

General merchants tend to do well here though some are conspicuously better than others. There are some specialist timber merchants and these are the places to look for unusual species. Check Yellow Pages under Timber Merchants.

Roof trusses

Many timber merchants run up roof trusses as a sideline and this is a good line of approach. There are specialists though they are few and far between. One with a good reputation and near nationwide coverage is Scotts of Thrapston.

Insulation

There are many specialist suppliers in this field and they usually undercut the general merchants. Check Yellow Pages under Insulation materials. Don't overlook the Insulation Installers section; many of these offer very good value either for supply only or supply and fix.

Roofing

Another area where specialists reign supreme as both suppliers and subcontractors. Most Yellow Pages have several pages of both Roofing Materials and Roofing Services.

Guttering

Buy from general merchants unless you want something better than the industry standard uPVC fittings.

Lintels

Again buy from general merchants.

Steel beams, reinforcing

Usually the steel stockholders offer the best value. They have their own Yellow Pages section.

Glass

Again the specialists usually offer the best value, certainly cheaper than buying your glass with your joinery. Check Yellow Pages under Glass Merchants and Glaziers. Norman & Underwood have a good reputation for sealed units and supply to most of S.England.

Plumbing

Plumbers buy from specialist plumber's merchants who get their own Yellow Pages section.

Electrics

Look in Yellow Pages under Electrical Supplies Wholesalers or Retailers.

Kitchens

As the section on kitchens, hopefully, makes clear, your kitchen could come from any one of a huge number of sources: joinery shops, general merchants, kitchen specialists, you name it. There are also worktop specialists, appliance wholesalers and more than 1,000 kitchen unit manufacturers, many supplying direct to the public. Details of some of these suppliers are in the section Kitchens in Chapter 11, 'Room by Room'.

Plastering

General merchants pick up the great bulk of sales to plasterers. However the Yellow Pages, Plastering & Screeding, is a good source of contacts for hiring plasterers and dry-liners.

Paints, stains

Decorators' Merchants get a listing in Yellow Pages but for many people a general merchant or even a DIY shed will be just as cheap and more convenient.

Ironmongery

There are specialist stockists offering wholesale prices but a one-off housebuilder is still going to do better by buying the right amounts rather than chasing extra keen prices. General merchants discount heavily on bulk orders and do well here. Also check local Bolt and Nut stockists in Yellow Pages. One firm which sells all manner of lightside building materials, delivered direct to small sites throughout England and Wales is R&J Builder's Hardware. Another is Screwfix who specialise in mail order nails and screws. Note that at most general merchants, price breaks for screws very often don't start till you've purchased more than 1000, so if you need just nine screws of a particular size there really is little point buying a whole box of 200.

Door furniture

If you want anything unusual, check out Architectural Ironmongers in the Yellow Pages.

Ceramic tiles

Check under Tile Manufacturers & Suppliers. United Ceramic Tile is a nationwide supplier and a very good source for basic ceramics – many builder's merchants buy from them.

Garage doors

Check under Garage Doors.

This list is by no means exhaustive but I hope you have gleaned that in many cases the Yellow Pages is an essential reference tool both for digging out materials and for finding subcontractors. For items like central vacuum cleaners, underfloor heating and heat recovery units, where there may well be no local agents, the obvious place to look is in the selfbuild magazines, where the nationwide businesses actively seeking work are likely to be advertising. The directory at the end of this chapter includes head office phone numbers for all contacts that I've mentioned.

Salvage

One other important area I've not touched

Scaffolding Key Rates

- Scaffolding is conventionally hired out for 8 weeks at a time on a supply and fix basis.
- To estimate a price, first work out the length of the scaffold run (usually the perimeter of the building)
- Then work out the number of visits required to fit and to re-arrange the scaffolding
- Roughly speaking, this equates to the number of storeys you are building

The metre run rate is for the standard eight week hire	
Single Storey	£ 8 per metre run
Two storey	£ 12 per metre run
Three storey	£ 14 per metre run
Subsequent weeks are normally charged at 8% of the first 8 weeks' rate	

Benchmark House Scaffold Costs

Perimeter of house	60 m
Two storey rate	£ 12 per metre run
Basic cost	£ 720 (Perimeter x rate)
Extra weeks	£ 60 (8% of 8 week rate)
Extra weeks taken	8
Overrun cost	£ 480 (8 weeks at 8%)
Final bill	**£ 1,200**

on are the salvage yards. Time was when salvage yards were a source of cheap building materials, but there has been a flight to quality in this market and these days you are much more likely to be sniffing around expensive architectural gems which you probably won't be able to afford. If you are seriously into using salvaged building materials, you would do well to identify as early as possible what exactly it is you are going to get because incorporating changes to materials specification during construction can be very costly. There are hundreds of reclaimed building materials yards all over the country, varying in size from a couple of sheds in a back garden to multi-acre sites better equipped than the average builder's merchant. If you want to look further afield than your local Yellow Pages area, contact Salvo who keep a good database of material recyclers all over the UK. They are also one of the very few organisations in this book to run a cool web page – http://www.salvo.co.uk

■Hiring in plant

Tool and equipment hire is a rather specialised area that deserves a section to itself. As with most things in the field of project management, a little planning beforehand will reap dividends along the way. What equipment you need to hire (or buy) depends very much on how you plan to manage your build. For instance, if you are entrusting the whole shooting match to a main contractor, then you really shouldn't need anything at all. But if you are acting as the main contractor and hiring subcontractors to complete the various trades, you will need to discuss each subcontractor's requirements beforehand.

It can be a confusing area. For instance, some subcontractors – notably plumbers, electricians and most carpenters – tend to come fully fitted out with toolkits and access equipment: others, typically bricklayers, expect you to provide everything other than their trowels and their levels. With groundworks, you tend to hire the kit and the labour together as a single unit – thus when a JCB is quoted at £200 a day you are getting both a JCB and a driver for that price.

Scaffolding

A specialised area of plant hire that is normally undertaken by either dedicated scaffolders or sometimes roofing gangs. A standard scaffolding contract would specify an agreed price for a hire period of eight or, perhaps, ten weeks; if the hire continues beyond the agreed period, a surcharge is levied – typically eight per cent of the original price per week. The original price would include for three or sometimes four visits from the scaffolders to erect the different levels (known as lifts) needed for the other trades to put up the house.

Single-storey houses (and detached garages) will typically need only one lift but its level will have to be adjusted between brickwork and roofing; a two-storey house needs two lifts, each being adjusted in level at some point. Guide prices for scaffolding are £6 per metre run per lift and to calculate the relevant metre runs add 15 per cent to the perimeter measurements of the buildings you wish to scaffold to get the scaffolder's lengths. A guide price for a four-bedroomed house with detached garage would be around £800 for ten weeks' hire, followed by a £64 a week surcharge for longer hire periods. If you want to take control of the scaffolding process itself, there is a system called Kwikstage by Kwikform UK which just slots together, rather similar to erecting an aluminium tower scaffold, making it particularly suitable for those who are taking a more hands-on approach and want to have scaffolding erected for much longer than the normal time span. Kwikform provide some training for people who have never used scaffolding before or, alternatively, can provide an erection service. Rental prices for a four-bedroom house sized project work out at around £50 a week.

Skips

Part of your build plan should involve a close look at how you plan to dispose of waste; for many small builders a skip is a practical and economical solution. The basic cost of a builder's standard sized skip has all but trebled since the introduction of Landfill tax in 1996. By 2004, this tax had risen to £14 per tonne, equivalent to £112 per skip. Ouch. Who said stealth taxes were dead? The days of the £200 skip cannot be far off but even so it may still make sense to use one on tight sites if you wish to run a clean and efficient building site.

Skips come in three sizes:

■ Large hold 6.2 cu m (8 yards), equals around 7-8 tons and will cost £150-180 for one week and £4 extra for each subsequent week
■ Medium hold 3 cu m (4 yards), equals around 5 tons and will cost £100 for one week
■ Mini-skips hold 1.5 cu m3 (2 yards), equals up to 2.5 tons and are usually only hired for

two or three days max, at a cost of around £70.

The rental element is usually surprisingly small (typically £5 per week) and so you don't save money by delaying the arrival of a skip – you simply end up having to handle your rubbish twice over. Given that all building sites produce copious quantities of rubbish, I think that having a skip on site (certainly during the latter stages of the build) is essential: if you disagree, then at least have some coherent alternative strategy worked out for waste disposal.

Site fencing

There are an increasing number of sites where some sort of perimeter fencing is advisable, if only to stop unwanted visitors clambering all over your building site and walking off with your tools. The CDM health and safety regulations have also meant that professional builders are being forced to examine their policies in these areas because of accidents occurring with children playing on sites. Though a selfbuilder will be largely exempt from these regulations, that is no reason for ignoring their importance and if you are unable to provide round the clock supervision to a site, you should consider some form of fencing if your site is vulnerable.

You can hire steel fencing for about 50p per metre per week (less for long periods) but it is the province of the specialist. Check out SGB's Heras Readifence, which is about six-foot high and is very easy to assemble yet surprisingly secure. If you need security fencing for more than five months, it will probably pay you to buy it and resell when you have finished.

Tool hire shops

If you want to stay ahead of the game, then make sure you have opened trading accounts with a couple of tool hire shops because you will save yourself an awful lot of faffing about. For many novice project managers, tool and plant hire is one of those things that you just stumble into once the project is up and running. But after you've been and hired three

Even though they are undoubtedly expensive, most professional builders still use skips to organise their waste.

things and left £50 deposits which did or didn't get credited to your final bill and anyway you've gone and lost the paperwork which was in the front of the car but now you can't find it...you'll wish you had opened a trading account at the hire shop too. If you do, you will be able to take tools for as long as you want without having to pay any deposit. Deliveries and collections are also much easier to organise – most hire shops will deliver and pick-up for a small charge (around £5-£10).

Generally, the hire charges are structured so that you pay the highest rate over the first 24 hours, then the daily rate falls significantly if you hire for longer periods. After about ten weeks you will have paid as much in hire charges as it would cost you to buy, so hiring really only makes sense over shorter periods. The number of things you can hire never ceases to amaze me and rather than bore you with a long list, if you are interested get hold of a catalogue yourself – Hewden Stuart's is particularly good.

Hiring v buying

Which begs the questions: what should you hire and what should you buy? There are a few basic bits of kit that it would seem near essential to have with you permanently and therefore you should buy if you haven't already got them.

I would include in this basic hand tools like a 5m tape measure, hammer, saw, screwdriver, 1.2m spirit level, the sort of thing you need to put up shelves or assemble flat-pack kitchen units. I would also place a good, beefy (£70+) power drill, a good extension lead (£10) and a 6m ladder (£120) on my list of essentials; this equipment will be useful for ongoing maintenance, not just for housebuilding.

How much else it is worth buying is really only a question you can answer. It depends on how quickly you plan to build, how much direct involvement you will have in the building process and whether or not your selected subbies will have their own equipment. A brickie gang will, for instance, very often expect you not only to supply tea but also a cement mixer, and it may well make good sense to buy one that you can sell on at the job's end (though don't expect very much for a used mixer). If you work in the trade or have serious DIY pretensions, then you will probably have all of the above plus a lot more and you may view your project as a wonderful opportunity to expand your range of tools. But if you don't intend to carry on building after you've finished your house, then it is pointless to lay out thousands to buy tools which will only ever fill up your precious storage space and provide rich pickings for would-be thieves.

Most builder's merchant delivery lorries come with a built-on crane, known as a HIAB.

Whether you hire or buy, the proportion of your total bill going on either hiring or buying equipment is large (often around two per cent of total build costs) and can be one major hidden cost to creep up on the unwary. Also note that selfbuilders are not able to reclaim VAT on tool purchases or tool and plant hire, including such items as scaffolding and fencing.

■ Trucking

Moving materials around the country is expensive. A lorry with an off-loading crane (usually a HIAB, pronounced high-ab) and driver will cost around £150-£250 to make a trip of more than half a day – although this will be less with an ordinary flat-back truck without a crane. This sum will be the same whatever the load and so from the buyer's point of view it makes good sense to get as near to a full load as possible. The best economies come when ordering 20 tonnes, which is usually a full payload.

What's in a Full Load?
A 20-tonne lorry can shift:
■ about 8,000 standard bricks
■ or 7,200 block pavers (144 sq m)
■ or 1,440 dense blocks (144 sq m)
■ or 2,400 clinker blocks (240 sq m).

Aerated blocks (like Thermalite or Celcon) are so light that the capacity constraint on haulage tends to be volume rather than weight. 20 tonnes of super-lightweight blocks would be about 6,000 blocks, which would be 36 double packs.

There are no industry standards as to how masonry materials should be packed, although there is a tendency to use shrink-wrapped plastic (which keeps watertight) and to pack in weights and quantities that fit on to a pallet. A forklift can handle more than two tonnes and a common pack size is around 1 tonne (which allows two packs to be lifted at once). When ordering direct loads, you'll have to accept the nearest pack size quantity so if, for instance, you wanted 8,000 bricks and your selected brick is packed in 410s (as many are), you would have to settle for either 19 packs (19 x 410 = 7,790) or 20 packs (20 x 410 = 8,200).

Packs will either come palletted or with fork holes for forklift off-loading. The chances are a fully laden 20-tonner will not be able to get off the road, so hire of a rough-terrain forklift may be the best solution for unloading. A rough-terrain forklift and driver should be available at around £150 for a half day and is usually money well spent if the site is big enough to warrant one. Bricks and blocks can (sometimes) be set around site, making labouring much quicker and easier. A JCB with forks can be used as an alternative to a rough-terrain forklift.

Plasterboard

The plasterboard manufacturers all pack in the same sizes. Better prices are usually negotiable on full packs. A 22-tonne direct load would be enough for three or four large timber frame houses – probably a bit too much for your average individual builder – however, by buying in full pack sizes you should be able to make savings.
■ 1200 x 2400 x 9.5mm plasterboard comes in packs of 80 (1.76 tonnes)
■ 1200 x 2400 x 12.5mm plasterboard comes in packs of 60 (1.66 tonnes).

Timber

Timber has to be purchased in 20 cu m lots to take advantage of bulk discounts and 20 cu m is an awful lot of timber. Furthermore, CLS studwork, which is perhaps the commonest size of timber used in timber frame buildings, has to be ordered in 40 cu m lots. The average timber frame house uses around 1,000m of CLS – a paltry 5 cu m! Full loads of timber can undercut merchants' best prices by as much as 30 per cent, but you have to have some site going to justify such orders. By and large, you'd do better to try and concentrate on buying good rather than cheap timber.

Pallets

Many builder's merchants now charge a £15 deposit on pallets supplied to site with tonne loads of cement or whatever. This can soon mount up to a substantial sum. Reclaiming the deposit is straightforward if your paperwork is in order – i.e. you can't just take the pallets back, you need to prove that you actually paid a deposit before they will refund.

The practice of charging a deposit on pallets does not yet appear to have extended to supplies which arrive direct from the manufacturers so you may well end up with some pallets which have a deposit on their heads whilst others are free spirits.

■Concrete

Site Mix v Readymix

One person working with an electric or diesel mixer will mix 1 cu m of wet concrete in about an hour. Making concrete on site in a mixer will cost between £40 per cu m (Mats £28, Lab £12) and £60 per cu m (M £46, L £14), largely dependant on how cheaply the aggregates (i.e. the sand and gravel) are bought, which itself depends on the quantity of aggregates bought. In largish (10 tonne+) loads, they should be obtainable at around £6 per tonne; in loads under 2 tonnes, this may rise to around £15 per tonne. Another factor to consider is availability of mixers (usually hired at £10 a day). As a rule, readymix will be cheaper when more than 2.5 cu m is needed. Readymix loads are always going to be preferable where consistent concrete strength is important. Really, for anything other than laying the odd patio, it has to be site-delivered readymix concrete every time.

Strengths

Traditionally the design strengths of concrete

Pallets usually come with a deposit on their heads. At around £15 a time, this lot could net you enough for a good holiday.

have been expressed in ratios of volumes cement:sand:gravel (as in 1:3:6). However, things are stirring in the sleepy world of concrete and there are now at least three other labelling systems in operation. If you are mixing concrete on site, the old ratio system, as described, is fine and is actually very useful as you can use it to gauge how many shovels need to go into the mixer, although note that it is usually most convenient to have a sand and gravel mixture delivered to site – ask for 'all-in ballast'. If, however, you phone up for a readymix delivery you may do well just to explain what it is you want the concrete for and let them work out which mix it is you need:

■ Foundation mixes: 1:3:6 is traditional for on-site batched concrete. In readymix terms, this is now known as a GEN 1 mix

■ Floor slab mix: 1:2:4 is traditional volume way of looking at it – i.e. it's a bit stronger than the foundation mix. The readymix equivalent is usually referred to as a GEN 3. If you are screeding over your slab, you may be able to use a GEN 1 instead of a GEN 3. Basically, the lower the GEN number, the cheaper the mix. GEN 3 and GEN 4 are about five to ten per cent more expensive than GEN 1. There are lots of other more specialised mixes around. Reinforced work requires reinforced mixes, designated RC. Driveways and paths have their own mix known as PAV 1. If in doubt, ask the readymix rep.

When you add water to readymix, you weaken it. It often leaves the readymix yard in a perfect condition and is watered on site, making a joke of its original spec. Watered concrete is the biggest single cause of concrete failure.

If you take any off this on board you will already be ahead of the game. My friendly local readymix supplier, Allen Newport, told me: '99 people out of a 100 who phone up here haven't got a clue what type of concrete they want. Even with the professionals, it's only about 50 per cent who know what they need.'

Charging for air

Readymix lorries mostly carry 6 cu m, though some are 5 cu m. Much of the cost involved

with readymixed concrete is transport so the amount you pay depends very much on how far the truck has to travel so it pays to buy local. Prices for basic mixes like GEN 1 currently vary from around £45 per cu m up to over £60 per cu m in and around London. But be aware that on your first two truckloads you will be charged something for the empty carrying space on each lorry. So if you were to order 8 cu m of GEN 1, for instance, you'd pay for 8 cu m of concrete and 4 cu m of unused capacity, often at around a third the price of the concrete itself. If you order over 12 cu m (more than two loads) this charge is usually waived but be sure to find out beforehand how it is to be applied.

Concrete pumps

To hire a concrete pump, allow around £150-£200 per session. They pump a full load (6 cu m) in 20 minutes, about three times quicker than three men barrowing might do. Concrete pumps make financial sense on jobs with more than 30 cu m of concrete to be poured but there are other reasons for using them, notably when speed is important or access is difficult. If using a pump be sure to let the readymix supplier know, because the mix design is wetter and the through-put of lorries is much faster than on a normal job. It's also a little more expensive.

Foundation Flow

RMC have introduced a self-placing foundation concrete called Foundation Flow. It saves on having to barrow, dump or pump concrete around your foundation trenches. It sells for ten per cent premium but they reckon you can claw back the costs through labour and/or plant savings.

■*Steel*

Steel can be used in a wide variety of applications in new housebuilding and there are moves afoot to introduce steel framing as an alternative to timber framing. However, most housebuilders use it sparingly, preferring to use the traditional materials brick, concrete and timber wherever possible. Steel is the No 1 choice for standard fixings like nails and screws but elsewhere its use is restricted to a few specialised areas.

Reinforcing

The commonest form of steel reinforcing used in housebuilding is A142 anti-crack mesh, which is often set in concrete floor slabs to add strength. The mesh costs between 75p and £1.20 per sq m, depending on quantity needed but note that you'll need bolt croppers on site in order to cut it. It is usual (though by no means universal) to lay this in garage floor slabs. It needs to be located towards the bottom of the concrete layer in order to do its work properly. There are many other forms of steel reinforcing used in concrete but you are unlikely to come across them in housebuilding unless you are having to lay specialised foundations.

Lintels

Though reinforced concrete is much cheaper, for many years now steel has been the preferred material for bridging the openings in outer walls made by doorways and windows. The problem with concrete is that, in insulated new houses, it remains a large cold bridge through the wall, which is bad news thermally and attracts condensation. Also, when viewed from outside, concrete lintels look crude and cheap. In contrast, steel can be insulated and the outer leaf support is hidden seamlessly over the top of the window or door. The market is dominated by two Welsh steel businesses, Catnic and IG, and designers usually specify their products. Alternative suppliers do exist and Dorman Long and Keystone (used on the benchmark house) can often be ten to15 per cent cheaper. The most commonly used IG lintel is the L1/S, very suitable for bridging openings in cavity work with cavities up to 65mm. There is a heavy duty version, known as the L1/HD. They are made in lengths from 600mm to 4800mm and they increase in 150mm increments. The

minimum end bearings must be 150mm so that an opening of 900 would need to be bridged by a lintel of 900 + 150 + 150 = 1200mm. Standard lintels tend to cost around £20-£25 per lin m. The benchmark house spend on lintels was just under £700, and £300 for steel beams used under the first floor bedroom walls.

In contrast, concrete lintels still tend to be the preferred choice to bridge internal doorways. Here the lintel is completely covered and the heat loss/condensation issue is irrelevant. The steel lintel manufacturers do produce an internal door lintel but it is not widely used. Timber framers tend to use timber lintels, but note that where a brick skin is specified for the external wall, there are special steel lintels designed to do the job of just supporting the outer skin.

Cavity wall ties

Where the facing material is brick, block or stone you need approx 3.5 wall ties per sq m. If the inner skin of the cavity is timber frame rather than blockwork, the wall ties are a different shape and you need slightly more (about 4 per sq m). Look to pay between £8 and £20 per 100 for wall ties depending on type and quality. As a rule, go for stainless steel rather than cheaper galvanised. The benchmark house would have used around 500.

■*Mortars*

The standard building cement, packed in 25kg bags, is known as OPC, which stands for Ordinary Portland Cement, and sometimes this is referred to as Portland Cement. The cement (and concrete) market is dominated by a small number of firms (RMC, Rugby, Blue Circle, Castle) and, being a mature industry, you'll find that there is remarkably little variation in cement prices – though cynics may have an alternative explanation for this. By all means shop around – current prices are hovering around £100 per tonne (£2.50 per 25kg bag) – but note that it is worth sticking with the same manufacturer once you've made your decision; cement colours vary and you can ruin face brickwork with a nasty change in mortar colours. Our benchmark house will have absorbed something like 6 tonnes of cement (excluding concrete) so, with a total value of under £600, cement purchase is never going to be a bank-breaker.

Mix Designs

How strong do you want it? Strong mixes (one part cement to three parts sand, henceforth 1:3) are used where the mortar must stand on its own (i.e. a floor screed) or is likely to get very wet (i.e. some underground work); for brick and blockwork and for wall renders, it is important not to get an over-strong mix and also to get some plasticity into the mix. This is usually accomplished by using additives (such as FebMix or Cementone) or by substituting lime for some cement. Given the choice, many bricklayers like to work with hydrated lime in the mortar but it's not universally admired; it's bulky and easily wasted and transporting split bags is a pain. Also mixing has to be carried out more accurately as the addition of a third ingredient adds to the likelihood of changes in mortar colour.

Masonry cements

There are several other options available, all designed to make on-site gauging a little easier and a little more accurate. Masonry cement,

Mortar: Key Costs

Cement (OPC)	£ 2.50 25kg bag	£ 0.10 kg
White Cement (OPC)	£ 4.75 25kg bag	£ 0.19 kg
Hydrated Lime	£ 4.50 25kg bag	£ 0.18 kg
Hydraulic Lime	£ 15.00 25kg bag	£ 0.60 kg
Lime Putty	£ 15.00 per 18 lts	£ 0.83 lt
Sand	£ 12.50 per tonne	£ 0.01 kg
Plasticiser	£ 3.00 per lt	£ 3.00 lt

Mortar: What's in a Cubic Metre of Mortar

		SAND			CEMENT			LIME			PLASTICISER	
	Cost per m³	Lts	tonnes	Cost	Lts	Kg	Cost	Lts	Kg	Cost	Lts	Cost
Screed Mix (1:3)	£ 66	1000	1.6	£ 20	330	462	£ 46					
Masonry Cement Mix (1:5)	£ 48	1000	1.6	£ 20	200	280	£ 28					
Plasticiser Mix (1:6)	£ 48	1000	1.6	£ 20	175	245	£ 25				1.2	£ 4
Snowcrete Mix (1:6)	£ 70	1000	1.6	£ 20	175	245	£ 47				1.2	£ 4
OPC/Lime Mix (1:1:6)	£ 63	1000	1.6	£ 20	175	245	£ 25	175	105	£ 19		
Hydrated Lime Mix (1:3)	£ 56	1000	1.6	£ 20				330	198	£ 36		
Hydraulic Lime Mix (1:3)	£ 139	1000	1.6	£ 20				330	198	£ 119		
Lime Putty Mix (1:3)	£ 295	1000	1.6	£ 20				330		£ 275		

Mortar: How far does a cubic metre of mortar get you?

			m³ mortar/m²	lts mortar per m²	Basic Cost/m²
		m³ of mortar lays			
Bricks, single skin work, with frogs up, 10mm bed	1800 No or 30 m²		0.03	33	£ 1.70
Bricks, single skin, frogs down or no frogs, 10mm bed	2800 No or 47 m²		0.02	21	£ 1.10
100mm Blockwork, single skin, 10mm beds	1400 No or 140 m²		0.01	7	£ 0.40
12mm Render	80 m²		0.01	13	£ 0.60
50mm Screed	20 m²		0.05	50	£ 3.30
65mm Screed	15 m²		0.07	65	£ 4.30

Mortar: Benchmark House Mortar Costs

		Area in m²	m³ needed	Cost per m³	Total
Brickwork	Snowcrete Mix	246	8.2	£ 70	£ 580
Blockwork	Plasticiser Mix	292	2.1	£ 48	£ 100
Render	Plasticiser Mix	208	2.6	£ 48	£ 130
65mm Screed	Screed Mix	110	7.3	£ 66	£ 490
			Rounded Total for All Mortar		£ 1,300

Mortar Mix Chart

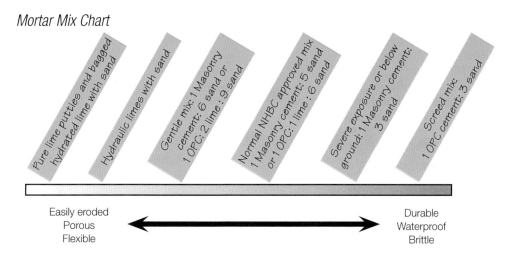

Pure lime putties and bagged hydrated lime with sand

Hydraulic limes with sand

Gentle mix: 1 Masonry cement: 6 sand or 1 OPC: 2 lime : 9 sand

Normal NHBC approved mix 1 Masonry cement: 5 sand or 1 OPC: 1 lime : 6 sand

Severe exposure or below ground: 1 Masonry cement: 3 sand

Screed mix: 1 OPC cement: 3 sand

Easily eroded
Porous
Flexible

⟵⟶

Durable
Waterproof
Brittle

sometimes called Wallcrete, is probably the best known; it consists of 85 per cent OPC and 15 per cent filler, usually crushed limestone. It's not as strong as OPC and doesn't behave as well as a sand:lime:cement mortar. This is because the modern, pure limes, when gauged, behave in a way that makes the mix 'fatty' and they help to cure the finished mortar, leaving it ever so slightly plastic enabling movement joints to close up. Wallcrete's fillers do not do this.

A better alternative is a product from Buxton Lime Industries called Limebond which, as its name suggests, uses lime and not fillers and is in effect a pre-gauged package to which you just add sand. Note that Limebond is relatively new and many merchants have never even heard of it. Yet another option is to use a pre-mixed mortar (i.e. even the sand is mixed in for you) – RMC can supply these at around the £15-£20 per tonne mark either in skips or tipped off lorries.

Idiot-proof cements

All these masonry mortars are designed for low-strength applications like brickwork, blockwork and renders, and their mistaken use in concrete mixes can present major structural problems. In contrast, Blue Circle's Mastercrete and Castle's MultiCem are designed to be completely idiot proof. They can be used in all the major cement applications (concrete, brick mortars, renders and screeds) and will go fatty enough in a mixer to be used without any additional additives. One brickie I know is very uncomplimentary about them, to the extent that if I were to print his comments, all you would see would be a whole bunch of asterisks.

Lime

There is no compulsion to use cement for the construction of new buildings and there are many restoration projects where it would be advisable to avoid it altogether. The use of cement in housebuilding did not become widespread until the Twenties. Before that people used lime-only mortars which never set as hard as cement, and one of the big advantages of lime mortars is that the mortar can be cleaned from the brick, making it possible for some bricks to be reused in other buildings. In contrast, most cement mortars cannot be removed from bricks and cement-bedded bricks are good for nothing more than hardcore. Another advantage is that lime mortars remain slightly plastic and this provides a certain amount of flexibility to walls, which helps to withstand subsidence and cracking.

However, it's not that simple just to switch to lime as a replacement for cement. The really traditional limes, sold in liquid 'putty' format in tubs, are around six times as expensive as

OPC cement and cannot readily be used below temperatures of 10°C: use that on your external brickwork and you'll be hanging around forever waiting for the stuff to set. There are different types of bagged lime available which you can use instead: hydrated lime is relatively cheap and readily available from builder's merchants but lacks strength without a little cement to bind it, whilst hydraulic limes can be used instead of cement but have to be imported from France.

If you want the lime look without the lime hassle, then you can cheat big time and use white cement, sold as Snowcrete. At £5.00 per 25 kg bag, it's twice the price of OPC but still much cheaper than using lime. The benchmark house is built this way. I leave the last word on this to its builder, Steve Baldwin. 'I use a 1:6 Snowcrete: sand mix with added plasticiser. I am not a great believer in lime: it doesn't do much for me.'

Quantities

I find it helpful to calculate how many cubic metres (cu m) of mortar are needed in each application and this is how the accompanying table works. I have made some assumptions about just how far a cubic metre of mortar will go; if, for instance, you are laying a double-thick 215mm blockwall rather than the normal 100mm thick one, you would do well to adjust your quantities so that your coverage is halved. The table is also complicated by the fact that there are several different mortar mixes commonly used on building sites; if you want to convert volumes (by which they are gauged) into weights (by which they are bought), look at the section called Crucial Measurements at the end of this chapter. Another big imponderable is waste; just how do you go about allowing for it, how much will you waste? The answer is usually a surprisingly high amount though this figure varies substantially. My coverage rates are fairly conservative, allowing for between 15-30 per cent of the cu m of mortar to end up somewhere other than you intend.

■Timber

You rarely see the price of timber advertised and you rarely see it on display in timber yards. This is because there is a wide range of prices charged for timber. The regular trade prices are usually around 33 per cent less than those charged to casual in-off-the-street customers and large orders will get another five to ten per cent off the regular trade prices. The way to get good prices is invariably to send your (hopefully) large order in for quotation at least two weeks before you require it. By all means include second-fix items like skirting boards which you may not need for several months; it makes you look more like a serious customer.

Carcassing

Most construction grade carcassing timber is spruce, usually referred to as carcassing, whitewood or deal – presumably because it's a good deal. It is relatively cheap and easy to work but it suffers from being one of the least durable timbers available. Of more interest to the builder is the strength of any particular piece of timber and there are several grading systems run by the timber trade for assessing this. The commonest form of grading at present is to see timber labelled as SC3 or SC4. SC4 timber is the stronger and the advantage of paying the five per cent more for SC4 timber is that you are allowed to use them over longer spans. For instance the longest distance you can bridge with a 50x175mm section of timber is 3170mm in SC3, but this length rises to 3380mm in SC4. SC3 and SC4 are British Standards and moves are afoot to replace them with Euro gradings, C16 and C24 respectively.

Kiln-dried timber

In 1995, it became compulsory to use low moisture timber in all internal structural applications – which means joists, studwork walls and roofs. Low moisture is defined as having a moisture content below 20 per cent and in effect this means using kiln-dried timber. The advantage of kiln dried timber is that it is dimensionally stable – it will not twist or warp as cheaper timber will, especially if it's been treated – and that it is regularised, which means that it has all been milled to an accuracy of 1mm. It is thus very much quicker and easier to put up accurate studwork and to fix flooring joists; non-regularised timber can sometimes vary in depth by 5mm or more and this is very noticeable when flooring is being laid over it. Having said that, there is a lot of supposedly regularised timber around which varies by plus or minus 5mm, sometimes even more, so the term is regularly abused. And in truth, 20 per cent moisture content is still much higher than the final settlement level reached in a centrally heated house (about eight per cent), so shrinkage still takes place. But kiln-dried timber is still a step in the right direction.

Timber treatment

Spruce is not classified as a durable timber and this means that it is liable to rot if exposed to continuous damp. This has led to the increasingly widespread use of timber preservatives to add durability. These preservatives can be applied by brush on site but more normally the timbers are immersed in a vacuum-pressure tank, which leads to them being referred to as having been 'vacuum treated'. There are two rival systems in regular use in the UK, Tanalising and Protimising. There is little to choose between them in price – they add around 10 per cent to the cost of the raw timber – but they do perform rather differently.

Tanalising is a water-based treatment which tends to dye the wood a light green colour although there is now a brown-dye version as well (useful if you plan to use brown or black stains); Protimising is spirit-based and usually leaves the wood uncoloured, although sometimes a red dye is added. You can usually tell if timber has been Protimised from the pungent, petrol-like smell. Generally tanalising is preferred in applications where there is contact with the ground, like fencing, and protimising is preferred for structural timber (and joinery) because it is less likely to cause

the timber to twist. Tanalising used to use arsenic as one of its ingredients; it has been reformulated to avoid this particular gremlin and is sometimes referred to by a different name, such as AC500. However, it will take a good few years before British builders get around to calling it anything other than tanalising.

Joinery grade redwood

The other commonly used wood in UK housebuilding is pine, or redwood as it is known. This is a denser and slightly more durable timber than spruce, and it is commonly used to manufacture windows and internal applications like skirting boards, floorboards and matchboard walling. It is more easily worked than spruce and it is most frequently seen in timber yards with a planed finish, usually referred to as Planed All Round (PAR) or Planed Square Edge (PSE). Scandinavia is the major supplier of redwoods.

You can use cheaper whitewoods for internal applications but they suffer from having what are called dead knots, which tend to work loose and fall out with time. Your mice may appreciate the odd dead knot in your skirting board but you will probably prefer to have timber with live knots that move with the timber as it expands and contracts.

Buying redwood 5ths

Scandinavian timber is quality graded into six groups, one being the highest and six being the lowest; one will be clear knot-free timber, six will have large knots and possibly waney edges as well. Most planed timber sold in the UK is sold as "Best" and includes anything from grades one to four, weeding out only grades five and six. Increasingly we are seeing grade five coming on to the market – known as '5ths' – and it sells for 25 per cent less than the normal, unsorted timber. Grade five timber is very much more knotty but most people find it perfectly adequate for their purposes. It is increasingly available for fascias, barge boards and skirtings. And whilst I'm on about skirtings, consider that there is another new development in this field and that is the use of MDF boarding to replace internal joinery items such as skirtings, architraves and windowboards (and soon door linings as well). MDF mouldings are about 15 per cent more expensive than best redwood (therefore about 50 per cent more than fifths); but they come in lengths of 5.4m, which can be a boon AND it comes undercoated ready for topcoat. If you are planning on a painted finish to your interior woodwork, then MDF is going to save you time and money.

Specialist softwoods

There are a number of more specialised softwoods:

■ Douglas Fir is particularly resinous and durable and it performs as well as many hardwoods. It is a favourite in high specification windows though one problem is that it doesn't hold paint well: wood stains are the solution.

■ Hemlock is another North American speciality softwood that is mostly used in door construction.

■ Cedar is particularly durable and really doesn't require any sort of on site treatment at all. However, its use is very limited, tending to be restricted to external claddings such as garage doors, and roofing, where it is known as shingles.

■ Parana Pine. This is a lovely looking South American timber, popular in several internal applications such as window boards and staircases. It is anything but durable and is very prone to buckling.

Hardwoods

Generally, hardwoods are not an alternative to softwoods. Rather, they tend to get used in particular applications like flooring and kitchen worksurfaces where softwoods are not commonly used. Joinery is the obvious exception to this rule: see the section 'Windows' in Chapter 7, Superstructure, where the pros and cons are examined. Also check Chapter 13, 'Green Issues', for the low down on tropical hardwoods.

■Joinery

The volume timber joinery business works very much on the principle of publishing list prices so that all and sundry can see, but then, in private, haggling over discounts obtainable off these list prices. Discounts are partially volume driven (i.e. the more you buy, the bigger the discounts) but they are also very sensitive to what the opposition are doing. To the novice builder this might appear to be a stumbling block because their design will more than probably specify a certain manufacturer's product and there may be only one supplier in the area. However, each manufacturer will almost certainly be producing a similar product that can be substituted. It's a complicated business because although the sizes and styles are often nearly identical, the reference codes are not.

Discounts

Most small builders will expect to get 30 per cent off the list prices shown in the catalogues as a matter of course and a selfbuilder should expect to get as much. The big boys will be looking to get 50 per cent off, and if your order is big enough (say 15 windows or more) you ought to be able to negotiate a discount larger than 30 per cent. Often the merchants will be more flexible than the direct outlets and they also often stock two or more manufacturers. Much of the uPVC market works in a slightly different way in that there are many more small suppliers who normally quote on your plans, rather than discounting off a list price.

Service

A further consideration is the speed and quality of delivery. In my experience this can vary enormously; sometimes the wrong items turn up, sometimes stock is damaged or parts are missing, often they are supplied later than promised. Furthermore, there seems to be little consistency; a factory or depot can supply everything correctly on time for one order and make horrendous cock-ups two months later.

A lot obviously depends on the staff at the dispatching end, and what state they are in one cannot know.

Ordering and correct delivery of joinery is one of the most crucial elements in the managing of a construction project because its absence can throw the job programme out of the window (or should that be window opening); on the other hand its presence on site too early creates storage problems – joinery is prone to site damage, to warping if poorly stored and to theft. If you do negotiate some whammo deal, check to see if you have to take all the items in one delivery because that may well not be the smartest move.

Delivery times

Another frequent problem comes when ordering some of the more obscure items from the catalogues. Delivery times of six weeks are sometimes quoted – which in reality means they haven't got a clue how long it will take. Even slump conditions in the building trade don't help much because joinery factories are then prone to taking longish holidays – watch out for the extended August break.

You can spend a long time and burn up your phone bill being shunted around from depot to depot trying to find out what has happened to your hardwood imperial French door frames. You'll get to talk to a lot of Geoffs, Steves, Daves, Sharons and Mandys but getting a fix on your missing order can prove virtually impossible.

If speed is of the essence it will pay you to stick to readily available products: the catalogues make it clear which they are.

One way around the problem of coordinating joinery deliveries is to have the items delivered to your nearest depot (or builder's merchant) and then either pick the stuff up yourself or arrange a second delivery. Note that some suppliers will not do this (as it obviously adds considerably to their transport costs) but note also that Magnet have no site delivery service at all and that if you purchase from them they will be obliged to hold the stock for you until you want it (unless of course they sell it on to another customer!).

Comparing Costs

Another problem is trying to evaluate the cost of finishing the joinery once it's installed in the building. Time was when it all arrived on site in the same condition; softwood frames with a single coat of primer on. Now things are a lot more complicated. The penchant for staining doors and windows instead of painting them has meant that the primer coat has been dropped in favour of a base coat of honey coloured wood stain which can be either painted over or stained.

The new thermal buildings regs have also caused some big changes for joinery in that it now needs to meet certain minimum energy efficiency standards, which generally mean that factory glazing is going to become a lot more common. And of course, timber joinery is now facing stiff competition from other products, most notably uPVC, which tends to get delivered to site ready glazed and pre-finished. As a result you can now buy timber joinery pre-finished (if you don't mind waiting for it); it's also usually available in an in-between state with some extra coats of paint or stain applied in the factory, all designed to reduce your onsite decorating costs.

Whether these pre-finished or semi-finished options are worth paying extra for rather depends on how much time and money you are prepared to bestow on the naked versions of your joinery; the pricing of these pre-finished units is usually calculated to make it as cheap as paying someone to decorate them.

Chapter 13
Green Issues

Construction audit
U values
Heat calcs and energy ratings
Energy saving tips
Low energy lighting
Kitchen & laundry
Saving water
Water treatment
Eco houses

Most of the interest in this field – and indeed, most of this chapter – is to do with saving energy. Our fascination with this topic really began during the 1974 oil crisis when people assumed – incorrectly – that we were facing a permanent fuel shortage and consequentially rocketing fuel prices. However, in more recent times, concern has grown that the ambient temperature of the entire planet Earth is gradually increasing, a phenomenon known to us all now as global warming. Why this should be is not yet understood but a very large finger of suspicion is pointing at us and, in particular, our habit of burning masses and masses of fossil fuels and thereby releasing carbon dioxide (CO_2) into the atmosphere.

Currently, each year we are burning up something like 400 years' worth of plant and animal growth from back in dinosaur times when all this fossil fuel was being made. This may (or may not) be causing a greenhouse effect which, in turn, may (or may not) be causing temperatures to rise which, in turn,

may (or may not) have catastrophic effects on Mother Earth. It's only a theory; all that's known for certain is that a) there is much more CO_2 in the atmosphere than there was even 50 years ago and b) global temperatures have been rising. The crux of the problem is that we won't know how much of this theory is accurate for another 50 years by which time it could be too late to do much about it.

Reckoning that it is probably better to be safe than sorry, governments the world over have been signing (and, in the case of the Americans and Russians, ignoring) accords – most notably at Rio and Kyoto – to reduce levels of energy consumption though, as environmentalists point out, not by very much and sometimes by nothing at all. As private households contribute about a third of our national CO_2 emissions, the effect of these undertakings is trickling down to the Building Regulations in the hope that stricter codes for new building will bring about some reduction in our energy consumption. Hence many of the recent changes to the building regs are to do directly with reducing CO_2 emissions.

What is interesting to the new housebuilder is that many of the energy (and therefore CO_2) saving features that can be built into a new home are also money saving features, and if you are concerned with ongoing running costs, then you can build energy saving into your home knowing that you will be saving money, as well as possibly saving the planet. Energy saving is, however, not the be-all and end-all of environmental concerns and I'll start the chapter by taking a look at some of the other issues, including an assessment of how much energy is used in actually constructing a new house.

■ Construction audit

This book may be green-tinged but it is not what anyone would call an eco-handbook. If you want to know more about green options then there are dozens of other titles available and I can especially recommend 'The Whole House Book' by Pat Borer and Cindy Harris, which gives a good overview of the many different ways there are to build.

Whatever your personal views on green issues, what can't be denied is that the green perspective has caused mainstream housebuilding to examine just what it does, and to look at ways it could be improved. For most of the 20th century, housebuilding in Britain was driven by the desire to make houses cheaper and easier to construct. Now the agenda is subtly shifting so that at last we are beginning to worry about what it is that we are building. Is it any good? How much damage does it cause in order to get built? How long will it last? Can it be safely disposed of when we've finished with it? In a word, sustainability. How does the benchmark house stack up?

Trade balance

Materials going into our benchmark house weighed around 300 tonnes, the vast majority of which will have been produced within 200

miles of the house. Timber (5 tonnes) is the only significant import by weight, though copper (used extensively in plumbing and wiring) and kitchen appliances were also imported. Traditional housebuilding remains an overwhelmingly British business. It is low-tech and uses a lot of very bulky materials that are costly to transport. Even where foreign companies achieve market penetration in Britain, production is usually UK based.

As a rule, Britain runs a trade deficit in building materials. We are net exporters of steel, wallpapers, paints, sanitaryware and even a few bricks (mostly to Japan), whilst timber accounts for around 90 per cent of our net imports, with heating and plumbing gear being the only other significant contributor on this side of the account. Take out timber from the equation and everything else pretty much balances out.

Embodied energy

Energy use involved in building any house can be divided into three areas: material production, transport and construction. Broadly speaking, the less a material is processed, the less energy it takes to produce, and the less distance a material travels the less energy is used in getting it there. On-site energy use is remarkably low, unless heating and lighting are employed – unusual when doing spec. housing. The table on the next page summarises the energy used in constructing the benchmark house and it is based on the following figures:

■ Natural materials take the least energy to produce. Sand, stone, slate and timber come into this group: production costs might be typically 100kWh per tonne.

■ Cement-based products like concrete and render are low on energy use because they have a high proportion of natural sand or stone mixed in with the cement. They consume around 300kWh per tonne to produce.

■ Clay-baked products like bricks and clay roof tiles use around 800kWh per tonne. Also included in this group are plasters and plasterboard. Note that the manufacture of concrete products consumes just half the energy

Benchmark House Construction Audit
Material Quantities and Energy Used to Construct House

MATERIAL	ENERGY USED in MANUFACTURING (in kWh/tonne)	MATERIAL QUANTITY	MULTIPLIER	WEIGHT (in tonnes)	ENERGY USED (in kWhs)
Concrete	300	40 m³	2.3	92	27,600
Bricks	800	15000 No	0.00	45	36,000
Lightweight Blocks	300	290 m²	0.1	29	8,700
Concrete Floor Beams	300	110 m²	0.15	17	5,100
Sand	30	32 t		32	1,000
Cement	1,500	7 t		7	10,500
Concrete Tiles	300	213 m²	0.05	11	3,300
Concrete Paving	300	100 m²	0.15	15	4,500
Hardcore and Gravel	30	30 t		30	900
Timber	100	7 m³	0.5	4	400
Chipboard/Plywood	300	0.2 m³	0.5	0.1	insignificant
Plasterboard	800	410 m²	0.01	4	3,200
Steel	13,000	0.7 t		0.7	9,100
Glass	9,000	42 m²	0.02	0.8	7,200
Plastic/uPVC	45,000	0.25 t		0.25	11,300
Sanitaryware	5,000	0.2 t		0.2	1,000
Others Materials	10,000			0.2	2,000
Timber Transport	Shipping 5 tonnes of timber across the Atlantic uses				2,000
Heavy Goods Transport	1 tonne uses 0.3kWh to travel 1km			15000 t x km	9,000
			TOTAL	288	140,000
COMPARISONS			Energy used/annum		kWh/annum
		Benchmark House Built to 2002 standards			23,000
		Benchmark House Built to Eco House standards			5,000
		Benchmark House Built to 1975 standards			90,000
		Family Car Doing 20,000km/annum			20,000
		Family of 4 flying to Spain and back			20,000

of their clay equivalents.
■ Glass: uses 9,000 kWh per tonne
■ Steel: uses 13,000 kWh per tonne
■ Copper: uses 15,000 kWh per tonne
■ Aluminium: uses 27,000 kWh per tonne
■ Plastic (inc uPVC): uses 45,000 kWh per tonne – but a tonne goes a long way.

Transport
In addition to the manufacturing costs, there are energy costs involved in getting the materials to site. As previously mentioned, most of these materials are locally produced. The one big exception is timber, which almost always is imported. Our joinery grade softwoods come mostly from Scandinavia, our carcassing from N. America, Scandinavia and Russia. Timber

boards like plywood and chipboard can come from anywhere, though note that Sterling Board is produced in Scotland and most of our MDF comes from Ireland.

Comparisons
The table breaks down the embodied energy that went into the benchmark house, which I calculate at around 140,000 kWh. This is equivalent to the amount of energy the house will take to heat, light and cook during its first five years of occupation or, looked at another way, about eight years' motoring in the family car doing 12,000miles per annum. The 2002 building codes mean that a new house is saving as much as 50,000 kWh per annum over the average of what older housing stock

would consume; that means that, if it was a replacement dwelling (which it wasn't), the energy consumed in production would have been recouped within three years. Arguably, many of the improvements built into new housing can be easily transferred into the existing housing stock, but on balance new housebuilding is still an energy saving activity. It could of course be even better – see the example of the German Passive House standard which represents the current best standard for low energy housing. On a scale of 0 to 10, with 0 representing the pre-insulated home (pre 1976) and 10 representing the Passive House standard, the current UK standard would score around 7.5. 75 per cent of the energy saving measures you could realistically apply to new homes are already in place: the last 25 per cent are the most difficult and expensive to achieve.

Environmental audit
Extraction of aggregates
Around 270 tonnes (over 90 per cent by weight) of the benchmark house is composed of sands and gravels and clays, mostly bound together with cement. With 170,000 new houses being built in the UK each year, around three cubic miles of materials are being extracted annually to meet this demand. That's an awful lot of holes in the ground and it's one area where new house building is particularly greedy. Quarries pose no long-term health risks and, arguably, the scars of quarrying are actually healed remarkably quickly. However, that doesn't make quarries attractive to nearby residents and new quarrying proposals are always hotly disputed.

Timber
The weight of timber used to construct houses is minute in comparison with masonry/concrete products. The benchmark house uses about 8 cu m (5 tonnes) of wood and wood-based products. Were it timber framed, this figure would rise to around 16 cu m (10 tonnes) and if the entire house were built from wood – cedar shingles on the roof,

weatherboarded exterior and pine-panelled interiors – the volume of timber would still only be around 40 cu m (24 tonnes), less than a quarter of the equivalent weight if masonry products were used. On the face of it, building from a renewable resource like timber would seem to be very desirable but there are a few snags:
■ Logging often has more in common with mineral extraction than agriculture; even so-called sustainable sources are often permanently damaged after the virgin crop is removed to be replaced by monotonous, species-thin plantations.
■ Almost all structural timber has to be imported into Britain, making it the one major building component not to be sourced in the UK.
■ Exterior timber and structural elements of timber frame housing have to be treated with preservatives, thus causing the manufacture of chemical nasties with associated health risks.

Tropical hardwoods
The problem with using tropical hardwoods is to do with the way in which they are harvested (or plundered) with acres of virgin rainforest being destroyed often to fell just one particularly nice mahogany tree. By and large this land is then cleared and used for rather poor cattle grazing. This sort of wanton destruction is going on all over the tropics and, in truth, is as much to do with burgeoning population growth as it is with extracting hardwoods, but there is no doubt that the hardwood trade plays a significant part. The building trade is, as ever, very slow to pick up on the potential problems here, and long after retailers have been selling furniture 'Made from renewable resources', there is little sign of any green awareness from timber merchants, possibly because tropical hardwoods are a nice little earner.

However, the environmental problems resulting from using these hardwoods in new housebuilding should not be exaggerated: their use is rare precisely because of their expense.

Brazilian mahogany is specified as standard as a cill detail on timber door frames but otherwise you have to go looking for materials – chiefly joinery – made out of tropical hardwoods. Another area where you may stumble across them is as constituents of better-grade plywoods (Far Eastern) and blockboards, but these are more commonly used for shelving than construction; MDF can be used as a cheaper substitute.

Health risks
Formaldehyde
This glue is used to bind timber panel products, chiefly chipboards, MDF and plywoods. Some people are known to react badly to the fumes which are released very slowly over a period of months after manufacture, a process known as off-gassing. However, adverse reactions are rare and exact causes are difficult to pinpoint. Almost all volatile organic compounds (VOCs) have come under suspicion – including carpets and clothes – and it remains a complex and poorly understood area. You can, of course, build and furnish a house from entirely natural materials but it is an expensive option.

Solvents
Solvents are used in oil-based paints, stains and varnishes, as well as adhesives and mastics. Many people actually like the smell of solvents but long-term exposure to them has been linked with brain damage. Occasional users probably need not be alarmed, but be aware that solvents are likely to be far more damaging to young children than to adults; if youngsters (and pregnant women) are present then you would do well to consider using water-based paints and stains indoors.

Wood preservatives
One normally associates timber treatment with remedial work carried out on old houses, but a great deal of new timber gets pre-treated with either water-based tanalith or solvent-based protim. The tanalising treatments used to be based on the copper-chrome-arsenic compounds (CCAs) whilst the spirit-based systems use a cocktail of chemical nasties such as lindane, pentachlorophenol (PCPs) and tri-butyl-tin-oxide (TBTOs). Neither is particularly pleasant and the tanliths have been reformulated as AC500 (minus the arsenic). They serve a dual purpose: one is to reduce risk of fungal infestations such as dry rot, the other is to reduce risk of insect attack such as woodworm and death watch beetle. The idea is that treated timber will taste so foul that insects and fungus will steer well clear: the danger is that these chemicals won't do us much good either.

External joinery is pre-treated as a matter of course and NHBC regulations require that timber in exposed walls is treated. There is a potential long term hazard, although this is rather along the lines of the formaldehyde and VOC threat – i.e. no one can say what it is – but there is also a more immediate danger to site carpenters who inevitably come into physical contact with treated timbers. Wearing gloves is not really an option for a chippie: the best precaution is to ensure that the timber is dried properly before it is worked; sometimes it arrives on site still dripping with the chemical preservatives, having just come out of the vacuum tank. Some commentators maintain that if the design detailing is good then the timber does not need preserving, but preservation is now an industry standard. Note that timber frame kit houses tend to come with pre-treated timber specified everywhere, whether it's actually needed or not.

Asbestos
In many ways, asbestos was a great product: lightweight, stable and with incredible fire resistance. But, and it's a big but, asbestos fibres are a proven killer and great care should be taken when handling the product. Asbestos related products are no longer available in the UK – the cement-based tiles were only phased out in 1999, However, you are at potential risk when removing asbestos products from old houses because this is where you are most likely to come into contact with the dust. There

are three different types of asbestos, known by the colours brown, blue and white. The dust from the brown and the blue are killers, whereas white asbestos has never been shown to have harmed anyone (which isn't quite the same thing as saying that it's harmless). Mostly the construction industry used white asbestos in products such as Artex and roof tiles and wall panels so the risks are pretty low, if not negligible, but the problem is how do you accurately assess what's on your site.

The legal situation regarding asbestos removal from the home is, to say the least, ambiguous. Domestic premises are excluded from the Asbestos Regulations published in 2002 so you could, in theory, work away on your own behalf without taking any precautions. But you can't bury it in your garden and you can't take it to a tip and you can't get anyone else to do it for you without triggering some aspect of the regulations which then require licensed contractors to come on board and make risk assessments and don space suits and charge whatever they feel like for taking the asbestos away.

No distinction is made between the different kinds of asbestos; as far as the regulations are concerned, everything must be treated with equal suspicion. So it may be that if you have asbestos in your house to be demolished, you will have no choice but to get a licensed contractor to dispose of it. However, it's well worth asking more than one to quote for the work. The contractors will undertake their own risk assessment of the dangers involved and the resulting quotation is likely to be heavily influenced by what their risk assessments tell them.

MDF

The problems related to formaldehyde have already been touched on and are not unique to MDF. However MDF is the board that gets worked most and it tends to produce the finest dust which sails through the average dust mask as if it's not there. This combination is reckoned (by some) to make MDF a hazard on a par

with asbestos and moves are afoot to produce a similar board made with safer resins. Passive consumers of MDF products are unlikely to be at risk but you should look out if you work with a lot of MDF dust.

Cement

Human skin does not react well with wet cement and concrete mixes; there is no instant sign that burning is taking place and many people assume that it is therefore harmless. It's not; prolonged exposure will cause very nasty burns.

Fibreglass

Fibreglass insulation, together with the closely related mineral wool, are unpleasantly itchy on skin, and eyes like it even less. Thought by some to be similar to asbestos in effect, others claim that the fibres are generally too large to cause lethal irritation. Whoever proves to be correct, it makes sense not to be macho about it. Wear gloves and a mask when insulating.

uPVC

The use of uPVC has been growing steadily in housebuilding. You will find it in plastic guttering and drainage pipes, in electric cable and, of course, uPVC windows and doors. However there is a vociferous campaign (led in this country by Greenpeace) against the use of uPVC, principally on the grounds that its production is a dirty, polluting business leading to the release of dioxins and the dumping of chlorine. What is not clear is whether uPVC manufacture is any worse than the rest of the chemicals/plastics industry.

Eco homes

In an attempt to introduce some objectivity to a subject which, in the eyes of many observers, is reeling with subjectivity, Britain's premier building science body, the Building Research Establishment (or BRE) published two booklets in 2000 called 1) Eco Homes and 2) The Green Guide to Housing Specification. Together they look at the impact on the environment and human health and they develop some criteria which allow you to rate housing development from the point of view of overall sustainability, not merely energy saving. You end up with a score in, wait for it, sunflowers. One sunflower is a PASS, four sunflowers, the maximum, indicates a development 'which demonstrates exemplary environmental performance across the full range of issues'.

So what makes a home an Eco home? This is decided by an EcoHome Rating system which marks many aspects of your house design and performance. The maximum number of marks obtainable is 207. Energy efficiency measures only account for 40 points; you get almost as many for water efficiency measures (max 30 points) or specifying sustainable materials (max 31 points). Other point scoring features include being within 500m of a bus stop or railway station (four points) and improving the ecological value of the site (up to 16 points). To get the top EcoHomes award (four sunflowers) you need to amass 145 points.

I put our decidedly pale green house, 1992 vintage, through the checklist and had scored 56 points (just over pass) when somewhere in the penultimate section I stopped understanding the questions. I couldn't decide whether or not we'd made 'effective use of our footprint'. No guidance appeared in either publication on what they could possibly mean by this though I have a hunch that they'd like us to have built a room-in-the-roof or a basement – we didn't do either – but that's not the way the question was phrased, so at that point I gave up.

The assessment is not meant to be a DIY affair in any event: rather, the BRE are licensing organisations to carry out EcoHome ratings, in a similar manner to the energy rating schemes which have existed for some time. This may explain why the checklist is not at all easy to fathom – you need to be trained to understand it. Added to this, the two publications are being sold for a combined cost of £60 (exactly a pound per page) which clearly marks them out as not being aimed at the casual user. More's the pity because every wanna-be eco-home builder

needs to go through an evaluation process like this before they can be sure that their ideas of what is environmentally-friendly chime in with everybody else's.

Contacts
The Whole House Book is £29.95 plus p&p from Centre for Alternative Technology Bookshop 01654 702948
The Green Guide to Housing Specification £35.00; Eco Homes £25.00. Both these are available from CRC 0207 505 6622

■ U values

As far as building regulations are concerned, green issues begin and end with energy saving. Energy saving measures first became part of the British homebuilding scene in 1976 and they have been progressively tightened since then. In fact you can map the declining wall U values over time thus:
■ 1976: maximum U value first introduced at 1.0
■ 1981: maximum U value reduced to 0.6
■ 1990: maximum U value reduced to 0.45, unless double glazing was installed in which case you could still build to 0.6
■ 1995: everyone down to 0.45, double glazed or not
■ 2002: it's now 0.35 – Scotland plumps for 0.3.

The latest set of changes came into effect throughout the UK in 2002. The key points were as follows:
■ More insulation is needed in order to meet the new U value requirements
■ Windows and doors must be energy-rated and meet specific U value requirements. For the first time, this applies to replacement windows in existing dwellings. Doesn't apply yet in Scotland.
■ Likewise, boilers must be energy-rated and meet certain standards. Again this applies to replacement boilers for the first time. In addition to this, new heating systems must be switched by more sophisticated controls.

Section Through a Brick and Block Cavity Wall, showing the R value of each element

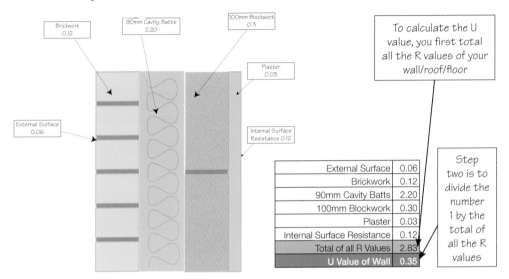

Brickwork 0.12

90mm Cavity Batts 2.20

100mm Blockwork 0.3

Plaster 0.03

External Surface 0.06

Internal Surface Resistance 0.12

To calculate the U value, you first total all the R values of your wall/roof/floor

External Surface	0.06
Brickwork	0.12
90mm Cavity Batts	2.20
100mm Blockwork	0.30
Plaster	0.03
Internal Surface Resistance	0.12
Total of all R Values	2.83
U Value of Wall	0.35

Step two is to divide the number 1 by the total of all the R values

Likewise, these boiler requirements don't apply yet in Scotland.

■ Energy saving lightbulbs will have to be used, though not exclusively or even extensively.

■ A new method of rating energy performance, called the Carbon Index, has been introduced. Previous methods have concentrated on heating costs; this one looks at CO_2 emissions.

Some of the details of the new requirements are looked at in their relevant sections. Thus boilers and controls are back in Chapter 8 and windows and doors are adrift somewhere in Chapter 7. And the lightbulb bit follows shortly (look under Energy Efficient Lighting).

It would be a waste of valuable paper to repeat them here. But the U value requirements, arguably the most important bit of the exercise, have only been skirted around and alluded to till now so it's time to get to grips with them. First an explanation of what a U value is. It's fairly dry academic stuff but it's not without its moments.

What is a U value?

Like most of the other values in our society, U values are declining; however, in this case,

declining values are broadly welcomed. You see, a U value is a measure of heat loss and a material with a low U value loses less heat than one with a high U value. Low U value materials are said to be thermally efficient and, therefore, green. In many ways, that's all you need to know. However, a U value is not like a moral value which you either have or haven't got; it's actually a scientifically derived measurement and knowing your U values will help you make a whole lot more sense of your decisions about how to build and heat your house.

A U value is a measurement of the heat flow (measured in watts) through a square metre (sq m) of a building element for every 1°C temperature difference between the inside and the outside. That reads like the horrible sort of definition you had to learn for Science A-levels, which is why you never did one. It's actually got three different bits to it and in an algebra lesson they'd call them a, b, and c and make it even more unintelligible. However the point that it's trying to make is dead simple: some things are better at retaining heat than others. It's something you know instinctively without ever having to ascribe a value to it – after all

MATERIAL	THERMAL CONDUCTIVITY	THICKNESS in MM	R VALUE		**MATERIAL**	THERMAL CONDUCTIVITY	THICKNESS in MM	R VALUE
INSULATION					BLOCKS			
Fibreglass/Mineral Wool					Clinker Blocks	0.57	100	0.18
Loose Quilt	0.04	100	2.50		Aerated (Celcon)	0.18	100	0.56
	0.04	150	3.75		Concrete Blocks	1.9	100	0.05
	0.04	200	5.00		Granite	2.9	100	0.03
Cavity Batts	0.03	50	1.32		Limestone	1.7	100	0.06
	0.03	65	1.71		Sandstone	2.3	100	0.04
Timber Frame Batts	0.03	90	2.37		Clay Tile	1.0	10	0.01
	0.03	140	3.68		Concrete Tile	1.5	12	0.01
Expanded Polystyrene	0.04	25	0.63		Roofing Felt	0.2	2	0.01
	0.04	50	1.25		50mm Screed	0.4	50	0.13
Extruded Polystyrene	0.03	25	0.83		65mm Screed	0.4	65	0.16
	0.03	50	1.67		100mm Concrete Slab	1.3	100	0.08
Polyurethane	0.02	25	1.00		150mm Concrete Slab	1.3	150	0.12
	0.02	38	1.52		Render	0.57	12	0.02
	0.02	50	2.00		Finish Plasters	0.57	3	0.01
Vermiculite	0.07	100	1.33		AIR GAPS			
OTHER MATERIALS					Cavity 25mm plus			0.20
Softwood	0.13	25	0.19		10mm or less			0.10
	0.13	50	0.38		Ventilated Loft Space			0.20
Hardwood	0.18	25	0.14		SURFACE RESISTANCE			
	0.18	50	0.28		External			0.05
Plywood/Chipboard	0.13	9	0.07		Internal			0.10
	0.13	18	0.14					
	0.13	22	0.17					
Plasterboard	0.25	9.5	0.04					
	0.25	12.5	0.05					
add for Foil Backing			0.20					
uPVC	0.4	2	0.01					
Clay Brick	0.77	102	0.13					

R Values of Common Building Materials

you know just how many clothes you need to wear to feel comfortable. The U value is just some poor sod's attempt at quantifying this fact.

In fact the U value of just about everything you could ever think of using to construct a house has been worked out under laboratory conditions. What they do is establish how quickly heat leaks out of any given material – the boffins call this thermal conductivity. The answer is expressed as a value, known as the lambda value, which is in fact the same as the U value for a one metre thick slab of this

material. The better the insulator, the lower the leakage rate. Our best insulators, things like polyurethane foams, have a lambda value of 0.025watts whilst a poor insulator like granite has a value of 2.9watts. From which you can deduce that polyurethane is around 100 times better than granite as an insulator or, put another way, a 1mm strip of polyurethane would keep you as warm as a 100mm wide granite brick.

The final U value of a material is found by dividing the lambda value of the material by its actual width in metres. Thus 50mm (or 0.05 m) of polyurethane foam (lambda value 0.025 remember) has a U value of $0.025 \div 0.05 = 0.5$.

Now that's all fine and dandy but there is a mathematical problem to be faced here. A wall

Ground Floor R and U Values

EDGE: AREA RATIO	R VALUE	U VALUE
0.2	2.8	0.36
0.3	2.0	0.5
0.4	1.6	0.6
0.5	1.4	0.7
0.6	1.2	0.8
0.7	1.1	0.9
0.8	1.0	1.0

Ground floor heat-loss calculations are a special case (see previous page). Edge:Area ratio is calculated by dividing the GF perimter length in metres by the GF area in m²

If you want to improve on these 'as built' U values, you need to add insulation. To recalculate the new U value, add the edge:area R value to the R value of your chosen insulation, then calculate the U value

is conventionally made up of maybe four or five different elements. Each one has its own U value and each contributes in some way to the insulating capabilities of that wall. Now in order to work out the cumulative U value of the wall you need some method of combining these values. You can't just add the U values together or subtract them from one another; you get a nonsensical answer. The trick is done by switching U values into R values, resistance values. R values are a mirror image of U values – the higher they go, the more they resist the passage of heat. To switch between U values and R values you always divide the number you are working with into 1. So a U value of 0.5 is an R value of 2.0 (i.e. $1 \div 0.5 = 2$). And an R value of 4 is the same as a U value of 0.25 (i.e. $1 \div 4 = 0.25$). Unlike U values, you can add R values together and get a coherent answer. When you've added all the R values together to give you a cumulative R value figure, you can then convert this total back to U values. It's not that difficult. I just explained it to my 11-year old son Adam who understood it but added 'it wasn't exactly easy'.

Interestingly, the Americans prefer to work everything in R values and you rarely see them refer to U values. Note however that if you get hold of some US building literature and you think their R values look amazingly high, it's not because they only build eco-cabins but because they use imperial measurements. A metric R value is worth 5.68 Imperial ones. R values are arguably a simpler concept than U values – the higher the better – but U values

are more useful because you can use them for whole house heat calculations.

Commentary

The R value table covers most of the regular building elements that you might meet in constructing a new house. You can use it to roughly work out your own construction's U values by adding all the R values together and dividing 1 by the result. I have used the most regular thicknesses, but if you are not using one of these, remember that R values can be scaled up or down directly in proportion to the

Diagram 1 **Summary of Elemental Method**

[a] if windows have wood or PVC frames
[b] if windows have metal frames
[c] includes the effect of the unheated space (see paragraph 0.8)

The 2002 Elemental U values for England & Wales, taken from Part L of the Building Regs thickness of the material so that you can readily calculate your own. And also bear in mind that in more complex layers, such as a timber stud wall where the voids are filled with insulation, you have to work out the average R value based on the proportions of the area that are timber and insulation – typically 20 per cent is timber and 80 per cent is insulation.

Eagle-eyed readers will be asking 'Where's the glass?' and the answer is back in the Glazing section in Chapter 7, 'Superstructure'. Glass is a special case; when it's sunny, it gains heat – indeed it's specified as a heat source in passive solar designs.

Ground floors

U values for ground floors are also a special case and the process for calculating them is quite different, largely because heat has difficulty travelling in a downwards direction. However the cold bridging effect around the edges of the floors is pronounced and so the key calculation is concerned not with the R values of all the bits of the floor but in establishing a ratio of the edge or perimeter of the floor with the area of the floor. You measure the length of the perimeter walls (heated area only) in metres and divide the result by the area of the floor (heated area only) in square metres. It makes no difference if your ground floor is suspended or ground bearing, timber or concrete. On the benchmark house the calculation looks like this.
■ Perimeter walls are 60 m long; ground floor is 110 sq m. 60 ÷ 110 = 0.55.

This ratio has to be looked up on a table from which the R value and the U value can be read off – remember the U value = 1 ÷ R value. Deconstruct the table and you can see that the bigger and squarer the building, the less heat it loses through the ground floor. A relatively small footprint like the benchmark house has a U value of around 0.75 without the addition of any underfloor insulation. This was acceptable practice until the 2002 thermal regs came into effect. Now it is virtually compulsory to have some dedicated floor insulation in order to get the U values down to around 0.25.

Radiant barriers

One other problem with all these measurements is that they are very good at measuring conduction through building materials but much less good at spotting the two other methods of heat transfer, convection and radiation. There are a number of new products around, noticeably the reflective barriers (also discussed in Chapter 7) which simply don't work in conventional laboratory tests used to establish thermal conductivity. In order to prove their effectiveness, they have to be trialled side by side with equivalent products, a procedure known as witness testing. The powers that be seem quite happy to accept witness testing but there remain serious doubts about just how these new products work and whether the tests are utterly bona fide. No one is suggesting that they are fiddled – just that maybe they are measuring some other aspect of energy saving, such as air tightness.

U values in 2002

The basic 2002 U value standards are clear enough to comprehend from the accompanying diagram. In Scotland, the wall U value is slightly lower than England & Wales – it's 0.3 rather than 0.35. In the Irish Republic it is lower still at 0.27. As we go to press, new, yet tighter, U values are under review, for implementation in late 2005.

You don't have to build to these U values slavishly. There is a little leeway and a little trading-off available. You may, for instance, be able to use less insulation in exchange for a more efficient boiler. And if you are renovating a listed building you may well be exempted from some of the measures, notably the requirement for energy efficient glazing. 'No way!' say English Heritage.

■ Heat calcs and energy ratings

To get a feel for what U values can do for you, I have run some simplified heat calculations through the spreadsheet (see the table Benchmark House: Calculating Specific

Benchmark House - Calculating Specific Heat Loss

Elements	Area	U VALUE	1975	2002	Eco
A: SLOPING ROOF	24 m²				
1975 - little or no insulation	x	0.8	19 w		
2002 standards 140mm Pu	x	0.2		5 w	
Eco House standard	x	0.1			2 w
B: EXTERNAL WALLS	191 m²				
1975 - no insulation	x	1.5	287 w		
2002 standards	x	0.35		67 w	
Eco House standard	x	0.1			19 w
C: WINDOWS & DOORS	42 m²				
Single Glazing	x	5.0	210 w		
Double Glazing to 2002 standards	x	2.0		84 w	
Eco House standard	x	0.8			34 w
D: UPSTAIRS FLAT CEILINGS	77 m²				
1975 - little or no insulation	x	1.0	77 w		
2002 standards 200mm quilt	x	0.16		12 w	
Eco House standard	x	0.1			8 w
E: FLOOR	127 m²				
No Insulation	x	0.7	93 w		
2002 standards	x	0.25		32 w	
Eco House standard	x	0.1			13 w
F: VENTILATION	459 m³ = volume of the heated space inside the house				
Specific Heat of Air	0.33 w/m³				
Heat required for 1 air change/hr	152 w				
2 air changes/hr(1975)	2.0		303 w		
2002 standard (0.8 air changes/hr)	0.8			121 w	
Eco House standard (with MVHR)	0.3				45 w

WHOLE HOUSE HEAT LOSS

		1975	2002	Eco
Specific Heat Loss (SHL)	A+B+C+D+E+F	988 w	321 w	121 w
Heat load required for 20°C uplift	SHL x 20 ÷1000	19.7 kW	6.4 kW	2.4 kW
20° uplift/m³	Heat load ÷ volume	43 w	14 w	5 w

Heat Loss) showing how it's all done. The measurements are taken from the benchmark house but the U values and the ventilation rates are adjusted with some licence. I have used three versions of the benchmark house.

■ The 1975 house reflects how we built homes then, with little or no insulation. As you might suspect, it leaks heat.

■ The 2002 house is built to the standards now in place in England and Wales.

■ The Eco House or Passive House standard is an example of an ultra-low energy dwelling which requires almost no heating. There are in fact many examples of what are sometimes called zero heat homes across the world but the Passive House standard is one of the best

known. It hails from Germany – there it is called Passiv Haus – and there are around 3,000 of them, mostly in Germany but also now in other countries across Europe. It's not prescriptive – it doesn't tell you how to build a house or what materials you should or shouldn't use; instead, it's a performance standard, a very exacting one. The principles are always the same. Increase the insulation levels to such a degree that lightbulbs, appliances and body heat (the so-called incidentals) cover the entire heat loss for the house right down to your designed for minimum external temperature.

The calculations work as follows.

1. You start with measuring the areas of the

different parts of the house fabric – i.e. walls, roof, floors, joinery. NB The walls and roof figure should exclude the area taken up by the joinery.

2. You then attribute a U value to each of these areas. The 2002 house shows the U values required to meet the current regs.

3. You multiply each area by its U value. The result is the specific heat loss (SHL) for each area. Thus a wall area of 120 sq m with a U value of 0.5 will have a specific heat loss of 60 Watts per 1°C temperature difference between inside and outside.

4. You then work out the specific heat loss for the ventilation. To do this you need to know the volume of the heated air space in the house in cubic metres. And you need to factor in the number of air changes per hour. It can vary from around two to well under a half. If you are building a new home you could probably hazard a guess that you would get to around the half air change per hour mark. Multiply the air changes per hour by the volume and you get the volume of new air passing through the house every hour. Multiply this figure by 0.33 Watts, the specific heat of air (or the heat required to lift 1 cu m of air through 1°C) and you have a specific heat figure for your ventilation requirements.

5. You then add all these figures together to give you a specific heat loss for the whole house. This is the amount of heat, in watts, that it takes to lift the entire house through 1°C. This is the crucial figure. The specific heat loss. It's sort of a sum of all the U values. The lower the SHL, the better insulated the structure is. As it's a measurements in watts, you can easily apply a multiplier to it to find out how much heat you need to keep the house warm on the coldest day. Normally we work to a design temperature of -1°C in England and Wales and -4°C in Scotland. Though you are under no obligation to stick to them, the industry standards for desired temperature in each room are as follows:

- Living rooms/kitchen   21°C
- Bedrooms   18°C
- Hall/stairs   16°C
- Bathrooms   22°C

Passive House Performance Standard	
Maximum annual space heating requirement	15kWh/m²
Max annual energy budget	120kWh/m²
Max heating load	10 watts/m²
Max U value for roof and walls	0.15
Max U value for windows and doors	0.8
Minimum efficiency on heat recovery systems	80%
Maximum air changes per hour (tested by blower door)	0.6 @ 50 Pascals

To make the calculations a bit simpler, you can even all these temperatures to get an average temperature of around 18°C, maybe 19°C if you're a bit of a wuss. In order to keep our homes say 18°C warmer than the minimum design temperatures you would multiply the SHL by 19°C in England & Wales and 22°C in Scotland. The results are always surprisingly small. Try and persuade your plumber that you only need a 5kW boiler in your five bedroom house!

Energy ratings

Energy ratings take the heat loss calcs one stage further and attempt to speculate about how much energy you will actually burn in your home each year. A full blown energy rating on a house is a complex beast involving many different interlinked calculations. The standard one used by the powers that be is the SAP Rating. Its full title is the Government's Standard Assessment Procedure for Energy Rating Dwellings, and it's forever being tweaked here and there as new products come on to the market. The 2001 edition consists of 106 separate measurements and calculations looking in great detail at things like the orientation of your windows, your likely draughts and the amount of heat you will lose in your hot water pipes. From these figures it's possible to make a stab at your probable energy usage per annum expressed in units of energy, financial cost and CO_2 emissions.

It's very easy to pull holes in energy ratings, if you want to. Much of it is incredibly detailed to an altogether anal degree. Yet other bits use broad brush assumptions that can only ever

Benchmark House - Energy Ratings

			1975 House	2002 House	Eco House
A	Specific Heat Loss (1°C temp diff)	kw	0.99 kW	0.32 kW	0.12 kW
B	Incidentals Heat Gains (body heat, electrics)	kW	1.5 kW	1.3 kW	1.1 kW
C	Incidentals ÷ SHL	B÷A	1.52 °C	4.05 °C	9.01 °C
D	Degree Days of Heating		2,500 dd	2,500 dd	2,500 dd
E	Reduction due to Incidentals (200/1°C)	200 x C	300 dd	810 dd	1,820 dd
F	Adjusted Degree Days	D-E	2,200 dd	1,690 dd	680 dd
G	Annual Space Heating Demand	Fx24xA	52,200 kWh	13,000 kWh	2,000 kWh
	Add for Domestic Hot water				
Ha	say 4 people at 1000kWh ea/annum		4,000 kWh	4,000 kWh	4,000 kWh
Hb	Passive House uses Solar Panels (50% off)				2,000 kWh
H	Net use for DHW	Ha-Hb	4,000 kWh	4,000 kWh	2,000 kWh
I	Combined Total for Space Heating and DHW	G+H	56,200 kWh	17,000 kWh	4,000 kWh
	Gas				
J	Allowance for Boiler Efficiency		68%	78%	90%
K	kWh Actually Consumed	I÷J	82,600 kWh	21,800 kWh	4,400 kWh
L	Unit Cost of Gas/kWh (in pence)	1.5			
M	Annual Cost (exc standing orders)		£ 1,239	£ 327	£ 66
N	Carbon Emmissions for Gas	0.19	kg/kWh		
P	Carbon emissions in kg/annum		15700 kg	4100 kg	800 kg
Q	Carbon emissions per square metre	162	97	25	5
R	Adjust by adding 45m² to floor area	207	76	20	4
	Carbon Index Score		0.8	6.4	10.0
	Oil				
J	Allowance for boiler efficiency		70%	85%	95%
K	kWh actually consumed	I÷J	80,300 kWh	20,000 kWh	4,200 kWh
L	Unit cost of oil/kWh (in pence)	1.9			
M	Annual cost (exc standing orders)		£ 1,526	£ 380	£ 80
N	Carbon emmissions for oil	0.27	kg/kWh		
P	Carbon emissions in kg/annum		21700	5400	1100
Q	Carbon emissions per square metre	162	134	33	7
R	Adjust by adding 45m² to floor area	207	105	26	5
	Carbon Index Score		0.0	5.6	10.0
	Dirty Electricity				
J	Allowance for efficiency		100%	100%	100%
K	kWh actually consumed	I÷J	56,200 kWh	17,000 kWh	4,000 kWh
L	Unit cost of electricity/kWh (in pence)	4.0			
M	Annual cost (exc standing orders)		£ 2,248	£ 680	£ 160
N	Carbon emmissions for elelctricity	0.41	kg/kWh		
P	Carbon emissions in kg/annum		23000	7000	1600
Q	Carbon emissions per square metre	162	142	43	10
R	Adjust by adding 45m² to floor area	207	111	34	8
	Carbon Index Score		0.0	4.4	9.6

approximate real energy use. For instance, hot water use is estimated to rise in proportion to the house floor area. Anyone can see that it's actually more likely to be affected by the number of people living in the house but a dumb spreadsheet can't speculate about that,

can it? So in order to be able to compare one house with another, floor area is used a lot. Yet energy ratings are a useful exercise if only to help us understand just how houses work and how they do and do not burn energy.

Rather than go through SAP 2001 step by

step, I have built a very dumbed down version in the table 'Benchmark House: Energy Ratings' which shows the basics. The big variables are the Specific Heat Loss (already worked out for three different standards in the table), the fuel used and the boiler efficiencies. Common sense really. The Carbon Index is now the preferred way of ranking new homes energy-wise: if you manage to match or beat 8.0 on the carbon index then your home is deemed to have passed the 2002 thermal requirements, however it is built.

Here are a few notes on the table to help make sense of it.

■ A: Specific Heat Loss (SHL). This is calculated in the table 'Benchmark House: Calculating Specific Heat Loss.' It the basis of the energy rating. Normally it's expressed in Watts (as this is what U values are) but here I've divided the watts by 1,000 to make it kilowatts because it makes better sense later on in the table.

■ B: Incidentals. This is the heat that you pump inadvertently into the house by way of lights, appliances, solar gains from sunshine, all those standby lights on computers and TVs and, of course, body heat. A person at rest gives off just over 100 Watts, whilst moderate physical exercise gives off around 400 Watts. In all incidentals probably contribute between 1,000W (1kW) and 1,500W (1.5kW) to a typical household. Like much in the world of energy rating, incidentals are very variable and so a vague approximate figure is used. At times (during parties, for instance) the incidentals could amount to several kW of heat being produced.

Carbon Index Table	
Carbon factor(CF) kg/m²	Carbon Index CI
7.17 or less	10
8	9.6
9	9.1
10	8.7
11	8.3
12	6
13	7.7
14	7.4
15	7.1
16	6.9
17	6.6
18	6.4
19	6.2
20	6
22	5.6
24	5.3
26	5
28	4.7
30	4.4
32	4.2
34	3.9
36	3.7
38	3.5
40	3.3
45	2.8
50	2.4
55	2
60	1.7
65	1.4
70	1.1
75	0.8
80	0.6
85	0.3
90	0.1
92 or more	0

And at other times (whilst you're away they could amount to nothing at all.

■ C: Incidentals divided by the Specific Heat Loss. Why? The SHL represents the rate of heat loss from the house for every 1°C temperature difference between inside and outside. If you wish to keep the inside of the house 20°C warmer than the outside, then you will require twenty times more heat than the SHL to achieve this. But if your incidentals are already providing some of this heat, then you need to subtract this amount from your overall heating requirement. So this figure tells you how much of your heating load will be accounted for by your incidentals. And the answer can be expressed in degrees Celsius because each SHL unit is 1°C. Neat, isn't it?

■ D: Degree days. Nothing to do with your daughter's impending graduation from the University of Wensleydale where she just squeezed a third in Cheesemaking. Degree days are in fact a measurement of how cold each place gets in winter. Everyday it gets one degree below an agreed base temperature (I thinks it's around 15°C) counts as one degree day. If it gets to zero, then that day would count as a 15 degree day. Total it up for the whole year and you get an annual degree days total. In Britain it varies from 1,800 DD at Land's End to 3,000 at John O'Groats. The figure of 2,500 DD is taken here, just above average. Just think, one of the benefits of global warming is that the typical DD figures will actually be falling year on year.

■ E: Reduction due to incidentals. Now here's

a tweak and a half. Read this one carefully. If your incidentals can be expressed in degrees of heating (see above), then it follows that they can be subtracted from the number of degree days you need to cover. In effect, they lower your 15°C base temperature. Each degree less heat required because of your incidentals amounts to roughly 200 degree days less over a year – in fact the relationship isn't directly proportional but this is a dumbed-down table – what did you expect?

■ G: Having done this calculation, you can then have a healthy stab at how much heat you will actually need in your home to keep it warm throughout the heating season. You take the adjusted degree days, you multiply by 24 because there are 24 hours in every day and then you multiply this by your SHL figure. Voila. You have an answer in kilowatt hours (kWh) used per annum.

What is fascinating here is to momentarily reflect on the role of incidental heating in all this. Although the actual amount of incidental heat doesn't alter a great deal between the three different houses I have examined, the reduction in degree days rises dramatically as you increase the insulation levels, thereby reducing the SHL. In the extremely well insulated Eco House, you need just over 1kW of incidental heat to cover the anticipated heating requirements for the whole house whereas in the 1975 house the same amount of incidental heat is (I can't resist it) virtually incidental.

Back to the task in hand.

■ H: Domestic Hot Water (DHW) requirements. As already discussed, this part of the calculation is largely guesswork. But 4,000 kWh is enough for 180lts of hot water every day of the year, about 2.5 bathfulls. That's probably what four people would use. I have given the Eco House some credit (2,000 kWh) for having half their hot water being supplied by solar panels – it's the sort of thing Passive House people would do.

■ I: Combine space heating and DHW and you have an estimate of annual energy demand (in kWh).

■ J and K: Boiler efficiency. Now boilers are not 100 per cent efficient – see Chapter 8, 'Boilers'. They have been getting more efficient and the latest, state of the art, condensing boilers have broken through the 90 per cent efficiency barrier, but you still need to factor the boiler efficiency into the calculations.

■ L and M: Fuel costs. Now we have a figure for consumption, we can calculate a fuel cost.

■ N to R: Carbon emissions. Each fuel has a carbon emission factor. From this you can readily work out the total carbon dioxide release for each house type, by fuel type. And divide by the floor area to get a kg of carbon dioxide per square metre, the basis of the Carbon Index. In fact there is one more little tweak that goes in here, one that I don't begin to understand but need to point out. In the SAP worksheet, they ask you to add 45 sq m to your floor area before you divide your carbon emissions by it. Why 45 sq m? It tends to give a better result to smaller homes (obvious when you think about it) so it may be a subtle drive by the government to stop us building big houses. Maybe not. The fact is if you don't indulge in this tweak, you end up with Carbon Index figures which don't tally. The conversion of carbon emissions to Carbon Index is given in the table on the page opposite.

■ *Energy saving tips*

The benchmark house was not designed as a 'green' house which would have fantastically low running costs, and yet it is interesting to note that the combined bills for space and water heating come to just 35 per cent of the total fuel bills. Much of the literature and advertising you see aimed at selfbuilders and professionals alike goes on and on about thermal-efficient this and energy-saving that and how you must have this gizmo to have low heating bills and save the planet; but a balanced view of all this will show you that you already have low heating bills in a new house and that if you want to lower fuel bills then it is best to concentrate on other areas.

The table summarises twenty-one commonly considered measures that can be taken by the householder wanting a low energy consuming house with low fuel bills. Details on most of these measures are looked at in greater depth in their relevant sections in other parts of the book, but here they are grouped together for easier comparison. The results I find rather extraordinary; the most cost-effective measures are generally the least talked about and the least advertised and, conversely, the products which tend to get 'sold' to us as ultra-green are often of very doubtful value.

Do without an Aga
It's not just Agas. Any cast iron stove will suck in power like Saddam Hussein. And belt out heat like it's Basra in August. They are fine in pre-1975 housing but you will cook faster than your dinner if you put one in a post-2002 house. If you must have one, think seriously about having a swimming pool as well. Then you'll have somewhere useful to put all that surplus heat.

Open Fires
Arguably, the single most effective energy saving measure a new housebuilder can take is to do away with any thoughts of an open fire at the design stage. Fires are a costly feature to build, they are inefficient in terms of heat output and, when not in use, the chimney sucks up warm air like a vacuum cleaner. Despite this, people (otherwise known as the market) love real fires and they are unlikely to go out of fashion for a while to come. Using an enclosed stove doubles the heating efficiency of an open fire but halves the enjoyment value. See the sections Fires and Chimneys (Chapter 7, 'Superstructure') and Alternative heating (Chapter 8, 'Services').

Passive solar design
Sounds very grand but all it means is orienting your dayrooms so that they face south. Usually the possibility of doing this is dictated by the site and, given the choice, most people would opt for it instinctively. A good passive solar design will

save around £30 per annum in fuel bills.

Off-peak electricity
Switch to an Economy 7 meter and, for an additional standing charge of around £20 per annum, you get seven hours night-time electricity at under 40 per cent of peak-rate cost. Buy appliances with timers (or buy separate timers for £20) and run appliances at off-peak rates. Potential saving: £50 per annum.

This is saving you money but isn't, strictly speaking, saving energy. Night-time electricity use is no different to daytime use in this respect. However the reason night-time electricity is cheap is that there is comparatively little demand for electricity at night and yet they can't shut down all the power stations – especially the nuclear ones – at the flick of a switch. So using electricity at night is saving energy indirectly because it would otherwise probably be wasted.

Gas tumble dryers
Buying a gas-fired tumble dryer will pay for itself within three years. One for gas customers only. See following section, Kitchen and Laundry.

Gas cooking
Gas cooking is much cheaper than electric. Gas hobs are priced the same as electric ones but gas ovens are rather more expensive. Doesn't suit everyone. See following section, Kitchen and Laundry.

Fuel choices
Oil and mains gas are currently the two cheapest fuels. Most people gravitate to these if possible. Electric heating is expensive in comparison though note the growing interest in ground-to-water heat pumps. Expensive to install but very cheap to run.

Draught proofing
Paying proper attention to draught proofing is well worthwhile and not expensive. See also Ventilation section in Chapter 8. Unplanned

Energy Saving Tips

	EXTRA COST	LIKELY ANNUAL SAVING
GOOD		
Do without an Aga	Save £5,000	£300
Do without Open Fire and Chimney	Save £2,000	£50
Passive Solar Design	No cost	£30
Run Appliances on Off-Peak Electricity	£20/annum	£70
Use a Gas Tumble Dryer	£50	£25
Cook by Gas instead of Electricity	£150	£50
Choose the Right Fuel	zero-£400	£120
Fastidious Draught Proofing	£200	£30
Fit a Gas-fired Condensing Boiler	£200	£30
Buy Efficient Electrical Appliances	£200	£40
MODERATE		
Switch to Timber Frame Construction	£0-£3,000	£50
Add an extra 25mm of Ground Floor Insulation	£60	£5
Add 25mm Extra Cavity Wall Insulation	£150	£20
Put 100mm of Extra Insulation in the Roofspace	£40	£5
Fit Better Space Heating Controls	£200	£20
Design an Energy Saving Lighting Scheme	£500	£45
Fit a Super-lagged, Quick Recovery Cylinder	£50	£5
POOR		
Fit High Performance Windows	£800	£20
Fit Solar Hot Water Panels	£3,000	£40
Fit PV Solar Electric Cells	£10,000	£150
Fit a Heat Recovery System	£1,500	£0

ventilation, as it is sometimes known, is likely to be a much bigger problem in complex shaped homes with lots of junctions.

Condensing boilers

A gas-fired heating system run off a condensing boiler will cost an extra £200 to install but should save £30 per annum on heating and hot water costs. Really alone of the high-tech green gizmos, the condensing boiler is genuinely cost effective. Oil-fired condensers are very much more expensive and, therefore, only rate as moderate. See section on Boilers in Chapter 8.

Efficient appliances

Washing machines, electric tumble dryers, dishwashers, each cost around £40 per annum in electricity to run. Fridges and freezers cost around £25 each. Specify 'low energy' models when buying new and you could save 25 per cent on these annual costs. See following section, Kitchen and Laundry.

Floor insulation

The 2002 standards require significant levels of insulation under the ground floor, typically either 50mm of polyurethane or 100mm of polystyrene. Upping the spec from this standard has very little impact on energy saving. See Flooring in Chapter 7.

Extra cavity wall insulation

Adding extra insulation in the external walls helps a bit but the building regulations have already gone past the point of simple economic return.

Extra loft insulation

Similar arguments apply here as to cavity walls. You may well be surprised by what the new standards for roof insulation are. A U value of 0.16 in the floor of the loft requires no less than 250mm of fibreglass quilt, to be laid in two rolls one between the joists and one above. Adding another 50mm of insulation to this blanket will still just about pay for itself in a few years but above 300mm the return falls away.

Heating controls

Almost all central heating controls are cost

effective, though the savings are hard to quantify. Generally speaking, it is worth spending money on good controls though some of the more advanced controls, like boiler managers and zone control, are not appropriate to every situation. Thermostatic radiator valves (TRVs) cost about £8 per radiator; system managers are available for an extra £100. See section on Heating Controls in Chapter 8.

Low-Energy Lighting

Annual electricity bill for lighting a four-bedroom house is likely to be around £130: compact fluorescent 'energy saving' bulbs are cost effective, but are not suitable in every situation. A well designed lighting scheme might save £45 per annum in running costs but is likely to cost £500+ to install. Note that new houses are now required to have some energy efficient bulbs. See following section, Energy Efficient Lighting.

Better hot water cylinders

All new cylinders are pre-lagged to reduce heat loss to a minimum, though some are better than others: look for one with 50mm of polyurethane insulation. A 'quick recovery' cylinder will cost an extra £50 to buy but will save £5 per annum in making better use of boiler output. See section on Domestic Hot Water in Chapter 8.

Switching to Timber Frame

This always used to be a sure-fire energy saver because a standard 90mm timber frame, stuffed with fibreglass or Rockwool, easily outshone most masonry walls in terms of insulation. But the new requirement for wall U values of 0.35 means that this method of insulating timber frame is no longer enough (it used to get a U value of around 0.4). There are several different ways of making up the difference, all considerably more expensive. It's probably rather fatuous to try and reduce this complex matter to a simple money in to money saved equation but I've done it, to make you think if nothing else. I still hold that for most people

(maybe not the Scots) timber frame is slightly more expensive and yet it's still going to tend to give better energy performance than block work. See Inner Skin section in Chapter 7.

Solar panels

Don't be tempted by solar panels unless they cost less than £300, not on cost grounds at any rate. Annual savings are likely to be less than £40. See Alternative Heating section in Chapter 8, 'Services'.

High performance windows

What were referred to as high performance windows in the last edition of this book are now bog standard windows – cf. Jeld Wen's Stormsure range. Again, the new thermal regs are behind this change. Low performance windows no longer cut the mustard. However you can still easily out spec Jeld Wen windows. There are many people making very high performance windows, notably a lot of Scandinavian triple glazed ones with U values down at 1.3 (as compared to 2.0 needed to pass the regs). The savings are unlikely to be more than £20 a year. See Windows section in Chapter 7, 'Superstructure'.

Heat Recovery Systems

These are justifiable in terms of energy savings but not in terms of financial savings. They cost a great deal (£1500+) and many of them cost more to run than they could possibly save. Even a system which saves three times the amount of energy it consumes may still end up costing you, because the energy saved costs around 2p per kWh whilst the energy used to run the thing costs over 6p per kWh (i.e. peak-rate electricity). See Ventilation section in Chapter 8 for more information about MVHR (as it gets referred to) and also passive stack ventilation, a non-mechanical alternative which is greener because it uses no power. Worth mentioning also that most of these MVHR systems do not sell themselves principally on their energy saving capabilities; rather they emphasise the benefits of controlled ventilation and filtered air.

The ground-source heat pump is an interesting energy saving option. In payback terms, it only rates as a Poor, costing as it does around £8,000 to install. But it is cheap and clean to run. In order to get the pipe into the ground, it is usually necessary to dig up the garden.

◼ *Low energy lighting*

Slipped into the 2002 thermal building regs was a little stipulation about lighting. For the first time, you are required to pay attention to the watts you burn through your lights. It's not terribly draconian but it is there – many people will find that offensive enough. There is a remorseless logic about it all, of which more in a minute, but first a look at what Part L requires of you if you are building a home or even just an extension. It asks you to install at least one fluorescent or compact fluorescent bulb for every three rooms you create. Hall, stairs and landings count as one room. Garages, lofts and outhouses don't. En-suite bathrooms and utility rooms – it doesn't say, leaving plenty of room to argue. So the benchmark house has approximately 12 rooms so it would be required to fit four CF bulbs (or tubes). No problem, you say. Stick a few bulbs in and replace them with something that looks nicer when the building inspector has finalled the project. Not so fast. They have thought of that one. They are stipulating that you have to use fittings that will only take a fluorescent tube or a CF bulb. It doesn't stipulate where you should fit these lights but you are expected to go for somewhere where you would expect to

get reasonably heavy use, like halls and stairs or living rooms and kitchens.

There's more. The regs extend to external lighting. This is a first too. You are no longer allowed to rig up permanent lighting without it being energy efficient. You can fulfil this requirement either by using CF bulbs or by installing it with daylight and movement sensors – i.e. so it's only on occasionally.

So what effect will it have and what of this remorseless logic? Lighting is energy intensive and relatively expensive because a) it is inefficient (95 per cent of the energy coming out of a standard GLS light bulb is heat) and b) it is using peak-rate electricity at around four times the price of oil or gas. The benchmark house has 60 lights fitted – mostly low voltage halogen downlighters – and in normal usage patterns about a third of these will be heavily used, a third will be lightly used and a third rarely used.

A typical usage pattern would look something like this:
◼ 20 lamps @ 35 Watts. 2,000hrs per annum. 1,500kWh used, cost £110.
◼ 20 lamps @ 35 Watts. 500hrs per annum. 350kWh used, cost £25.
◼ 20 lamps @ 35 Watts. 50hrs/annum. 30kWh used, cost £2.

Now if four of these heavily used lights are replaced by energy efficient lightbulbs, then you could anticipate savings of 45W per bulb or 360 kWh per annum. That's 20 per cent of the overall lighting bill. In terms of kWhs burned the lights amount to no more than eight per cent of the total burnt but because electricity is so much more expensive than gas or oil, this mounts up to nearly 25 per cent of the overall fuel bill. So it does appear quite logical for the building regs to concern themselves with lighting efficiency.

There is no reason why you have to stop at the building regs minimum. You could probably halve the power used to light your home, if you set your mind to it. How?

Concentrate on the areas of heavy usage, which are generally kitchens, living rooms,

Benchmark House: Anticipated Annual Fuel Bills

Figures for 200m² house built to 2002 regs

	kWh	%	cost	%
Central Heating (Oil)	15300	52%	£ 250	26%
Water Heating (Oil)	4700	16%	£ 80	8%
LPG Gas Cooking	500	2%	£ 20	2%
Household appliances	3060	10%	£ 200	21%
Lights	3000	10%	£ 200	21%
Other electrical equipment	3010	10%	£ 200	21%
Electricity Standing Charge			£ 25	3%
ANNUAL FUEL BILLS			£ 975	100%
Heating Oil			£ 330	34%
LPGas Bottles			£ 20	2%
Electricity			£ 625	64%
COSTS INCLUDE VAT @ 5%				

hallways, stairwells and studies; the areas of lighter use (typically bedroom and bathroom lighting) are unlikely to produce significant savings. You could substitute your 12 most heavily used GLS bulbs with compact fluorescent, energy saving ones.

The problem is that energy saving light bulbs are not always particularly suitable as direct replacements for GLS bulbs; they cannot be easily dimmed, the light quality tends to be a bit too cold for most people's taste, and they are generally not compatible with standard lampshades. Substituting fluorescent light for tungsten light makes for subtle changes in atmosphere, and ill-planned installation can end up putting people off energy-saving light bulbs for good. Energy efficient lighting doesn't have to be bad lighting but for too many people this is exactly what it becomes when they swap over to a compact fluorescent bulb. However technology has moved on since the early days of CF bulbs and the current crop are smaller, more efficient and give better light quality. A Which? report (Jan 2004) rated the Osram and Philips ranges: not only was light quality good but the bulbs are small enough to be exchangeable with GLS bulbs in standard light fittings. IKEA also scored highly with a 20 watt bulb costing just £3.

Kitchens
Fluorescent lighting can work well in the

kitchen – specialised lights can be used for both task and background lighting.

Living areas
In contrast, fluorescent lighting will not work well in living rooms and dining rooms. Low-voltage downlighting is an option (they use roughly half the power of a GLS bulb but twice the power of a fluorescent) but because of the tightly focused nature of the beams, you will end up using twice as many fittings which neatly cancels out their 50 per cent efficiency rating over GLS bulbs. Low-voltage does not have to be confined to downlighters and a well-designed scheme could achieve adequate lighting from half the number of lamps by using mini-spots and/or uplighters.

Hallways and stairs
The other areas of heavy use tend to be in hallways and stairwells. Arguably light quality is not so important here and there are numerous compact fluorescent (CF) fittings which will fit the task. Whilst you may struggle to get a CF bulb to look good in a lampshade, the small 9 W bulbs do fit into most uplighters and there are an increasing number of specialised low-energy light fittings becoming available: downlighters, glazed ceiling fittings and wall lights. They tend to cost around £30 where the conventional fittings might be had for under a tenner and so they need to be heavily used to justify the extra expense.

External
If you plan on external lights the 2002 regs require that you either control them with timed passive infra-red (PIR) switches or, if you want them on permanently, use low-energy fittings. As for utility rooms and garages, fluorescent lights are commonly used here in any event and they can't readily be improved on.

Intelligent switches
Don't overlook the fact that one of the best ways to save lighting bills is to turn lights off when they are not being used. However, if you've got

a house full of stroppy teenagers this may not be quite as easy as it sounds. You can, of course, fit time switches in hallways and stairwells but they tend to be a bit institutional. We are now quite used to seeing PIR switching used for external security but its use indoors to control lighting is still rare, but no more expensive than external PIRs (prices from around £25). Home Automation produce an informative price list which includes such things, as well as dimmers for low-voltage and compact fluorescent lighting.

Summary

A low-energy lighting scheme needs to be carefully designed to be successful. With potential extra savings of £50 per annum, it is worth spending money on too. There is precious little professional advice on the subject – many lighting consultants will specify lots of low-voltage halogen fittings that will cost you much money but which won't save on running costs. Many architects know next to nothing about lighting design, and electricians are taught only the rudiments of good lighting practice. How much you spend on energy saving features is entirely up to you but if your budget extends much past £500 on a four-bedroom house like the benchmark house, then you are unlikely to get cost effective savings.

■ Kitchen & laundry

Together with lighting, household appliances are the great unseen energy consumers. An examination of the fuel costs for a new home reveal that, even without specifying super-insulation levels and condensing boilers, fuel bills are actually higher for cooking, kitchen appliances and lighting than they are for space and hot water heating. Yet with a little application it should be possible to reduce running costs by nearly half.

The Annual Fuel Bills table includes a breakdown of estimated fuel costs for cooking and household appliances in the benchmark house using the standard arrangements and comparing them with the cheapest alternative.

The 'normal' arrangement assumes all electric appliances using peak rate power: the 'cheapest' assumes a mains gas supply is available. These are very much notional average bills; a 'dinky' household, without children, might well run up bills less than half this amount whilst a large family could easily double the sums.

Cooking

Gas cooking is way cheaper than using electricity; cooking by gas costs almost a quarter of what it costs to cook using peak-rate electricity. Many people prefer cooking on a gas hob (and most developers' packages offer them as an alternative at no extra cost) but gas ovens have an undeservedly poor reputation and they are now few and far between, particularly in the built-in market. Electric controls and electronic ignition have greatly improved the traditional gas oven and if you use a main oven or grill more than one hour a week, it will be worth paying the extra £150 to install a gas oven. Stoves, Canon, Parkinson Cowan, New World still produce them; British Gas showrooms (now called Energy Centres) display them although they are not cheap places to shop. MFI has a number of cheaply priced gas ovens (made for them by Philips and Stoves). If mains gas is not available, then LPG models will still produce 50 per cent savings on electric cooking.

If electric cooking is the only sensible option, there is currently very little one can do to reduce costs. Energy efficiency has yet to make any significant impact on this area, but note that microwaves are very efficient at cooking small quantities. Microwaves are quick and work at much lower power than conventional electric cookers: on the other hand, food bought ready for microwaving is expensive. It all depends on how you use them. The induction hob, described in Chapter 11 'Kitchen appliances', would also seem to offer efficiencies over an ordinary ceramic hob

Note that cast-iron stoves – and Agas in particular – are very heavy users of fuel. A gas or oil-fired Aga kept on all year would cost over £400 per annum to run.

Energy use for household appliances

Appliance	rating in watts	Hours used per annum	kWh used per annum	Annual running costs
Gas fired	costed @ 1.5p/kWh			
Gas Hobs	2000	200	400	£ 6
Gas Ovens	2000	300	600	£ 9
Gas Tumble Dryers	1000	300	300	£ 5
Electric	costed @ 6.5p/kWh			
Electric Hob	2000	200	400	£ 26
Electric Oven	2000	300	600	£ 39
Microwave	2000	100	200	£ 13
Fridge/Freezer	50	8760	440	£ 29
Small Fridge (120lt)	25	8760	220	£ 14
Dishwasher	1200	400	480	£ 31
Washing Machine	1200	350	420	£ 27
Electric Tumble Dryer	1000	200	200	£ 13
Kettle	3000	100	300	£ 20
Iron	2000	50	100	£ 7
TV	100	1500	150	£ 10
Computers	150	1500	230	£ 15
Stand-by Equipment/Chargers	10	8760	90	£ 6
Heavy-use GLS Lightbulb	60	1500	90	£ 6
Heavy-use Energy-efficient Light	18	1500	30	£ 2
Medium-use GLS Lightbulb	60	500	30	£ 2

Tumble dryers

If mains gas is available, then go for a gas-fired tumble dryer. Canon and Crosslee White Knight both produce reasonably priced gas tumble dryers. Expect to pay £220 plus which is 50 per cent more than the cheapest electric versions, and allow for gas plumbing, but they are very much cheaper to run – payback period is around five years. Green, but are they any good? My limited experience suggests they are desperately slow.

Off-peak electricity

If you are unable to get mains gas, then fit an Economy 7 meter and you can take advantage of electricity at around 40 per cent of the peak rate by arranging to use your appliances during off-peak hours. If you don't lead a nocturnal lifestyle, then buy equipment with delay timers or make sure that you can access the sockets and fit separate delay timers (cost £15-20). Despite the large savings to be had, delay timers still hardly feature as a sales aid: you have to go looking for them.

Off-peak electricity charges are complex to understand; each supply company (REC) sets its own charges.
■ All of them increase the standing charge (tariff) for letting you buy cheap rate supplies. Increased tariffs vary from £15 to £25 per annum extra.
■ All of them have an off-peak rate of around 2.5p per kWh (compared with peak rates of 7p per kWh or higher) at which you will be charged for all electricity supplies for seven hours each night.

The economies to be gained from using an off-peak tariff will vary from area to area, but if properly managed it should result in a reduction in electricity bills of 15 per cent, perhaps more.

Hot and cold fill

Look for dishwashers and washing machines which can be filled from your hot water pipes rather than heating their own water. This is now standard on new washing machines but is still rare on dishwashers (though Ariston make one). If using machines on delayed night-time switching, then separate H&C fill is of little benefit as the disparity between the costs of off-peak electrically heated water and boiler heated water is reduced.

Energy efficient?

Many manufacturers are jumping on the bandwagon in claiming to produce machines which save on electricity, water and detergents. This is a complicated area and many of the claims are at best marginal and depend on the user understanding just what is expected of them. To help spread a little light into this murky area, fridges, freezers and washing machines are now routinely energy labelled to help the customer make an informed decision about how much power they use. A visit to my local Curry's revealed a wide range of scores: a Bosch Economic fridge freezer scored A and reckoned to use just 120kWh per annum (cost £8) whilst a giant Hotpoint power guzzler scored G, estimated to use 540kWh per annum (cost £38). Whilst the accuracy of energy labelling (which is carried out by the manufacturers) has been called into question, the fact that there is now a comparative yardstick available on a range of white goods is a big boon. In fact the concept of energy rating bands from A to G looks set to grow: boilers are already sold that way and pretty soon you may see windows following.

Although these savings may not look individually very large, careful purchasing should be able to save £50 or more per annum of peak rate power and metered water. Water saving washing machines actually save remarkably little in cash terms and yet it is this feature which tends to be the strongest selling point on 'Green' appliances.

For most buyers, there will be a number of other factors which will determine which machines they purchase – notably servicing costs and standards, reliability record, easy-to-use controls or perhaps it just all came with the kitchen – and you may well be right to base your decision on these criteria, but don't be afraid to ask about water and electricity use. It is worth paying a little more for machines which perform well but, with the exception of cold storage, running the appliances during off-peak hours is by far the best option if you want to save on running costs. Don't be conned into paying out hundreds of pounds extra for 'eco' products which bring minimal savings to you or the environment; instead, ask why it hasn't got a delay switch fitted.

Use of appliances

Considerable savings can be achieved by using your appliances efficiently. Really these are no more than common sense measures such as drying clothes on washing lines whenever possible, setting washing machine temperatures as low as possible and turning off lights when rooms are empty. If you've a genuine interest in

If you've beeen shopping for white goods recently, you'll be familiar with Energy Labelling. The concept is now spreading to boilers and windows.

energy conservation – or just don't like paying bills – then at least part of the solution is in your hands.

Summary

Energy-efficient appliances – or more particularly energy-efficient use of appliances – can be planned into a new house. The presence of gas on site makes for large cost savings but, even on remoter sites where gas is not available, there are numerous actions you can take to increase fuel efficiency. There is a cost penalty (though it is hard to quantify because there are so many variables) but there are also appreciable savings to be made. However, unlike installing insulation or efficient heating systems, saving energy in the kitchen requires you to interact intelligently with your machines and for many people this is just too much hassle.

■ *Saving water*

Although 95 per cent of UK property is still charged for water and sewage by a rating system, newly constructed housing in England & Wales is invariably metered (not so in Scotland and N. Ireland). Living with a metered water supply is a novel experience for most of us and it takes some getting used to. If you are connecting your drains into the main drains as well as tapping into the local water supplies, your bills will be broken down into four sections:

■ Standing charge for water supply
■ Volume charge for water supply
■ Standing charge for sewage disposal
■ Volume charge for sewage disposal.

Properties that dispose of waste by other means (usually septic tanks) will have other costs to pay instead of sewage charges – see section on Drains, Chapter 6, 'Groundworks'.

Water charges

Unlike fuel prices, water supply charges have been going up. The average charge levied in England and Wales has doubled since 1989 and is only now beginning to level off. Average charge

for water by volume is 70p per cu m, although this can vary from 40p to over £1.00. In addition standing charges average £25 per annum.

Sewage disposal charges

Average charge is 90p per cu m, but this also varies from 40p to £1.50 per cu m in the South West. Welsh and Anglian also charge well above average. Annual standing charges payable for sewage disposal vary from £10 to £60 with an average of just over £30. As a rule, companies with high standing charges have low volume charges and vice versa, so it does tend to even out.

Metering: how it works

Only the water supply is metered. The volume of discharge you pour back down the drains is worked out from the amounts of water you consume: some companies reckon it to be 100 per cent, some 95 per cent and some 90 per cent. If yours works on a 95 per cent figure then, if you were to consume 100 cu m of water, you would be charged for 95 cu m of sewage.

A four-person household will typically use and discharge 185 cu m of water/annum (equivalent to 2300 baths, that's just over six baths a day). This is likely to cost them between £300 and £450 per annum depending on how much their water company charges. This 185 cu m figure is very much an average and a new house with lots of thirsty appliances like dishwashers and power showers, not to mention children, could easily use 50 per cent more. (Incidentally our household of five has all these thirsty appliances and we consistently consume 230 cu m of water per annum). Heavy demand from swimming pools, garden sprinklers and the like would be in addition to these figures.

Comparisons

The charges for average water usage are larger than the anticipated heating bills for a new home. Assuming the average 185 cu m per annum is consumed by our notional four-

How we use water in the home

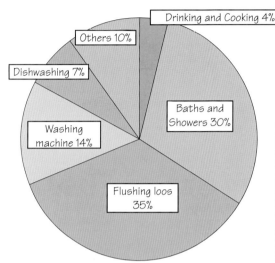

Drinking and Cooking 4%

Others 10%

Dishwashing 7%

Baths and Showers 30%

Washing machine 14%

Flushing loos 35%

1000lts of water = 1 cubic metre = 1 tonne. It's also equivalent to 220 gallons, about 12 bathfulls or 160 flushing loos

Water Appliance Consumption	
Av. Consumption/head	150lts/day
Flushing a Loo	7-10lts
Taking a Bath	80lts
Ordinary Shower	10lts/min
Power Shower	30lts/min
Washing Machines	70-100lts/wash
Dishwashers	25-50lts/wash
Garden Hose/Sprinkler	10lts/min
Tap Dripping Once a Second	5lts/hr

person household, the average bill, including standing charges, will be just over £300 per annum. However, in some high charging areas such as the South West this could rise to over £450 for the same volume of water. In comparison, the estimated space and water heating costs for the benchmark house are just £212 – including five per cent VAT which is not levied on water and sewage services. With so much attention focused on saving energy, let us try to redress the balance and look at reducing water consumption. The pie chart illustrates how we consume our water.

What immediately stands out about these figures is how little water actually passes into our bodies (five per cent) compared to how much is consumed largely to keep us and our homes clean and hygienic. Part of the justification for higher water prices is the cost of maintaining drinking water standards but, on reflection, it seems extraordinary that we should go to such trouble to purify our water supplies in order to pour 95 per cent back down the drains. In theory, at least, there is ample scope to use non-potable water, and ample savings to be made by avoiding relatively expensive metered supplies.

Use less

Before delving into esoteric water-saving schemes, there are a number of common sense ways that water consumption can be reduced without making you smell:

■ Wash yourself under showers, not in baths (impractical with small children)
■ Don't fit a power shower
■ Fit the smallest WC cisterns possible – the industry standard is now down to six litres per flush, thanks to a recent change in the water bylaws, but you may be able to source even smaller cisterns
■ Don't run washing machines and dishwashers unless they are full
■ Don't water lawns; water plants in the evening to avoid evaporation
■ Use water butts (though attractive ones are hard to find)
■ Don't build a swimming pool
■ Pee anywhere except in the loo – easier for some sexes than others.

Water saving

Water-saving schemes are sommat else. They can be divided into two areas: rainwater collection which replaces water you'd normally

Water Bills in England & Wales

ANNUAL CHARGES/ m³			WATER	SEWAGE	COMBINED
		Average Standing Charges	£25	£40	£65
		Average Volume Charges	£ 0.70	£ 0.90	£ 1.60
WATER USED BY 4-PERSON HOUSEHOLD			ANNUAL VOLUME CHARGES		
ACTIVITY	Litres/day	As %	WATER	SEWAGE	COMBINED
Drinking/Cooking	20	4%	£ 5	£ 7	£12
Baths/Showers	150	30%	£ 38	£ 49	£87
Flushing Loos	175	35%	£ 45	£ 57	£102
Washing Machine	70	14%	£ 18	£ 23	£41
Dishwasher	35	7%	£ 9	£ 11	£20
Others	50	10%	£ 13	£ 16	£29
TOTAL	500	100%	£ 128	£ 164	£292
STANDING CHARGES + VOLUME CHARGES			£153	£204	£357
VARIATIONS					
		4-person household, Highest charging area (South West)			£490
		4 -person household, Lowest charging area (Northumbria)			£290
		Average for 3-person household			£280
		Average for 2-person household			£210
		Average for 1-person household			£140

buy through your water meter, and grey water collection which recycles some of the water you have already used.

Rainwater collection

Even in dry lowland England (average rainfall equals 750mm per annum) a four-bedroom house plus detached garage will get around 100 cu m of rain falling on to it during the course of a year. Add in a paved yard and a drive and potentially you could collect your entire 185 cu m annual consumption from the skies overhead. In wetter areas to the north and west this figure could easily double as rainfall levels are so much higher. The potential is there; the problem is that rainfall is not only unpredictable but sporadic whereas household usage is basically quite constant. You need to build a reservoir capable of holding enough rainwater to supply basic household needs, which is exactly what your own water company does on a much larger scale. Starting your very own water supply business may be an appealing prospect for some but it is likely to prove expensive to build and time-consuming to run. The bigger your reservoir, the more effective your own supplies will be in replacing your metered supply, but the more problems you are likely to have with

construction and maintenance.

Rainwater harvesting has become quite trendy in no time at all and a surprising number of selfbuilt homes are fitting tanks, filters and pumps so that they can reuse at least some of their free rainfall in a similar fashion. The Germans have been doing it on a domestic scale for twenty years and three of their systems – IRM, Wisy and KSB – are now available in the UK. Prices quoted are between £1,000 and

There are various methods of designing rainwater harvesting systems. If you don't have a basement, then you need to bury the tank in the ground. This schematic shows the IRM system.

£2,000: for this you get underground storage tanks (either plastic or concrete), filters to take out most of the leaves and twigs and a pump to lift the water back up to the house. Most people use it just for flushing loos, installing a second plumbing system supplying the cisterns from the storage tanks. You can rig it up so that the storage tanks never empty – the mains water cuts in when the level falls too low. More sophisticated arrangements allow rainwater to be used as drinking water but this requires on site treatment which is a complex affair.

Grey water

Only a water recycling scheme will cut down both supply and discharge. Grey water is the term given to waste which is reusable, notably the waste from baths, showers and wash basins. There is potential to recycle this water in the garden and especially for flushing loos. Because the waste from baths and washing is much more regular than rainfall, the storage facilities do not have to be nearly as large to be effective. A large bath-sized tank will be enough to flush ten loos and should get refilled most days.

As with rainwater harvesting, there has been a small explosion of interest in grey water recycling and there are now proprietary systems available using pumps and a small holding tank which can be placed in the loft. The grey water is treated with cleaning agents and passed through a carbon filter. Grey water requires much less storage than rainwater harvesting to be effective but there are potential problems with contamination which need to be addressed. Trials are under way to see just how effective grey water is – if it is as effective as claimed, it will pay for itself in around ten years in a four-person metered household.

Potential

By combining rain-saving and grey water systems, the potential is there to reduce water demand in new housing by over 50 per cent. Whilst the legislation dealing with carbon dioxide emissions (our thermal building regs) has grown steadily more onerous on the housebuilder, water saving has yet to be seriously considered. Yet the harmful effect of CO_2 – the greenhouse effect – remains an unproven hypothesis (albeit with potentially catastrophic consequences), whilst the effects on the environment caused by reservoir building are all too tangible. The best that can be hoped for is that it could be given a much needed boost by exempting developments incorporating water saving schemes from the perilous infrastructure charge – see Chapter 3, 'Pitfalls'.

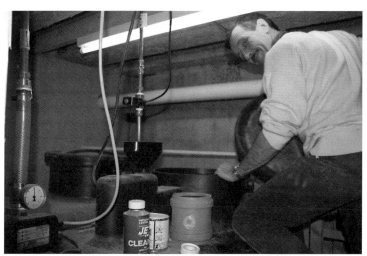

Housed in selfbuilder Adrian Thurley's basement are three rainwater harvesting tanks, supplied by Freewater UK. The cost for the whole system was around £2,500; it takes rainwater from the guttering and reuses it to flush the loos and to fill the washing machine. Adrian commented: "When it's working, it supplies about 60% of our household water. I calculate it's saving us about £7 a week which I am delighted with. The two tanks together hold 7500 litres and it takes just an inch of rain to fill them up."

Paying for leaks

Whilst the problem of a dripping tap is well known (and costly for metered households), it palls into insignificance compared to the potential nightmare of an underground leak. You, the householder, are responsible for all water consumption downstream from the water meter – which is conventionally located outside, close to the plot boundary. Spring a leak underground between the meter and your internal stop tap and you may know nothing about it until a massive water bill arrives on your doorstep (as much as six months later); if you are lucky, the water company will let you off paying the sewage charge, but even so a bad leak might lose as much as 20 cu m of water a day which would cost £1,500 by the time you get your water bill. Be warned that sloppy installation (and loose connections) of metered mains supplies can be very expensive.

Boreholes

There is another way of avoiding water company charges – and infrastructure charges – and that is to sink your own borehole and draw your own water supply up from under the ground. It's where most of the water comes from in SE England and in many other areas besides and, whereas your local water company has a monopoly on piped supplies, there is nothing to stop you tapping into the enormous natural groundwater reservoir directly. That's an oversimplification; there is the small matter of installation costs which vary from £1,000 and £10,000, depending on such matters as the depth of the borehole and the water pressure. For most people, that makes it an extremely expensive way of going about getting water and sends them straight back into the arms of their local water company.

If you are one of the small number who plan to draw their own water supply from under the ground, then you will be responsible for your own water quality. That's not to say that you won't have to submit your water for analysis to the local Environmental Health Inspector: indeed most councils will be around testing

you every couple of years or so. Simple bacteria tests tend to be done in local hospitals and cost around £30; however tests for pollution are more expensive – I was quoted £100 for a nitrate test. The Environmental Health Inspector has the power to condemn your supply but this rarely happens because almost everything can be filtered out – at a cost. My local inspector reckoned that ground water pollution was something of an overstated problem and that when he did come across it, it was very often the house itself that was the cause of the pollution; he advised not to use ground water supplies in conjunction with a septic tank. Obvious really.

■Water treatment

There are two very distinct processes here. You soften (or condition) water in an attempt to prolong the life of your domestic appliances, whereas you filter water in an attempt to prolong your own life. Both techniques are surrounded by a veil of mystery and intrigue which is hard to penetrate, and the whole subject is so rife with claim and counterclaim that it makes the job of the humble commentator akin to negotiating a minefield. Wish me luck as I go in.

Softening and conditioning

If you live in a soft water area (which includes most of Britain above a line drawn between the Humber and the Severn) then this section is one to miss. If in doubt, phone your water company to get figures on local conditions. Even if you live in a hard water area there is no need to panic. Households have been known to function quite adequately for years without so much as a hint of any water softeners about. However, many sane people swear by water softeners and insist that they produce tangible benefits – even if it's only to reduce the amount of soap powder they use in their washing machines

Traditional Softeners

Permutit are the best known name here though

there are a number of other manufacturers. For between £400 and £1,000 you get a big box into which you add salt – you need around three 25kg bags of salt per person per annum, so this alone will cost you £30 each every year. Softeners work by separating out the hard bits in the water, exchanging them for softer sodium bits. The box needs an electrical supply and a drain-off point. The long-term benefits include reduced water heating bills and savings on soap powders (combined unlikely to be worth more than about £25 per annum). Evidence that water softeners increase the lifespan of hot water appliances is – careful now – inconclusive but almost everyone who has one reckons they do make the water feel softer and the laundry appears cleaner.

As these boxes actually chemically change the water supply, their output should not be drunk or cooked with. Design your plumbing so that the kitchen tap, at least, comes direct from the mains.

Phosphate conditioners

These are a sort of junior version of the big water softeners. They are designed to stop hot water appliances from scaling up and they are usually sold in conjunction with combination boilers and/or mains pressure hot water cylinders. You will see them in plumber's merchants – look for names like Combimate

A phosphate conditioner plumbed into the feeder main going to a mains-pressure cylinder

and Combicare. They work by adding phosphate solution to the incoming water, which inhibits scale formation – they don't 'soften' the water as such but they are reckoned to prolong the life of water-heating equipment in hard water areas.

They cost around £80 and they don't need power or drainage facilities but the phosphate cartridges need replacing every year (cost £15 a time). Again the treated water is not ideal for drinking but these conditioners are normally only fitted to water heating devices.

Inhibitors

Unlike the two preceding methods – which are chemical treatments – inhibitors act by passing a magnetic or an electrical charge through the water which – it is claimed – prevents the hard bits in the water from sticking to the pipes. They are relatively cheap (£30-£60), easy to install and need no maintenance. Also they do not affect drinking water qualities. Some need electrical power, most operate without. But do they work?

You may figure they are so cheap that there is nothing to lose in trying and you may well be right. But how will you know that your investment does the biz? Another thing to ponder on during those long dark nights. During 1995, Which? carried out a survey on this very issue and reported back with a wide range of reactions from 'very pleased' to 'a complete waste of time and money'. If there was any conclusion at all it was that they work in some areas but not in others. Not really very helpful. Leading names are Salamander and Culligan, who both produce magnetic versions and electrolytic versions. If you want to know what the difference is (or what reverse osmosis is) then you sound like you're interested enough to make your own enquiries; start your investigations at the plumber's merchant.

Filtering

In the last few years, there has been an enormous growth of interest in the subject of tap water quality. Whereas the Victorians basked in the glory of the technical achievement of providing clean drinking water to all homes, we have now become blasé about this and tend to worry that much of this water runs through lead pipes and, in any event, doesn't taste very good. Added to which there are fears (in lowland England at least) that we are now getting nitrate and pesticide residues in our tap water.

There is now a huge choice of water filters available, ranging from the free standing plastic jug affairs which can be picked up in Boots for a few quid to expensive, in-line purifiers. There are no British Standards for water purifiers ('tap water's just fine, old boy') and there is little concrete evidence on the effectiveness of the various methods. There is also concern that many filters may themselves be health hazards, providing spawning grounds for micro-bacteria. Nevertheless, interest in water filters continues to grow and one of the more innovative companies working in this field is Culligans who supply the whole range of water treatment gizmos from softeners and scale reducers to filters and ultra-violet disinfection units. If you want to find out more, get hold of their Practical Guide to Water Conditioning.

■*Eco houses*

I looked at the two predominant schools of house architecture back in the Design chapter. Traditional is of course just that but modern design is getting a bit long in the tooth itself. Modernism first appeared in the Twenties and by the Fifties it had evolved as far as it was going. American architect Phillip Johnson famously built a rectangular glass box house for himself in 1949 and that was it really. After that, all glass box houses have been variations on an established theme and 'Modern' simply became the name of another school of architecture like Georgian or Arts & Crafts. In the commercial world trends have moved on, but in housing there has been very little new happening stylistically since then – almost everything has been harking back to popular styles of the past.

But in the past few years a new style has begun to emerge, the Eco House. I think almost everybody is aware of the term Eco House but it's maddeningly difficult to define what an Eco

House actually is. The concept first appeared in the Seventies shortly after the oil crisis begun to concentrate minds on the need to conserve energy – long before anyone had ever heard of global warming. Architect couple Robert and Brenda Vale are generally held up to be the pioneers behind it, at least as far as Britain is concerned. Back then they were called self-sufficient houses and the Vales lived in one and wrote books about how to do it. The Vales would be the first to admit that what they were building was hardly great architecture; it was more an example of environmental engineering. Yet the interest in what they were doing never went away and their influence has steadily grown. The Centre for Alternative Technology (CAT), based in a quarry in North Wales, also started in the Seventies and they began a programme (which continues to this day) of building ground breaking structures, moving away from simple energy saving to embrace a whole plethora of different techniques and materials. CAT is open to the public and each year thousands visit and this way slowly the seed has spread out through the community.

A style is born

In the past few years the number of Eco Houses being built has mushroomed. Society generally seems to be slowly greening and the younger generation in particular is more aware of environmental issues and seems to be prepared to put their money where their mouths are. But what has also emerged is an Eco House style, a sort of organic cottagey look, which is quite unlike any form of housing we've had in Britain before. The Eco House has moved on from the early pioneering days and has begun to develop a language all its own. The key elements are the use of loads of natural materials, preferably as unprocessed as possible. Timber and slate are in, concrete and plastic out. The house needs to be engineered so that it has a minimal environmental footprint; this translates as being not only super energy-efficient but also water-efficient as well – water recycling is becoming de rigeur. Internally, the styling tends towards

Vikki Martin's hi-tech approach. Note the PV cells on the garage roof and the solar water panel on the main house roof

the aesthetic – white walls, wood or stone floors, little ornamentation, ethnic furnishings. Surprisingly, an awful lot of the kitchens still come from IKEA.

There is a strong echo here of the Arts & Crafts movement which flourished in Edwardian times. That too was an upmarket affair – principles are expensive – but whereas the champions of that movement were highbrow art lovers, the Eco House builders are self-consciously looking to build a better world, rejecting the values of trashy consumerism. It's as though the hippie movement has grown up and got rich and translated their core values onto that ultimate bourgeois status symbol, the detached four bedroomed house. Enough of these contradictions.

I realised that the Eco House had gone mainstream when I visited Vikki Martin in 1999 in her newly built Green House in Cambs. Till then, I had never come across an Eco House that hadn't been the brain child and baby of the owner/builder. Vikki was different: she had been persuaded to build green by her architect. 'Previously I hadn't really known anything about it,' she told me. 'But Bill Miller thought it was a good idea and the more he talked about it the more I became convinced. The ideas seem so sensible.' The Green House is cutting edge techno green: it has photovoltaic solar cells on

the roof and the electricity they generate is sold to Eastern Electricity via a two-way meter – it's one of the first homes in the UK to do this. Unusual yes, but it's been built and it doesn't look like any other house in the village.

Eco houses are not yet the complete consumer item. But all it takes is a client who is prepared to spend a little more money, to take a longer view on how the building will work and what effect it will have on the environment and suddenly another one is underway. My estimates are that around 100 a year are now getting built in Britain and that this is increasing year on year at a steady pace. There are now dozens of architects and builders specialising in Eco Building – a very good place to find out about them all is the Association of Environment Conscious Builders (AECB) which publishes annual lists of practitioners as well as a useful magazine.

Besides the individual selfbuilders, there is growing interest from larger housing organisations, especially housing associations. We are also seeing a few green housing estates and even a few green villages popping up; the best known is the Beddington Zero Energy Village (or BedZed), brainchild of architect Bill Dunster which has emerged from out of an old sewage farm in South London – you can't get much more organic than that.

The much-photographed Black House in Prickwillow, Cambs, designed and built by architect Meredith Bowles qualifies on most counts as an Eco House. It certainly looks like nothing else!

Chapter 14
Apocrypha

Beware building costs
Accessibility
Future proofing
Security & safety
Sound advice
Barn conversions
Crucial measurements

The original Aprocrypha was written at the same time as the Holy Bible but was felt by the editors of that work not to be quite up to the mark, so they published it separately. This Bible's Apocrypha consists of a few odds and ends that simply don't fit into the rest of the book. Analysing housebuilding as an activity is a bit like trying to figure out where every strand of spaghetti begins and ends. Some are easy to spot, some take some figuring out and some you just can't do, no matter what. So these are the bits to go into the Aprocrypha. All essential stuff, just doesn't fit neatly into the jigsaw. A number of other items which don't fit neatly into the Housebuilder's Bible or which have come to light since this edition went to press are being published in a regular update which is available on subscription. To subscribe you can visit www.ovolopublishing. co.uk/update or call 01480 896834 (24 hours) or email info@ovolopublishing.co.uk. The book website www.housebuildersbible.co.uk also has a section called Aprocrypha which contains an archive of earlier misfit articles.

■*Beware building costs*

You may have a very good idea of what you can afford but, unless you are an experienced developer, you are unlikely to have much idea of how much and what sort of house that money will build. The going rate for new homebuilding varies as you travel around the land – currently the magazine 'Homebuilding & Renovating' publishes a useful table showing average build costs across the country which vary from over £1,000 per sq m for a top notch job in the London area down to under £400 per sq m for a basic job with lots of DIY input somewhere cheap.

Novice builders often make the mistake of clutching at building costs like these and assume that they should divide their budget by the going rate and the answer is the size of house they should build. For instance, if your building budget is £80,000, then – by dividing £80,000 by say £500 per sq m – you could build a 160 sq m house. You may be very happy with this outcome, but it is also just possible that a 120 sq m house built to a much higher specification would have suited you better. You don't just judge cars by their size and you shouldn't judge houses that way either.

Trouble is that all of these figures which are casually bandied about – none more so than unit area build costs expressed either as £ per sq m or £ per sq ft – are themselves very casually defined. There is no British Standard number to define what a building cost actually is and there isn't really such a thing as an industry standard either. Neither is there complete agreement on just how floor areas of houses should be measured. Different businesses use different methods and this makes a minefield out of the task of comparing costs and setting budgets.

Measuring floor areas

You might at first think that how you go about measuring a floor area is a little bit academic. It is, if you aren't basing your budget and/or designs on some cost per unit area, but the evidence is that a huge number of builders do

just that. And for those contemplating buying a timber frame kit, the floor area measurements are habitually used to compare one supplier's product with another, despite the fact that there is every chance you will not be comparing like with like.

The most widely used floor area measurement in Britain is the one which refers to the internal floor area of the house. It expressly excludes the area of the external walls, although (largely for convenience when carrying out the measurements) the area taken up by the internal partition walls is included. This measurement is also known as the net floor area.

Gross v net

There is another floor area measurement commonly in use, the gross floor area, which includes the area of the external walls. The effect of including the external wall areas in the calculation is to increase the apparent size of the building by up to 15 per cent as external walls are, these days, usually constructed at thicknesses of 240-300mm. On the Continent,

Which method of measuring?

External Walls are 280mm thick, usually 12-15% of the gross floor area

One bungalow, three different methods of measuring it. The net area – I think this is the correct one – shows a floor area of 60.6 sq m. The gross area adds the external walls and comes out at 70.3 sq m. Whilst the third way adds the attached garage, making the floor area total nearly 40 per cent more than the net area.

it's the gross floor area that people usually refer to and many of the kit home suppliers use gross floor areas in their sales literature without being explicit about the fact and there is often no way of telling which area they are talking about other than by measuring it up yourself with a ruler. Using a gross floor area will appear to reduce unit area costs by 15 per cent – which is an illusion.

Garages

Garages should not be regarded as living space, even when they are integral to the rest of the house. Again, there is no check other than you and your ruler and you need to be very careful when evaluating sales literature to see that any integral garage is not included in the overall floor area. In contrast, detached garages are unlikely to be included as part of the floor area of a house in such literature, but here the trick is to exclude their building costs from any overall budget calculations. As a garage will typically cost between £5,000 and £8,000 to build (which may be as much as 20 per cent of the total building cost), either its inclusion in floor areas or its exclusion from building costs will have a dramatic (and wholly misleading) effect on apparent unit area cost.

Added to possible confusion over net and gross floor areas, the lack of a consistent benchmark for measuring floor areas means that a four-bedroom house with an integral garage could be given as 150 sq m by one method and as much as 200 sq m by another.

Grey areas

There are a number of other features worth examining. When you get into the swing of measuring house sizes off plan, you will undoubtedly come across features which are not clear cut. Again there are no hard and fast rules but I would suggest the following assumptions are fair.
■ Cupboard space: storage space such as under-eaves cupboards which are common when your upper storey is built into the roofspace, should be excluded from internal floor area.

However, built-in full height wardrobes should be included as normal living space.
■ Utility Areas: normally these would be included as part of the living space. Sometimes it is hard to judge where a utility/storage area ends and a garage begins; if you're in this position don't worry too much because at least you understand what the issues are.
■ Internal Walls: conventionally, these are measured straight through and they are included as part of the internal area.
■ Stairwells: normally measured straight through on both floors and therefore included as internal floor area as if it was regular circulation space. The exception comes when you have a large open plan arrangement, not often seen in new houses but common in barn conversions where large openings have to be preserved. How do you decide when your ordinary stairwell becomes extraordinary? The rule is that if the upper floor opening is restricted to just the functioning stairwell, then measure straight through on both floors; if the open area extends beyond the immediate staircase, then you must exclude the entire stairwell area from the upper floor area.

Building costs

So much for defining the internal floor area. The 'building costs' are even harder to define. There is no official standard but there is a sort of British way of defining building costs, as detailed in the accompanying table. Making long lists and producing definitions is all very well, but what I am trying to get at is that building costs are really just a subgroup of development costs and that to concentrate on building costs to the exclusion of other costs is potentially disastrous. Like building costs, development costs can vary enormously and in this respect there is no greater variant than the price paid for your building plot. Some building plots are far more expensive to develop than others; problems can arise with bad ground, slopes, difficult service connections, difficult access, trees, legal covenants, intransigent planners — you name it! Now, the art of property developing is to be able to predict these problems and to negotiate a price on the land which reflects the cost of getting around them.

All housebuilders must pay close attention to these extra costs. One advantage a selfbuilder has over a professional is that they have more potential to control the project cashflow. For instance, you may not need to build a garage at all, which could bring substantial savings. You can defer certain non-essential works such as landscaping for many years if cash is tight. You can substantially reduce your financial commitments by roughing it a little bit whilst the house is being built. And, of course, you can reduce costs by undertaking some of the work yourself. But all of this will pale into insignificance if you fail to budget the project correctly in the first place; to achieve significant savings, you need to buy and develop your plot appropriately, be very organised and be able to stick tightly to a budget.

◼ *Accessibility*

Provision for disabled access in housing became part of the building regulations for the first time in October 1999. The bit of the regulations which covers access issues in England and Wales is called Part M (Part Q in Scotland) and the changes have been greeted with enthusiasm by disability campaigners but have had a lukewarm reaction from both the housebuilders and the general public who feel that this is political correctness run riot. Personally, I'm torn between the extremes. The little Tory in me reacts negatively to having meddlesome legislation shoved across my soon-to-be-levelled doorstep; then I find myself talking with a builder whose wife is confined to a wheelchair and, as he describes the struggles they both have in coping with her disability, I suddenly chide myself for being so mean-spirited and wish that the regulations went much further than they do. These changes were in fact first mooted by the Tories in the early Nineties – they may appear to be very New Labour but they have been

welcomed by politicians of all persuasions as a way of increasing the independence of both disabled and elderly people. Although Part M has been phrased in such a way as to make you think they are designed solely for wheelchair users, the groups who are expected to benefit from the changes are far reaching, including the blind and partially sighted and families with pre-school children.

Part of the problem is that there are actually very few severely long-term disabled people around, so making every new house conform to a rigid set of standards in order to meet their requirements seems both expensive and illogical. Perhaps. Perhaps not. It actually costs very little extra to build a Part M compliant house – in contrast it's always frighteningly expensive to retrofit such measures into an existing house. We are building homes which may well have a life expectancy stretching well into the 22nd century and during this lifespan there is every chance that several occupants will come to appreciate some of the 1999 Part M changes. Whatever your feelings about it all, Part M in housing is here and we are going to have to learn to live with it.

What's in Part M?

To comply with Part M:
◼ Each house will have to have one level threshold – ideally, but not necessarily, the front door. This doorway should have a minimum clearance of 775mm between frame and opened door, which translates as having to use an 838mm door (the old imperial 2 ft 9 in size). A level threshold is defined as one which has a bump of no more than 15mm under the door.
◼ This entrance should be easily approachable from the outside. In practise this means there should be no steps and no incline of more than 1:20.
◼ Every home must have a downstairs toilet. This room doesn't have to be big enough to accommodate a wheelchair. It's just the door has to be wide enough to get a wheelchair through (2 ft 9in or 838mm again).

■ Ground floor corridors and doorways must be wide enough to allow wheelchair users easy access. There is a trade-off here; wider corridors can have narrower doors but the rule of thumb which seems to be developing is to have all ground floor doors 838mm wide and to have corridors at least 1050mm wide.
■ Power sockets and switches must be placed no lower than 450mm and no higher than 1200mm above finished floor level throughout the house.

Level thresholds

This is the feature that is giving designers and housebuilders the most sleepless nights. The standard (pre-1999) British front door involved stepping up from the ground into the house – indeed the internal floor level is typically 150mm – that's two brick courses – higher than the external ground level. Like many standards, this front step had never been a regulation but was simply a detail that had evolved, primarily as a way of keeping water from flowing in under the door. The level threshold changes all. It requires the doorstep to be re-engineered. Many builders will chose to provide a ramped access up to the level threshold but in situations where this is not possible, it will be necessary to sink the entire house by two brick courses. Don't shout it out too loudly but there is

Hepworth's Threshold Drain is the most ingenious solution yet to the problem of marrying level thresholds with maintaining a damp proof course under the door cill

actually a small potential cost saving here.

Detailing a level threshold so that it is watertight is in itself a challenge. One of the authors of the new Part M, Dr Andrew Burke, admitted in a seminar I attended that there were no designs which were totally foolproof: I find that worrying. You need to pay attention to rainwater ingress and to rising damp – the damp proof course around the door needs careful attention, as does thermal cold bridging and, in some cases, radon and methane penetration into the surrounding cavity. It's easy to install waterproof barriers underneath the front door only for the carpet fitters to come and rip them off later when they find that they can't actually open the door once the carpet has been fitted. This is another problem to be faced. If you pay close attention to your front door detailing, you will probably be fine but, traditionally, it's been a part of housebuilding design which has usually been sorted out on site. Traditionally front doors open inwards and traditionally floor covers have not been an issue because of the step. But level thresholds force you to consider carefully how you will finish the floor internally. Consider it carefully. A sunken matwell seems to be a good solution for many. This covers the area where the door opens and you can start your floor cover on the inside of the matwell.

In fact, we have already accumulated a wealth of experience in building level thresholds, mostly in the social housing sector. Habinteg is a housing association which has been specialising in special needs designs since 1970. They have fitted level thresholds to around 2000 properties and have not experienced any notable problems. Occasionally, they have to fit a gully across the threshold to collect rainwater but this can normally be avoided by creating a small (one in 40) slope away from the door.

Habinteg's standard detail satisfies the requirements for waterproofing, draught proofing and thermal bridging as well as level access. Instead of a timber cill, they use a precast concrete threshold, chamfered on the leading edge so that water runs off. Unlike a

My previous benchmark house used ramps as a way of meeting Part M obligations for a level threshold. It looks ugly and it's arguably a little dangerous as you stagger home late from the pub. There are better ways of getting there.

conventional timber cill, this concrete threshold sits below the damp proof course – the damp proof membrane is lapped up the inside face of the threshold. The cold bridge is stopped by a 20mm strip of insulation placed against the inside face of this threshold: this is in turn bridged by quarry tiles.

The joinery manufacturers all produce Part M compliant entrance frames which take most of the sweat out of how to specify them. However it still leaves the problem of providing a level access up to the door. The way that most builders are 'doing level thresholds' is by putting in a ramp outside the front door. This can look completely ridiculous and can also be something of a hazard itself. My last but one benchmark house (in the Millennium edition) was a prime example of this – see picture above.

Nothing else in Part M involves anything new or unusual. The regulations about ramp gradients and corridor widths are spelled out in the approved document and house designers should soon be up to speed on how these measures should or should not be incorporated into the home.

What is less clear is just how and where exceptions are to be made. Officially, Part M excludes only extensions and alterations to existing dwellings. All new dwellings in England and Wales are meant to comply with Part M access whether they be new builds or conversions. However, there are a number of cases where there may be an opportunity to waive at least some of the obligations. Most prominent amongst these is the issue of people building flats: there is no requirement to provide lift access to the upper stories, so effectively the disabled will be no better off. There is also expected to be some provision for steeply sloping sites which otherwise might not be developable without recourse to using stepped access. What is less clear is what will happen to people wanting to build upside-down houses or townhouse designs where the main living accommodation will be on the first floor.

Lifetime homes

From the point of view of the disabled, Part M is very tame. It concentrates on making new homes 'visitable' but it does little to make them more 'usable.' Disability campaigners would like to see Part M extended in scope to include further measures, building what are usually called Lifetime Homes (after an influential report by the Joseph Rowntree Foundation).

My 98/99 benchmark house was built with removable ducting laid into the floor. Very few builders go to such trouble.

What would turn a Part M compliant home into a Lifetime Home?

■ Attention is paid to car parking: you need a space at least 3.3m wide to enable wheelchair users easy access to cars
■ Thresholds should be illuminated as well as level; the main entrance should be covered
■ The upper storeys should be potentially visitable as well; to do this, space should be left where a lift could be fitted in the future.
■ All the house controls should be within reach, not just sockets and light switches; this includes things like window catches and trickle vents and central heating controls
■ Drainage should be provided for floor showers in bathrooms and WCs and baths should be capable of being adapted to take handrails.

Open building

The open building movement is the ultimate stage on this road. It proposes that homes are built like office buildings with maximum flexibility in mind. You start by building a shell and then you fit it out to the occupants' wishes. You don't start with an interior design fixed, just a very flexible construction which allows you a number of possibilities. If you sell up and move out, the next occupant can easily

disassemble what is there and fit it out the way they want it. So room partitions can be moved and services re-routed. Disabled access is built into the shell so it doesn't have to be thought of in any special way.

To date open building in the UK only happens in the commercial sector. The Dutch and the Japanese have done a fair amount of open residential building but their housing markets are pretty different to ours – typically they see it as a way of customising apartments (which is what they mostly build). Still it's food for thought.

■ Future proofing

Accessibility is often thought of as a way of building in measures to help the disabled. But there is another side to the coin and that is just how we access all the services we place inside a new house. It's something which modern building techniques have made increasingly difficult and there is a tendency to hide everything in walls and floors and to use materials like chipboard and plasterboard which make future access difficult. As the number of wires and pipes running around our homes multiplies, we are actually making it harder and harder to get at them, quite the opposite of what we might anticipate. It's certainly a long way from the idea of Open Building which, in its purest form, is all about being able to easily rearrange not just the services but the very structure of the house so that, for instance, rooms can be open plan or subdivided. But for many people it's more a question of being able to access cable and pipe runs, a way of leaving your future options open.

The trouble is, open access to services is both difficult to achieve and surprisingly expensive. Most houses can accommodate a major service run duct from, say, ground floor up into the loft space. The problems come when you want to get to the actual sockets. Both floors and walls tend to be pretty unremovable: you can adapt them but it is not easy. For instance, you can lay floor ducting into screeds which is fine if you cover the floor with carpet but not so useful if you put tiles or hardwood floors down: these can be taken up but not without a good deal of grief. Similarly you can build boxed-out skirting boards which can double up as cable ducts but this still leaves you with the problem of how to get to the back of the sockets, and also presents problems at door openings.

Of course these problems have all been addressed in the office environment where all the cabling gets hidden in false ceilings and behind removable perimeter trunking. Though you can use such systems in the home, it does tend to look pretty industrial. People go to great lengths to conceal such things as waste pipes and soil stacks and this makes it seem somewhat retrogressive to start surface-mounting plastic trunkings. But it is an option. If you were prepared to say definitely just where the workspace in each room should be located, you could easily equip each room with a short section of trunking which would allow you the flexibility of later fitting data terminals, phone sockets, TV outlets or even good old mains sockets, bearing in mind that mains power is best kept a short distance away from data cables as you can get interference between the two. With a little forethought you should be able to plan access panels, ducting and cable runs into

your home at the design stage.

Perimeter trunking can be made on site if you fancy your hand at second-fix carpentry. Alternatively, you can buy pre-assembled trunking from Centaur, Mita or any of the electrical wholesalers listed in your Yellow Pages. Trunking tends to come in 3m lengths and costs from around £15 per m upwards depending on depth and finish specified. And to be readily accessible you have to sort out the vertical drops as well so that, ideally, you can lay new cable without disturbing any of the fittings in the house. In fact, both Centaur and Mita produce vertical columns designed to run from floor to ceiling (called Powerpoles) through which you can easily feed new cable and add as many outlets as you require.

The downside with this approach is that again you have to make some prediction about just how you are going to use the house in years to come. Will you want a TV or a computer or a phone in every bedroom? Will there be problems if you install them in some rooms but not others? And just where in each room should the outlets be?

In the meantime, at least pay attention to the idea of a wiring closet (see Chapter 9, TV, phones and cables, for an explanation). Whereas your electrician might persuade you to fit your fusebox under the stairs, if you have more room it is a good idea to set aside some wall space to take more complex gear in years to come. And provide some ducting between the floor beneath and the outside world.

Secret plumbing

Exactly the same issues occur with plumbing. Indeed future accessibility is arguably more important because plumbing can leak. Piped water runs are often placed under the floor but this can be difficult if, as in the benchmark house, you have a power floated slab which goes down at the beginning of the construction process. If you lay a screed on your floor then you can fit ducting: check out Pendock Profiles who produce a range of galvanised steel channels which can accommodate water pipes and have a screwed plywood covering. They are designed to fit into either a 50mm or a 70mm screed: I estimate that fitting Pendock Profiles to the ground floor of the benchmark house would cost around £200 in materials: this would have been enough to take all the radiator pipes around the radiators downstairs. Whatever you do you should be aware that they are at their most useful when the ground floor gets a carpeting. Tiling of any description and tongued and grooved timber floors cannot be taken up without a good deal of disruption and it will be impossible to replace them as before.

Security & safety

The average private dwelling currently suffers an attempted break-in every 12 years and over half of these attempts are successful. Furthermore, the amount of burglary has nearly doubled since 1983 and if the crime rate continues to grow at this sort of pace, then by 2025 it will have risen to one attempted break-in at every home every other year.

Whether this Doomsday scenario ever comes about is open to doubt because it would involve an army of a quarter of a million burglars each breaking into a house every week. Whatever the future holds, burglary is not a problem that is likely to go away and anyone considering building a new house would be foolish not to consider the matter very carefully. Some inner city areas already suffer appallingly high burglary rates, making house contents insurance extremely expensive and sometimes even impossible to obtain.

The burglar

As you might suspect, the typical burglar is a young male but you might be surprised to learn that he is not part of a well-organised gang but usually a lone wolf whose break-in is often done almost on the spur-of-the-moment, when he sees the opportunity arise. There is really no reason to adopt a fatalistic attitude because, although it's entirely true that if someone really wants to get into a house they can, 90 per cent

of the time they won't bother if you go to the trouble of making life difficult for them. Our young burglar's main concern is not to get caught in the act and to this end he values being able to get in, and out, quickly and preferably unseen. Another surprising statistic thrown up is that as many as 20 per cent of burglaries take place while the home is occupied. You'd think this would be amazingly risky for our burglar but it only takes a few seconds to come in through an open door and walk out again with something like a radio or a camera and you may not even realise that you've been burgled. If you are worried about this sort of thing happening, get a dog.

With regards to new housebuilding, current thinking focuses on the following areas:
■ Site layout
■ Preventing access to the rear of the house
■ Decent locks fitted to ground floor windows and doors
■ Burglar alarms where risk is high
■ Security lighting.

Site layout

Though this area has more relevance to estates than to single dwellings, it's worth mentioning what they are on about. Dark corners and unlit alleyways should be avoided and houses should be sited where their neighbours can see who is coming and going. There is often little the individual housebuilder can do about this, though it is possible that consideration can be given to the issue when there are two or more houses to be sited near each other.

One obvious point that the professionals have tended to overlook is to locate the most widely used room in the house – usually the kitchen – at the front of the house, so that the occupants can see who is coming and going out on the street. However, this arrangement remains an extremely unpopular layout in this country; we still prefer our kitchens to be by the back door.

Restricting access

The rear of the house is the preferred area of entry for burglars. This is largely because the back of the house is almost always more private and is often very well screened from neighbours. A burglary often starts with a casual casing of the front of the house; if it looks as though there is no one at home, the second stage will be to go round the back and take a closer look. Only when they're convinced the coast is clear will the break-in proceed. If access to the back of the house is impeded, then the would-be burglar may abort the job at this early stage in the hope of there being easier pickings further up the road.

A 2m fence and a stout gate – even without a bolt – will provide a considerable measure of defence against unwanted prowling. Back gardens can be protected, to a lesser extent, by walling or hedging them in. Plan in any obstructions that will at least slow down the progress of a potential burglar. However bear in mind that a fully enclosed garden, once breached, makes an ideal spot for our burglar to force an unseen rear entry so if your garden is going to be enclosed for security reasons, you need to do it well.

Robust locks

It is now an NHBC standard to have five-lever locks on all external doors and to have window locks as well. At least one exit – usually the front door – must be protected by a night latch (Yale-type locks) which can be opened from the inside without a key; this is to aid escape in case of fire. The idea is to lock the door on the night latch when the house is occupied and to use the five-lever mortise lock when the house is empty. Window locks are now fitted as standard on most volume joinery, so all new houses will – or should – be built to these security standards now and there is no further action that need be taken at the design stage.

French and patio doors

It is marginally easier to force a door inwards than to prise it out but it is likely to be rather noisy. Most front doors open inwards. However, note that double-doors (French doors) are particularly easy to force in or prise outwards;

most French doors open outwards and if you fit them be sure to fit decent sliding bolts to the top and bottom of both doors. For extra security, make these lockable bolts. Sliding patio doors are generally a much more secure (and draughtproof) alternative (though not half as elegant); however, many break-ins have occurred where the patio door frame has been levered out of its seating, having only ever been held in by six short screws or, sometimes, nothing more than mastic sealant.

Glass

The current building regulations will ensure that you have to fit double-glazed sealed units, and the safety standards on glazing insist that safety glass is fitted to all doors, windows next to doors and all glazing less than 800mm above the internal floor level. Safety glass is expensive, costing nearly twice as much as ordinary float glass. It comes in two varieties, toughened or laminated, and they perform slightly differently.

Toughened is harder to break but when it breaks it collapses into small nodules, whereas laminated glass has a sheet of plastic sandwiched between two layers of ordinary glass; this makes it harder to break through (from the burglar's point of view) and is therefore slightly more secure. The police are big fans of laminated glass, suggesting that it should be fitted wherever there is glass next to an accessible lock, but as this includes virtually every ground floor opening window it would be an expensive option.

New security standards

Factory-glazed windows are available which meet a new British security standard, BS 7950. Rather than just testing the individual locks or the glass, BS 7950 tests the whole window assembly in situ. Typically such a window will have laminated glass on the external face and shootbolt espagnolette locking mechanisms. To get windows to this standard, they really need to have been factory glazed but this doesn't mean they have to be plastic – most of the big timber joinery manufactures now produce BS 5750 windows.

Burglar alarms

There is a huge variety of different alarm systems out there and it's not easy deciding what to fit. It is usually cheaper to install a wired system, which is particularly well suited to new housing as the wiring can be concealed during first-fix stage. Installation quotes for a four-bedroom house are likely to vary from £500 for a basic system based on a mixture of internal infrared detectors and contact points to over £1,000 for external vibration detectors which are triggered by interference with doors and windows. Should you not want to go to the expense of installing an alarm, as an alternative, the wiring can be first-fixed in a day for between £100 and £200, so that the intruder detectors can be fitted at a later date without disruption to the decorations. Burglar alarms are eligible for zero-rating of VAT when building a new home.

Fixing a burglar alarm should not be beyond the capabilities of a competent DIYer and there are a number of systems designed for just this. DIY alarms usually consist of a control panel, the detectors and an external siren. The wired systems are the most reliable and are probably best suited to new builds. However, wireless alarms have their advocates and are easily fitted as an afterthought. The standard wireless systems still need mains connections for both the control panel and the siren but the latest generation work entirely on radio signalling: the siren and the control panels are solar powered and you activate the alarm by using a remote control. Response Alarms produce a totally solar powered alarm called the Sola costing just over £100 but it's fairly basic in its capabilities.

More features tend to add to the cost but it is still possible to get a well-featured wireless system for under £200, such as Yale's High Security Alarm System which can handle up to 24 zones. Zones are the areas covered by individual detectors and most burglar alarms allow you to arm or disarm any of your zones individually. This is useful if you have pets or if you want only the downstairs armed when you are upstairs at night. Better systems have a capability of checking that all component parts are working – a feature sometimes referred to as a 24 hour zone.

Detectors

The detectors on which burglar alarms are based come in a number of guises. The two commonest are the passive infrared (PIR) detector, which is triggered by movement across its path, and the door- or window-opening detector which is set off when a magnetic contact is broken. You can also get detectors based on pressure pads – typically these would be under a doormat and would be triggered when someone unexpected treads on it. You can give great thought to just which detector to put where and still get it all wrong. Many a break-in now occurs via an upstairs window: the thieves never go downstairs because they reckon it will be alarmed, so they just ransack the bedrooms before leaving the same way they came in. So maybe it pays to have lots of detection zones but possibly only if you are very confident in your ability to operate the system.

If you've never lived with a burglar alarm, you might be forgiven for thinking that they are the last word in home security. However, the consequences of fitting an alarm can be fairly tortuous for the householder and their neighbours. All systems are set to make a loud noise for a few minutes; false alarms will make you very unpopular and false alarms do happen, so a burglar alarm is not without its problems. A recent police estimate reckoned that no less than nine out of ten ringing alarms are actually false alarms and the police in some areas are now refusing to respond to ringing alarms, particularly if the alarm in question is known to be a repeat offender.

Monitored alarms

If you have a very remote site or are not entirely

happy about a 105-decibel alarm ringing when a mouse crosses the floor, the next step up the security ladder is to get a monitored alarm. These link your house via the phone lines either to the local police or to a security firm. If you want the police to monitor your alarm, then the system must be installed by a company approved by one of two bodies; NACOSS (National Approval Council of Security Systems) or SSAIB (Security Systems and Alarm Inspection Board). Needless to say NACOSS or SSAIB approved systems cost rather more than unapproved ones. Or as one wag put it, it's daylight robbery what these guys get away with. Monitored systems also carry an annual charge which is likely to be in excess of £150; they are only available if two key holders besides the occupants live close by and are prepared to be called out in the middle of the night.

Movement sensors

Alarm systems don't have to just concern themselves with making loud noises or sending messages off to police stations. You can also rig up detector beams running across the front and the back of your house which set off a buzzer inside when they are crossed. They vary in sophistication from simple passive infrared beams like the ones used to trip lights, to multi-height beams running between two concealed posts which aim to be cat and fox proof. The well designed systems will give you fairly reliable intruder alerts: a poor system, tripping out every time a bird flies by, will just make you paranoid.

Why bother with a movement sensor? Well, I would have tended to ask the same question until my mum had one installed a few years back. She loves it; she has one out the front and one out the back and she can tell the difference between the postman and the paperboy by the time they take to cross the beam. At night, the system is switched from buzzer to warning light in the bedroom and once it picked up a prowler round the back of the property and enabled her to alert a neighbour before any damage was done.

Car parking

Both integral and detached garages can be included in whole house intruder alarm systems, but this tends to be very inconvenient; the car has to be left outside whilst the alarm is deactivated (usually inside the house). It rather defeats the purpose of these remote control devices for garage doors.

Other measures

Door chains (from £3) and viewers (from £4) are becoming more common, and are recommended by the police. Surely the most cheeky is the fake 'Protected by Burglar Alarm' bell casing which you screw on to your outside wall. Available at around £8 from DIY sheds.

Security lighting

Passive Infrared (PIR) detectors, similar to the ones used on internal movement sensors in burglar alarms, are also used on external lighting. These can be very useful around dark entrances although the halogen bulbs (sometimes 500 W) can be so bright that you dazzle passers-by and tend to make them think you live in a high-security prison. Installation of a good PIR security light will cost around £80 (Mats £40, Lab £40). There are some very cheap versions on the market (at around £10-£15) which are best avoided; at around £30 you start to get ones where it is possible to change the bulb. Better forms of external lighting exist which can be wired to PIR switches, as well as manual override switches, which give pleasant external illumination as well as some form of security (see Chapter 9).

There are also a number of products which can be used to give the effect of occupation when the house is empty. For around £20, you can buy a gizmo which fits in between a lightbulb and its lamp holder which acts as a light-sensitive switch, useful for simulating occupation when you are away.

Shutter protection

To fit security roll-down shutters to every opening on the benchmark house would cost over £6,000 so no way is this a cheap and cheerful option. Indeed it looks pretty severe as well, but if you are away a lot and have particular reason to fear intruders, then shutters are very secure. They don't work well with outward opening windows (think about it) and are best designed around either sliding sash style or tilt and turn windows. On the Continent, shutter protection is often taken as a given, but then on the Continent windows only ever seem to open inwards. Strange to reflect how different something as basic as a window can be.

Safes

Home safes are available from £150 for a wall fitting one and from £200 for one bolted to the floor. Placing a safe in an existing house can be awkward but in a new house it's a doddle – if you've planned ahead for it.

Fire safety

The fire brigades get called out to around 60,000 house fires every year and around 500 people die each year in house fires in this country. And many of these deaths could be easily prevented with a few basic precautions. Fortunately, most of these have been encoded in our building regs so if you are undertaking a newbuild or a major renovation, you will have to build them in.

The purpose of the fire safety regulations is not to stop buildings burning down but rather to allow the occupants time enough to escape from them when they do start burning down. One of the long held prejudices against timber-frame building is that people think it will be more likely to catch on fire but this really is not so as the timber elements are almost always enclosed in a layer of inert plasterboard which is enough to delay the onset of fire by around half an hour.

The real danger in house fires is caused when soft furnishings catch fire, and the smoke quickly engulfs the occupants. Whilst there has been a steady introduction of non-flammable materials into the home furnishing

market, the biggest step forward in the world of housebuilding came in 1992 when smoke detectors became mandatory. Since then, all new homes have been required to have smoke detectors not just fitted but mains-operated with a battery backup as a fail safe.

Smoke detectors cost around £20 and can be wired into the house lighting circuit. Electricians are by now au fait with what's required. The regs are that there should be smoke alarms on each storey and that they shouldn't be further than 3m from any bedroom door, so that some larger designs will require two or more on the upstairs landing. The benchmark house has three fitted, one in the sun lounge, one in the entrance hall and one upstairs on the landing.

What the regs don't go into is the different types of smoke detector you can choose. The cheapest and commonest are the ionisation detectors which are very sensitive to small particles of smoke produced by flaming fires, such as chip pans, and will detect this type of fire before the smoke gets too thick. But you can also specify optical ones as well which are more effective at detecting larger particles of smoke produced by slow-burning fires, such as smouldering foam-filled upholstery and overheated PVC wiring. Optical detectors are more prone to going off in error; either the mirror gets dirty or thunderflies get in.

A third and possibly more useful type is the heat sensor which gets triggered when temps reach around 55°C – fit it in the kitchen but not too near the cooker. Whatever you choose, they have to be interconnected so that when one is triggered, they all go into action. Some smoke alarms have additional capabilities, such as emergency lights and silence buttons to override false alarms.

Other safety features you might choose to look at are the provision of fire blankets in the kitchen (around £30) and extinguishers in garages and near open fires (£70-£100). Your best bet is to stick with local firms which offer maintenance: look in Yellow Pages under Fire Extinguishing Eqpt.

Egress windows

Since 2002, there has been a requirement, embedded within the building regs, to have a means of escape window in all habitable rooms above ground floor. These are known as egress windows – no, I'd never heard of them before, either, but egress is apparently the opposite of access so you can see the logic. The building regs are quite specific about what constitutes an egress window:

■ must have an openable area not less than 0.33 sq m

■ the opening dimensions must be at least 450mm wide and 450mm high

■ the opening must be within 1100mm of the floor

■ if it's a sloping roof, then the distance between the cill and the eaves shouldn't be more than 1700mm.

For many windows, this doesn't present a problem but a few designs have had to be re-engineered to make them pass muster. The simulated sash windows which open outwards aren't acceptable in their original format and neither are narrow windows with fixed vertical bars. However with a bit of imagination, they can be reconfigured – there is in fact a detail now known as a flying mullion which sounds like a fish but is actually a bar built into the opening casement.

Three-storey houses

Provided every room opens onto a hallway or corridor, a two storey house is not going to have any problems meeting fire safety regulations. But there is a critical safety level, defined as having a floor 4.5m above ground level, when it becomes necessary to beef up your escape procedures. One of the principal requirements relates to how your main staircase runs through the house. Ideally, the staircase should lead directly to the front entrance door within an enclosed hallway: what is frowned upon are open-plan arrangements, particularly when the staircase exits via the kitchen (reckoned to be the highest risk area).

You also need to consider how to protect the stairwell from encroaching fire. There are two options. The first is to make the entire stairwell what is called a fully protected enclosure; this means that the walls around the landing and stairwell must be rated at 30 minutes fire resistance and the doors opening onto the landing must be rated at 20 minutes. The second option doesn't insist on fire doors but instead requires that you design at least one window in the top floor as an escape window, allowing the fire brigade to get a ladder safely under it. You also need to consider the floor construction which also needs to meet the 30 minute fire rating.

If you are undertaking a new build or a major renovation, it's not difficult to meet these standards; in fact in terms of walls and floors it's quite difficult not to meet them. The only place where you are likely to come unstuck is on the doors. Not only do you need a thicker door – most fire doors are 44mm thick, the same as external doors, but you will also be required to fit them with door-closers. The least obtrusive solution here is the Perko door-closer which is fitted into the hinge side of each door and connects to a plate fixed to the door frame. They are cheap to buy (around £7 each) and a pain to fit and adjust – at least I find them painful – but they do the job. Fire doors are also much more expensive than regular doors: Premdor Crosby are a good source for fire check doors. If you are converting an existing house, there are fireproof (or intumescent) paints that you can apply to doors to upgrade them; check out Environmental Seals.

■ Sound advice

Of all the sections in this book, it's this one, on sound, which has proved the most troublesome to write over the various editions. I keep changing it and keep adding new bits and in the next edition I discard them and try something different. Getting a handle on sound and, more particularly, sound reduction measures is tricky; try as I might, I am still not really sure that I understand it. It's one of those subjects where the more you learn about it, the more you realise how little you know.

The essence of the problem, from a builder's point of view, is that our appreciation of sound is very personal and therefore highly subjective. What annoys some people gives pleasure to others. There are sounds which most people wouldn't even notice that can drive others completely nutty. How do you legislate for such a state of affairs? With a great deal of difficulty, of course. It falls on Part E of the English & Welsh building regs (in Scotland, it's Part H) to provide guidance and it is a very complicated part indeed and has recently been rendered even more complicated by our boys in Whitehall trying to upgrade it.

This section looks at the background behind sound reduction measures for builders. Guidance on how to achieve better soundproofing is to be found lodged in two earlier sections on internal walls and internal floors, both back in the Chapter 7. But do try to wade through this section before you decide what to do about your walls and floors; I think it will be worth it, if only to learn what the hell a decibel is.

Acoustics for beginners

Sound is a form of energy. It moves in waves through the air and it can be absorbed and transmitted through solids as well. The human ear is adept at picking up sound in a range of frequencies and at different volumes. There are more qualities to sound than just frequency and volume but we'll concern ourselves with just these two, as it's their interplay that makes much of the debate about soundproofing so intriguing.

Frequencies are measured in hertz (Hz) and kilohertz (kHz): these correspond to the wavelengths that various sounds travel at. Low frequency sound has a very long wavelength; high frequency sound consists, conversely, of energy moving at very short wavelengths. Humans tend to hear sounds between 50 Hz and 15,000 Hz (15 kHz); this upper limit reduces with age.

Sound energy is measured in decibels, routinely written down as dB. The decibel scale is non-linear: it double every 3dB . However, what we perceive sound is a little different: humans perceive a doubling or halving of volume roughly every 10dB . Thus a 60dB noise would sound, subjectively, twice as loud as a 50dB one, which, in turn, sounds roughly twice as loud as a 40dB one.

Whilst the ability to hear sounds is regarded as one of life's more pleasurable experiences, we also worry inordinately about hearing noises we don't want to hear. Noise is defined as unwanted sound. As regards building design, our concerns are usually to minimise sound transfer between walls and floors.

Sound energy is said to transfer through buildings in three different ways. The easiest to understand is airborne sound. This is how sound gets to us when we speak to one another. If there is a wall between us when we speak, then some of the airborne sound gets absorbed by the wall and the amount of sound absorbed by the wall is said to be so many decibels of sound reduction. Thus, if a wall is said to have an airborne sound reduction level of 40dB, it means that, should a 60dB conversation were taking place on the other side of it, you would only hear about 20dBs worth on your side.

But sound is capable of travelling through solids as well. In certain instances, walls and, in particular, floors have a nasty habit of not absorbing sound at all but instead acting as a conduit for sounds. Impact sounds, as we call them, are usually mechanical in origin: tapping, hammering, drumming or just walking across floors in heels. The actual volume of the sounds may not be that high but a floor without adequate impact sound insulation may as well not be there.

The third cause of sound pollution is usually referred to as flanking sound. It occurs when airborne or impact sounds get to you via an indirect route. Consider for a moment the soundproofing between two adjacent rooms. Your first concern is to look at the performance of the wall that divides them. Sound transfer

Paul Goring, head of NHBC's acoustic department, seen here with an impact testing device

through the wall may be airborne or impact (i.e. lightswitches going on and off) but, either way, it's direct. But sound can also travel between the rooms via other routes. It can come in through doors and windows for instance.

It wasn't until I spent an afternoon witnessing an acoustic test that I really began to understand the difference between the different sorts of sound transfer. Paul Goring (above), currently NHBC's head of acoustics, was testing a floor between two flats in a newly built nurses' hostel and it took him a good couple of hours to do it. On floors, it is routine to test for both airborne sound and impact sound and the procedure for testing them is a little different and worth describing.

To measure airborne sound transmission through a floor, he placed a multidirectional loudspeaker in the upper room and set it to pump out 100db of noise: 'pink noise' it is referred to as, a horrible cocktail of every audible frequency you can think of. At 100db

you really don't want to be in that room for a moment longer than you have to be: even with ear defenders on, it's physically unpleasant.

The measuring equipment was in the room below. Airborne sound insulation is measured by taking the difference between the output from the pink noise and the sound in the receiving room. Your rating for the floor in question is the difference between the two measurements. Straightforward enough. The airborne tests consist of five different samples from around the receiving room, each taken from two different locations for the pink noise box in the room above – i.e. 10 measurements of 15 seconds duration.

Impact noise is measured in a different way. The noise is made by a series of hammers inside a wooden box, resembling a mechanical drum machine, which you sit on the floor and then let rip. Impact noise is conventionally measured directly: you don't subtract the noise made in one room from the noise received in another: you just make a British Standard sort of impacty-noise from the drum machine and measure how much gets through the floor. Impact noise is only ever considered on floors.

So there is an important distinction here. When you see decibel-rating tables, the airborne decibel ratings are for sound reduction capabilities. Therefore the higher the decibel rating on airborne sound reduction, the better: a 50dB-rated floor is much better than a 45dB-rated one. But for impact sound ratings, the reverse is true. The rating just tells you how much sound got through the floor so that a 62dB impact rating is better than a 64dB one.

Flanking sound isn't measured directly, but it contributes to the overall scores and makes significant differences to the scores between lab tests and field tests. In lab tests you only test the wall or floor because there are no flanking paths whilst in field tests the wall and floor are physically connected to the surrounding structure so the test is carried out in the presence of flanking. You don't experience flanking sound as something different to airborne sound or impact sound but when there is a lot of noise being made, you can sometimes be aware of it. In my case, I was able to actually feel the walls vibrating when the pink noise machine was on. This was flanking sound in action.

Measuring up

The equipment that measures sound – or noise, as it would be referred to in this instance – is expensive and sophisticated. Paul Goring uses a Danish system costing around £15,000. It measures sound at 16 different frequencies and gives 16 different readings that have to be interpreted and analysed. This is where things start to get very complicated. Legislators want a yes or no answer to the question, 'Does this floor or wall meet a defined sound reduction standard?' The regs invariably hone in on a pass rate expressed in decibels but the data comes in measured over 16 different frequencies, some of which may look OK and others not.

What has evolved over the years is a number of calculations that offer a 'best fit' answer to the riddle of how much noise is being made at any one time. None of them are perfect and there are big debates about which measuring systems should be used. Normally, this really wouldn't be of concern to anyone outside the cosy world of acoustics but during 2003 this debate took centre stage in the formulation of the latest set of building regulations, because the different ways of sampling decibels give some widely different results.

There are four main methods of measuring sound reduction used in Britain. If proof were needed that acousticians do not come from this planet, these different methods are referred to by a complex sequence of letters and punctuation marks, some italicised, some suffixed. When they speak English, these labels roll off their tongues in capitals and don't sound so weird, so I will be anglicising them, if only to help my typesetter.

The simplest rating, written as Rw and referred to by all as 'RW' is derived from simple laboratory measurements. It's a useful tool for considering the best performance you can

get out of a particular construction detail but it doesn't look at the likely performance of a wall or floor in a building: flanking noises are ignored. By way of example, a timber joist floor with 18mm chipboard over it and 12.5mm of plasterboard nailed under it, will have an RW sound reduction rating of around 35-38dB. For the technically minded RW is the weighted sound reduction average across a sample of different frequencies of sound through a wall or a floor element but it only concerns itself with airborne sound reduction through an individual wall or floor element.

The next sound reduction rating, written as DnT,w (known as 'DNTW') is derived from the measured performance of the wall or floor element on site, rather than in a lab. On site you tend to get added noise coming through the structure – flanking sounds – and therefore, not surprisingly, the DNTW ratings tend to be lower than the Rw ratings, usually by around 5dB. DNTW ruled the roost as far as the building regs went until the 2003 changes. But because of various bits of research undertaken in recent years, it was felt simple DNTW didn't adequately reflect the types of noise that are currently being made through our party walls and floors so a variation, giving far more emphasis to low frequency sounds, has been unveiled, known as the Ctr or CTR bias.

Ctr is additional to, not a replacement for, DNTW so that the new regs require you to provide 45dB of sound insulation (DnT,w + Ctr). It's complicated, but not that complicated, and if you look at it long enough you can begin to see the funny side. The point about DNTW plus CTR measurements is that it creates a higher standard to meet because low frequencies are harder to block. However, the Ctr effect is not uniform: on some structures, it may make the figure just 2 or 3dB lower; on others it may be as much as 10 or 15dB lower. Our basic timber floor is particularly badly affected by Ctr bias: its sound reduction rating, depending on the low frequency performance, can fall to around 20dB airborne sound reduction.

Engineered 'I' joists minimum depth 240mm supported by timber framed walls

Floating floor treatment No 1

Sub-deck board
(minimum 15mm)

10mm mineral fibre based
quilt (10-33kg/cu m)

Minimum 240mm engineered
timber 'I-joist'

Resilient bar

Ceiling of two or more layers
of gypsum-based board
(min 24kg/cu m)

The Robust Standard Details show methods of building in 50dB sound reduction into walls and floors. Here's the RSD for timber I joist floors, showing that it can be done, even if it is multi-layered and therefore rather expensive.

There is a fourth measuring scale used solely for impact sound. It's written L'nT,w: gets called LNTW. Impact sound is only measured on floors and, as already discussed, is measured directly rather than being subtracted from a source sound, so the lower the dB rating, the less noise gets through the floor.

In summary, let's take our very basic floor and see how it stacks up on the different scales. It's a timber-joisted floor with just a chipboard cover and plasterboard nailed to it underneath. It scores:

■ 38db on the RW airborne scale
■ 33db on the DNTW airborne scale, (roughly −5dB difference between lab and field)
■ 20dB on the DTNW plus CTR airborne scale (Ctr of, say, -13dB)
■ 70dB on the LNTW impact scale

None of these are any good at all! To find out how to improve them, check the section called sound advice back in Chapter 7.

Ministry of sound

You can, hopefully, see that sound reduction levels expressed in simple decibels don't actually mean very much unless you know which scale they are referring to. The latest switch to the added Ctr measurements has divided the acoustics community; though everybody agrees that bass sounds are more prevalent, not everyone agrees that this new measurement system is the best way of approaching it. When the building regs were revamped in 2003, the actual sound reduction levels appeared to get less but this was because of the new method of measuring them. However, the changes are not uniform and there are some constructions that would have failed the old regs that now pass the new ones, so the improvement in standards is not consistent or universal.

However it was another aspect of the changes in Part E which took centre stage in 2003. That was the insistence that not only should party walls and floors be built to the new standards but that they should be heard to do so; acoustic testing was to become part of the scene.

But when the powers-that-be first ran their suggestions past the housebuilders, pandemonium broke out. Not only was acoustic testing reckoned to cost around £600 per test, but also rectifying failures in already completed schemes would be a real nightmare. Years and years of acoustic testing had shown that there is often a large gap between the designed-for sound reduction and that actually achieved. The acousticians felt strongly that it wasn't enough simply to tighten the old standards: to improve matters significantly, you had to test, which, coincidentally, was jolly good news for acousticians.

Well a fudge was worked out. After much badgering and a very rushed research programme during 2003, the government accepted a Super Level sound proofing standard, to be known henceforth as the Robust Standard Details or RSDs. This sets an airborne soundproofing target a full 5dB higher than that required just to meet the regs for new party walls and floors but – crucially – doesn't call for any testing.

So what emerged at the beginning of 2004 when the regs were set in stone were four different levels of soundproofing:

■ Level 1: 40dB (Rw scale) airborne sound reduction. Applies to internal walls and floors within individual homes. No testing required.
■ Level 2: 43dB (DNTw + Ctr scale) airborne sound reduction plus (floors only) 64dB (LNTw scale) maximum impact noise. Applies to party walls and floors between flats and attached houses when they have undergone renovation. Requires testing.
■ Level 3: 45dB (DNTw + CTR scale) airborne sound reduction plus (floors only) 62dB (LNTw scale) maximum impact noise. Applies to party walls and floors between flats and attached houses if they are newbuild. Requires testing.
■ Level 4: 50dB (DNTw + CTR scale) airborne sound reduction plus (floors only) 57dB (LNTw scale) maximum impact noise. A series of approved robust standard details (known as RSDs) that can be used by new builders (only) who wish to avoid the expense of testing.

How you go about meeting these new standards really lies beyond the scope of this book. Both Part E (Part H in Scotland, Part G in Ulster) and the new RSD documents are available free on the web at the Office of the Deputy Prime Minister website so you can check out all the many details required. There is an awful lot of detail on the junctions between walls and floors where flanking sound tends to come into play. The RSD documents have details for walls and floors made out of timber and steel as well as the more obvious masonry materials. What is worth pointing out is that there is a big jump between Level 1 and Level 2. It may look like a mere 5dB difference but notice that the scales are different and 40dB on the Rw scale is probably only about 30dB on the more exacting DNTw + CTR scale. So there is lots of room to improve the very basic standard found in Part E2 of the regs, which applies to individual homes.

■ Barn conversions

Many people reading this book start out with a dream of living in the countryside in a house built to their own designs. It's a widely shared aspiration but, for the majority, it will never become more than an aspiration. Britain has some of the tightest rural planning rules in the world and it's simply not possible to pitch up in Chipping Butty and build a house in Farmer Giles's meadow. What building plots do come up are more likely to be the back garden of an existing house which may not be quite what you had in mind.

But there is a chink in the planning armour. Whilst the planners won't countenance building from scratch, they are keen to see existing rural buildings get a new lease of life. There are several hundred thousand farms dotted around the British countryside. Virtually every one has outbuildings used to store cattle or grain or for various farmy type things and a huge number of these are now lying empty and unused. Now conservation bodies love these old barns and want to see them survive in some form but there is simply no call for them with modern farming. Such is the demand for rural building plots that people are willing to pay enormous sums to convert these barns into homes. In doing so, they have created an entirely new form of housing that seems to be unique to Britain. It is both ancient and modern. Ancient in that it involves restoring centuries old structures often using traditional techniques. Modern in that the space being created is often far more like an urban loft apartment than a traditional home as served up to us by the mass market developers.

The world of converting redundant buildings is very different to new housebuilding. You have to be prepared to have things imposed on you which you might think are unreasonable and unfair. The very fact that we are allowed to convert redundant buildings rather than just pulling them down demonstrates that we are engaging with the British obsession with preserving the past, and the planners have a number of ways of making sure that certain rules are adhered to in exchange for the right to create a home in a place you otherwise would not be able to. Chief amongst these is the idea that what you build should continue to look like what was there before. And not in any way look like a conventional house. This goes for conversions of nearly all redundant buildings with some degree of historic interest; chapels, schools and pubs to name but three. But the bulk of single home conversions are going on in rural barns as these are by far the commonest rural structure up for conversion.

The Rules
■ reuse existing doorways, even if they were designed for carts
■ don't block up existing openings
■ no masonry chimneys – stainless steel flues acceptable only if kept away from the ridge
■ as few new windows as possible – and any new windows should as plain as possible
■ no changes to the roof. Certainly no dormers and preferably no rooflights. If rooflights, preferably on the side no one sees
■ repair the original material wherever possible. If replaced, use something similar. If

it's timber, it must be timber that matches the old style.

What a lot of barn designers end up doing is building in a large glazed screen area where once stood the main barn door. This is often inset into the structure – this borrows a little extra light for the rooms opening off the hallway behind the glazed screen. No matter that what you end up with doesn't look a bit like a farm building, it does make a very attractive structure. In fact the barn conversion, particularly the timber barn conversion, has rapidly attained iconic status as a fashion item in its own right. Whilst the history of the original barns has been documented by the likes of RW Brunskill, the history of barn conversions has yet to be written.

Barns tend to come in two distinct flavours,

Barn quiz

From a planner's point of view, this is the barn conversion from hell. There are at least ten conversion rules broken here — see if you can spot them. Answers on the next page.

timber and stone. Timber predominates in the south and east where they tended to be built for threshing and storing corn. Stone barns are more common in the north and the west – the Scots refer to them as steadings – where they were most often used as cattle sheds. As cattle don't like going up stairs, the stone barns tend to be single storey, the timber ones are routinely two storey or, more accurately, high enough to accommodate a second storey. There are of course masses of exceptions to this rule of thumb and there are also masses of sheds and barns built of other interesting materials like cob and clay lump. After a penal brick tax was removed in 1857, you start to see a lot of brick barns being built which are also now ripe for conversion. I have even seen steel framed agricultural buildings (you can hardly call them barns) dating from the Fifties getting the modern barn conversion treatment, complete with stained weatherboard exterior. Another example of planning gone mad, perhaps. But why not?

If you see a barn on the market with planning permission for conversion, the chances are that it has already been subject to a thorough examination in order to have obtained that permission.

Unlike virgin building plots, you can't obtain Outline permission on a barn conversion – it has to be Detailed which means that the design is closely scrutinised by the planners before any approval is granted. The planners would ideally like to see redundant farm buildings given over to some commercial use with the hope of creating some rural employment. In fact there

are grants of 30 per cent or more available for conversion if you can find a viable business use for the building – this can include farm shops, workshops or even holiday lets. Diversification, that's the name of the game. Trouble is that for a huge number of barns there simply isn't any viable option other than residential conversion for resale (for which there is currently seems to be an insatiable demand). However in order to prove this, you have to carry out a business viability survey, assessing likely income from the converted building.

Brian Belton, a surveyor with Durrant & Sons, based in Diss in Norfolk, handles a large number of these applications every year and he says: 'I've yet to find a barn in my patch, the Waveney valley, where the economics of a commercial conversion stack up. You need to show a return of 14 or 15 per cent before banks will be willing to finance and you only ever seem to get around seven or eight per cent returns showing through on the surveys, even with the grant money thrown in.'

Only by showing a commercial conversion is unviable do you open the door to a residential conversion. But before such permission is forthcoming, a detailed structural survey also needs to be undertaken to see whether the barn is 'permanent and substantial'. In Durrant's practice, this involves measuring every timber and inspecting all the joints. Most timber barns are in need of a large amount of restoration but very few are unsalvageable. The rule seems to be if it's standing, it's salvageable. Typically the timber along the bottom edge – the sole plate – has rotted and sometimes twisted, causing the base of the barn to move outwards, but the sole plate can be replaced and the plinth can be reset. The very fact that a barn has stood for so long is usually a testament to how well built it was in the first place but sometimes decay can be rapid, especially if the roof cover has been removed or has blown off. On occasion, conversion has to be carried out in double quick time in order to save the building. If it collapses beyond repair, there will be no hope of obtaining permission to rebuild.

Before and during. The above shot, taken in Feb 2000, shows a timber barn on its last legs. By June that year, the whole structure had been transformed. You could easily be mistaken for thinking this was a new house taking shape: basically, it is. Only the original posts and beams remain from the original structure.

This raises another intriguing problem: insurance. Redundant buildings are intrinsically liabilities, not assets. What's of value here is the development potential, not the structure itself. But the development potential hangs on the structure continuing to at least exist. There a danger of buying a barn for conversion and losing everything when it burns down or gets blown over before you've started work. This insurance risk is at least recognised and specialist selfbuild brokers such as Holbrook offer cover for this. But do bear in mind that most planning consents for barns conversions specifically state that the consent will become invalid if more alterations or repairs are carried out than were agreed – hence the need for a good survey and plenty of shoring up.

Timber barns

With a little luck, your barn survives long enough for you to make a start on the conversion. What needs to be done? Start with the foundations. Rarely will any of these buildings have what we now call foundations in any shape or form. Stone or brick plinth walls just tended to spread a little below ground; there were never any attempts to dig down a metre of so on to hard bearing ground.

However the barns have stood the test of time so the principle to be observed is that, if you don't change any of the loadings, there really shouldn't be any need to alter what exists. Given that the alternative is underpinning and that underpinning tends to cost a minimum of £500 per linear metre (likely to work out at over £20,000 for a barn), then it's well worth avoiding new foundations if possible. So if you wish to build in an upper storey, you have to find a way of keeping the added load of this new floor off the existing walls. The solution lies in building a platform inside the barn; this can be achieved with stud walls underneath or, more commonly, using a series of beefy posts which themselves get bedded on concrete pads.

Then consider the ground floor. The condition of these varies from compacted earth through to level concrete in good condition. Concrete sounds like an advantage but bear in mind that in order to meet the latest U value requirement for floors you will almost certainly have to put insulation on top of it and consequently you may be losing significant height; sometimes it is better to dig out an existing floor and put in a new one.

There are two additional points to consider here. You don't want to go down so deep that you expose the base of the walls otherwise you will suddenly find yourself in an underpinning situation – a couple of exploratory test digs should reveal how far down your walls go under the ground.

On the other hand, if you are planning on building an upper deck, you may find that you have to negotiate a tie beam, tying the roof trusses together. Ideally you want your finished ground floor level to be at least 4.5 metres below any tie beams otherwise you will be having to go on hands and knees to get under the tie beams.

Incidentally, there is no minimum height for rooms or doorways encoded in our building regs, but realistically you need 1.8m clearance on doors to make them comfortable to pass through. If you haven't got a reasonable clearance there may be ways around the problem by gaining access to the different bays from half landings or maybe installing a second staircase. Physically, you may be able to lower the floor a little or you may even be able to jack the entire building up a little – though for God sake keep quiet about this, the planners would have a fit!

Actually, it is perfectly acceptable to jack a timber structure up when carrying out restoration work. Expected even. The procedure is to strip away everything that you don't intend to keep. Often this means reducing the barn to nothing more than a timber skeleton. You then build an internal scaffold cage and then place pins under the header plates at the top of the walls which take the weight of the roof. The whole structure then gets lifted gently off the supporting walls at the bottom and this then allows you to get to work restoring these walls and go about replacing the sole plates.

If all the bottom joints between the sole plate and the wall studs have rotted, it is standard practice to cut the wall studs shorter and fix a new sole plate (usually green oak) in a slightly higher position than the old one.

If other pieces of the original frame are missing or damaged, now is the time that the replacements are made. You will then have to add a couple of courses of brick or stone onto the plinth wall underneath to make up the difference. At this point you would be expected to let the structure down again to sit on the repaired plinth.

From here on in, the timber barn conversion becomes a new build. The walls will normally get covered in plywood or something similar and you need to add insulation to the structure – in this respect a converted barn must perform to the same standards as a new house. In timber barns, most people want to see as much as possible of the original timbers and therefore the tendency is to find insulation systems which wrap around the exterior. The reflective foil insulations like Actis are gaining ground in these markets as they take up so little space. Normally a timber barn will get a new weatherboarded exterior.

Stone barns

Stone barns pose rather different problems. There will certainly be no jacking up of the structure, rather there may have to be a painstaking repair of what is there. And the requirement for good insulation levels means that one face, usually the inside, will have to be covered over. You may need to underpin, especially where new openings are formed and the wall loadings are altered – it very much depends on the ground conditions beneath.

An additional problem is making the structure watertight, something which it was doubtless never designed to be in the first place. A typical stone barn consists of two skins of sorted stone separated by a rubble filled cavity. The existing walls will often be as much as 450mm thick so, on most barns, it's quite impractical to build another skin on the inside. So you have to work with what is there. It's difficult to install an effective damp proof course and it can be difficult to stop rain penetration through the walls as well.

The planners are unlikely to accept a waterproof render being applied to the outside face, the best you can realistically hope to do is to point up the gaps between the stones. And accept, perhaps, that you are not living in a new build and that you may have to put up with the odd damp patch from time to time.

Cost

Barn conversions cost rather more than new housing on a square metre basis. On a like-for-like basis, the unit area rate works out at between 30 per cent and 50 per cent more than undertaking new builds. Durrants are currently budgeting around £900 per sq m for converting timber barns and of course this figure does not include the purchase price. An upper deck will be slightly cheaper to construct on a square metre basis making two floor barns cheaper than single storey ones. But the saving is not that great.

Stone barns will tend to be a little more expensive because stone is always time consuming and therefore expensive to work with. Modern (brick) barns will be cheaper because the structure is usually in better condition. The more exceptional the barn, the more it is likely to cost to convert.

Most barns are not listed unless they happen to be in the grounds (or the curtilage, in planning speak) of a listed farm in which case there may well be extra features to consider (such as thatch). Generally speaking, most barn conversions are undertaken by selfbuilders. Spec builders tend to shy away from them because they don't like the unpredictability – though one or two plucky ones will go as far as importing barns from France in order to get the right feel in a property.

Despite the costs and the risks involved, barn conversion opportunities don't hang around. As Brian Belton commented: If somebody wants a home deep in the country, there often isn't that much choice so when barns for conversion come onto the market they are currently snapped up, usually within two weeks, four weeks maximum. And most of the people buying barns are doing it for their own occupation.

HISTORY LESSON

Most of the timber barns coming onto the market in SE England were built to thresh and store corn. They were designed to take a horse and fully laden cart in through one door and out empty on the other side – occasionally this is reflected by having a high door on one side and a low one on the other but more often you get two similar sized barn doors facing each other. Despite every barn being seemingly different, there are some surprising similarities. They are routinely made up of bays, defined by the principal posts and trusses. The roof pitch often gives a clue to the age of the barn; the older the barn, the steeper the pitch. Thatch – widely used in parts of England in Tudor times – requires a pitch of more than 50° whereas pantiles and the like work with pitches of 35-40° and when slate arrived in the 19th century the pitch could be dropped to 30°.

■ *Crucial measurements*

What's in a ton?

Conventionally when the word is written Ton it refers to an imperial ton. When it's written Tonne, it's a metric ton(ne). The old imperial ton was 20 cwt (hundredweight): the metric tonne is 1,000 kilogrammes. The imperial ton is just 1.6 per cent heavier than the metric tonne and therefore, to all intents and purposes you can ignore the difference.

Not so the differences between cubic metres and tonnes. Now quarries or merchants can sell by using either method. In fact many suppliers use both – volume up to 10 cu m and tonnes above that level. The conversion on sand is 1cu m equals 1.6 tonnes but be warned that sand is much heavier when wet and so you'll be getting up to 20 per cent less if you are buying by weight in wet weather. However, at £6-£10 per tonne for 10 tonne loads, it's cheap enough to not worry unduly over. Other importaant volume to weight conversions are noted in the Material Densities section of the adjacent table.

Note the critical one is water, which is used to define the relationships between metres, litres and tonnes. Materials with a density greater than 1 are heavier than water and will sink, whilst materials with a density less than 1 will float. Try dropping a Celcon areated block in a bath full of water: it will amaze the kids, if nothing else.

Crucial Measurements

Weight		
1lb = 0.454kg		
1kg = 2.2lbs		
1 imperial ton = 1016kg		= 1.016 tonnes

Length		
1 millimetre (mm) = 0.039 inches		
1 metre (m) = 39.4 inches		= 1.094 yards
1 inch = 25.5mm		
1 foot = 305mm		
1 yard = 914mm		= 0.914m

Area		
1 sq. metre (m²) = 10.76 sq.ft		
1 ft² = 0.93m²		
1 hectare = 10,000m²		= 2.47 acres
1 acre = 4047m²		= 0.4 hectare
Area of triangle = half base x height		

Volume		
1 UK gallon = 4.5 litres		
1 cubic metre (m³) = 1000 litres		= 220 gallons
1 m³ of water = 1 tonne		

Heat		
1 kiloWatt (kW) = 3410 British Thermal Units (BTU)		
1 kilowatt hour (kWh) = 1 kW burned for one hour		
1 joule = 1 watt burned for a second		
1 gigajoule (GJ) = 278kWh		
Specific Heat of Air = 0.33watts/m³/1°C		

Material Densities		
1m³ water @ 4°C = 1 tonne (by definition!)		
1m³ of dry sand = 1.6 tonnes (up to 20% more wet)		
1m³ of aggregate = 1.8 tonnes		
1m³ of cement = 1.4 tonnes		
1m³ hydrated lime = 0.6 tonnes		
1m³ concrete = 2 tonnes		
1m³ clinker blocks = 1.6 tonnes		
1m³ bricks = 1.2 to 1.6 tonnes		
1m³ aerated blocks = 0.6 tonnes		
1m³ softwood = 0.45 tonnes		
1m³ hardwood = 0.65 tonnes		
for more conversions, check out www.simetric.co.uk		

Getting it square

Only in a right-angled triangle is the square of the hypotenuse (the long side) equal to the square of the two shorter sides. This basic rule of geometry (Pythagoras' Theorem) allows us to get our corners dead square using nothing more than a tape measure. Most carpenters are taught this bit of geometry via the 3-4-5 rule which they use for squaring up frames but it is just as useful when setting out foundations. The classic 3-4-5 triangle calculation is demonstrated in the diagram but, of course, the calculation will work with any lengths, just as long as you can work out the squares – tip: get a calculator with a square root function.

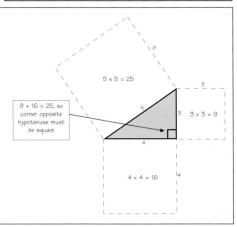

5 x 5 = 25

9 + 16 = 25, so corner opposite hypotenuse must be square

3 x 3 = 9

4 x 4 = 16

Contacts	Phone	Web	Area of Interest
Abbey Pynford	01923 211160	www.abbeypynford.co.uk	Foundations
Actis	01380 730195	in french	Insulation
ADM Ventilation	01756 701051	www.admsystems.co.uk	Whole House Ventilation
Advanced Showers	01483 295930	www.advanced-showers.com	Showers
AECB	01559 370908	www.aecb.net	Eco-builders Organistaion
Aga Rayburn	08457 125207	www.aga-rayburn.co.uk	Range Cookers
Allied Manufacturing	0208 205 4188	www.kingswood-allied.co.uk	Kitchens
Altro Safety Floors	01462 707600	www.altro.co.uk	Floors
Amazon nails	01706 814696	www.strawbalefutures.org.uk	Straw Bale Housing
Amptec Boilers	01256 363417	www.electroheatplc.co.uk	Electric boilers
Andersen Windows	01283 511122	www.andersenwindows.com	
Anki Chimneys	01983 527997	www.anki.co.uk	Chimneys
Architects Registration Board	020 7580 5861	www.arb.org.uk	
Arcon CAD software	01420 520023	www.3darchitect.co.uk	
Arrow	01905 363000	www.arrow-distributors.co.uk	Kitchen Appliances
B&Q	0870 010 1006	www.diy.com	DIY store
Basement Information Centre	web site only	www.basements.org.uk	Basements
Baxi Potterton	08706 060623	www.baxi.co.uk	Boilers
Beco Wallform	01652 651641	www.becowallform.co.uk	Polystyrene houses
BIAT	020 7278 2206	www.biat.org.uk	Architectural technologists
Bio Bubble	01243 370100	www.bio-bubble.com	Off mains drainage
Blanc de Bierge	01733 202566	www.blancdebierges.com	Pavings
Border Oak	01568 708752	www.borderoak.com	Oak houses
BPAC	01592 882202	www.bpac.co.uk	SIPS houses
BRE Bookshop	0207 505 6622	www.brebookshop.com	
Brickability	01656 645222	www.brickability.co.uk	Brick factors
British Earth Sheltered Housing Assoc	01639 701481	www.besa-uk.org	
Build It	020 7772 8300	www.buildit-online.co.uk	Self build magazine
Buildstore Mortgages	0870 870 9991	www.buildstore.co.uk	
Buildstore's Plotsearch	0870 870 9994	www.buildstore.co.uk/plotsearch	Plot searches
Burdens (WTB Group)	0117 986 1766	www.burdens.co.uk	Drainage
Buxton Lime Industries	01298 768467	www.buxtonlime.co.uk	Limebond
Caradon Wintun	0141 889 5969	www.wintun.co.uk	Level thresholds
Carpenter Woodland Oak	01225 743089	www.cowco.biz	Oak houses
Carpet Foundation	01562 755568	www.carpetfoundation.com	
CED Stone factors	01708 867237	www.ced.ltd.uk	
Celcon Jamera	01732 886333	www.celcon.co.uk	Block houses
Celotex	01473 822093	www.celotex.co.uk	Insulation
Centre for Earthen Architecture	01752 233630	ask for Linda Watson	
Chelmer Heating	01245 471111	www.chelmerheating.co.uk	Thermal stores/UFH
Classical Flagstones	0117 9371960	www.classical-flagstones.com	Pavings
Clear Skies Grants	08702 430930	www.clear-skies.org	
Community Selfbuild Agency	0207 415 7092	www.communityselfbuildagency.org	
Conservation Engineering	01359 268340	www.conservation-engineering.co.uk	Heating design
Construction Resources	0207 450 2211	www.constructionresources.com	Green builder's merchant
Cress Water	01905 422707	www.cresswater.co.uk	Reed beds
Crosslee Appliances	01422 203585	www.crosslee.co.uk	Kitchens
Croydex H20 Showers	01264 367224		
Culligan (formerly Liff)	01484 512537	under construction	Water conditioning
Customs & Excise Advice Line	08450 109000	www.hmce.gov.uk	
DCD Heating Controllers	01753 882028	www.dcd.co.uk	
Design for Homes		www.designforhomes.org	Find an architect
Devi ElectroHeat	01359 242400	www.devi.co.uk	Electric underfloor heating
DMS Insurance	01909 591652	www.selfbuild.armor.co.uk	
DPS Heat	01372 803675	www.heatweb.com	Thermal stores
Durrant & Son	01379 642233	www.durrants.com	Suffolk Estate Agents
Eaton Electrics	0161 652 1111	www.memonline.com	Home Automation/Wiring

Contacts	Phone	Web	Area of Interest
Ellis-Miller, Jonathan	01223 359000	www.ellis-miller.com	Architect
Encon	01937 524200	www.encon.co.uk	Insulation
Environment Agency	08459 333111	www.environment-agency.gov.uk	Services
Environmental Seals	01304 842 555	www.envirograf.com	Fire proofing paints
Esse	01282 813235	www.esse.com	Ranges
Excel Industries	01685 845200	www.excelfibre.com	Insulation
F.P.Herting	020 8606 7000	www.fpherting.co.uk	Ironmongery shopping
Fermacell	0870 6090306	www.fermacell.co.uk	Wall boards
Fernhill Stone	01207 521482	www.fernhillstone.com	Stone claddings
Fireplace Design Consultancy	01889 500500		
Freewater UK	0870 2416964	www.freewateruk.co.uk	Rainwater Harvesting
Hafele UK	01788 542020	www.hafele.co.uk	Kitchen ironmongery
Hanson Jetfloor	01636 832000	www.hanson.co.uk	Insulated flooring system
Harris & Bailey	020 8654 3181	www.harris-bailey.co.uk	Stone factors
Harrison McCarthy	0161 794 9021	www.diyboilers.com	Plumbing supplies
Hewden Stuart	0800 371565	www.hewden.co.uk	Tool Hire
Holbrook Insurance	01483 521650	www.holbrook-insurance.co.uk	Insurance
Homebuilding & Renovating	01527 834406	www.homebuilding.co.uk	Selfbuild magazine
Hormann	0800 0834639	www.hormann.co.uk	Garage doors
Housebuilder XL	08708 502444	www.hbxl.co.uk	Project Management
Huf Haus	08702 000035	www.huf-haus.de	German prefab houses
Ice Energy Heat Pumps	01865 882202	www.iceenergy.co.uk	
Idrosplit	via Plumb Center	www.plumbcenter.co.uk	Chillers
IP Homenetworks	0121 766 8460	www.iphomenet.com	Structured cabling
Ironmongery Direct	0845 450 0020	www.IronmongeryDirect.com	
Isokern	01202 861650	www.isokern.co.uk	Chimneys
Jablite Roof Element	0208 320 9100	www.jablite.co.uk	SIPS roofs
Jackson's Fencing	01233 750393	www.jacksons-fencing.co.uk	
Jeld Wen (John Carr)	01302 394000	www.jeld-wen.co.uk	Joinery
Jewson	0800 539766	www.jewson.co.uk	Large builders merchant
John Davidson Pipes	01228 791503	www.jdpipes.co.uk	Drainage
Johnson & Starley	01604 762881	www.johnsonandstarleyltd.co.uk	Warm air, passive stack
Keystone Lintels		www.keystone-lintels.co.uk	
Kingspan	01544 388601	www.insulation.kingspan.co.uk	Insulation, SIPS
Knauf Insulation	0800 627465	www.knauf.co.uk	Insulation
Lafarge Roofing (Redland)	08705 601000	www.lafarge.roofing.co.uk	
Landbank Services	0118 9626022	www.landbank.co.uk	Plot search
Lindman	0117 961 0900	www.lindman.co.uk	External doors and pultruded windows
Machells	0113 250 5043	www.machell.co.uk	Salvage
Magnet	various	www.magnet.co.uk	Joinery
Mattick, Stephen	01799 541695	no	Superior house designer
MFI	0870 609 5555	www.mfi.co.uk	Kitchens
Milbank Roofing	01787 223931	www.milbank.co.uk	Roofing. floors, basements
Modece Architects	01284 761141	www.modece.com	Hemp Homes
Mortgage Guarantee	01744 886884		Finance
NHBC Solo	01494 735363	www.nhbc.co.uk	Warranties
Norman & Underwood	0116 251 5000	www.nandu.co.uk	Glass
Norwich & Peterborough	0800 883322	www.npbs.co.uk	Finance
OFGEM		www.ofgem.gov.uk	Electricity
OFWAT	0121 625 1300	www.ofwat.gov.uk	Water
Osma	01249 766600	www.wavin.co.uk	Drainage
Passivent	0161 962 7113	www.buildingproductdesign.com	Passive stack ventilation
Pendock Profiles	01952 580590	www.pendock.co.uk	Trunking
Pineland Kitchens	01299 271143	www.pineland.co.uk	Kitchens

Contacts	Phone	Web	Area of Interest
Plotfinder	09065 575400	www.plotfinder.net	Plot search
Potton	01480 401401	www.potton.co.uk	Timber frame houses
Premdor	0800 026 0760	www.promdor.co.uk	Joinery
Premier Guarantee	0151 650 4343		Warranty provider
Project Builder	020 7716 5050	www.projectbuilder.com	Insurance, warranties
QED Systemline	01483 747474	www.qed.co.uk	Audio
R&J Hardware	01254 52525	no	Ironmongery
Rackhams	01924 455876	www.rackhamhousefloors.co.uk	Beam and block floors
Radiating Style	0870 072 3428	www.radiatingstyle.com	Plumbing & Heating
Real Door Company	01462 451230	www.realdoor.co.uk	
Redbank	01530 270333	www.redbankmfg.co.uk	Flues, roofing
Retrotec	01453 836700	www.retroteceurope.co.uk	Blower door testing
RIAI	016 761703	www.riai.ie	Irish Architects
RIAS	0131 229 7545	www.rias.org.uk	Scottish Architects
RIBA Clients Advisory Service	020 7307 3700	www.architecture.com	English Architects
RICS	020 7222 7000	www.rics.org	Design
Riley Associates	01259 726650	www.riley-associates.co.uk	Finance
RMC Foundation Flow	0800 667827	www.rmc.co.uk	Concrete
Rockwool	01656 862621	www.rockwool.co.uk	Insulation
RSAW	02920 874753	www.architecture-wales.com	Welsh Architects
RSUA	02890 323760	www.rsua.org.uk	Ulster Architects
Rytons	01536 511874	www.vents.co.uk	Ventilation
Salvo		www.salvo.co.uk	Salvage directory
Scottish Building Standards		www.scotland.gov.uk/build_regs/	Design
Scotts of Thrapston	01832 732366	www.scottsofthrapston.co.uk	Roof trusses
Seconds & Co	01544 260501	www.secondsandco.co.uk	Insulation
SEDBUK boiler ratings	web site only	www.boilers.org.uk	
Selfbuild & Design	01283 742970	www.selfbuildanddesign.com	Selfbuild magazine
Self-builder.com	0800 018 7660	www.self-builder.com	Insurance
Shackerley	01257 273114	www.shackerley.com	Glass blocks
SIPTEC	01234 881551	www.siptec.com	SIPS houses
Sound Reduction Systems	01204 380074	www.soundreduction.co.uk	Soundproofing
Spanish Slate Quarries	020 8961 7725	www.ssq.co.uk	Roofing
Speedframe	01709 888005	www.speedframe.co.uk	Windows
Steve Baldwin	01638 507248		Benchmark house builder
Storm King Plastics	01827 311100	www.stormking-plastics.co.uk	Porches
Tarmac Topfloor	01223 837838	www.tarmactopfloor.co.uk	Beam and block floors
Taylor Lane	01432 271912	www.taylor-lane.co.uk	Timber frame houses
The Lime Centre	01962 713636	www.thelimecentre.co.uk	Lime experts
Thermonex Basements	01204 559551	www.thermonex.com	Basements
TJ Crump Oakwrights	01432 353353	www.oakwrights.co.uk	Oak houses
TLC	01293 565630	www.tlc-direct.co.uk	Electrical wholesaler
Tudor Roof Tiles	01797 320202	www.tudorrooftiles.co.uk	
UK Timber Frame Association	01259 272140	www.timber-frame.org	
Unico Warm Air	07785 985876	www.unicosystem.com	Warm Air Heating
VAT Selfbuild reclaims	0121 697 4000		
Velfac	01223 897100	www.velfac.co.uk	Composite windows
Velux	0800 3169893	www.velux.co.uk	Roof windows
Villavent	01993 778481	www.villavent.co.uk	Whole house ventilation
Vincent Timber	0121 772 5511	www.vincenttimber.co.uk	Cedar cladding merchants
Walter Segal SelfbuildTrust	01668 213544	www.segalselfbuild.co.uk	Community selfbuild
Wickes	0500 300 328	www.wickes.co.uk	Builder's merchant
Woodalls	0208 458 6434	www.we-sell-it.co.uk	Kitchen Appliances
X10	information on	www.kevinboone.com/x10	Home Automation
Zehnder	01342 317171	www.zehnder.co.uk	Radiators
Zurich Custombuild	01252 387594	no	Building warranties

Index